IT'S
N SNATCHING
SON AGAIN.

3,400 transit police.
ywhere, all the time.
keep it, don't flaunt it.

WE'RE WORKING TO
THINGS SAFER.
YOU CAN HELP.

M

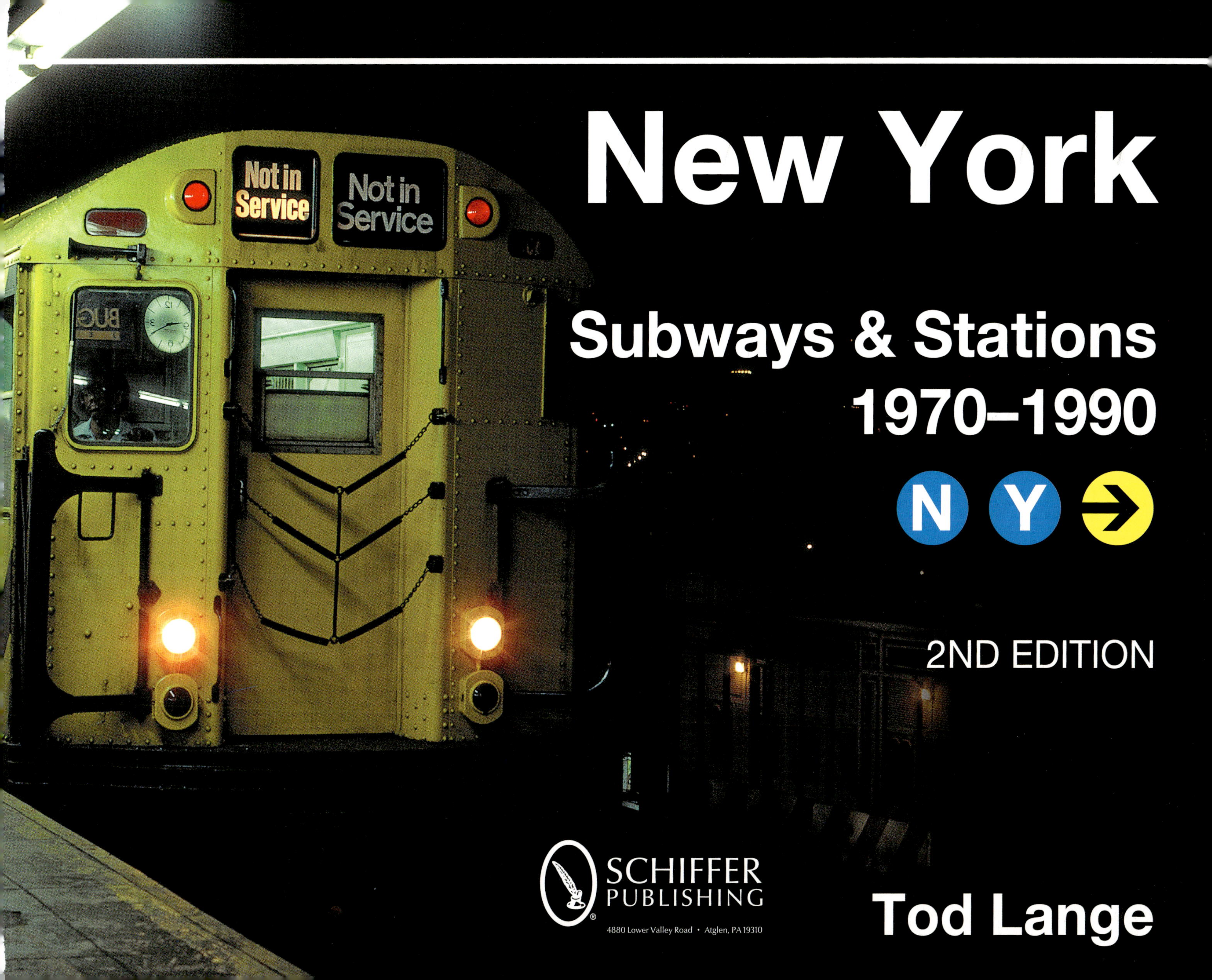

New York

Subways & Stations 1970–1990

2ND EDITION

SCHIFFER PUBLISHING
4880 Lower Valley Road • Atglen, PA 19310

Tod Lange

Other Schiffer Books by the Author:

Vintage New York City Subway Signs: 1920s–1980s, 978-0-7643-6920-9, $39.99

Born to Run: NYC Subway Graffiti on the IND and BMT Lines, 978-0-7643-5642-1, $34.99

Other Schiffer Books on Related Subjects:

Iron Trails of North America: 1978-2008, Robert W. Burns, 978-0-7643-3262-3, $49.99

Library of Congress Control Number: 2025930168

Designed by Justin Watkinson Cover by Jack Chappell
Type set in Helvetica / Minion Pro
ISBN: 978-0-7643-6984-1
ePub: 978-1-5073-0603-1
Printed in India

For our complete selection of fine books on this and related subjects, please visit our website at www.schifferbooks.com. You may also write for a free catalog.

Schiffer Publishing's titles are available at special discounts for bulk purchases for sales promotions or premiums. Special editions, including personalized covers, corporate imprints, and excerpts, can be created in large quantities for special needs. For more information, contact the publisher.

Published by Schiffer Publishing Ltd.
4880 Lower Valley Road
Atglen, PA 19310
Phone: (610) 593-1777; Fax: (610) 593-2002
Email: Info@schifferbooks.com

Photo Credits

Bill Myers: 7, 8, 42, 61, 76, 87, 103, 111, 126, 169, 189, 191, 193, 199, 217, 223, 225, 227, 230, 236, 238
Bill Pollman: 15, 28, 101, 109, 121, 123, 149, 152, 158, 170, 183, 254
Steve Zabel: 16, 32, 43, 46, 57, 59, 63, 64, 65, 81, 130, 131, 132, 160, 202, 219
William Madden: 21, 25, 133, 256
Douglas Grotjahn: front and back cover, 23, 27, 45, 47, 48, 49, 50, 51, 58, 134, 143, 163, 164, 171, 178, 179, 180, 181, 185, 196, 200, 201, 203, 216, 241, 242, 243, 244, 245, 246, 247, 248, 249
William Mangahas: 129, 161, 162, 165, 239
Frank Florianz: 40, 41
Joel Shanus: 60
Harold Smith: 69
All other photos from the author's collection

A special thank you to Douglas Grotjahn and Brian Merlis

Contents

Introduction

New York Subways & Stations 1970–1990

With the success of the first edition, we are presenting a new look at two great eras in transit history. With the assistance of photographer Douglas Grotjahn, I was able to rework this revised edition. Douglas and I reviewed countless boxes of vintage 35 mm slides and hand-selected images that have never been published. We added many new photos and a chapter on subway car interiors.

During the early '70s, crime was rampant. Financial hard times took a toll on the city and altered its landscape. Some neighborhoods were reduced to rubble and resembled a war zone with burnt-out buildings, stripped and abandoned cars, and a subway system that looked like the aftermath of an apocalypse. The 1970s and '80s represented a remarkable time in the city. I'm talking about the old New York! The filthy, not politically correct place I used to call home. This book will show you a time that will probably never again be repeated. The subway system was very dirty and colorful at the same time. During rush hours, cars would be so packed that moving to the next one was out of the question. The heat would only intensify the body odor of the sweaty sardines on their daily commute. The homeless, the hookers, and street hustlers were all permanent fixtures in New York. The subway system was used for more than just traveling. The homeless would sleep in the cars, stations, and tunnels. If you rode at night, you would encounter a Who's Who from a bad science fiction movie. The strangest and oddest things would play out right before your eyes. This was reality TV at its best.

The subway system was no stranger to Hollywood, either. The majority of films that featured subway scenes always depicted it as a dangerous place. Violent vigilantes and ruthless street gangs sought out victims. The Fresh Pond train yard in Queens was the location of a variety of films. *A Stranger Is Watching*, *Beat Street*, *Dreams Don't Die*, *2019: After the Fall of New York*, and *Wild Style* were all shot at that yard. Walter Hill's 1979 classic *The Warriors*, set the stage for one of the most accurate portrayals of the New York subway system. As this movie played in theaters, the crime wave was spreading out of control in real life. The film captured the raw, gritty awareness that the system was in a hopeless state of decay. Years of deferred maintenance put great strain on an already weakened system. They said, "Your train was more apt to break down than you to be mugged on the train." The Lexington Avenue Express was given the title "Muggers Express." In 1979, a group called the Magnificent 13 patrolled the Number 4 line from 8:00 p.m. to 4:00 a.m. The Magnificent 13 went on to become the Guardian Angels and expanded its patrols throughout the city. Regardless of all the negative attributes that surrounded the system, it could not have been more perfectly situated than in a city such as New York. The people, infrastructure, and era each played roles in what was going on, and what was about to happen next. The innocence of yesterday is gone, much like the trains in this book.

Nearly all of these trains were cut up for scrap metal or ended up at the bottom of the ocean as artificial reefs. This book was never intended to be a technical or scholarly survey of the subway system. Yet, I have attempted to offer an unapologetic view of the city as it was seen through the eyes of its people. Good, bad, frustrating, and scary, it's what made New York, New York!

The Seventies

New York
Subways & Stations
1970–1990

CHAPTER 1

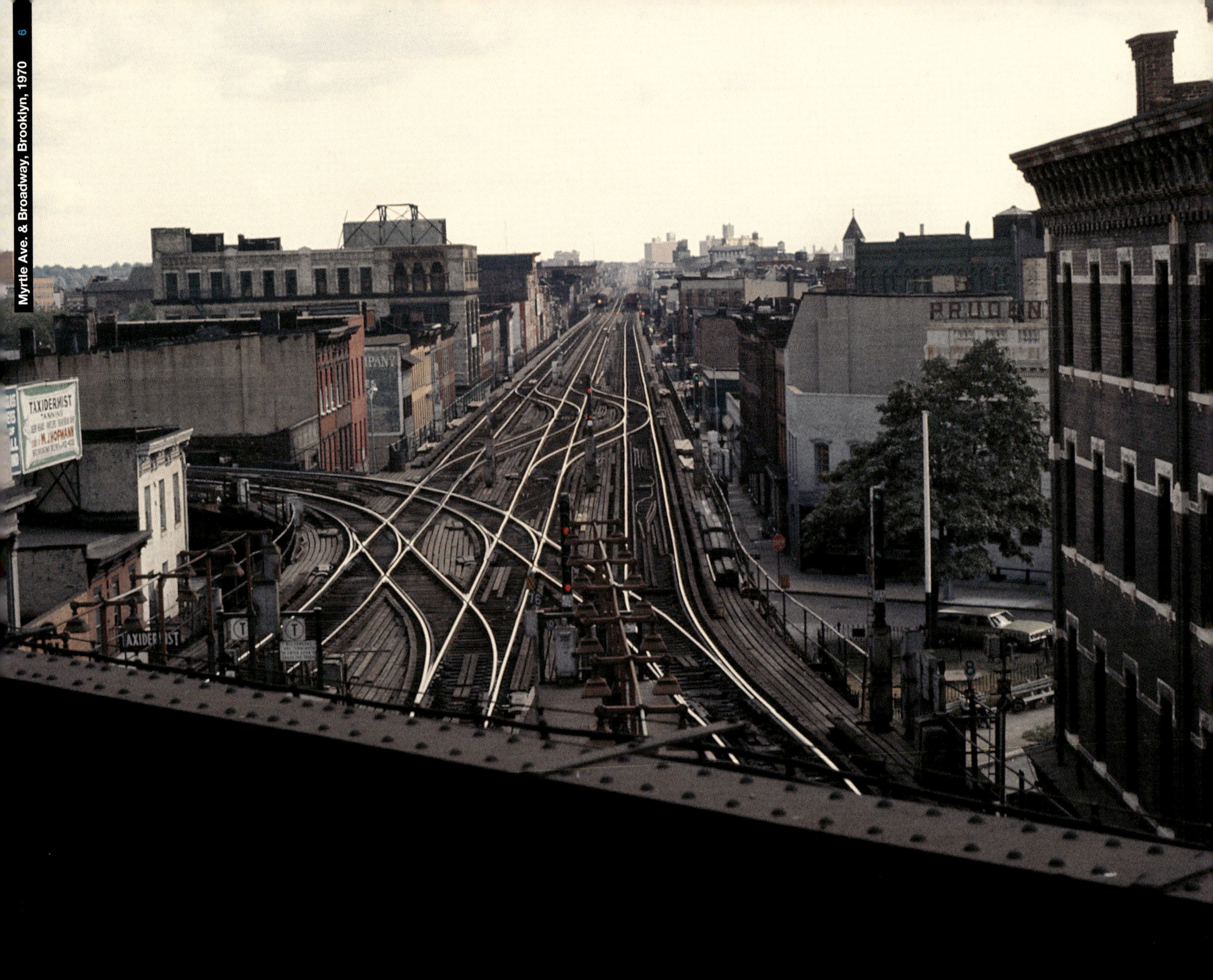

Myrtle Ave. & Broadway, Brooklyn, 1970

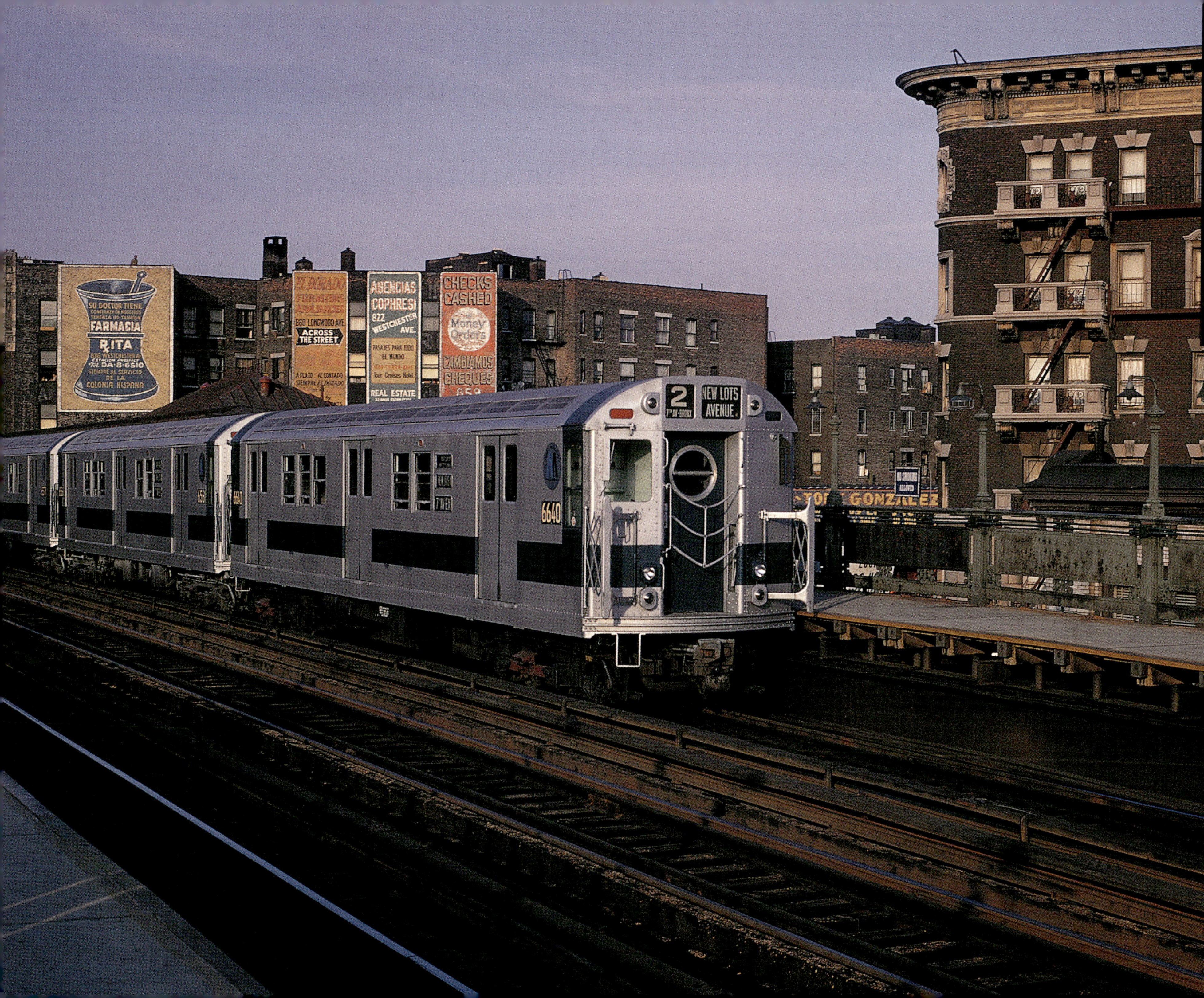

7 R-17s, No. 2 line, Prospect Ave., Bronx, 1970

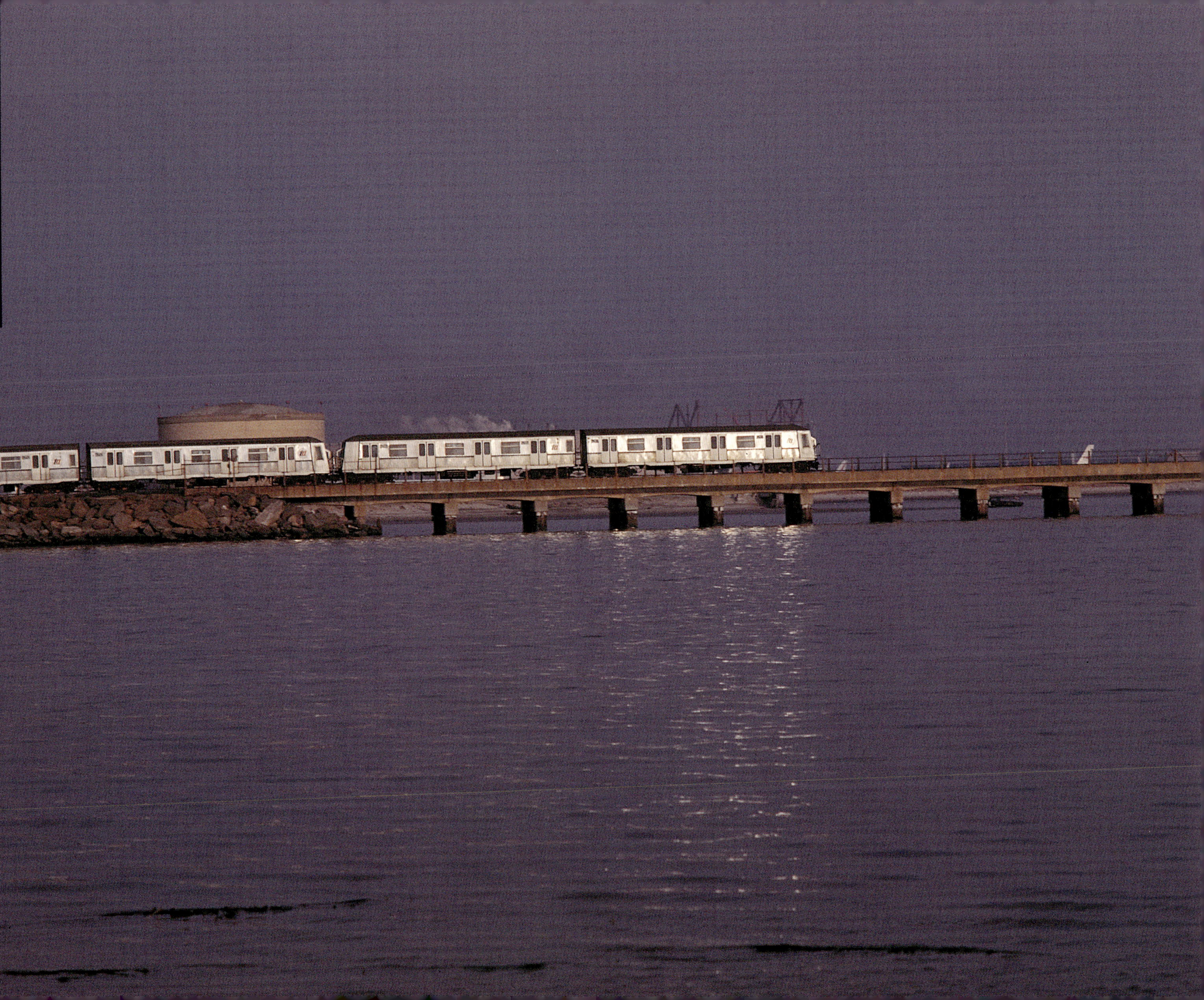

R-40s, A line, Jamaica Bay, Queens, 1970

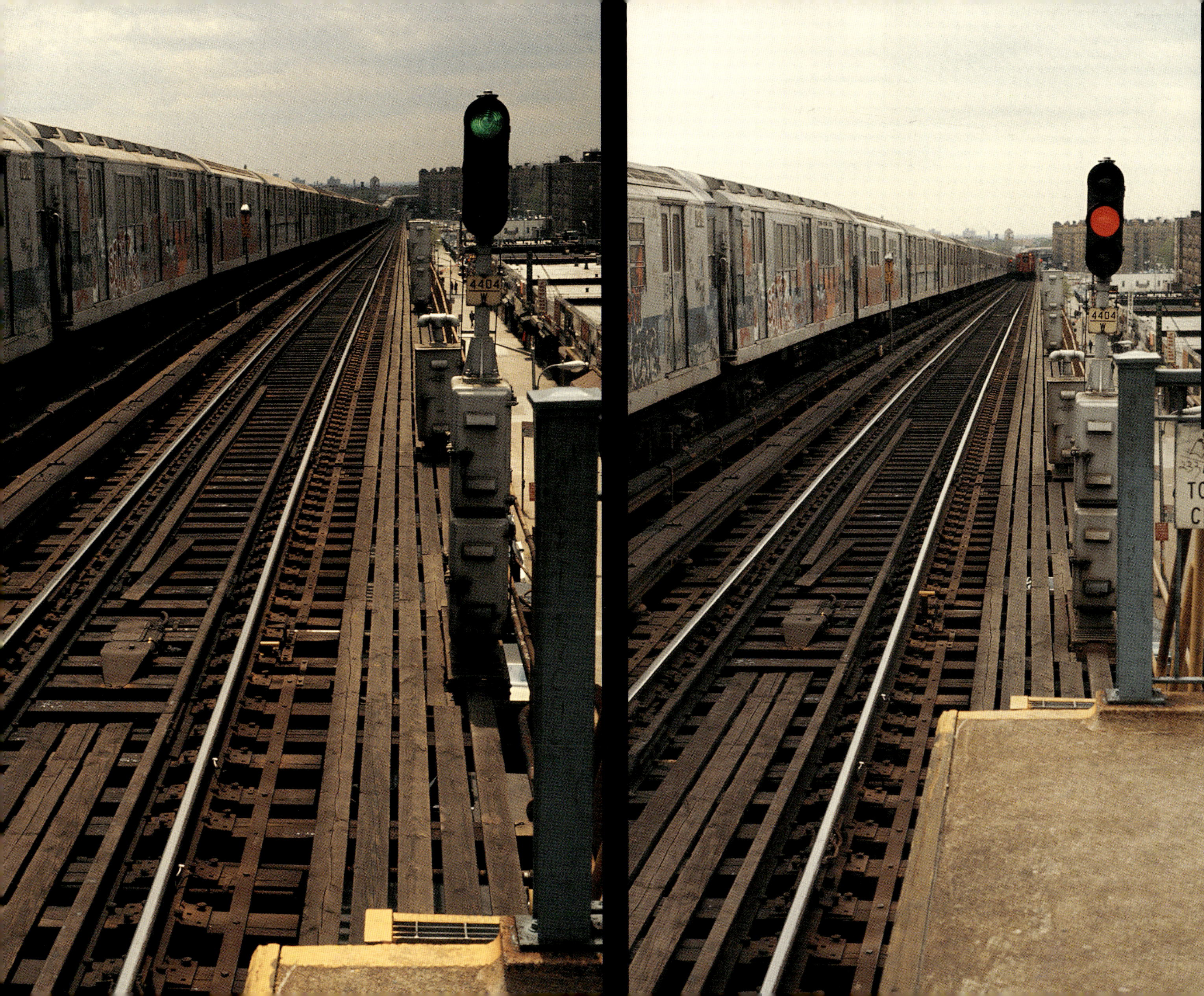

9 White Plains Rd. line, Pelham Parkway Station, Bronx, 1973

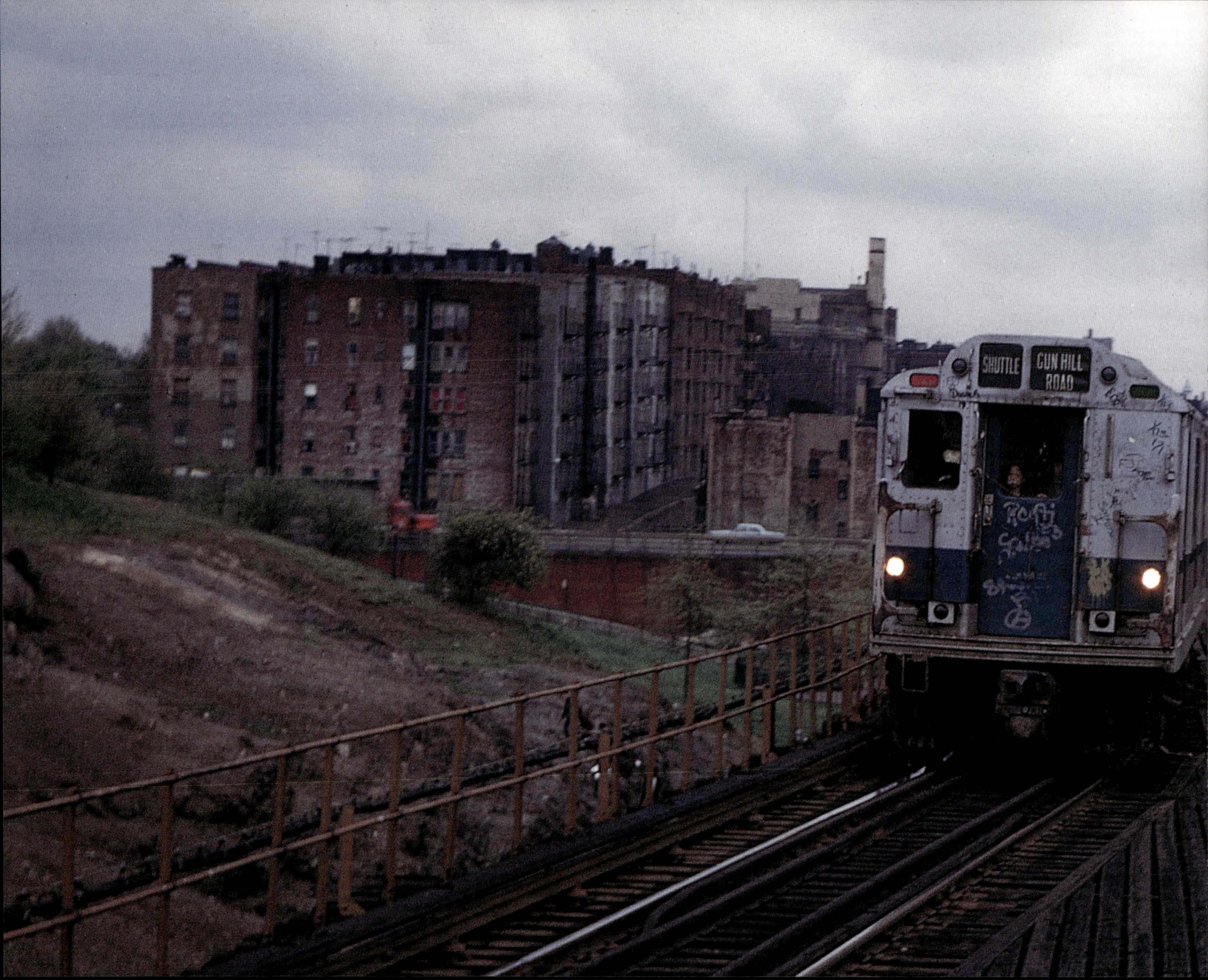
SHUTTLE
GUN HILL ROAD

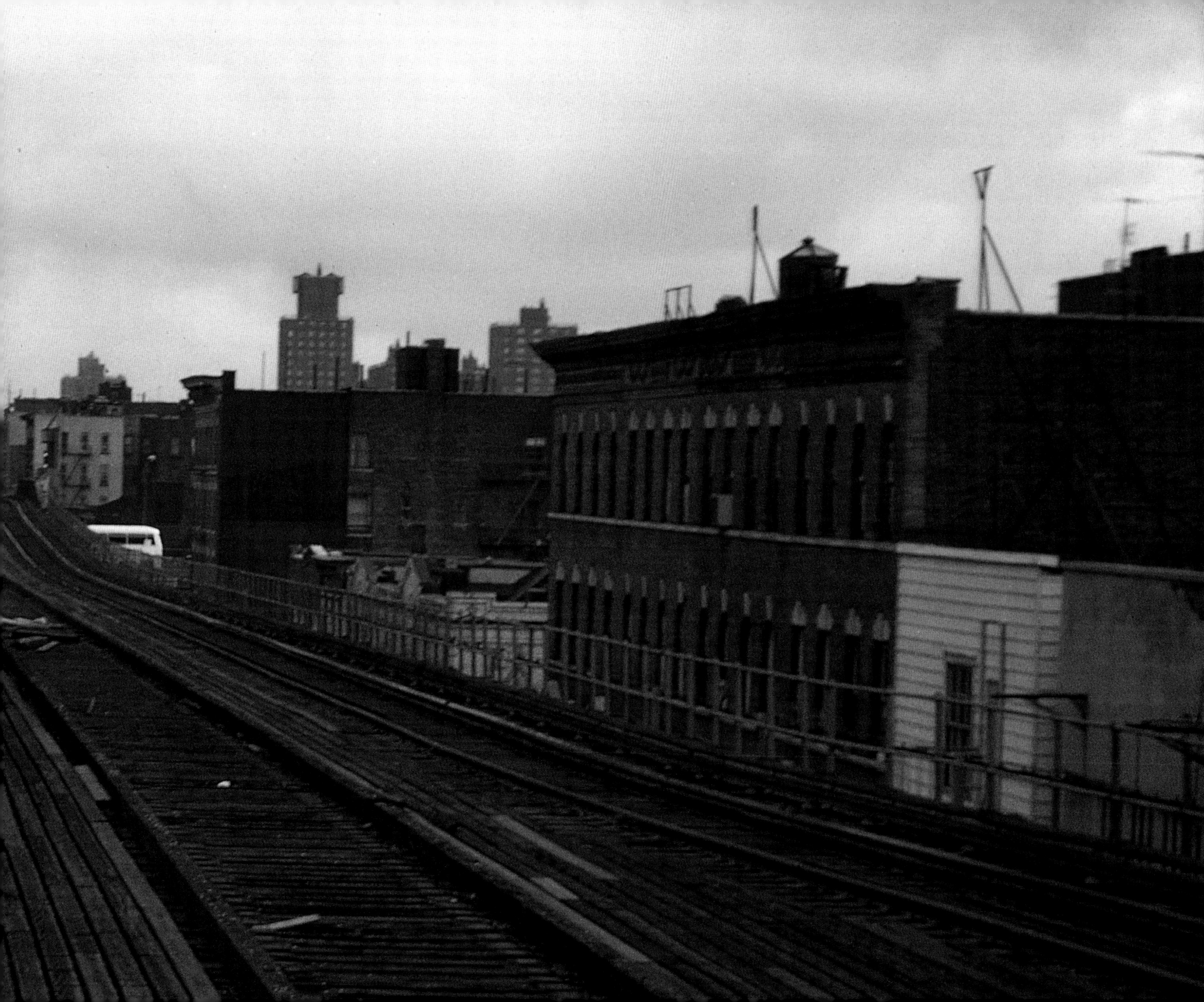

R-12s, 3rd Ave. El, Bronx, 1973

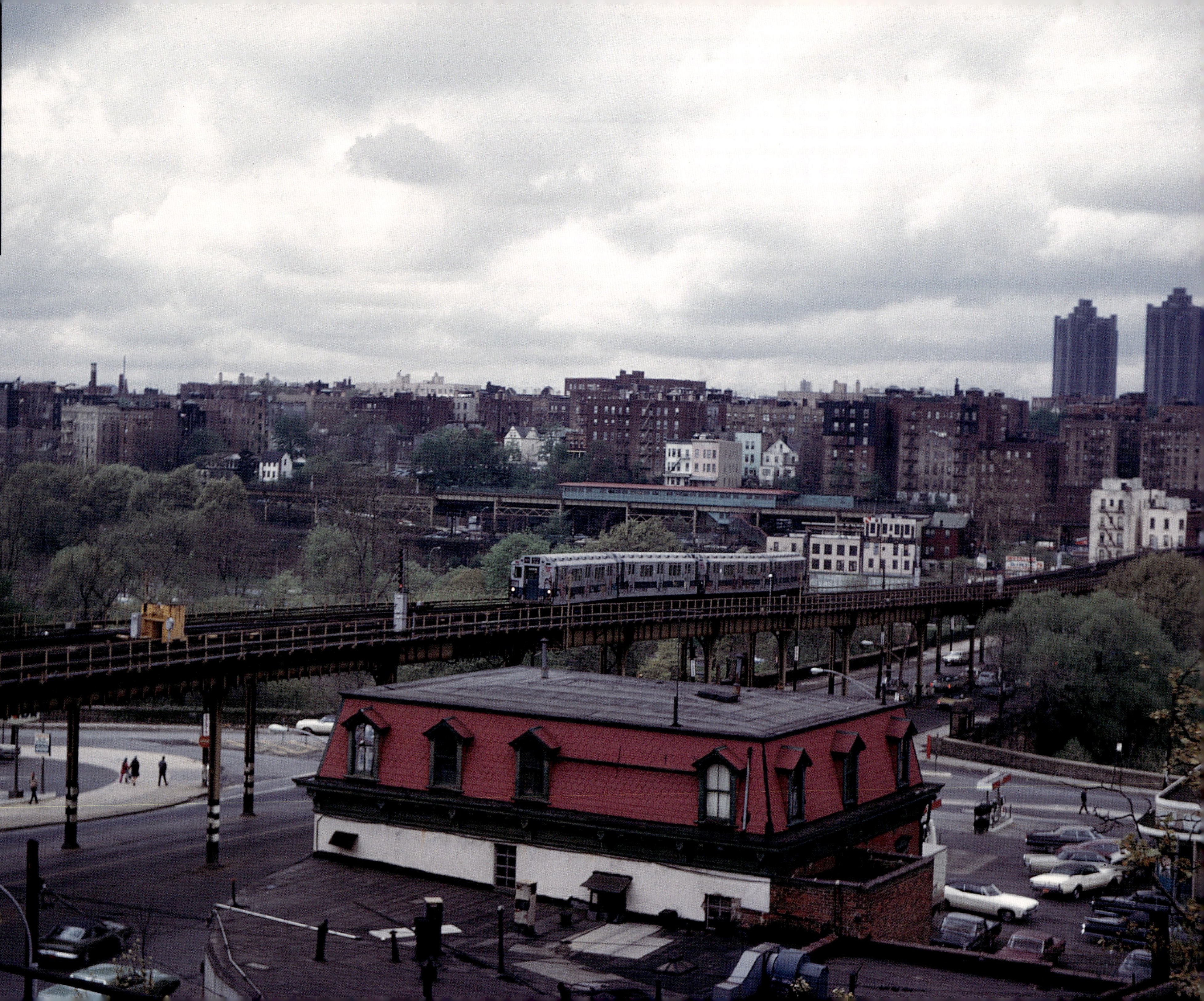

R-12s, 3rd Ave. El, Bronx, 1973

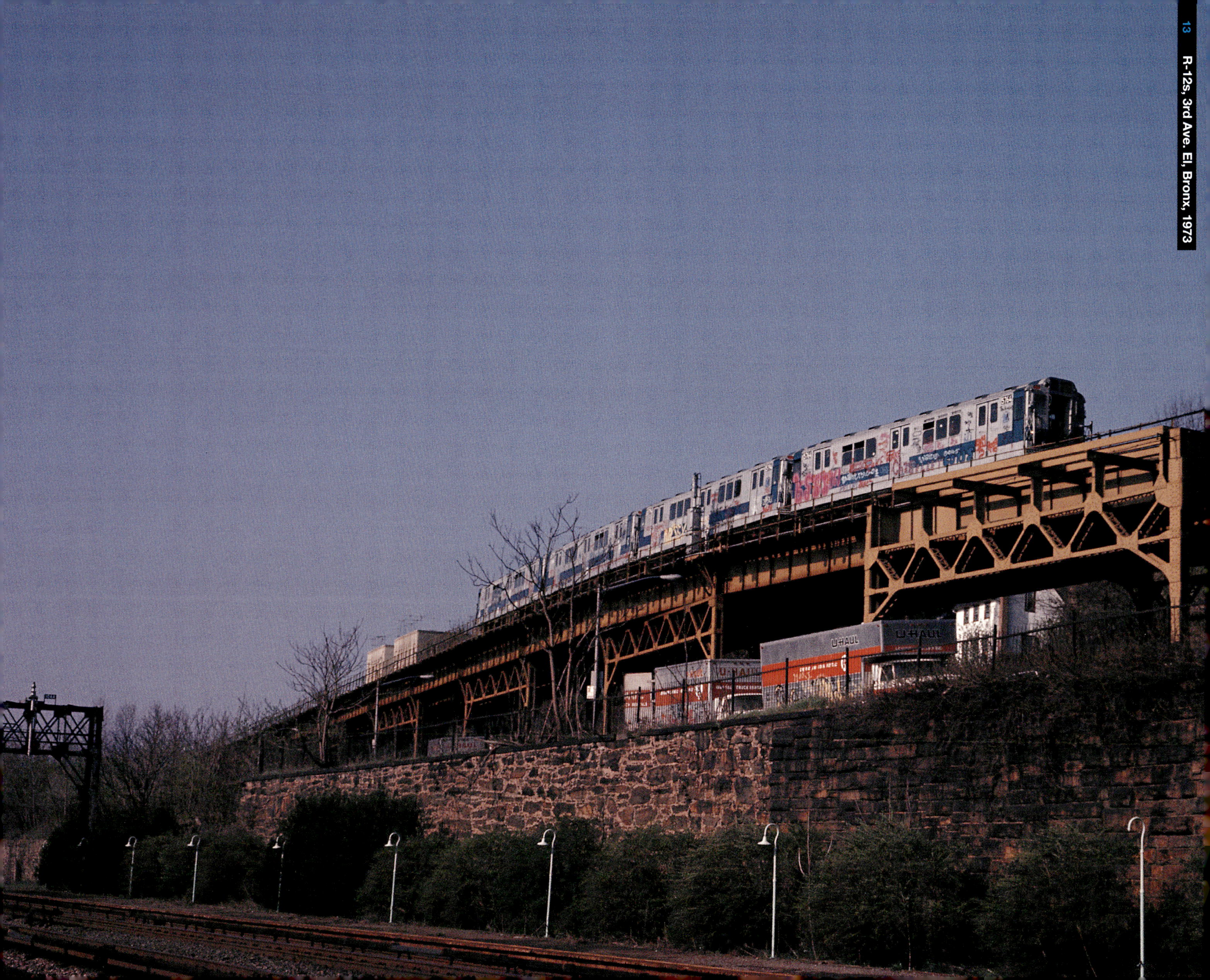

R-12s, 3rd Ave. El, Bronx, 1973

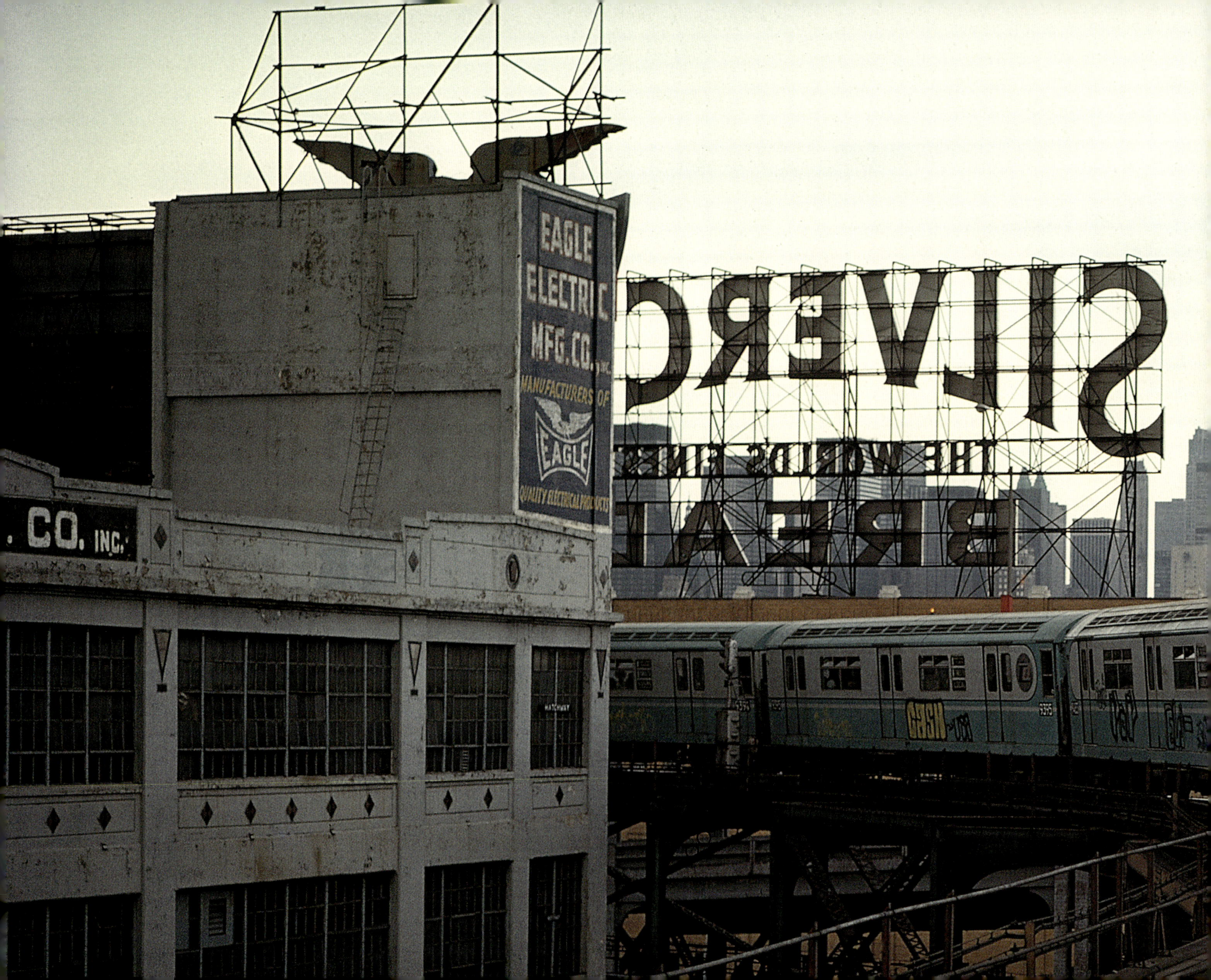
EAGLE
ELECTRIC
MFG. CO. INC.
MANUFACTURERS OF
EAGLE
QUALITY ELECTRICAL PRODUCTS
. CO. INC.

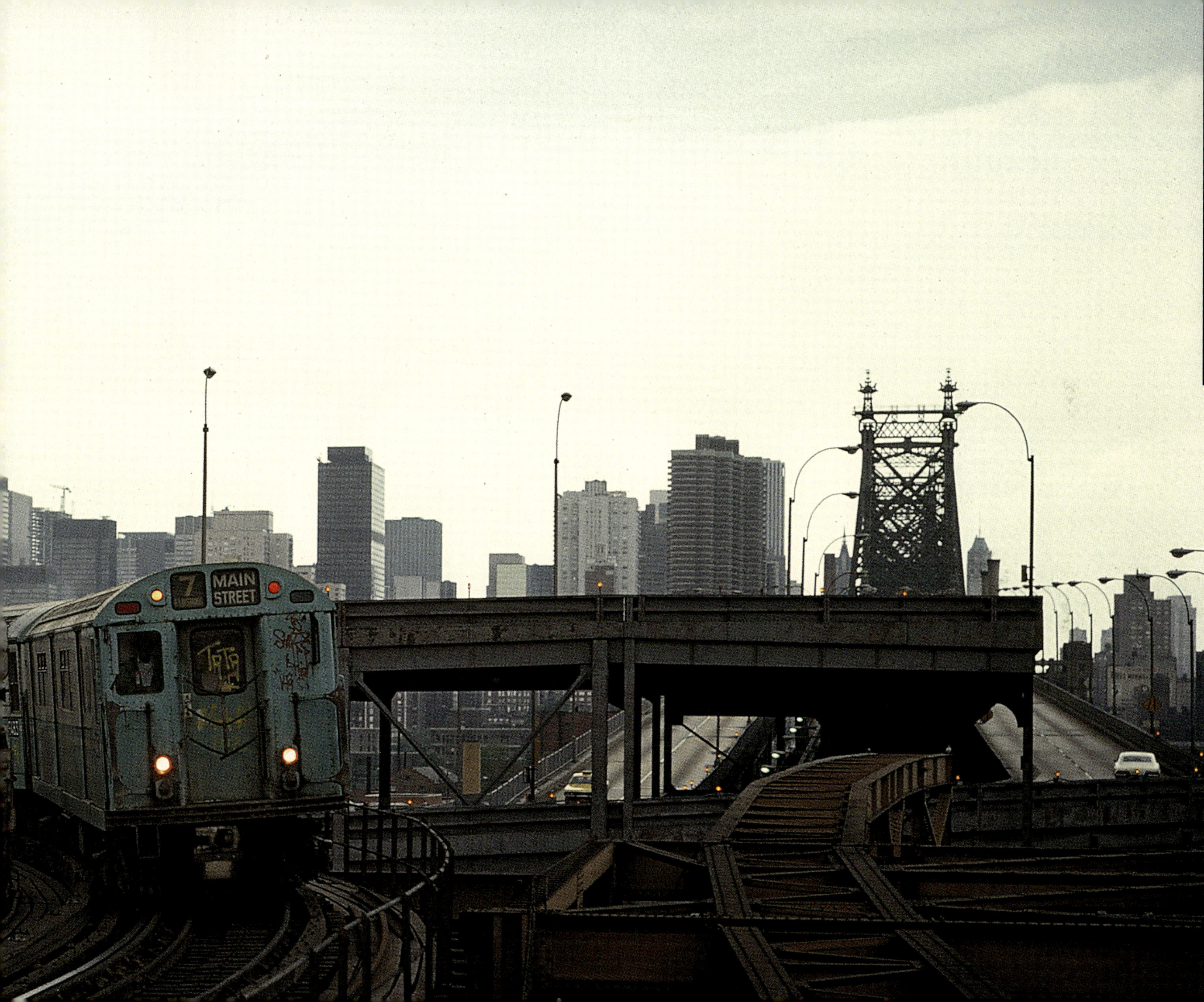

R-36s, No. 7 Flushing Line, Queensboro Plaza, 1974

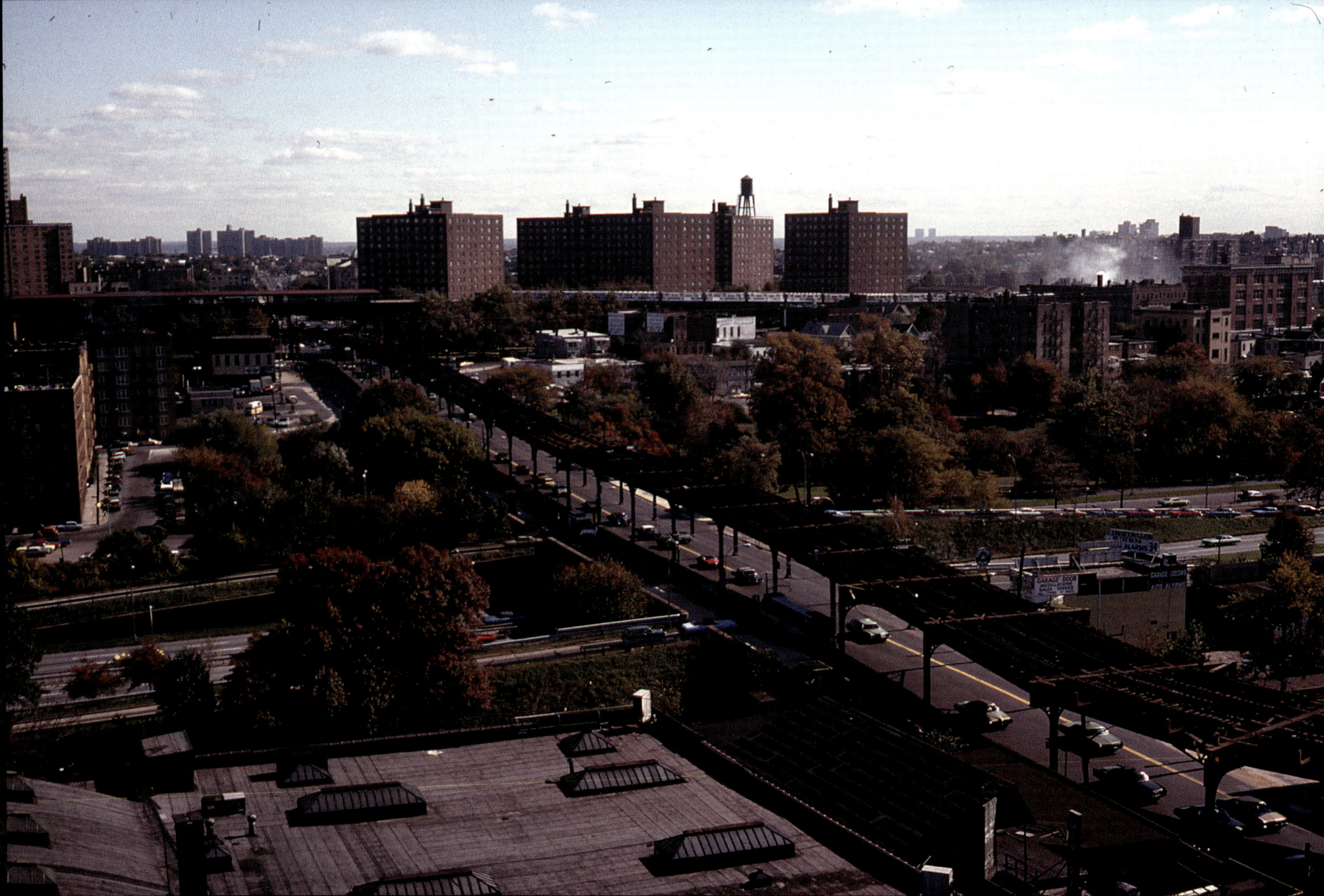

3rd Ave. El demolition, Gun Hill Rd., Bro

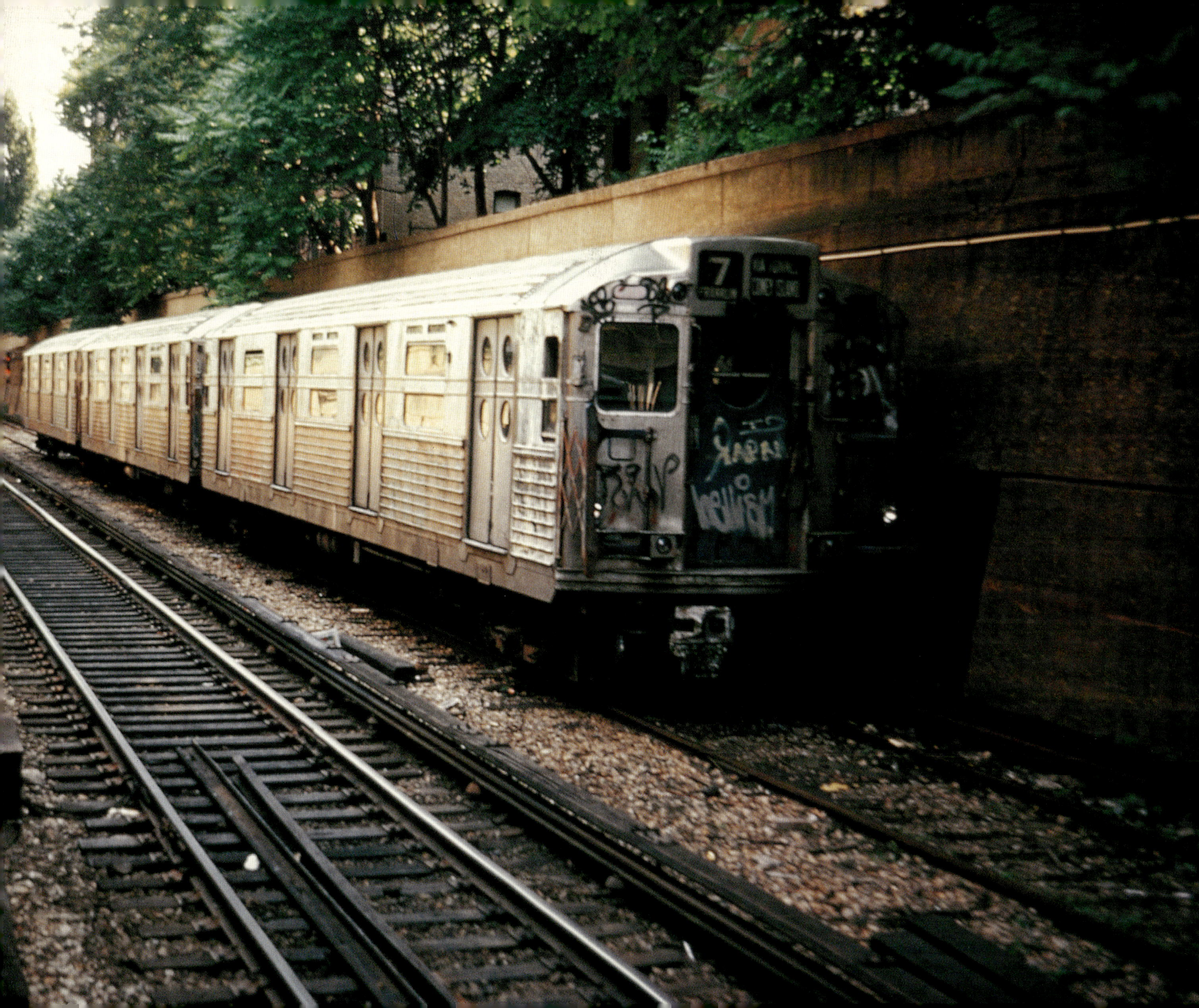

R-11s, Franklin Ave. Shuttle, Brooklyn, 1975

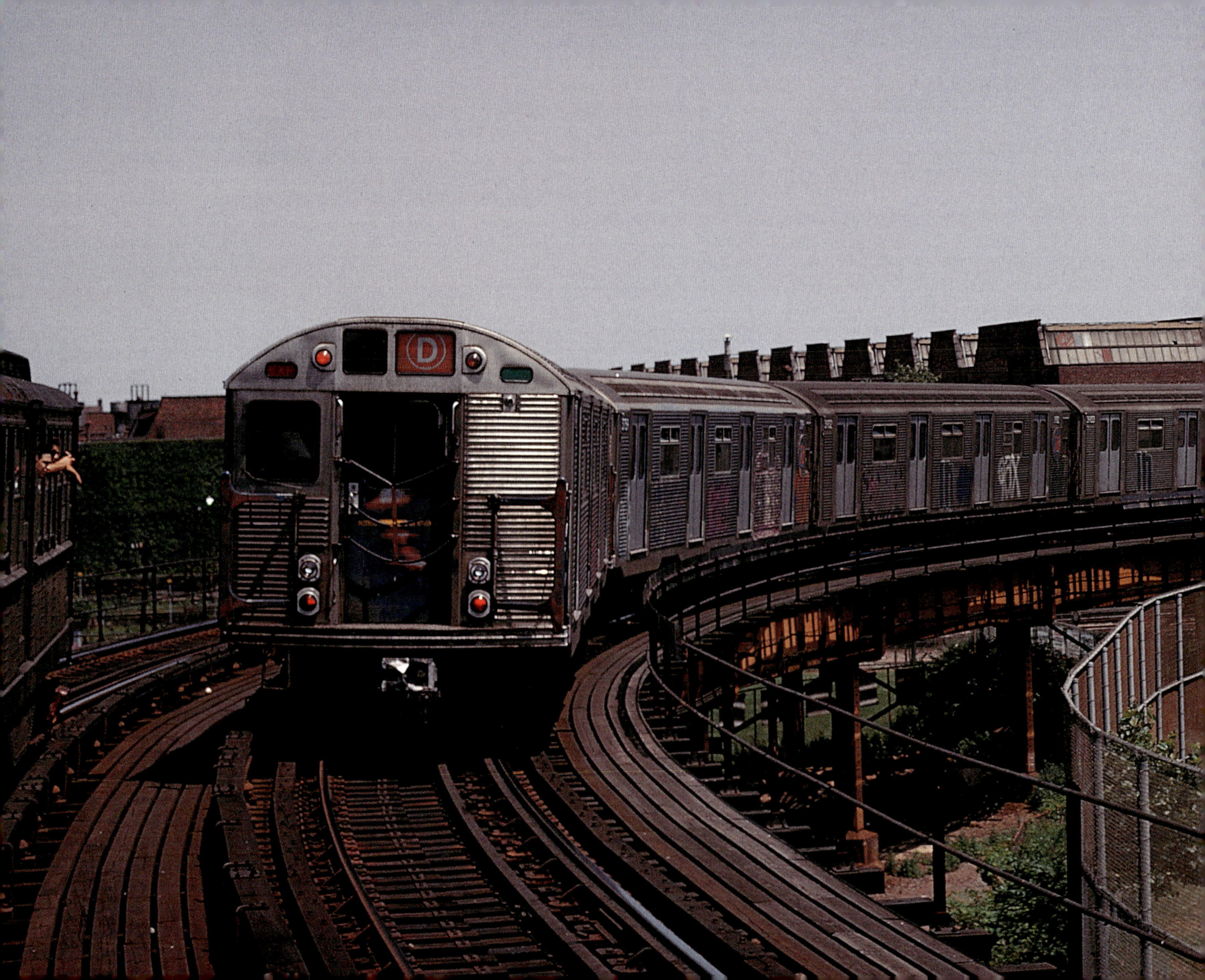

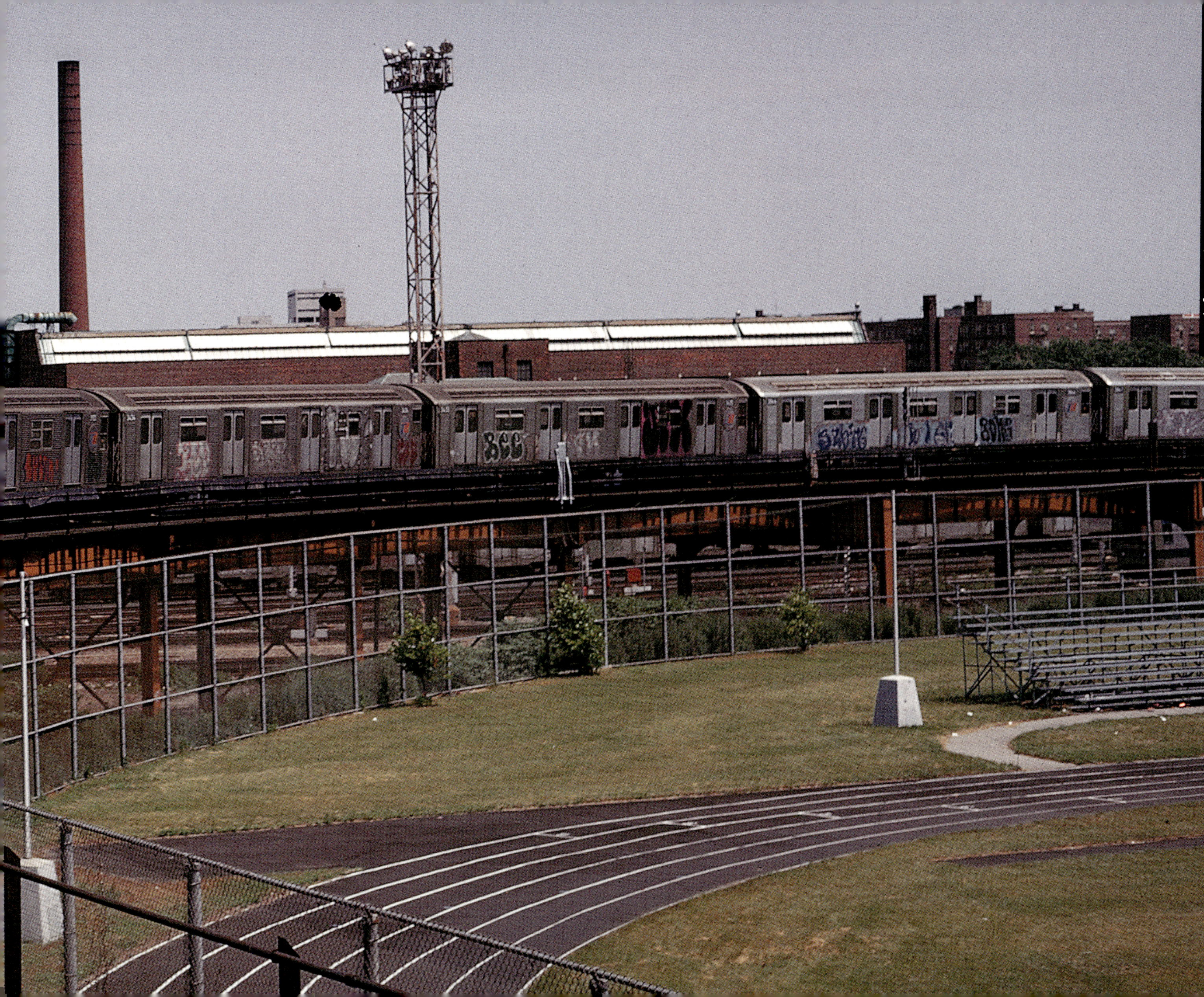

R-32s, near Coney Island Yard, Brooklyn, 1975

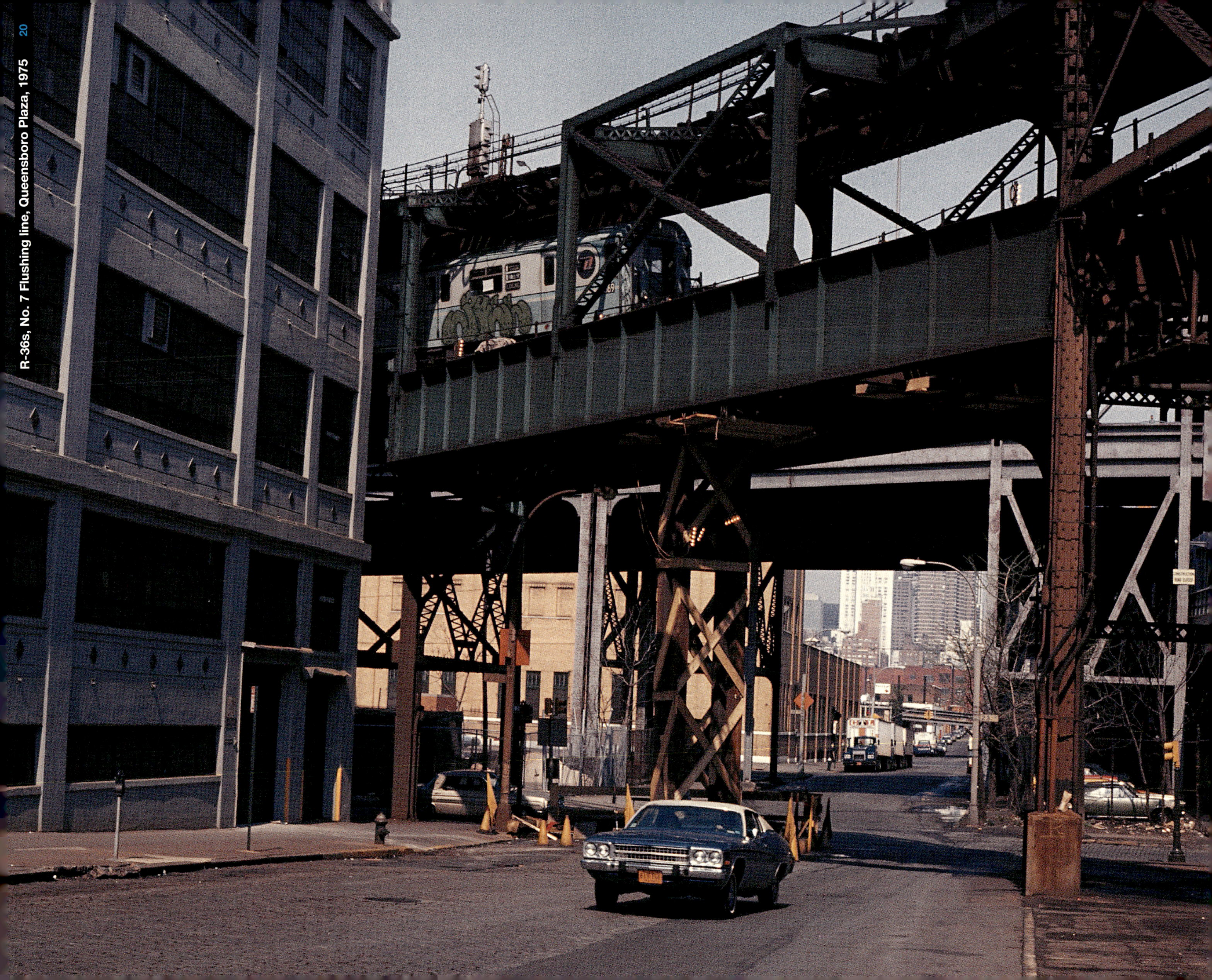

R-36s, No. 7 Flushing line, Queensboro Plaza, 1975

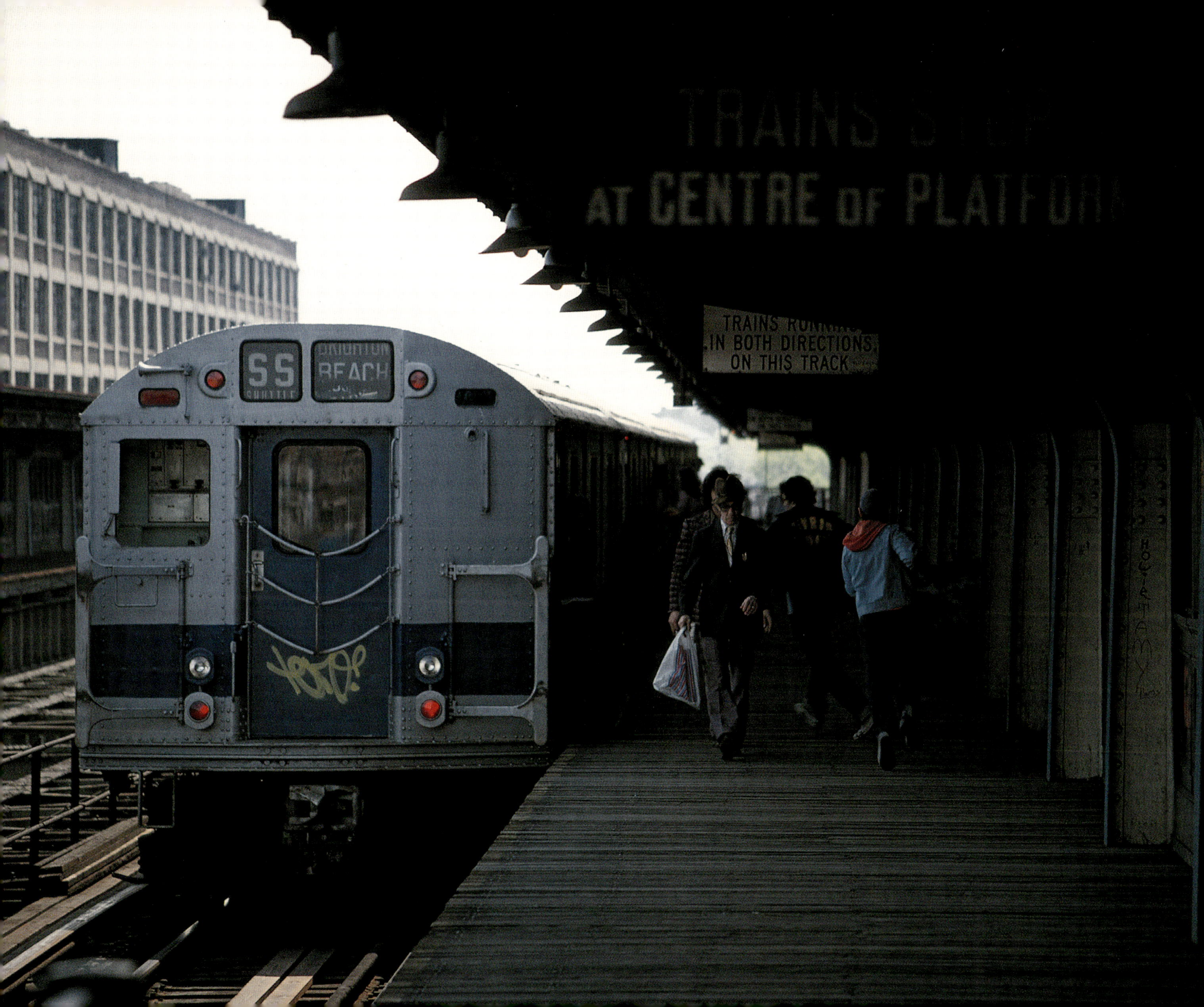

R-27s, Culver Shuttle,13th Ave., Brooklyn, 1975

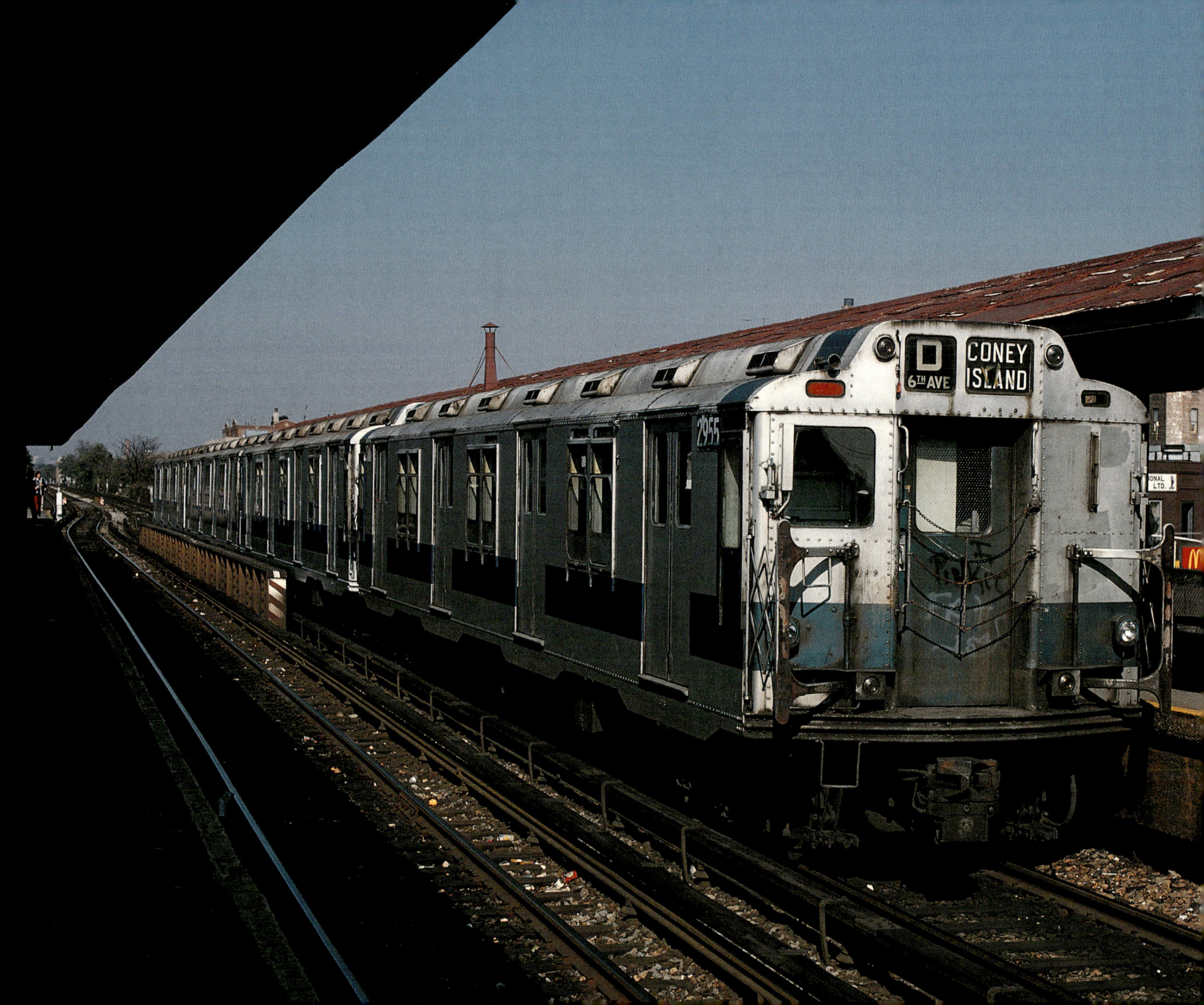

R-10s, Brighton line, Kings Highway, Brooklyn, 1976

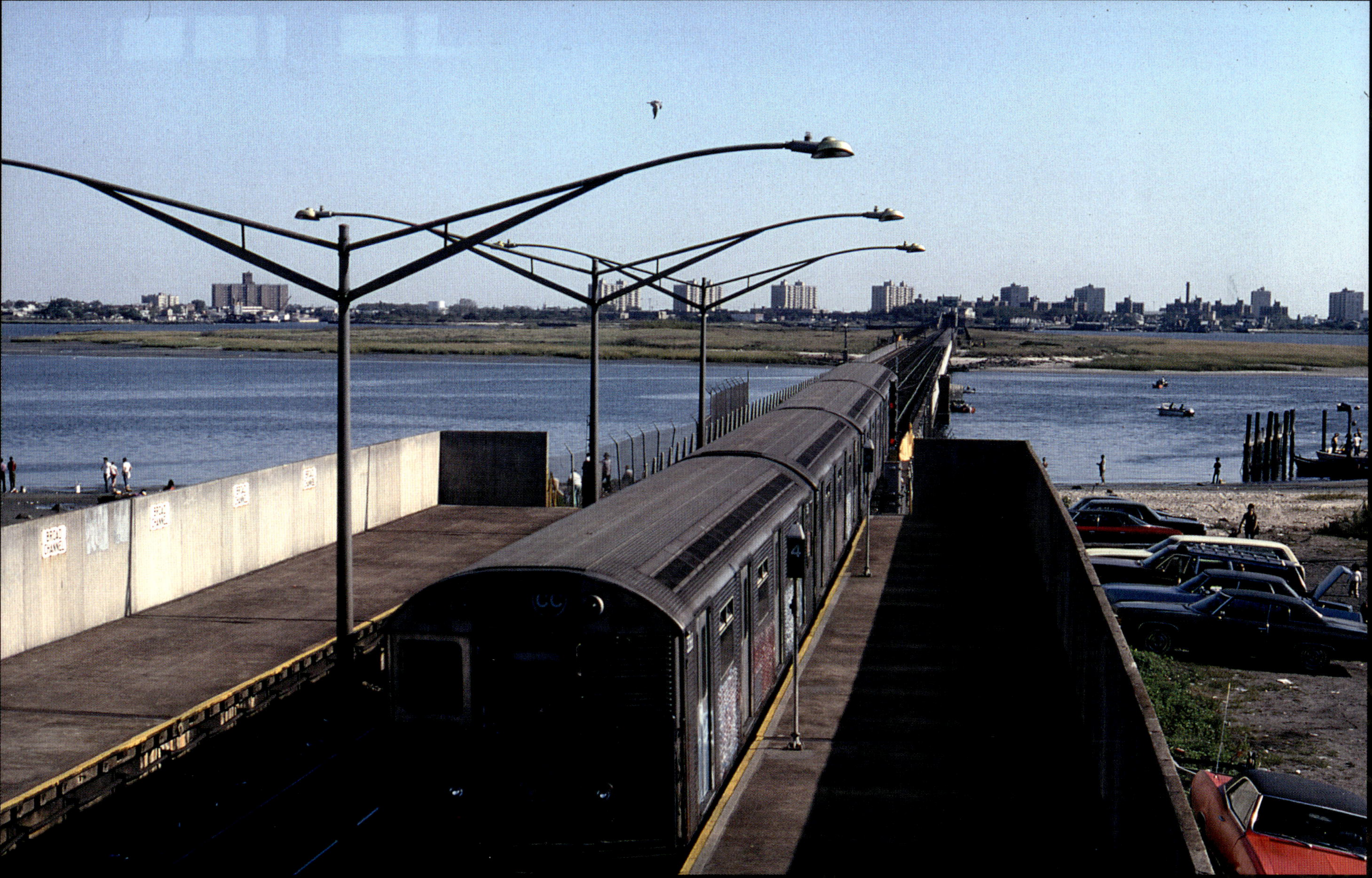

Shuttle, Broad Channel, Queens, 1976

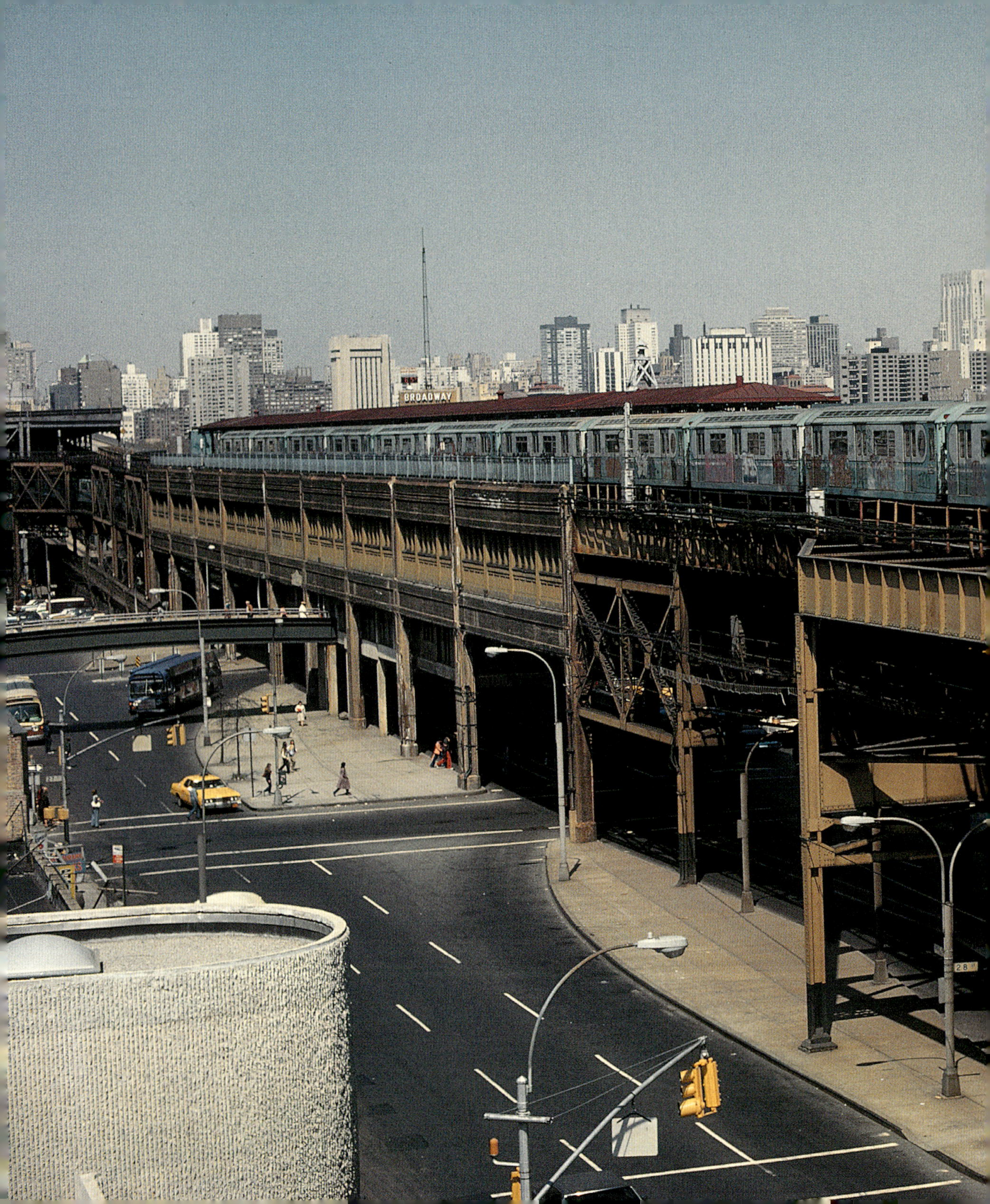
BROADWAY

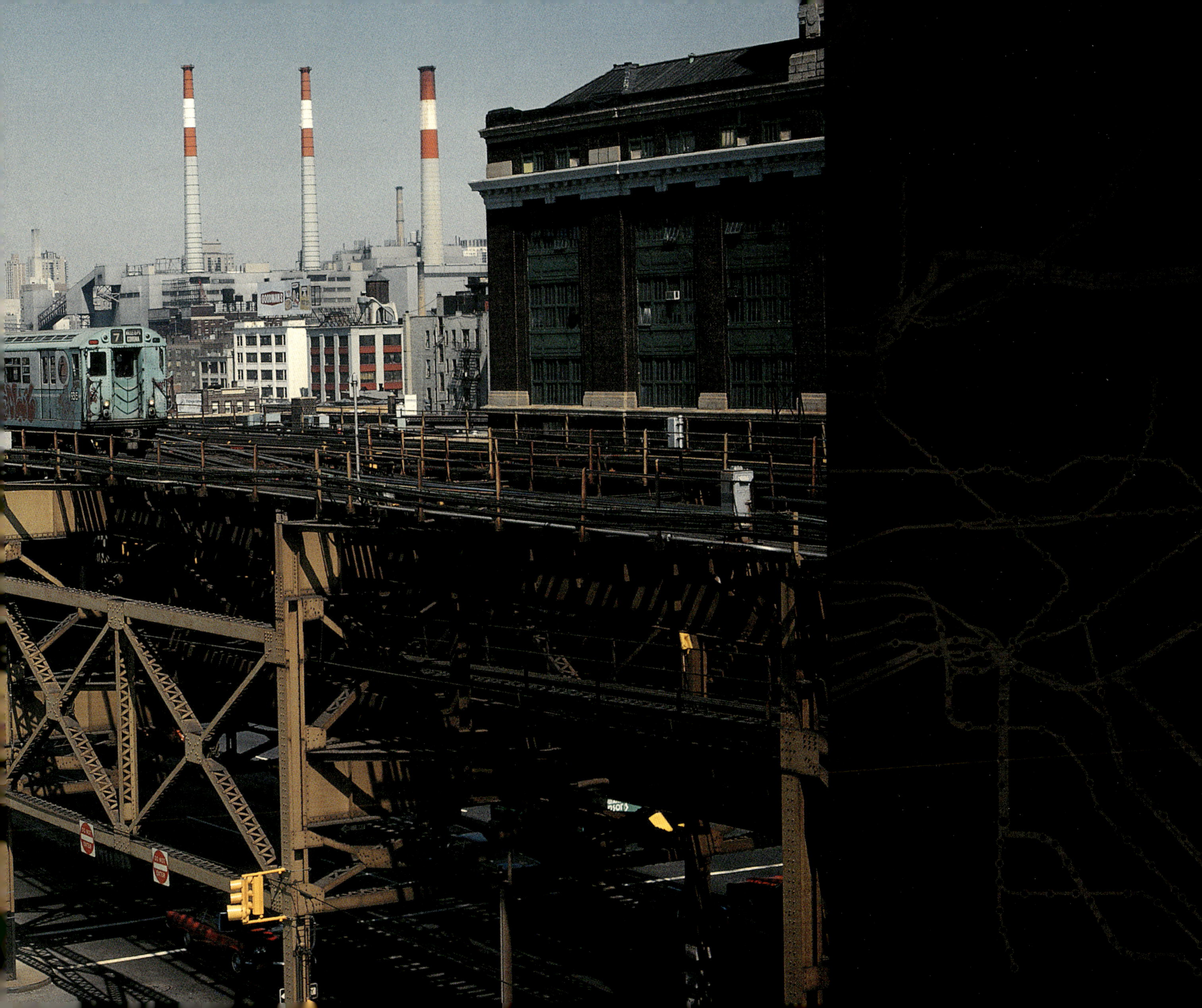

No. 7 Flushing line, Queensboro Plaza, 1976

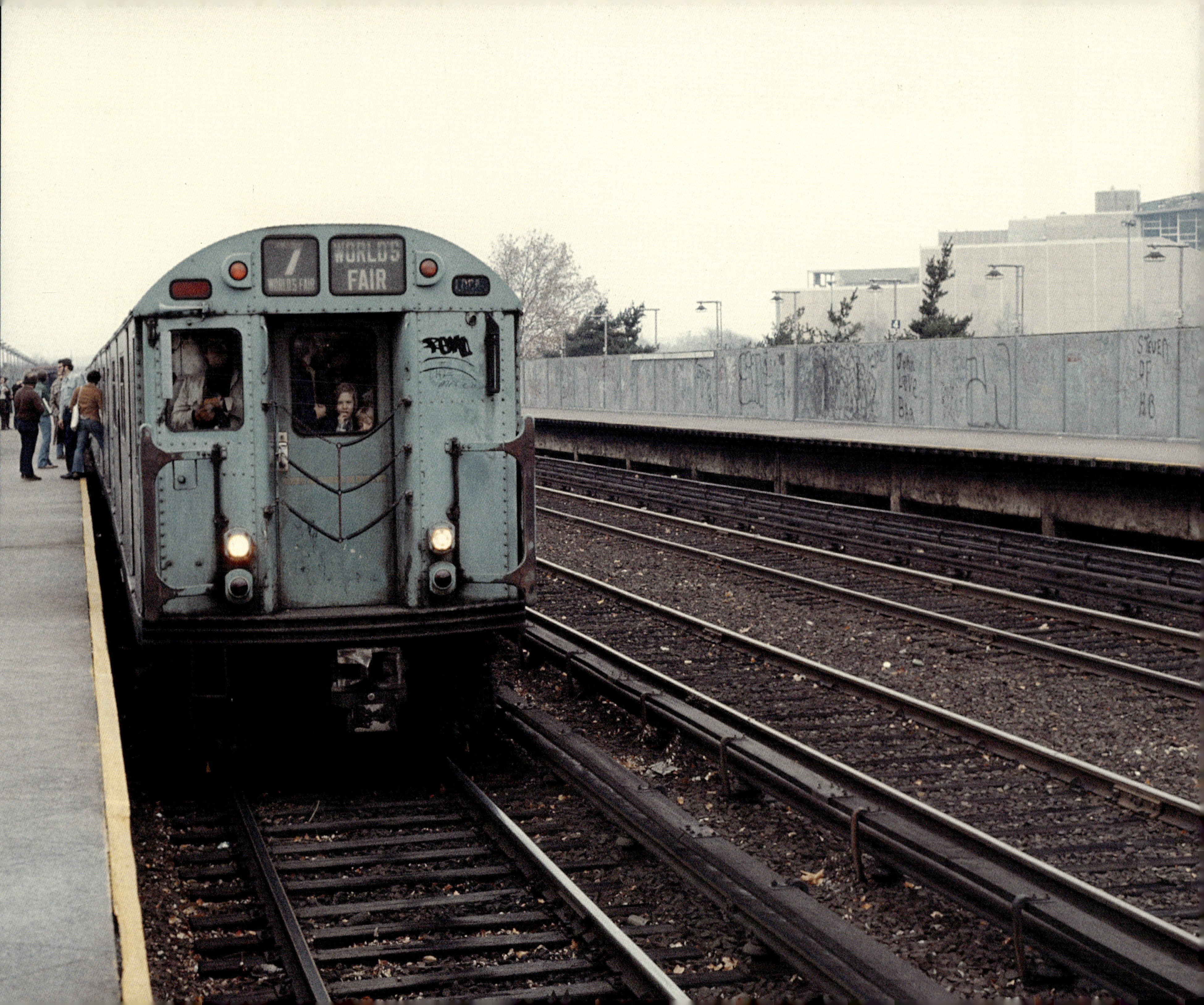

R-33 / R-36s, Rockaway line fan trip, Aqueduct—N. Conduit Ave., Queens, 1976

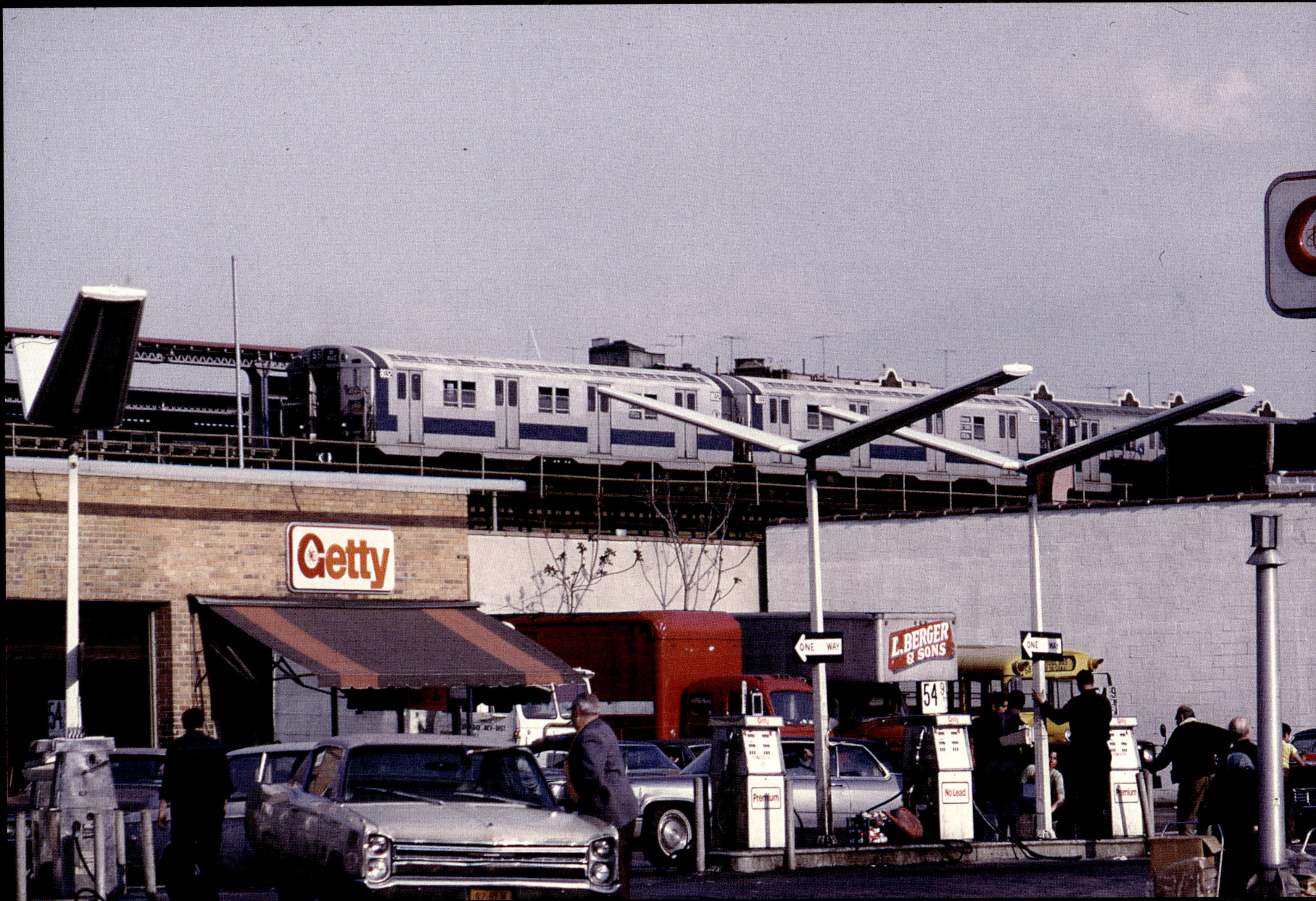

R-27s, Culver Shuttle, Ditmas Ave., Brooklyn, 1975

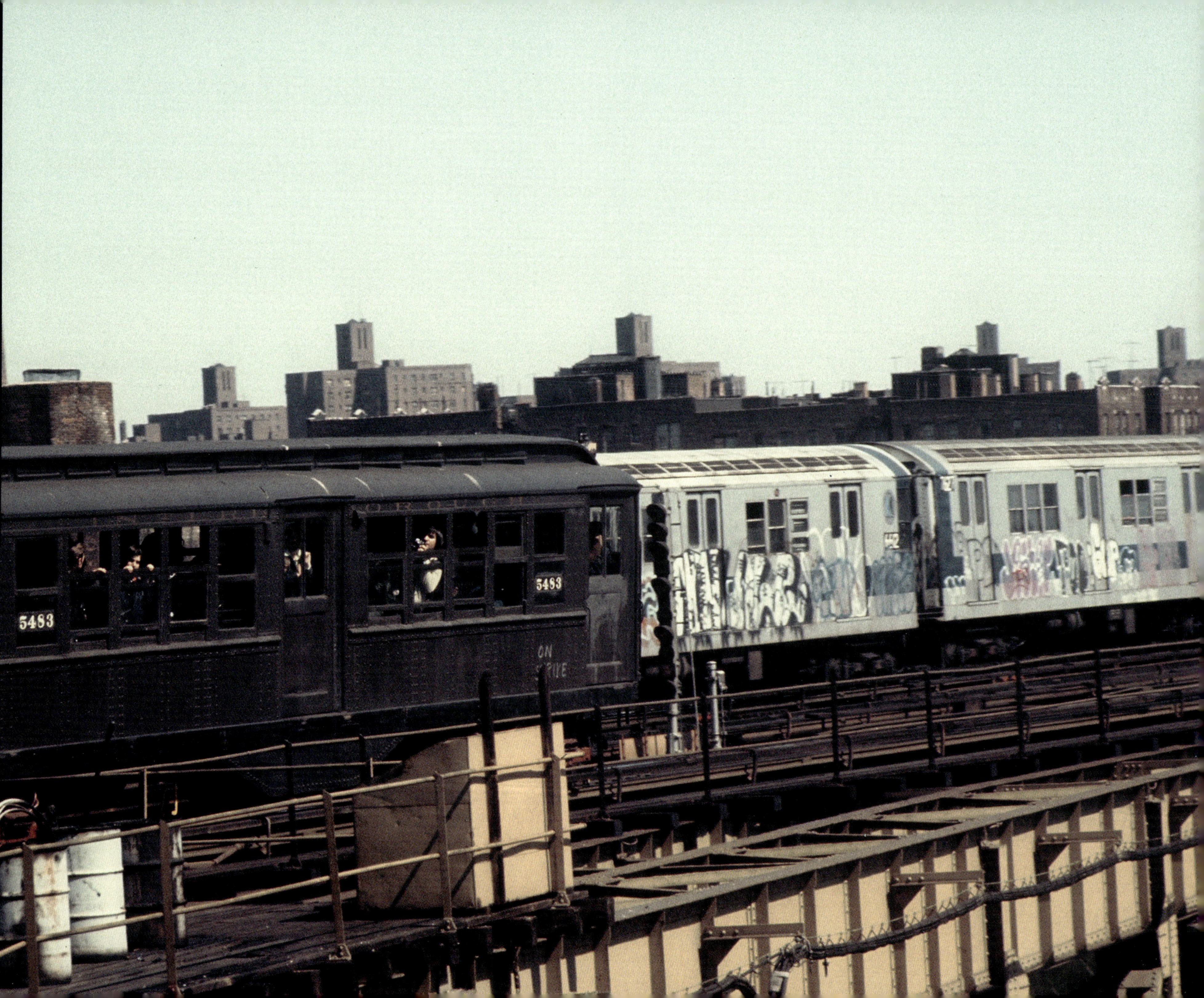

Low Vs passing R-17 & R-22s, West Farms Sq.—E. Tremont Ave., Bronx, 1976

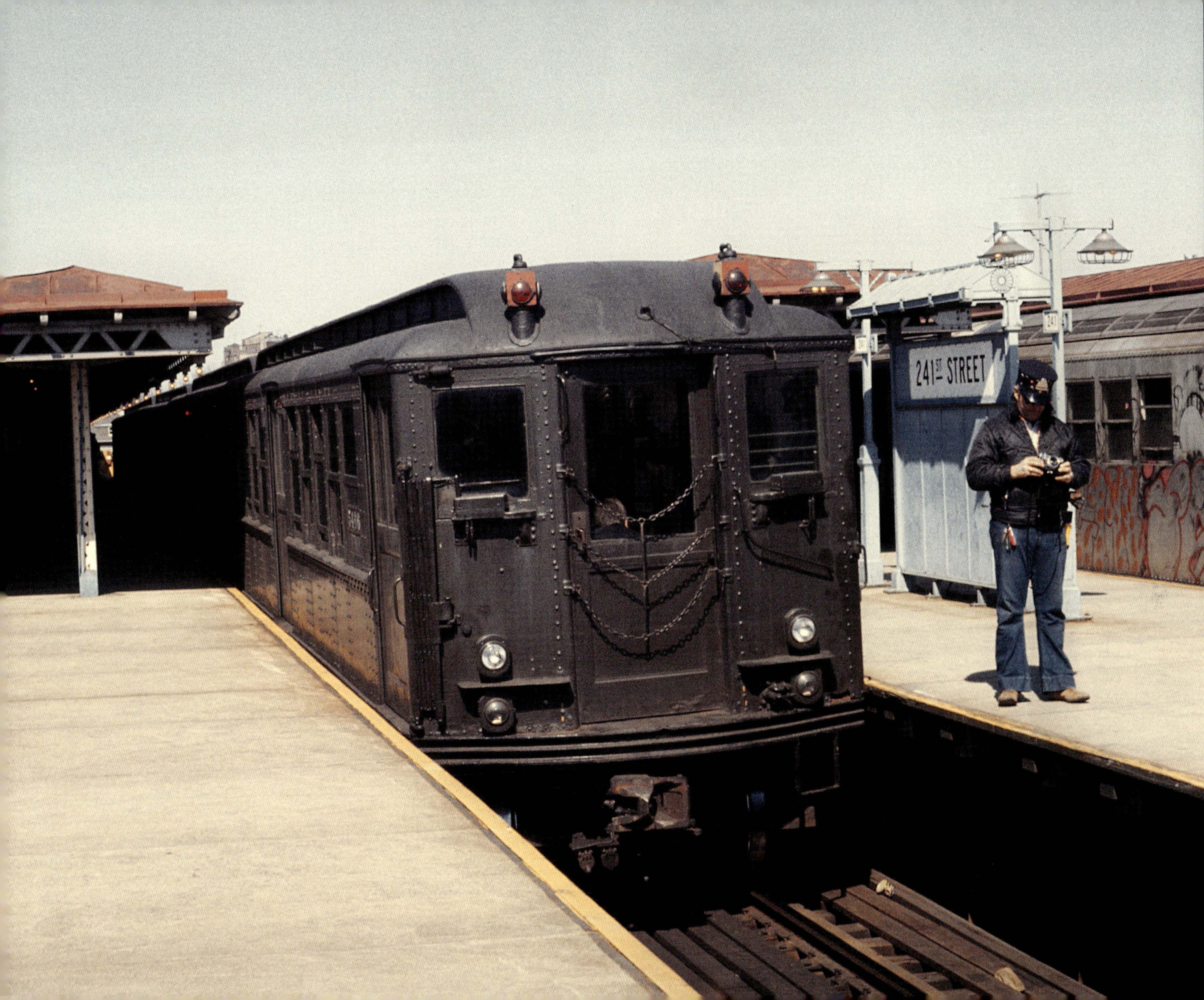

29 Low Vs, 241st St., White Plains Rd. Line, Bronx, 1976

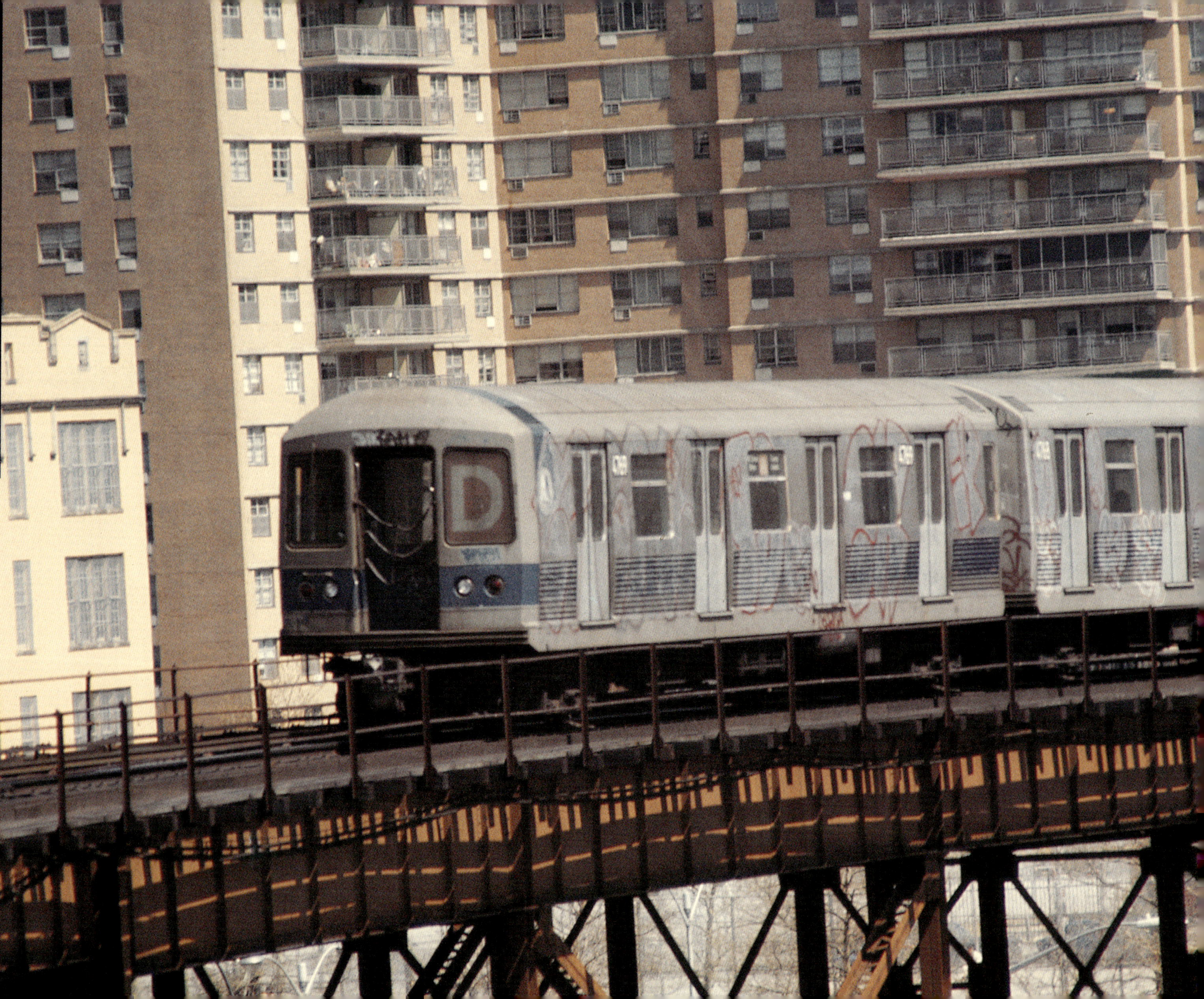

R-42s, D line, between W. 8th St. & Ocean Parkway, Brooklyn, 1977

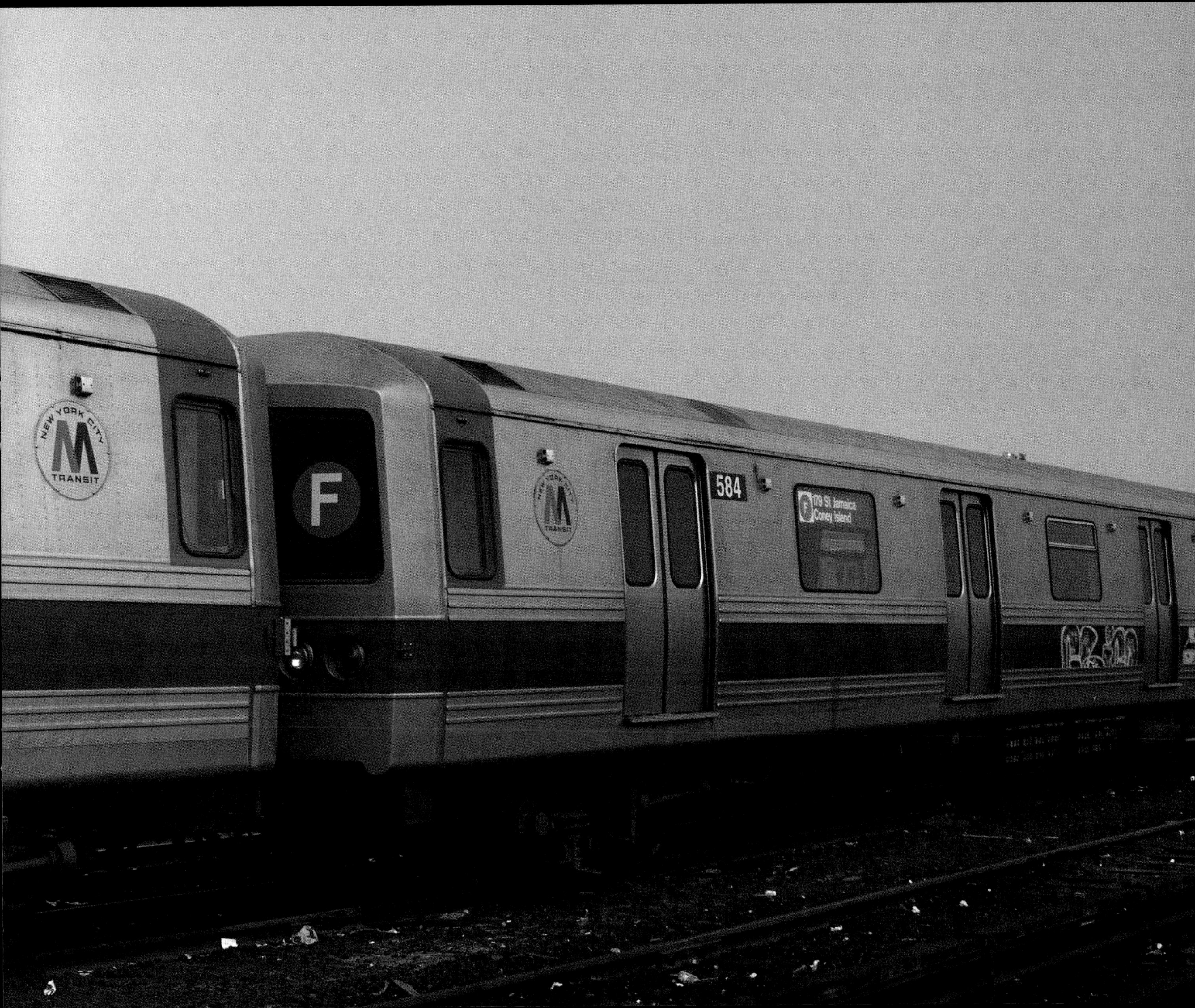

R-46s, Coney Island Yard, Brooklyn, 1977

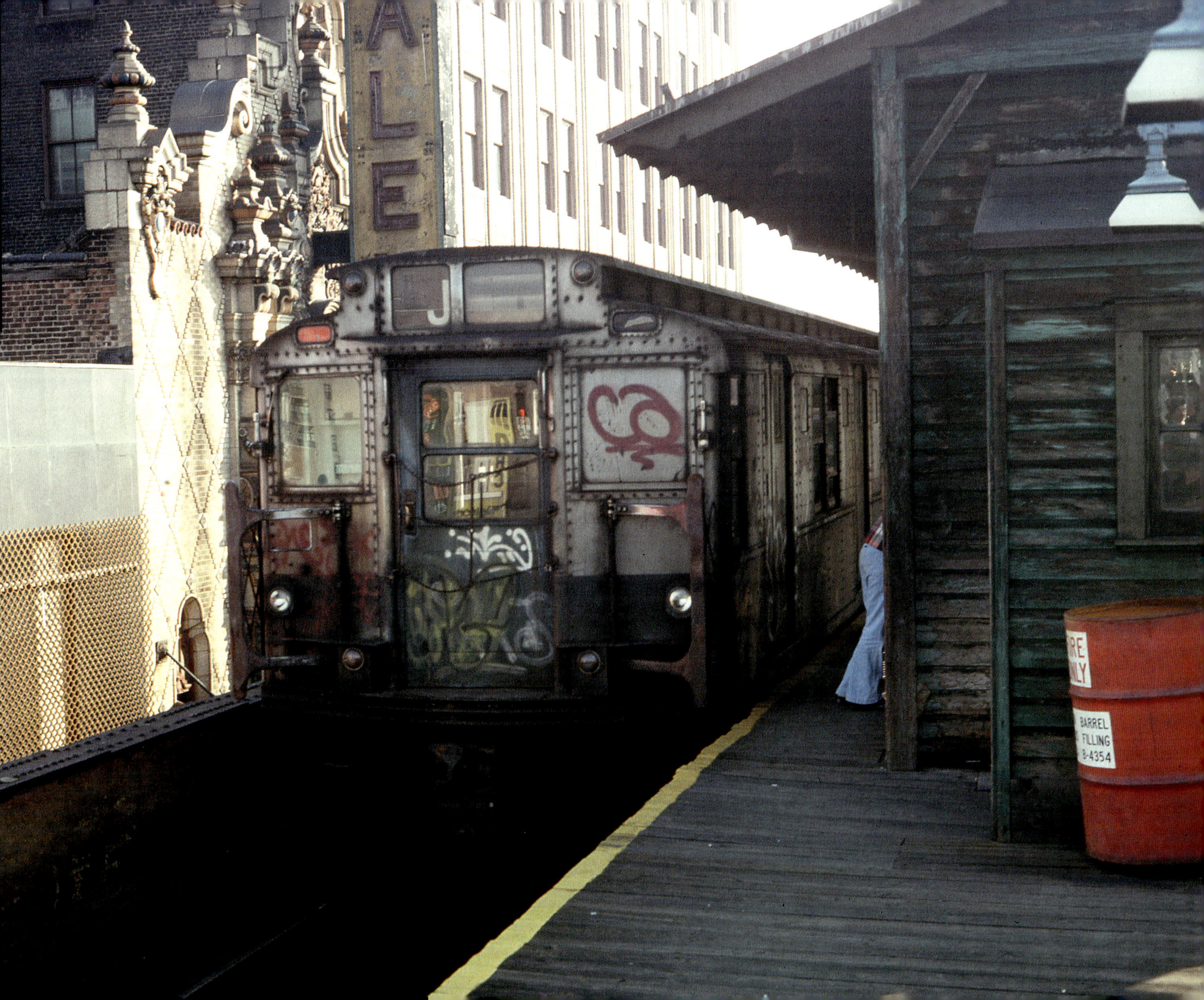

R-9s, 168th St, Jamaica line, Queens, 1977

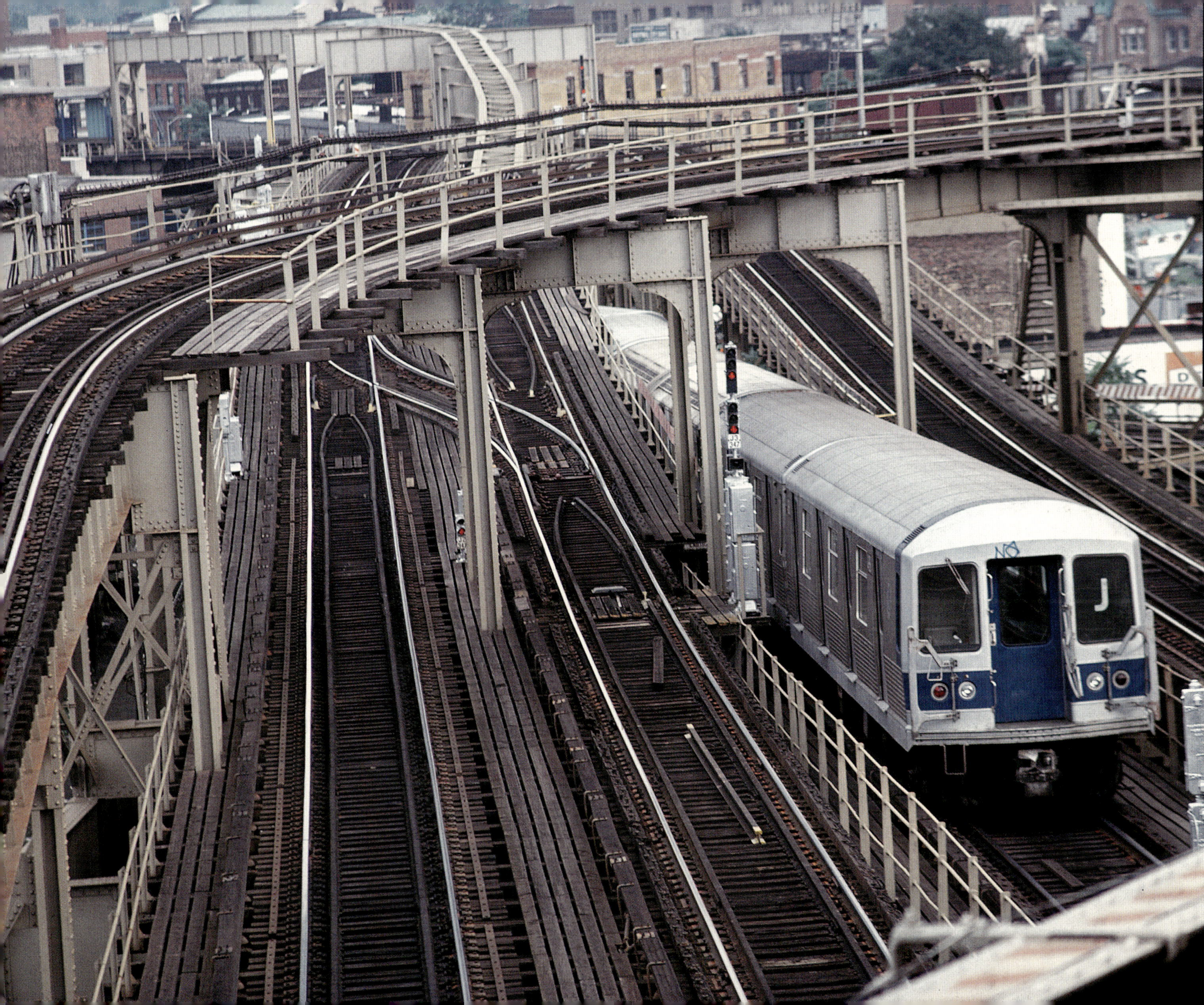

R-42s J line, entering East NY Yard, Brooklyn, 1978

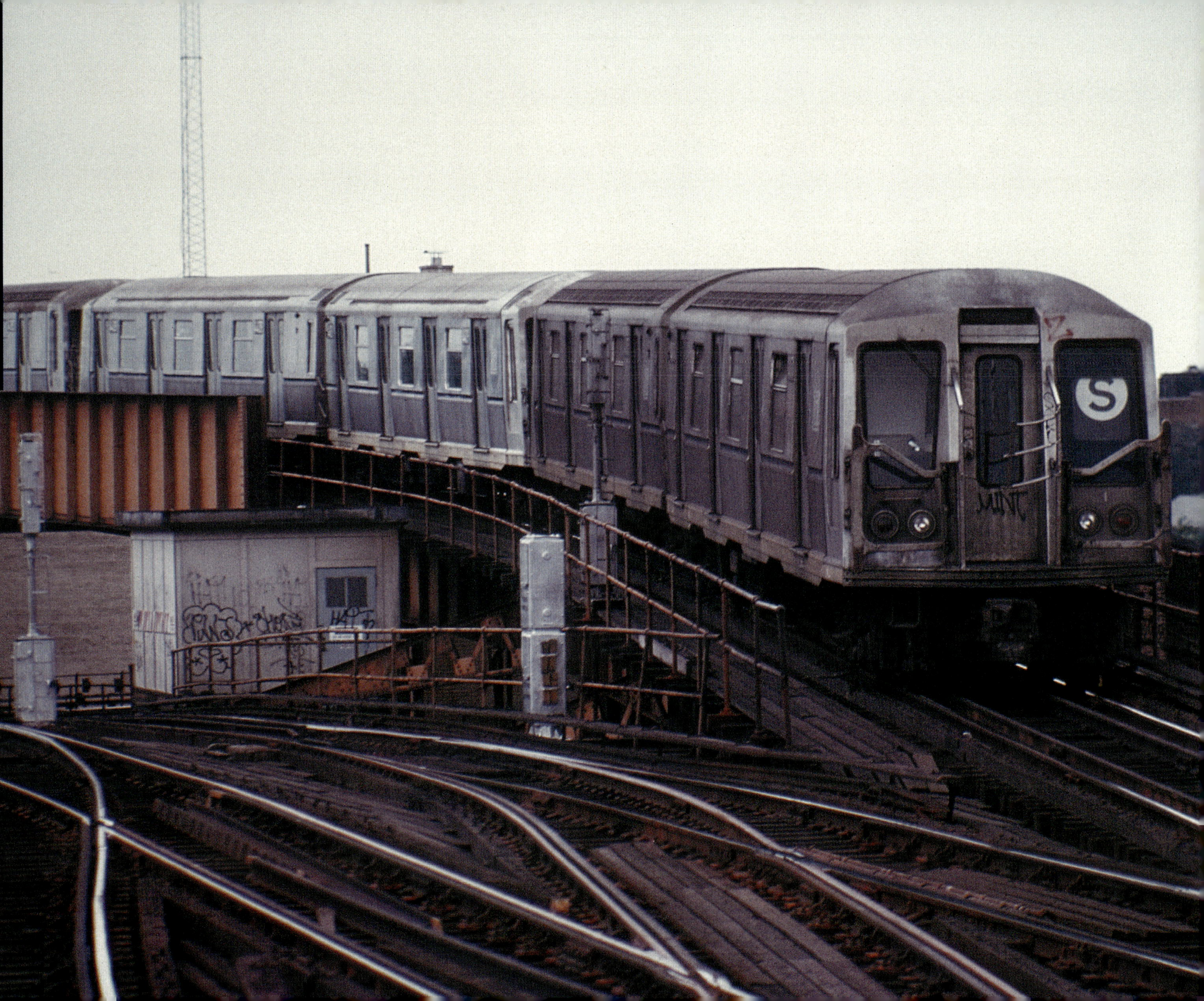

R-40s, A line, east of Rockaway Blvd., Queens, 1978

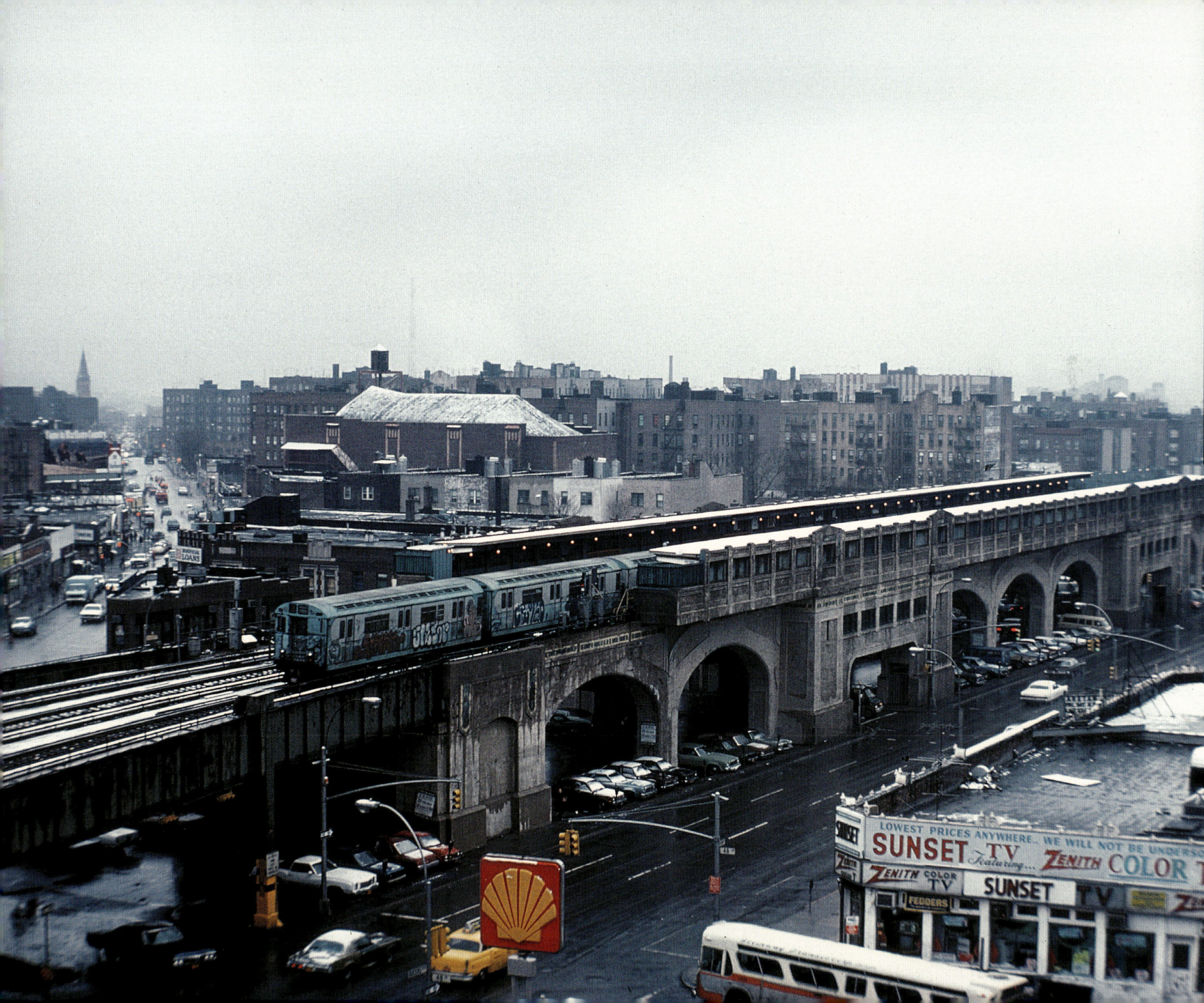

R-33/R-36s, No. 7 Flushing line, 46th St.–Bliss St., Queens, 1978

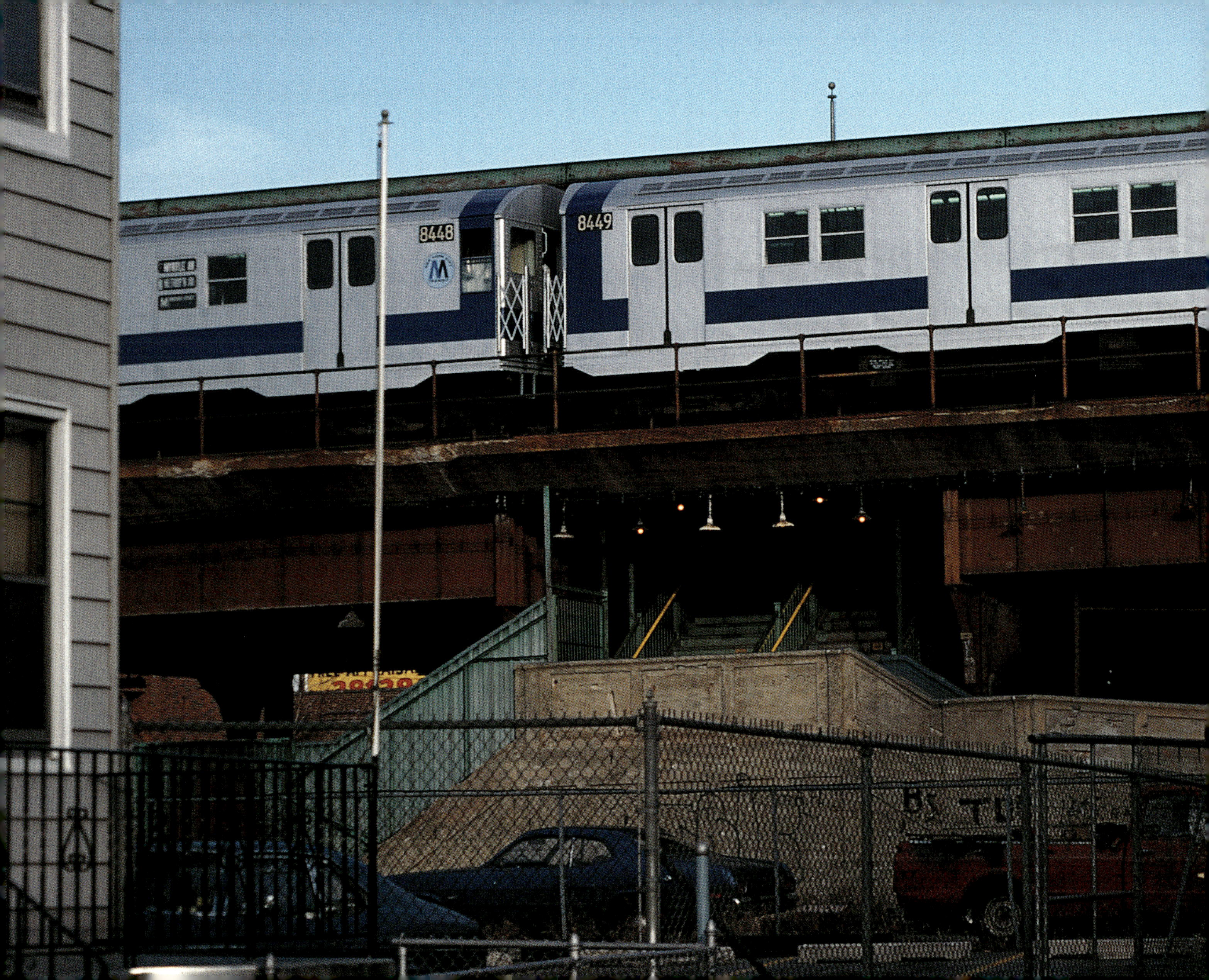
8448
8449

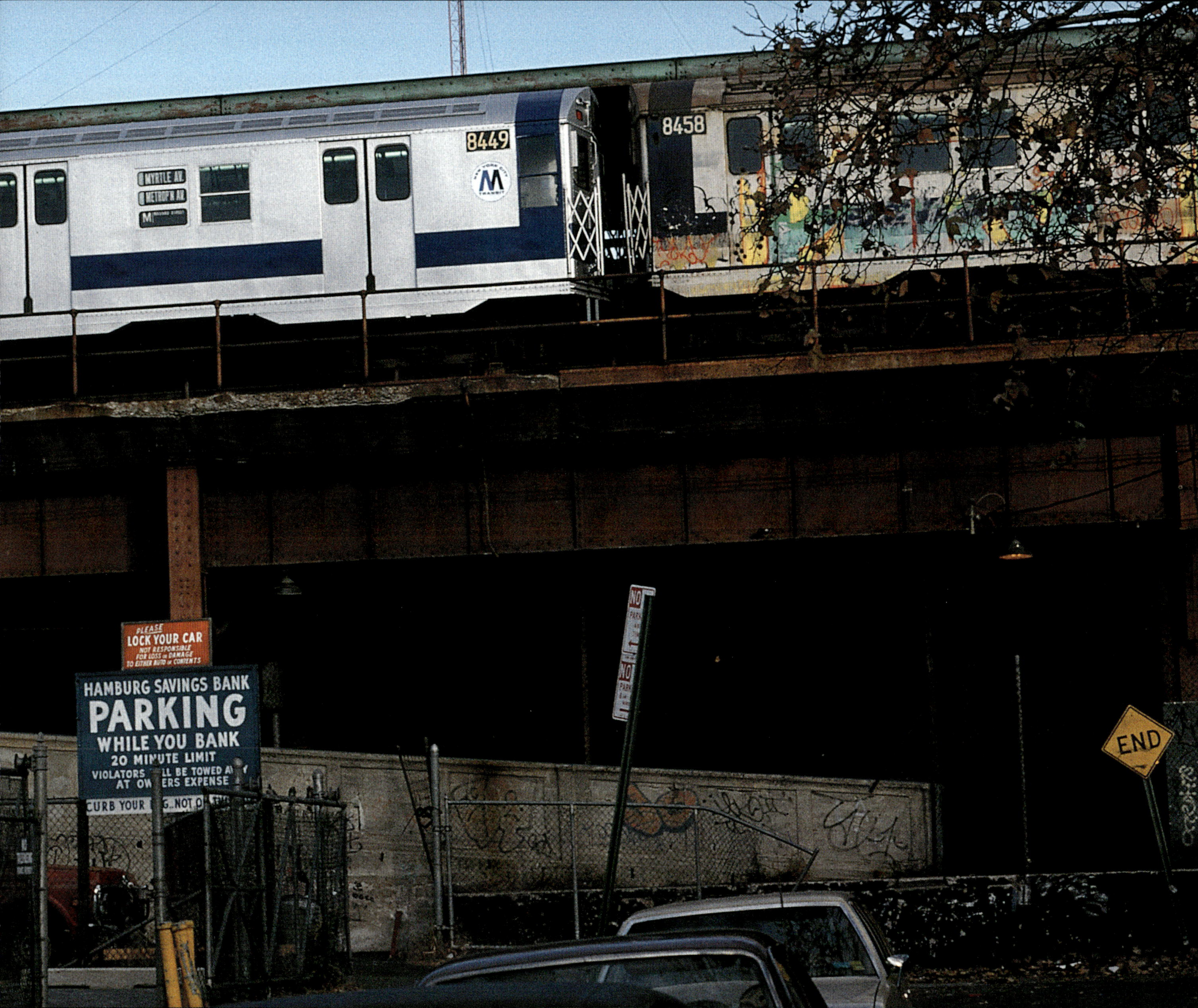

R-30s, Myrtle Ave. line, Fresh Pond Rd., Queens

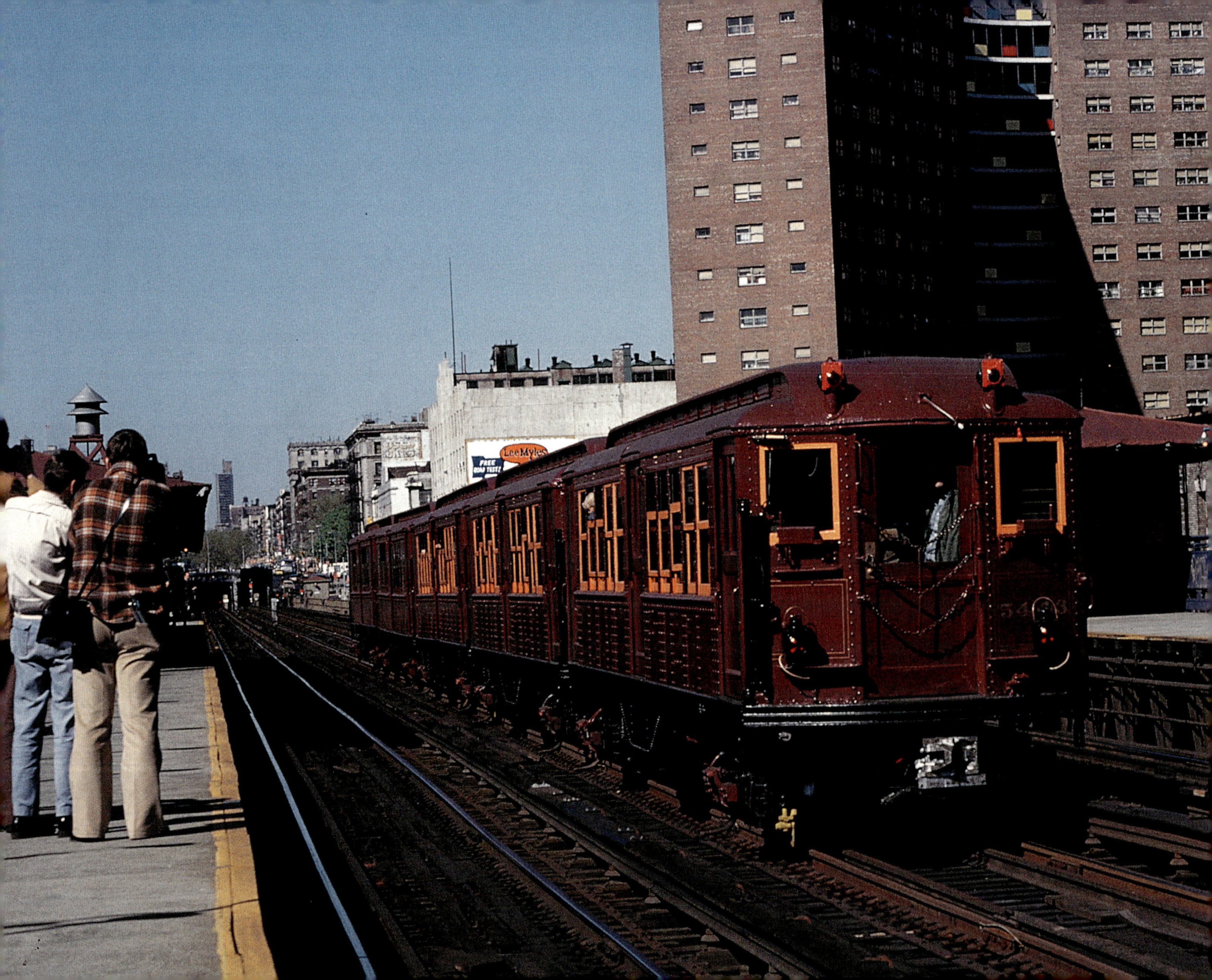
LeeMyles

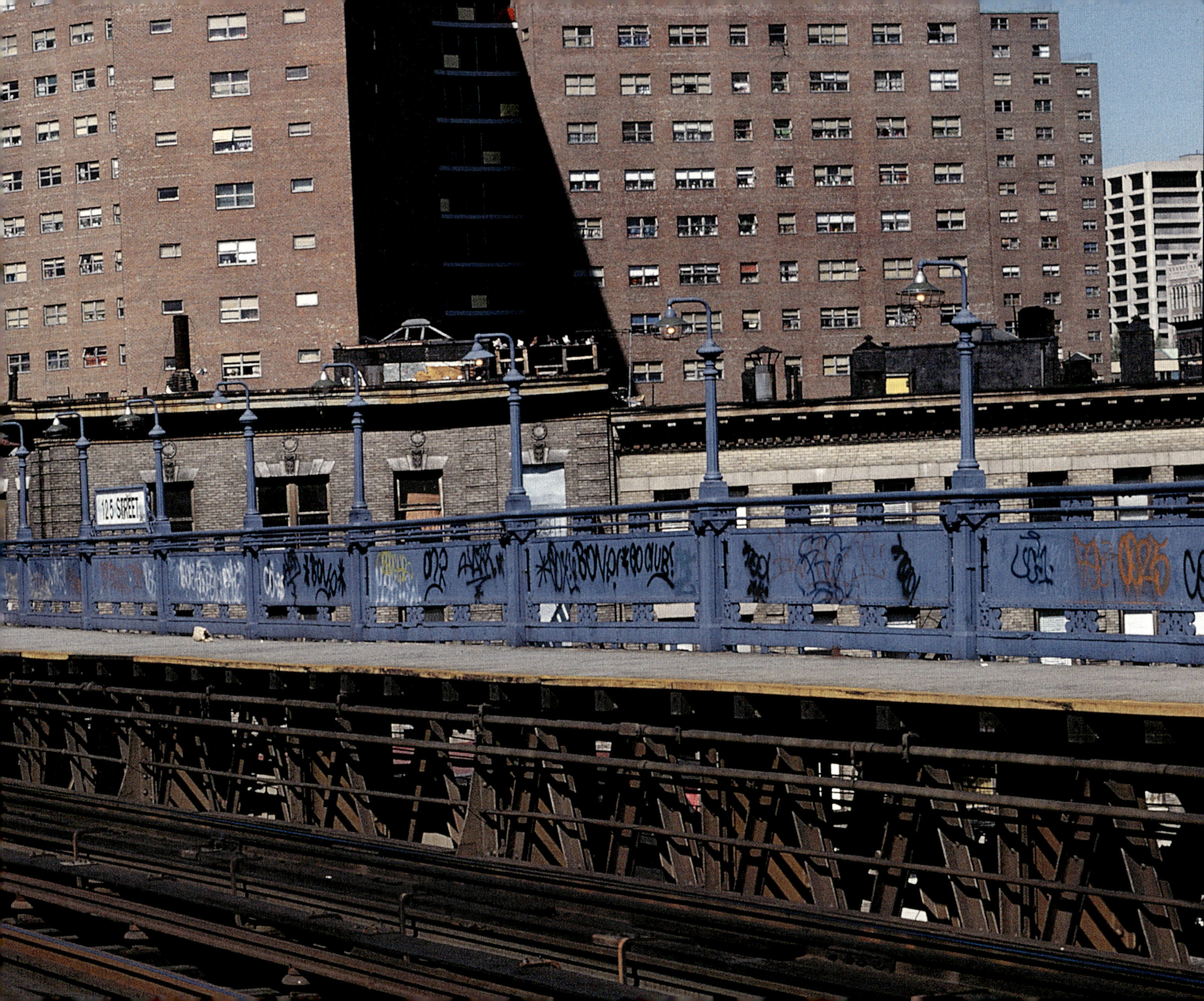

Low Vs, Broadway line, 125th St., Manhattan, 1979

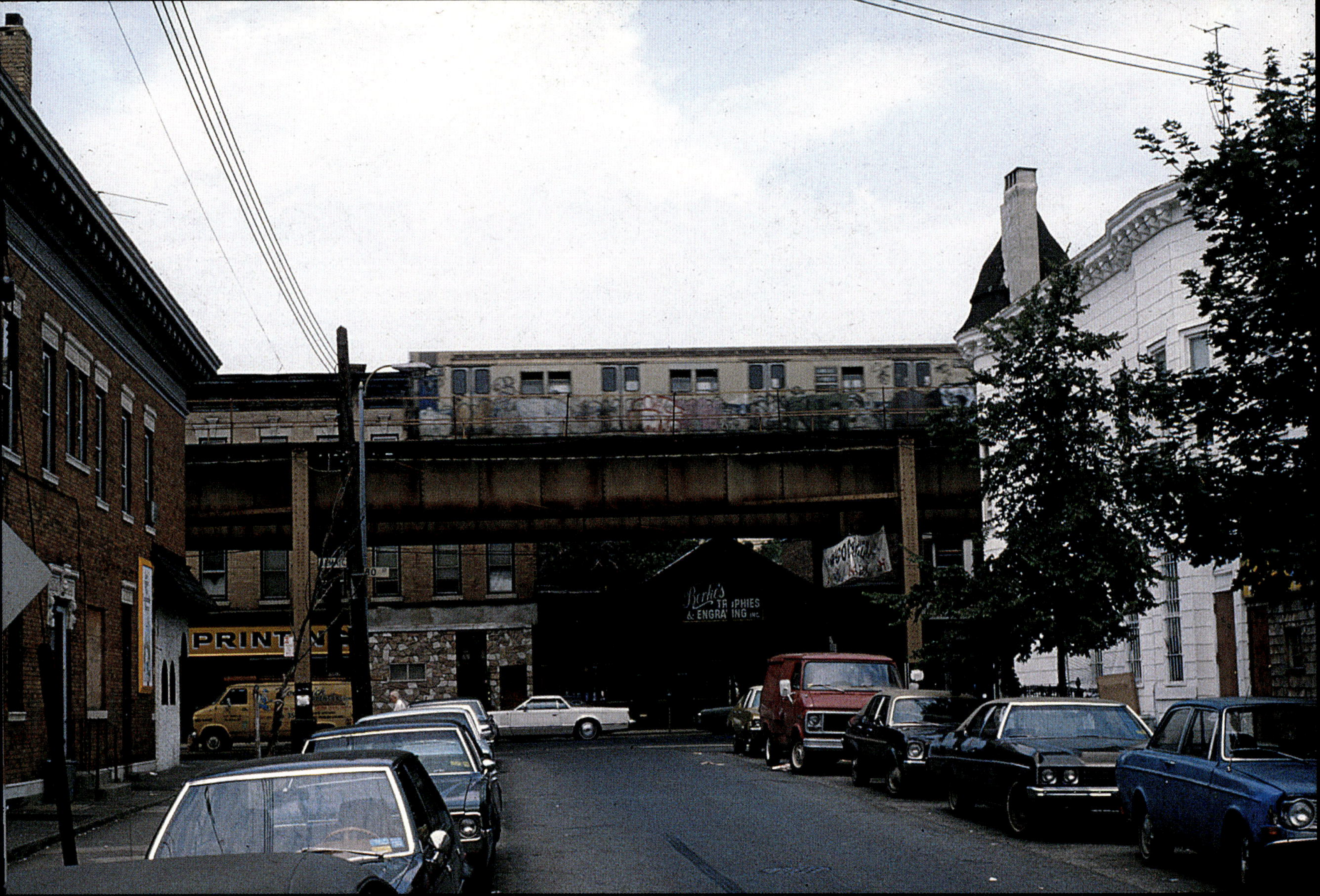
PRINTIN

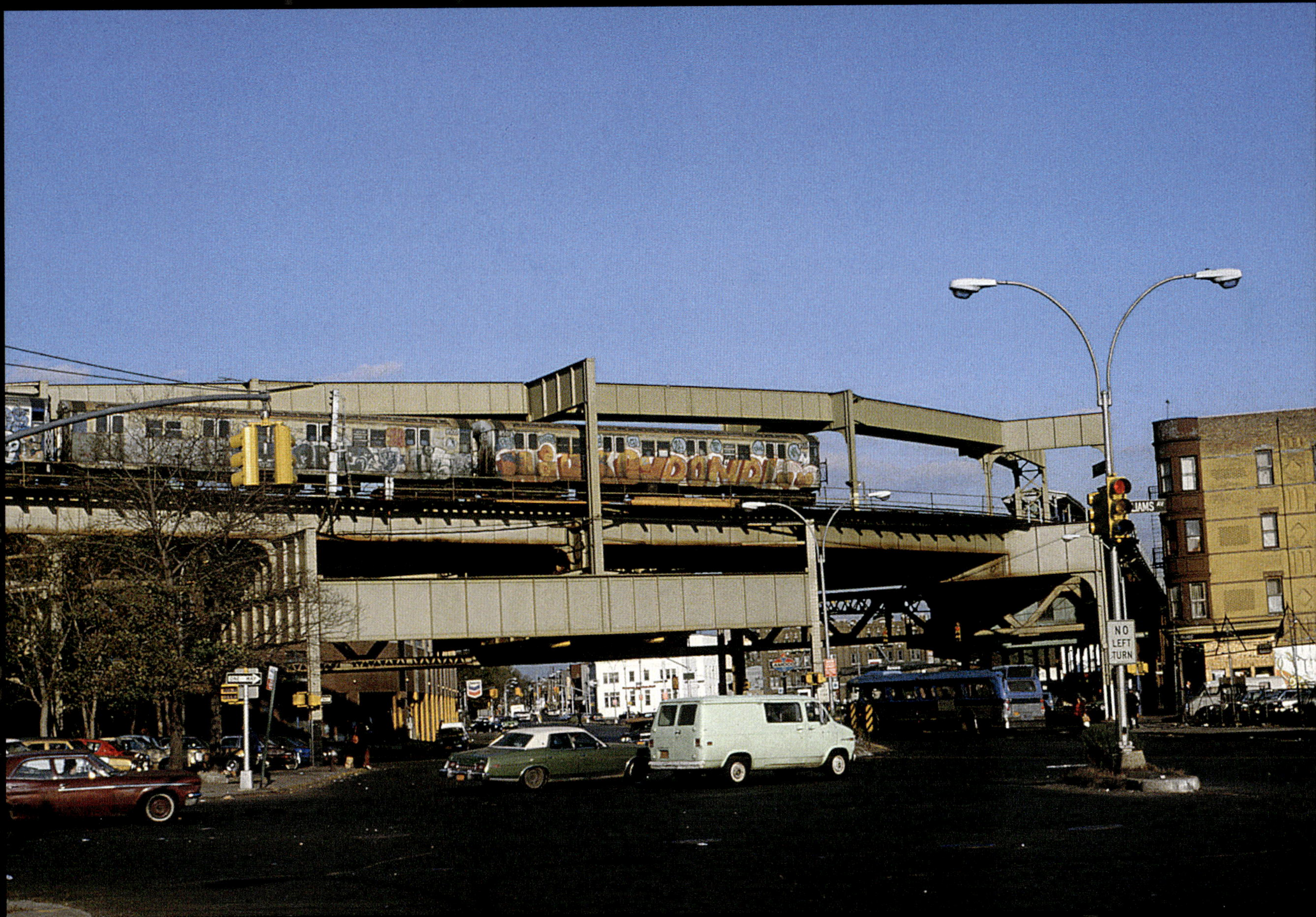

R-27/R-30s, Jamaica line, Alabama Ave., Brooklyn, 1979

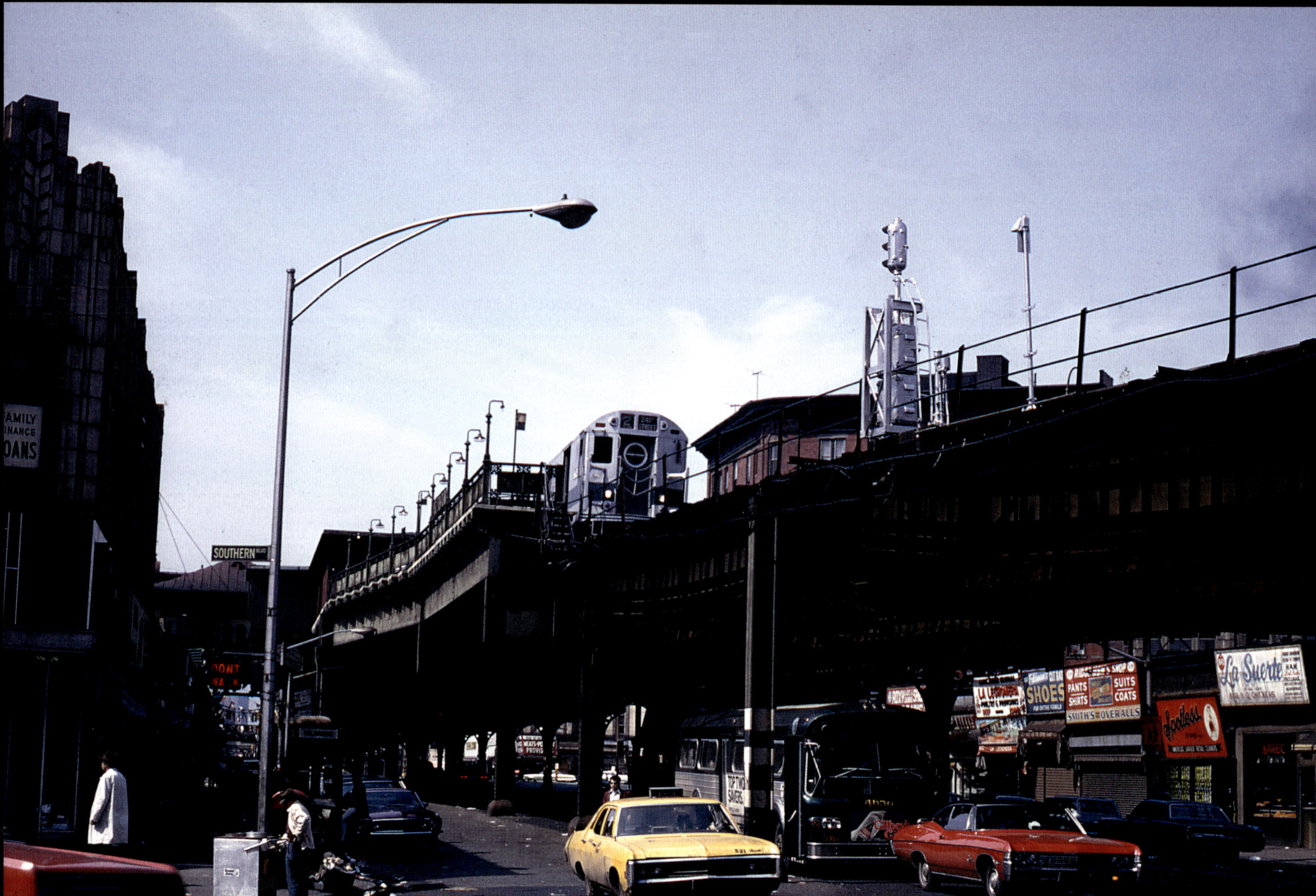

R-17, No. 2 line, Simpson St., Bronx, 1970

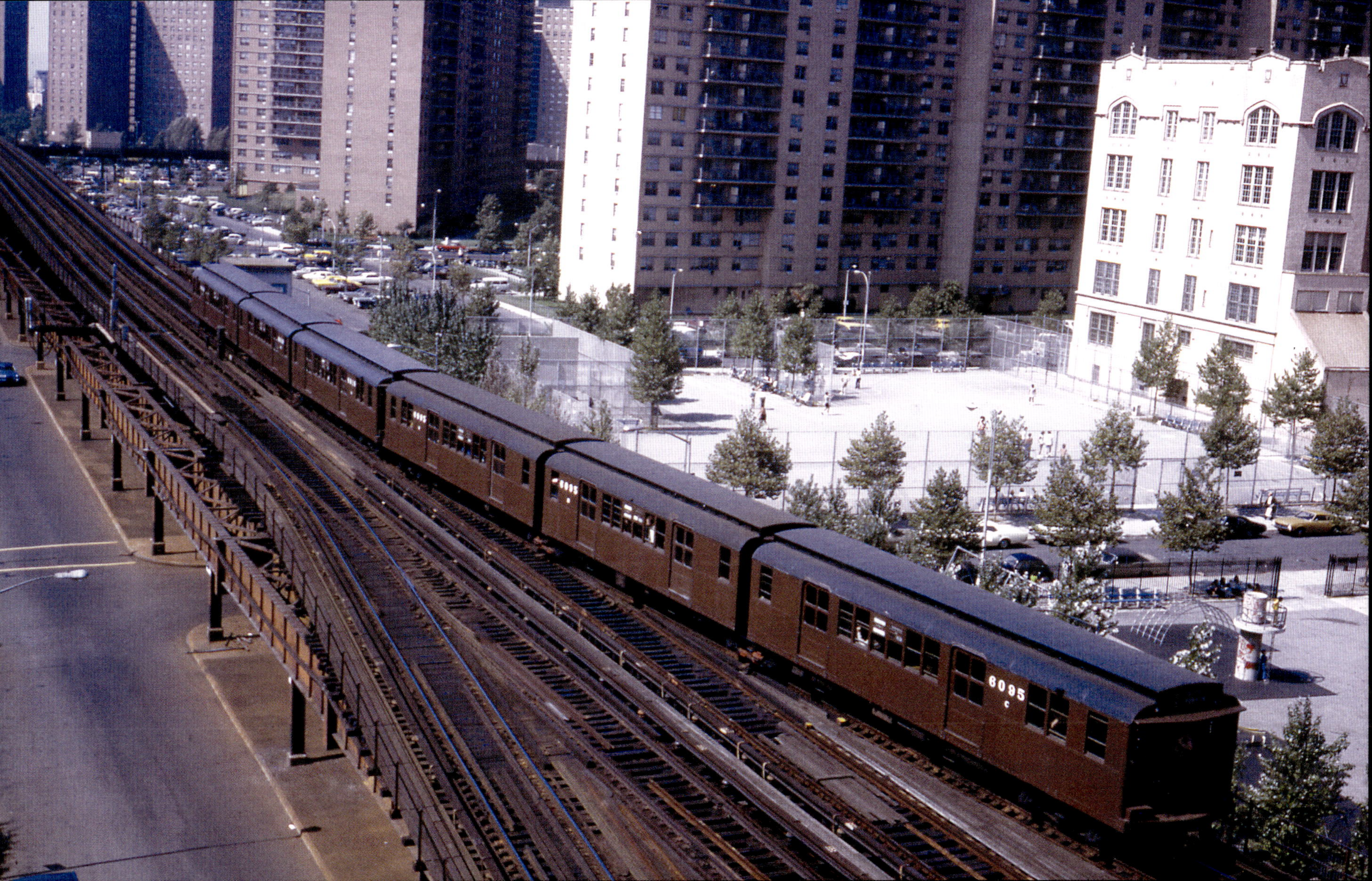

trip, Brighton line, Ocean Parkway, Brooklyn, 1970

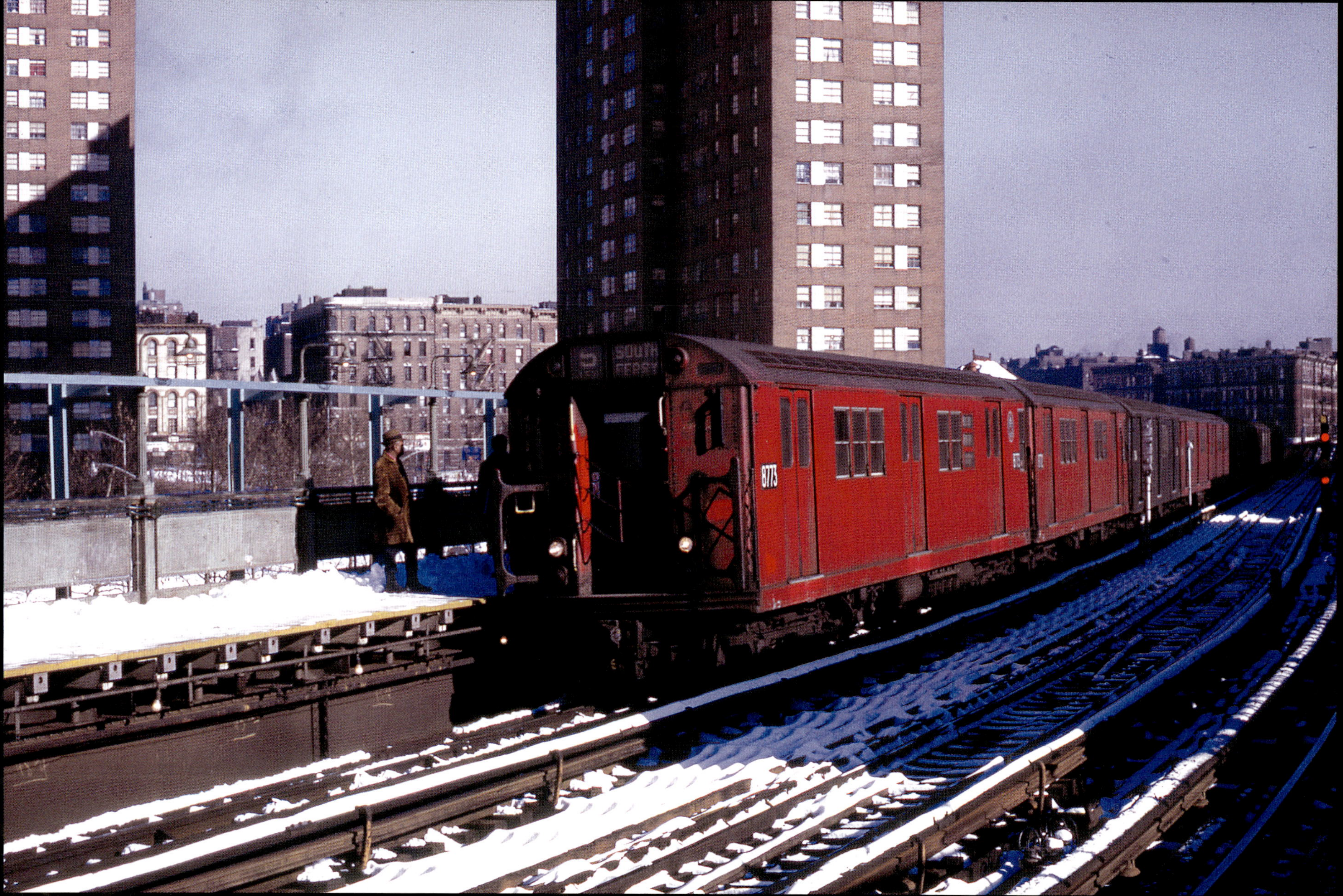

R-29, No. 5 line, Jackson Ave., Br

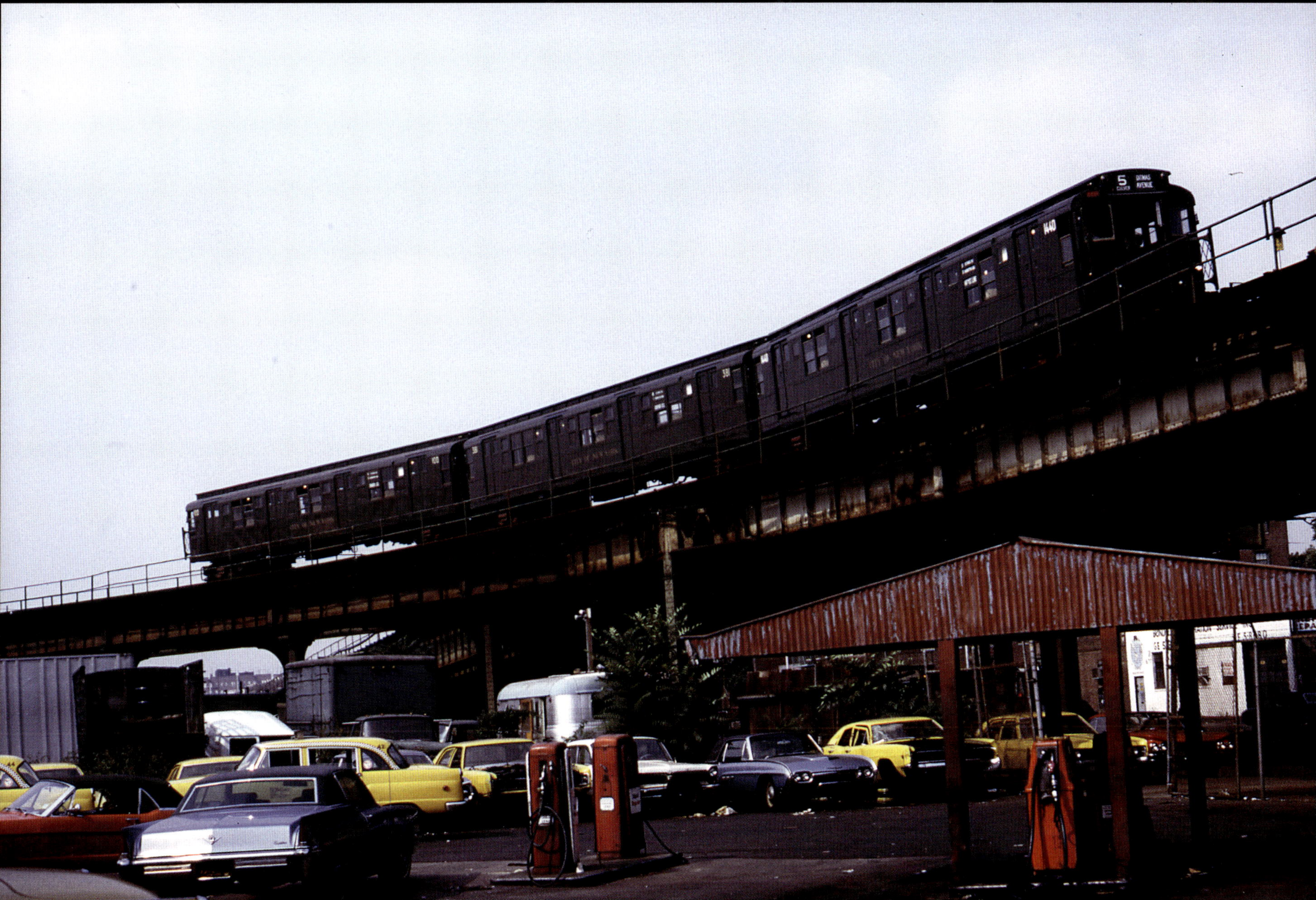

R-7, R-1s, Culver Shuttle, Ditmas Ave., Brooklyn, 1971

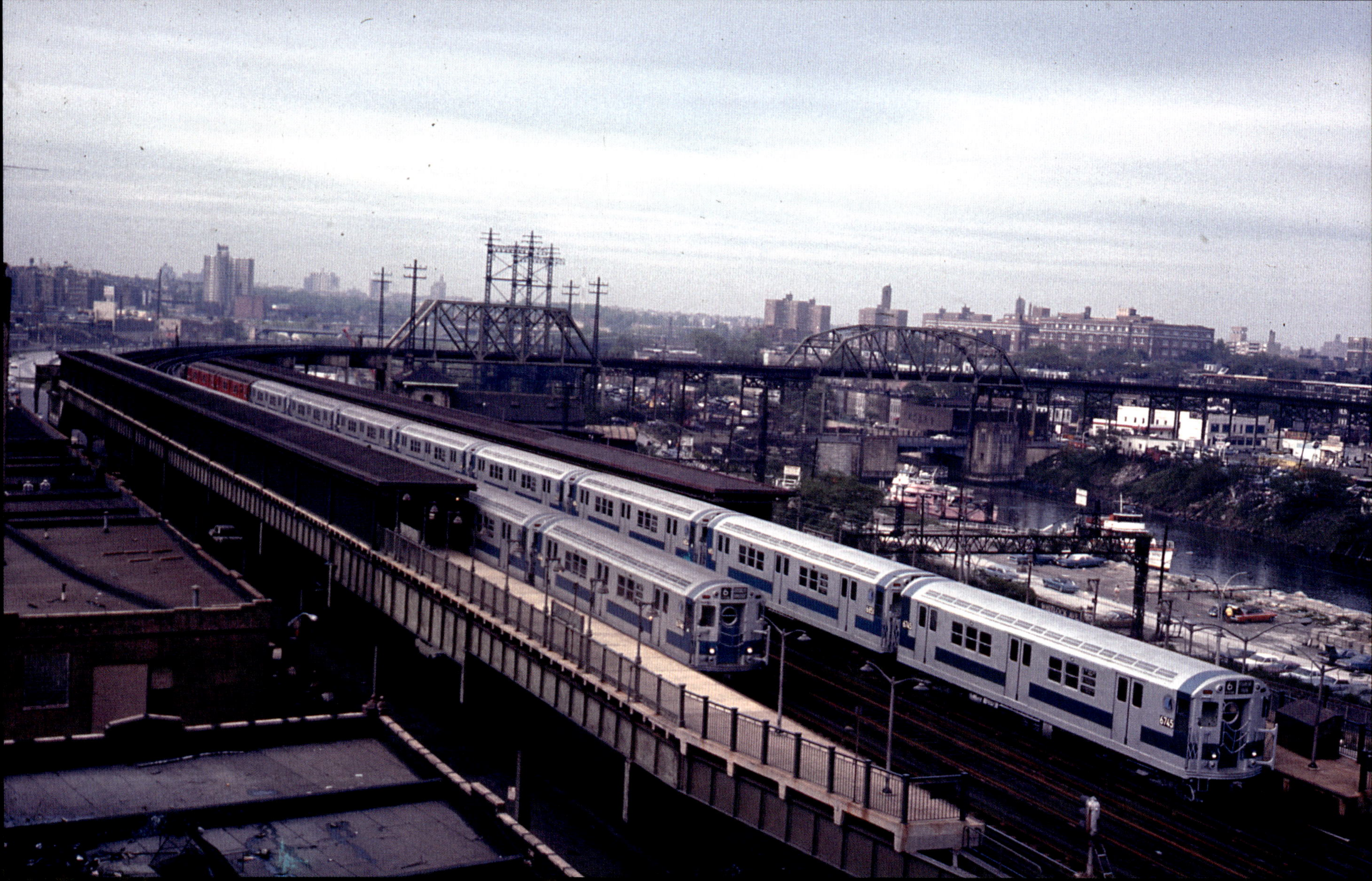

R-17s, No. 6 line, Whitlock Ave.,

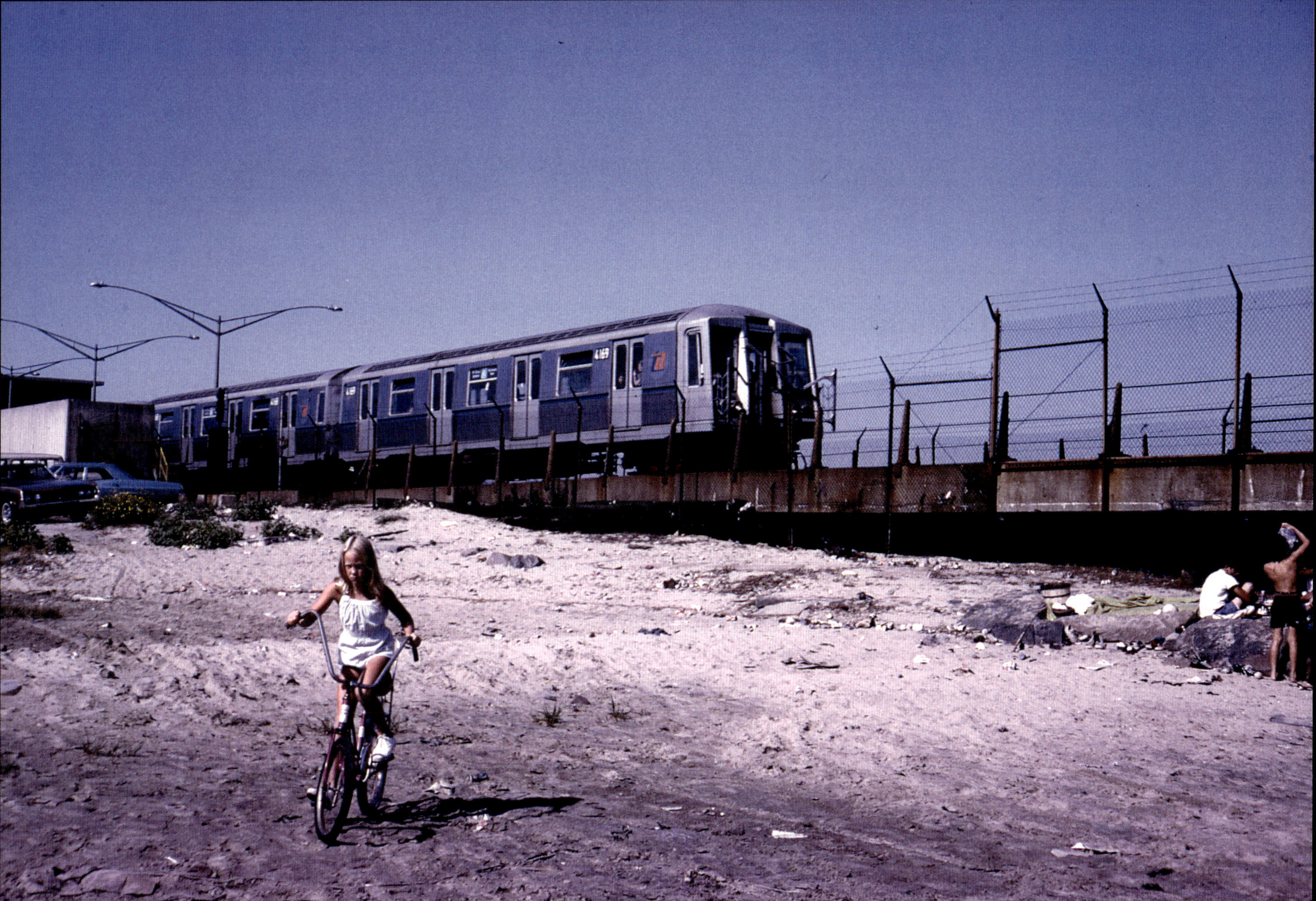

H, Rockaway line, Broad Channel, Queens, 1972

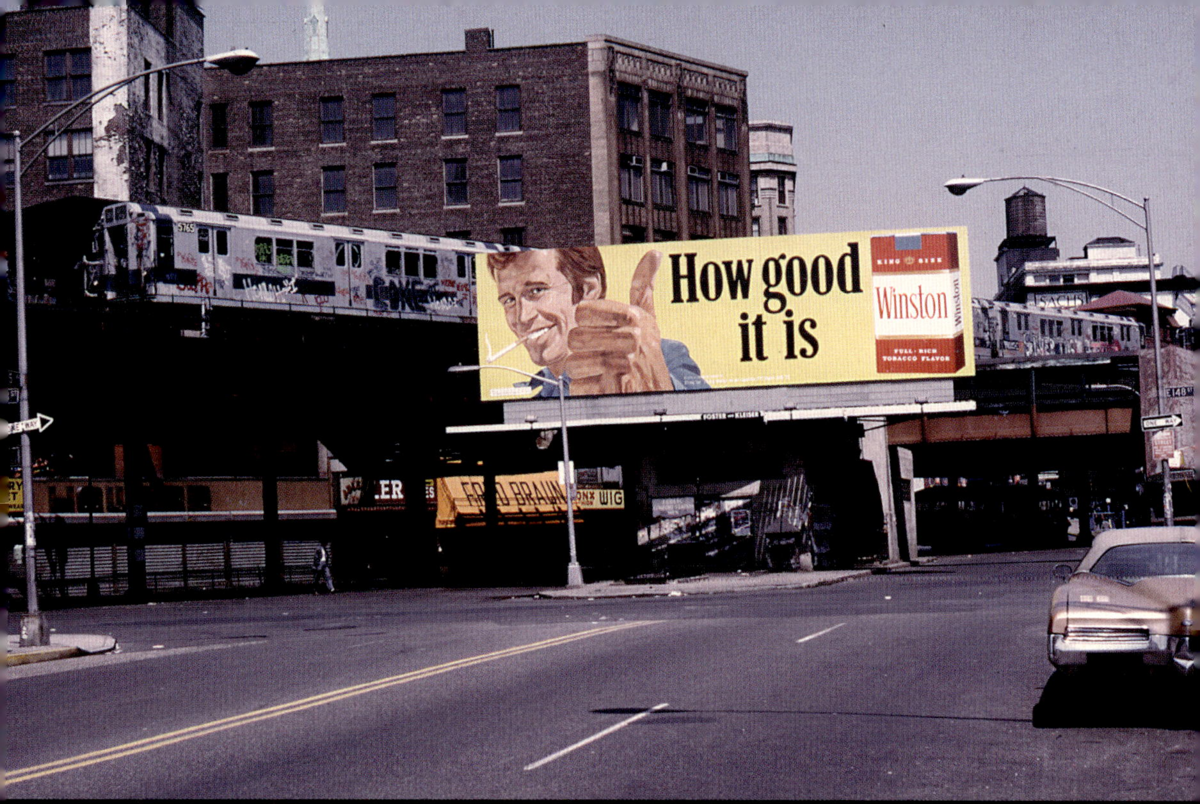
How good
it is
Winston
FULL-RICH TOBACCO FLAVOR

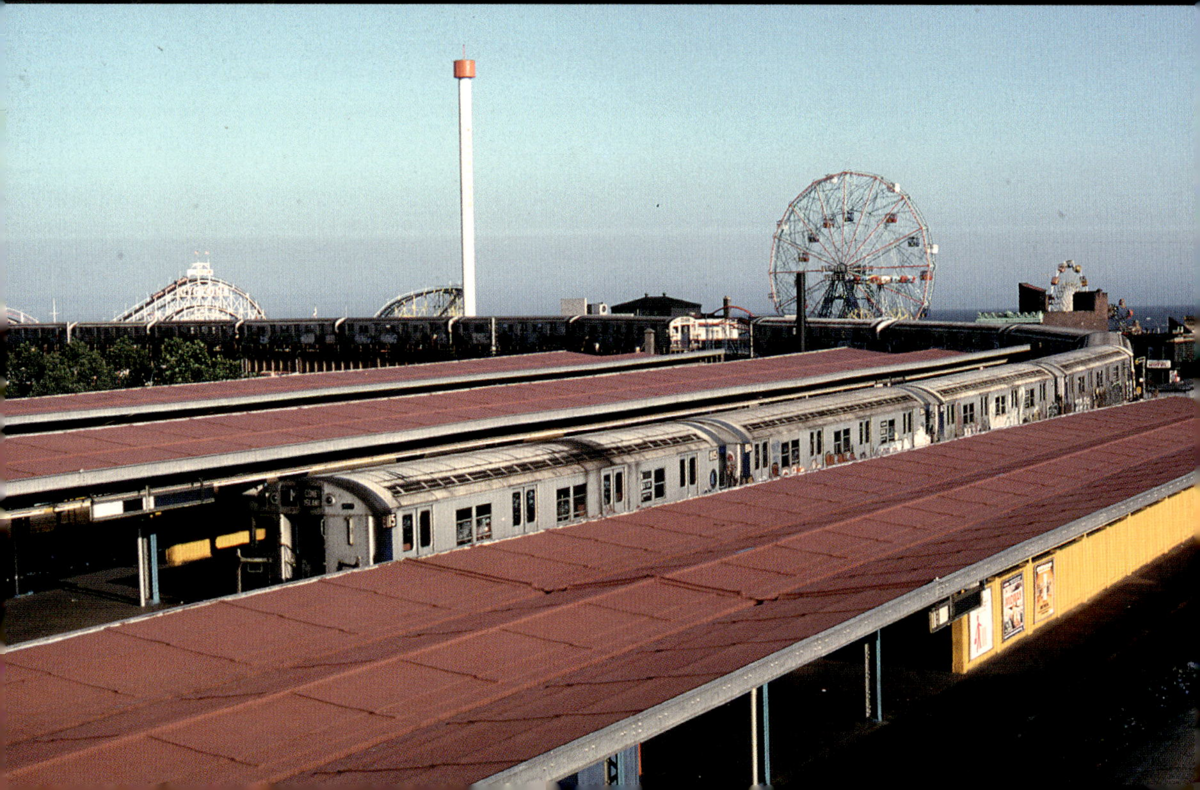

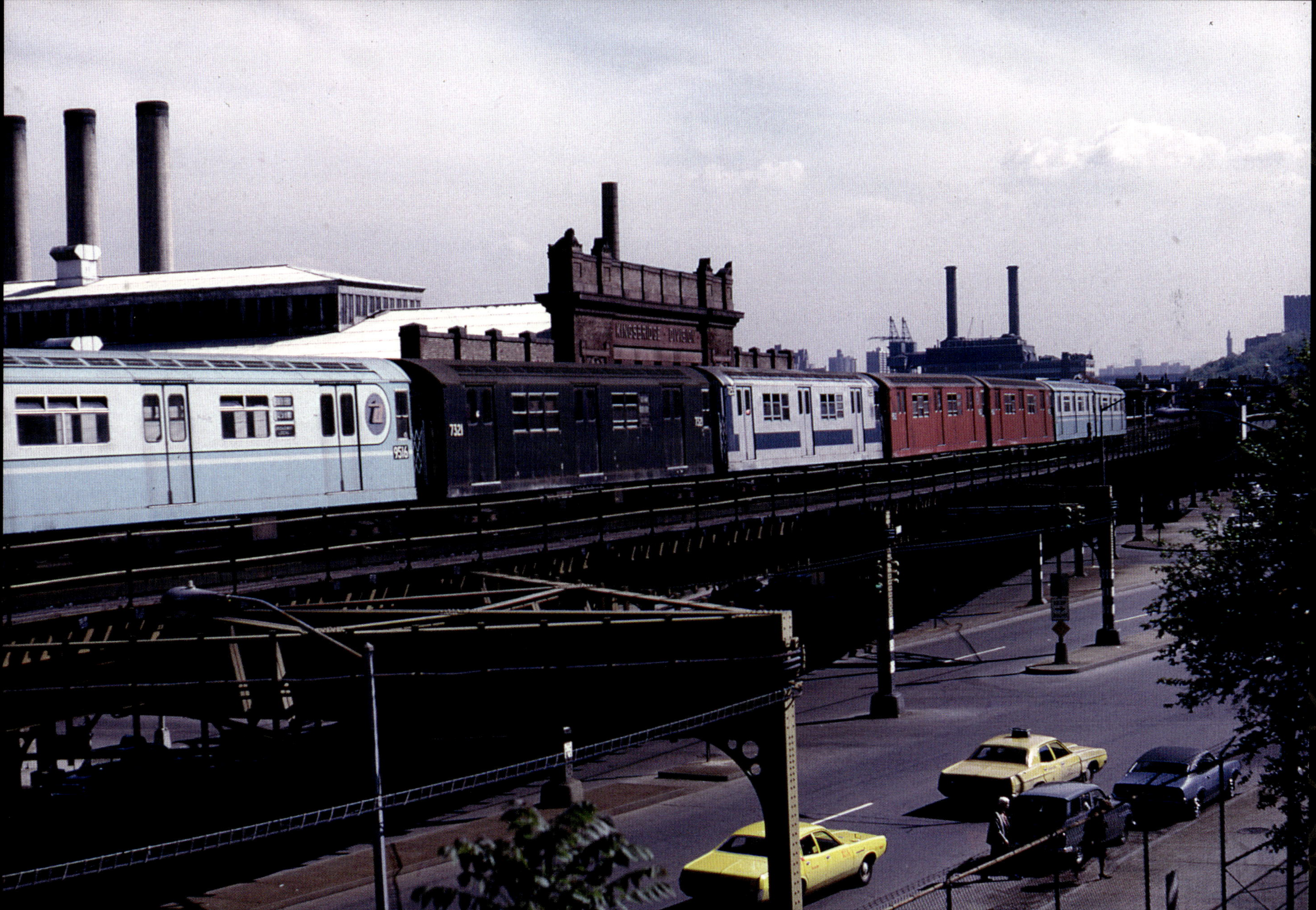

Broadway line, near 215th St., Manhattan, 1972

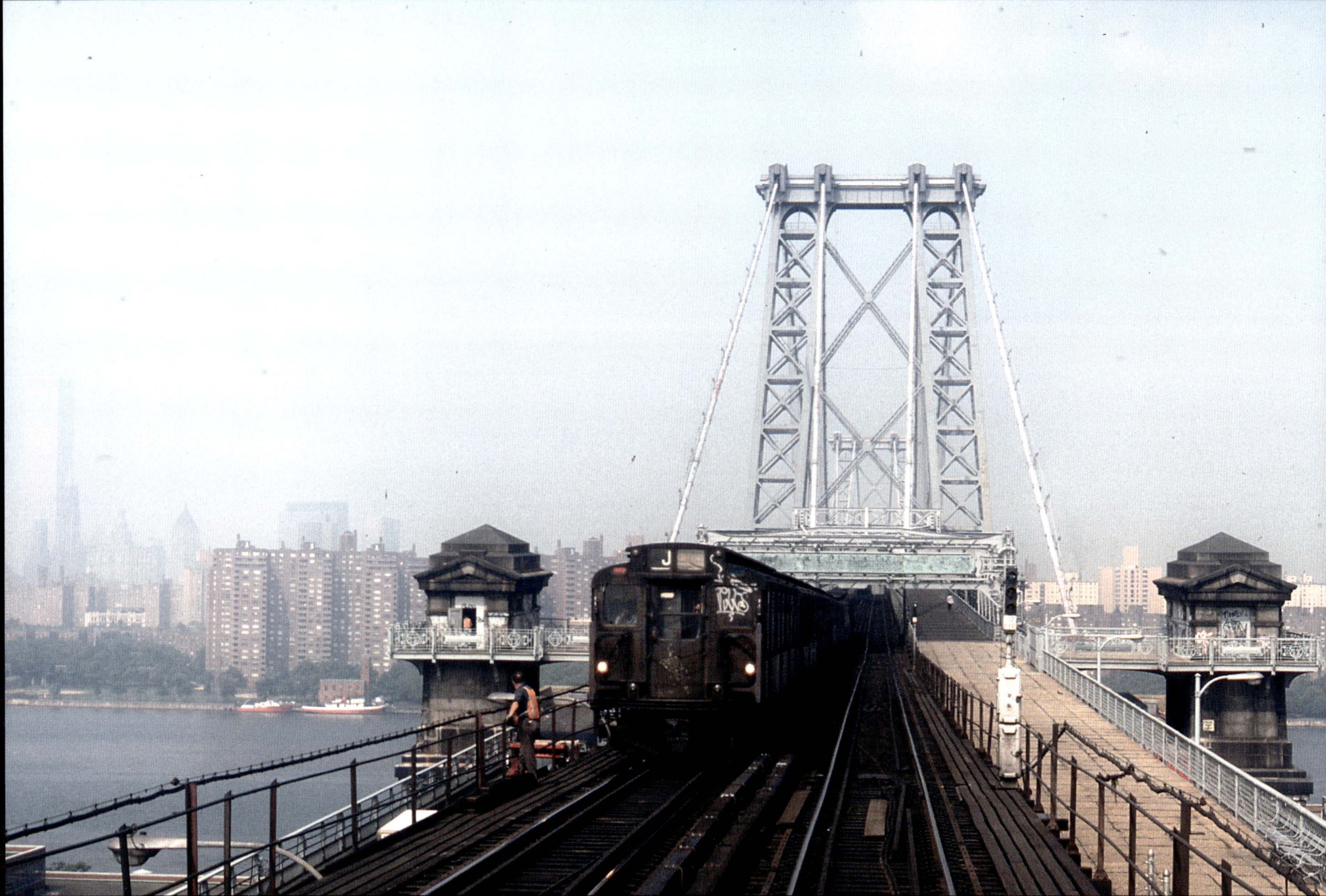

R-7, J line, Williamsburg Bridge, Brooklyn s

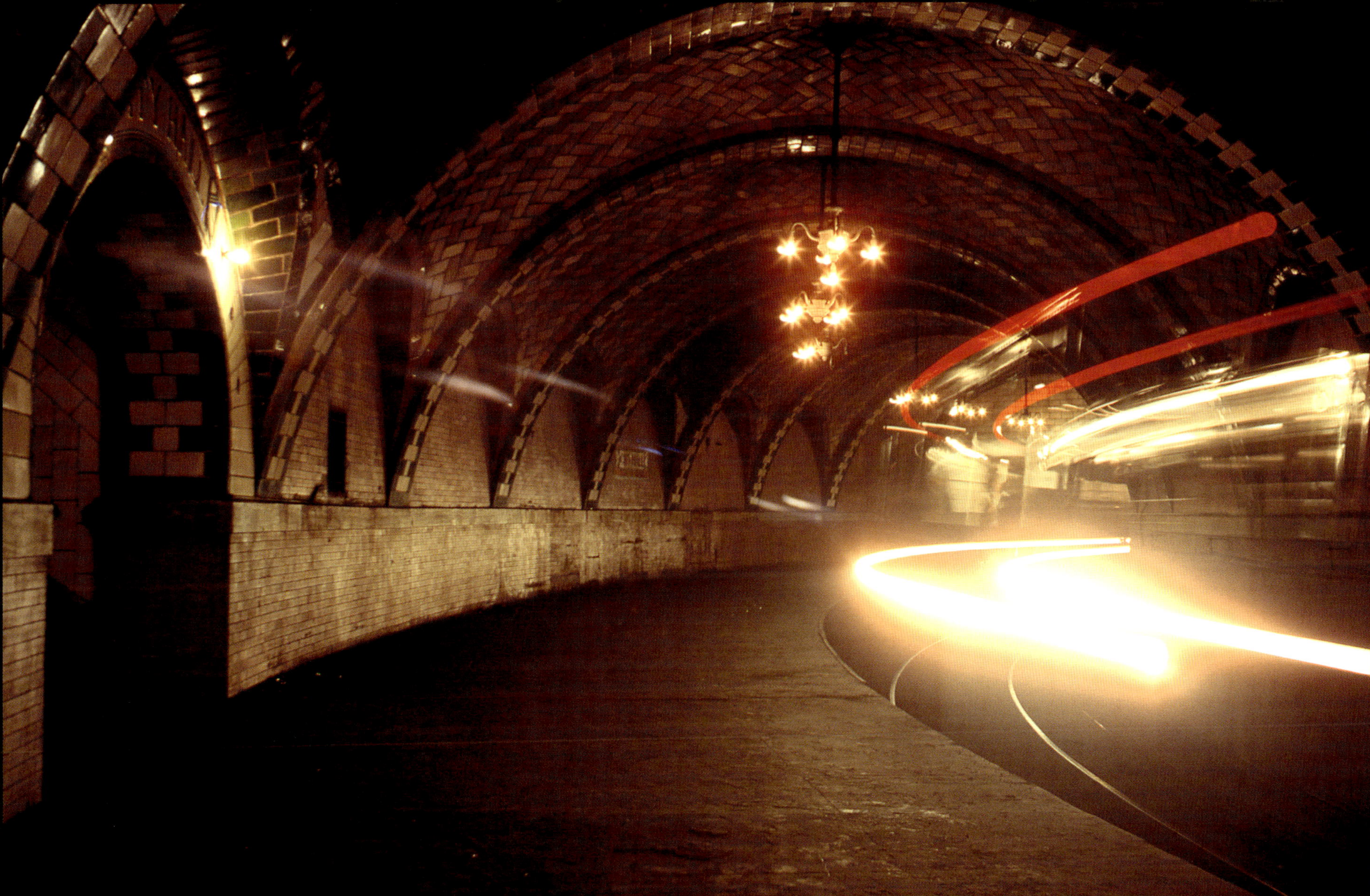

IRT City Hall Station, Manhattan, 1979

The Eighties

New York Subways & Stations 1970–1990

CHAPTER 2

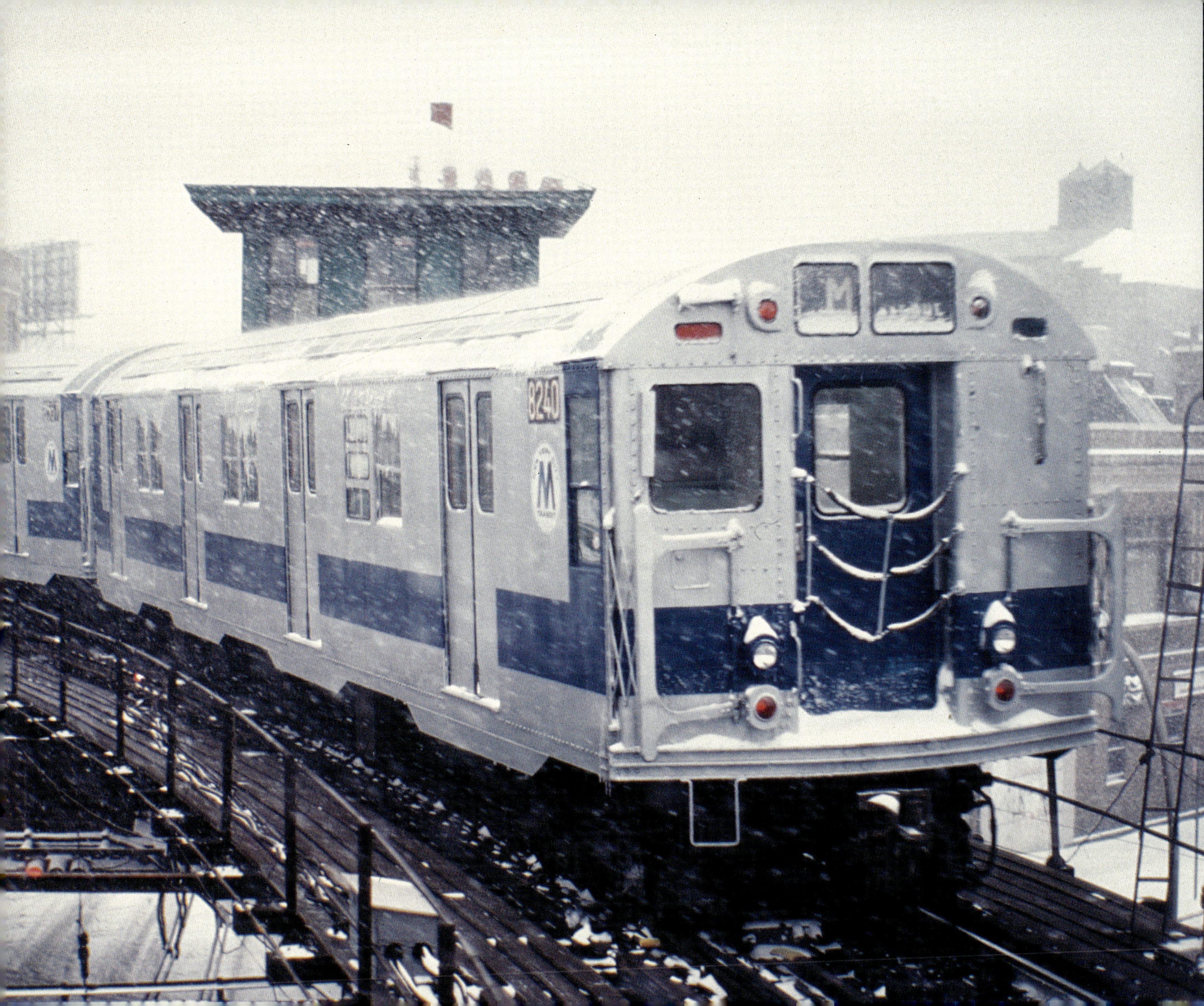

R-27s, Myrtle Ave. line, Wyckoff Ave., Brooklyn, 1980

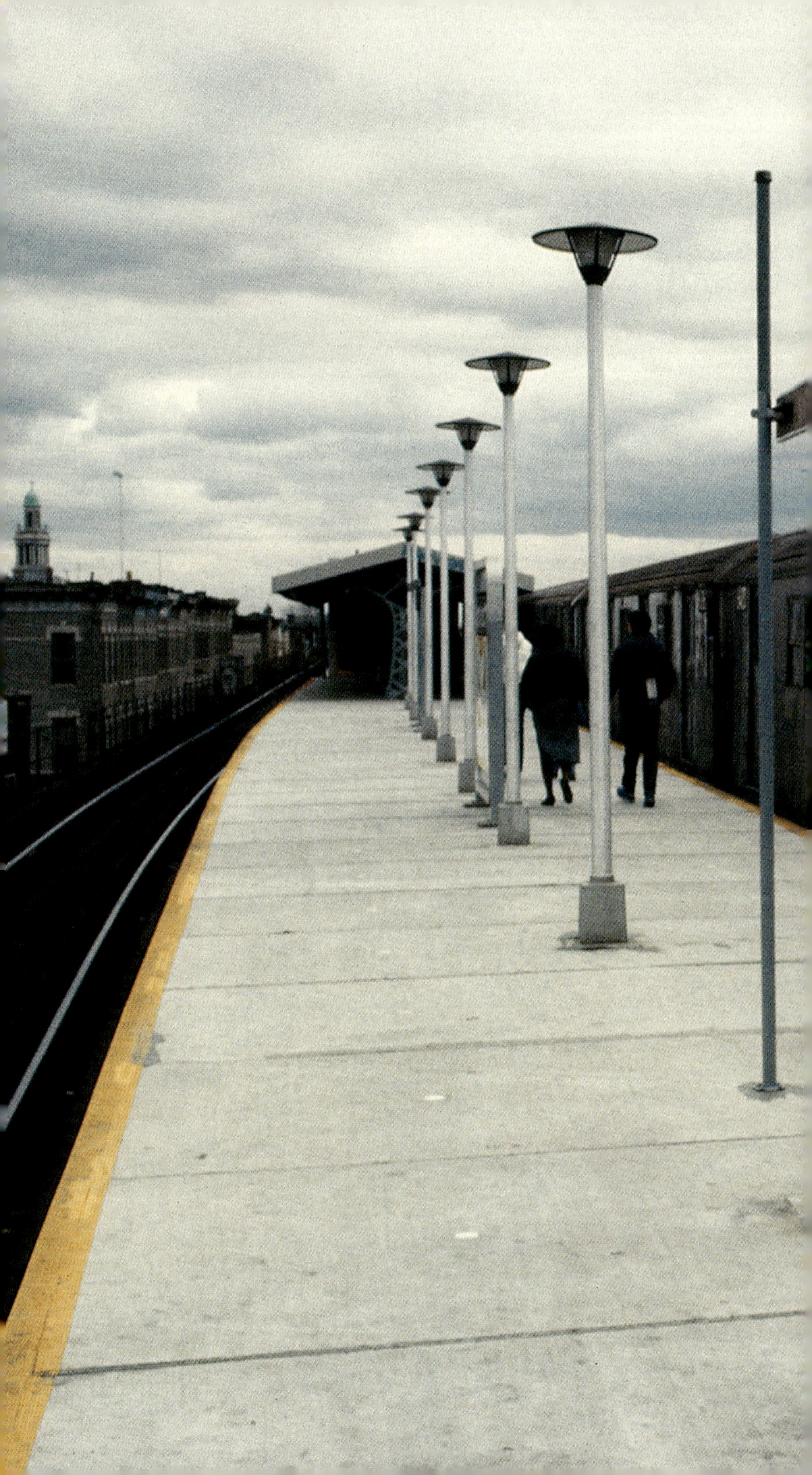

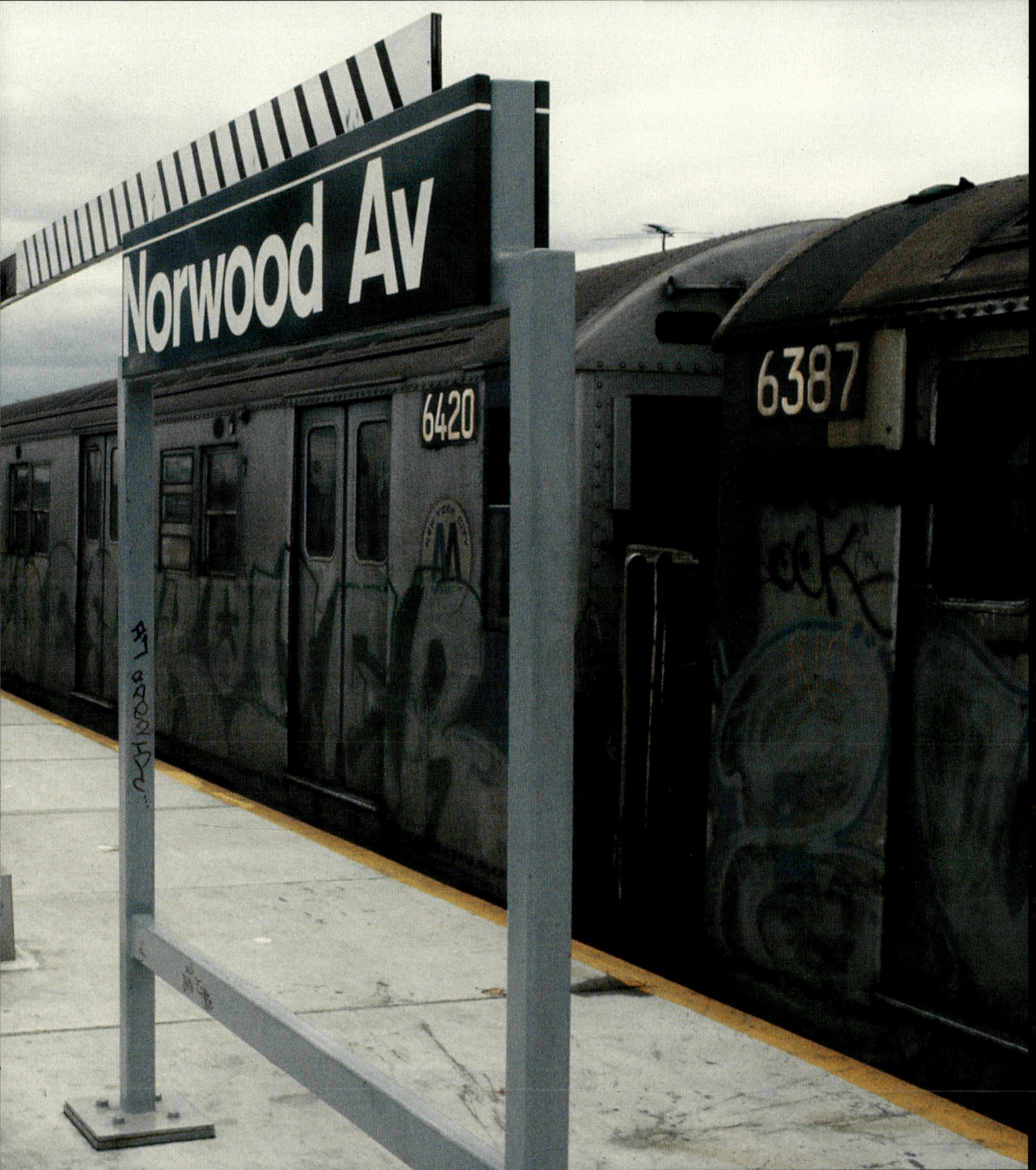

Norwood Av
6420
6387

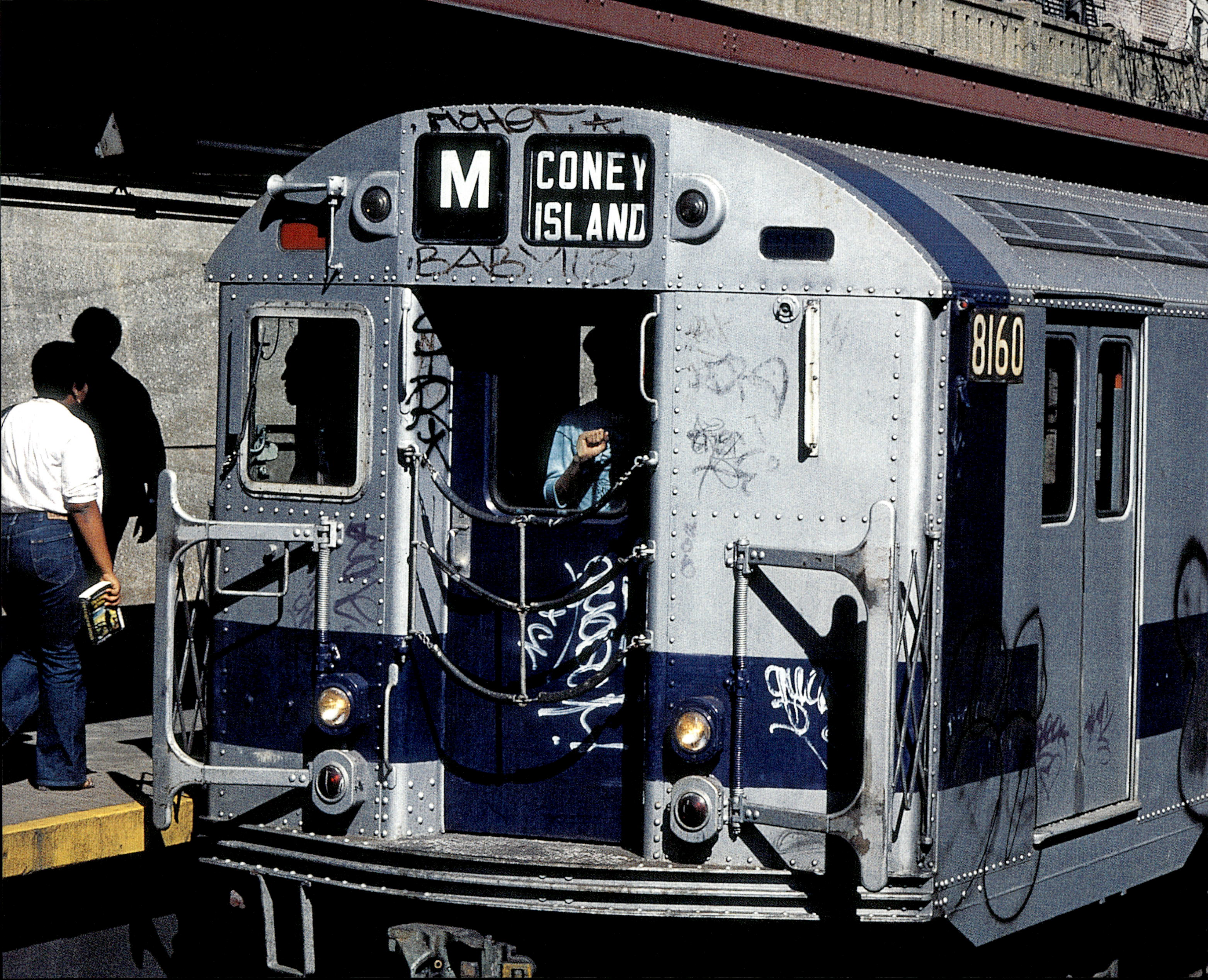
M
CONEY ISLAND
8160

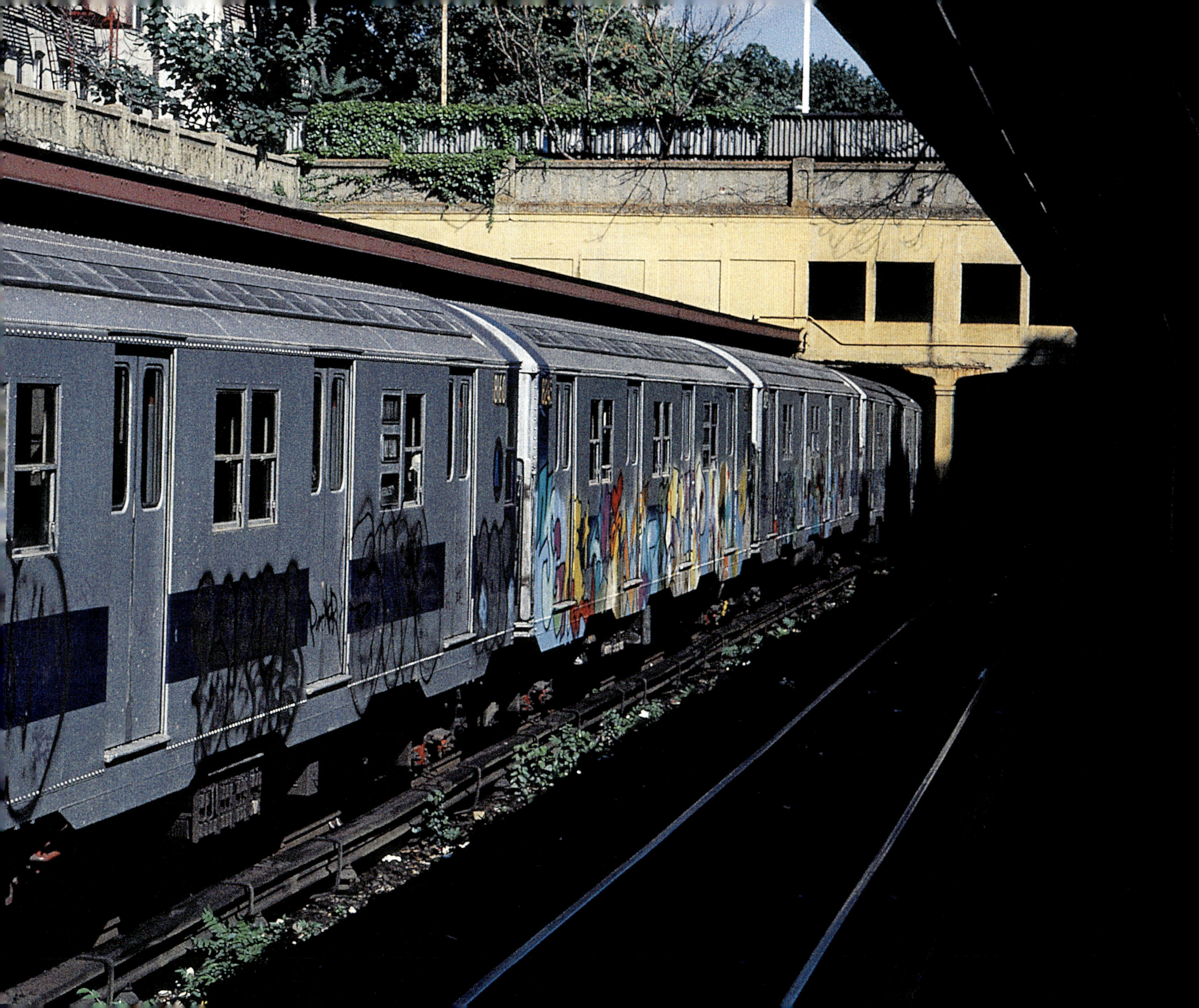

R-27s, Brighton line, Prospect Park, 1981

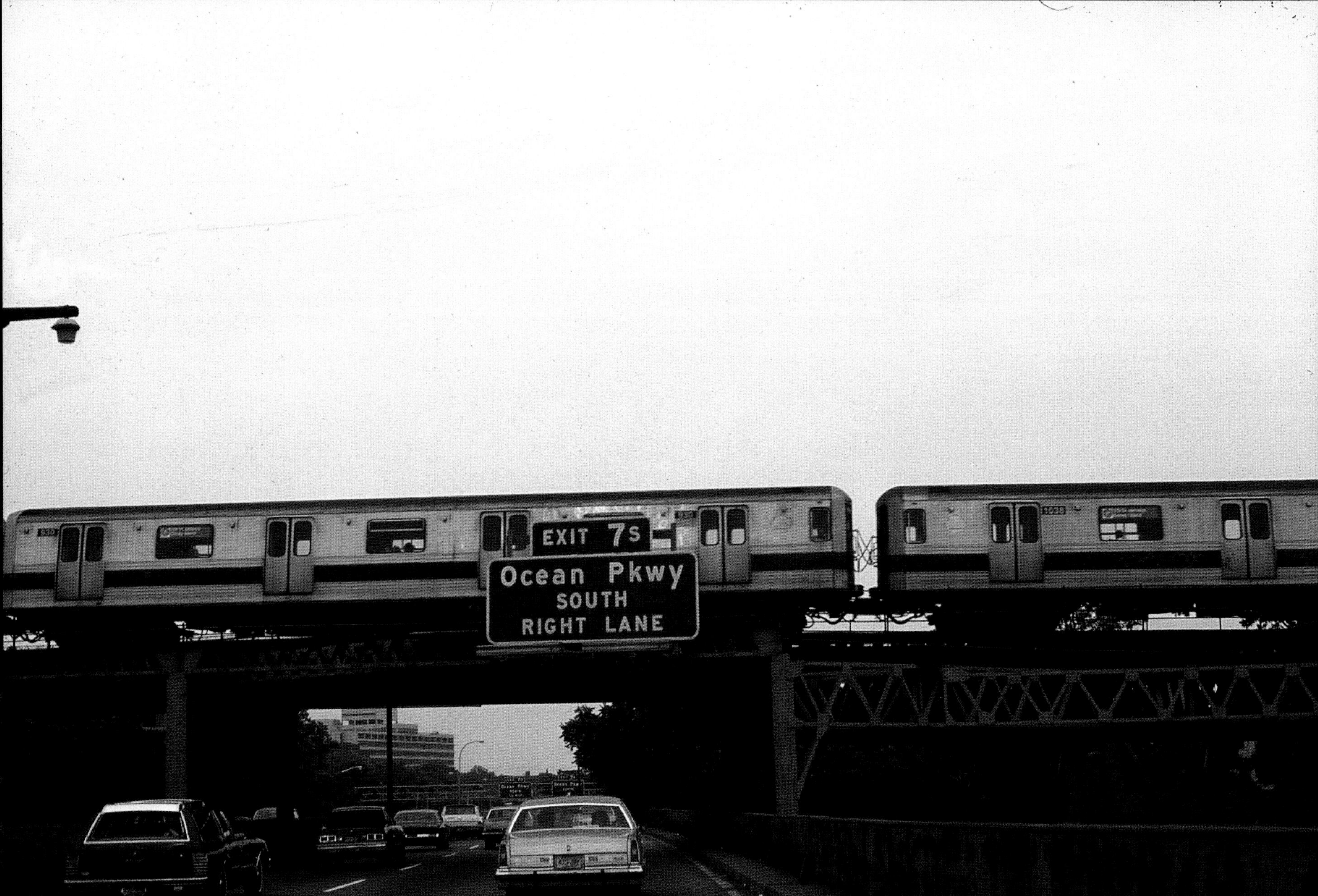

R-46s, F line, near Neptune Ave., Brookl

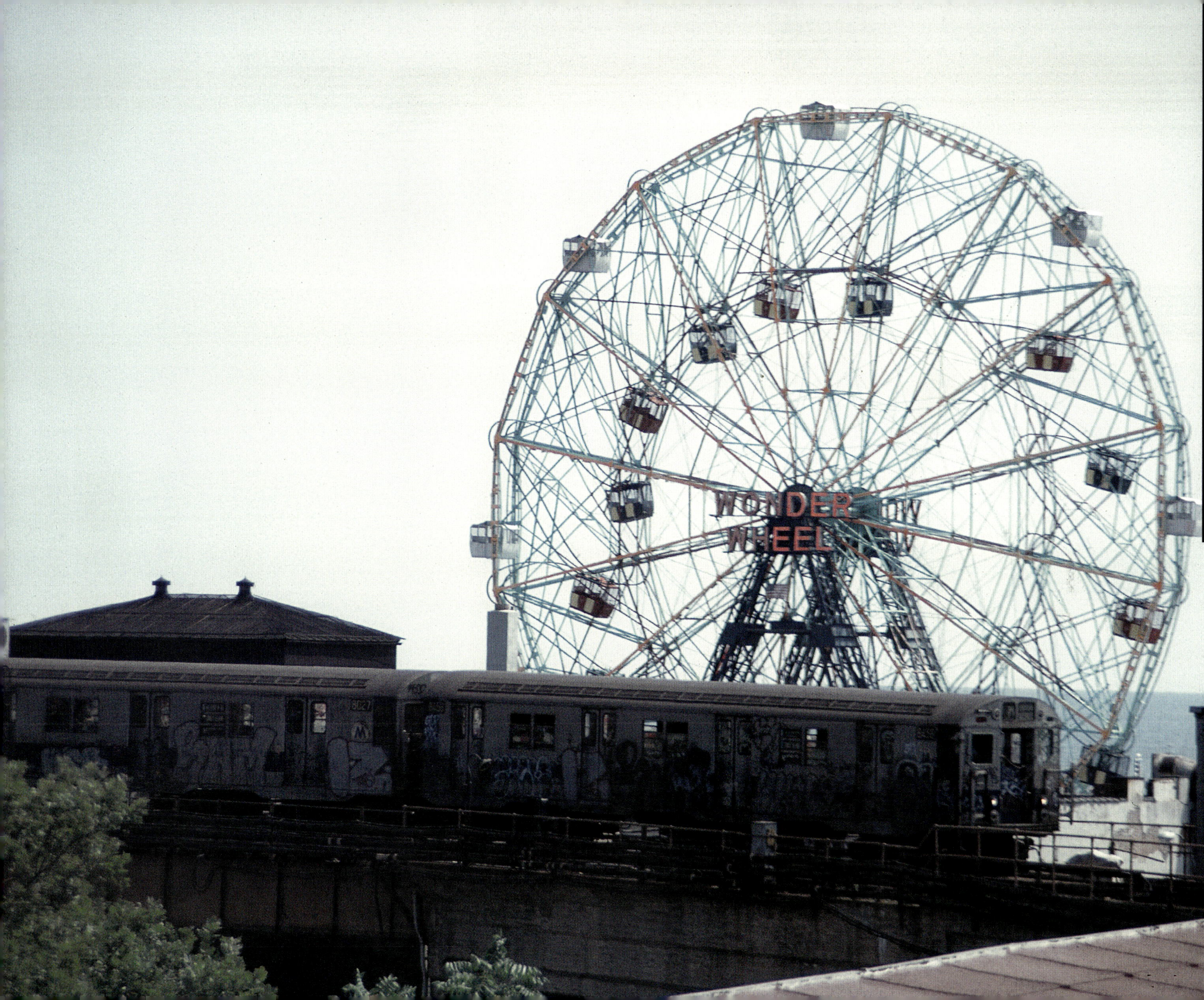

R-30/R-27s, M, Brighton line, Wonder Wheel at Coney Island, Brooklyn, 1981

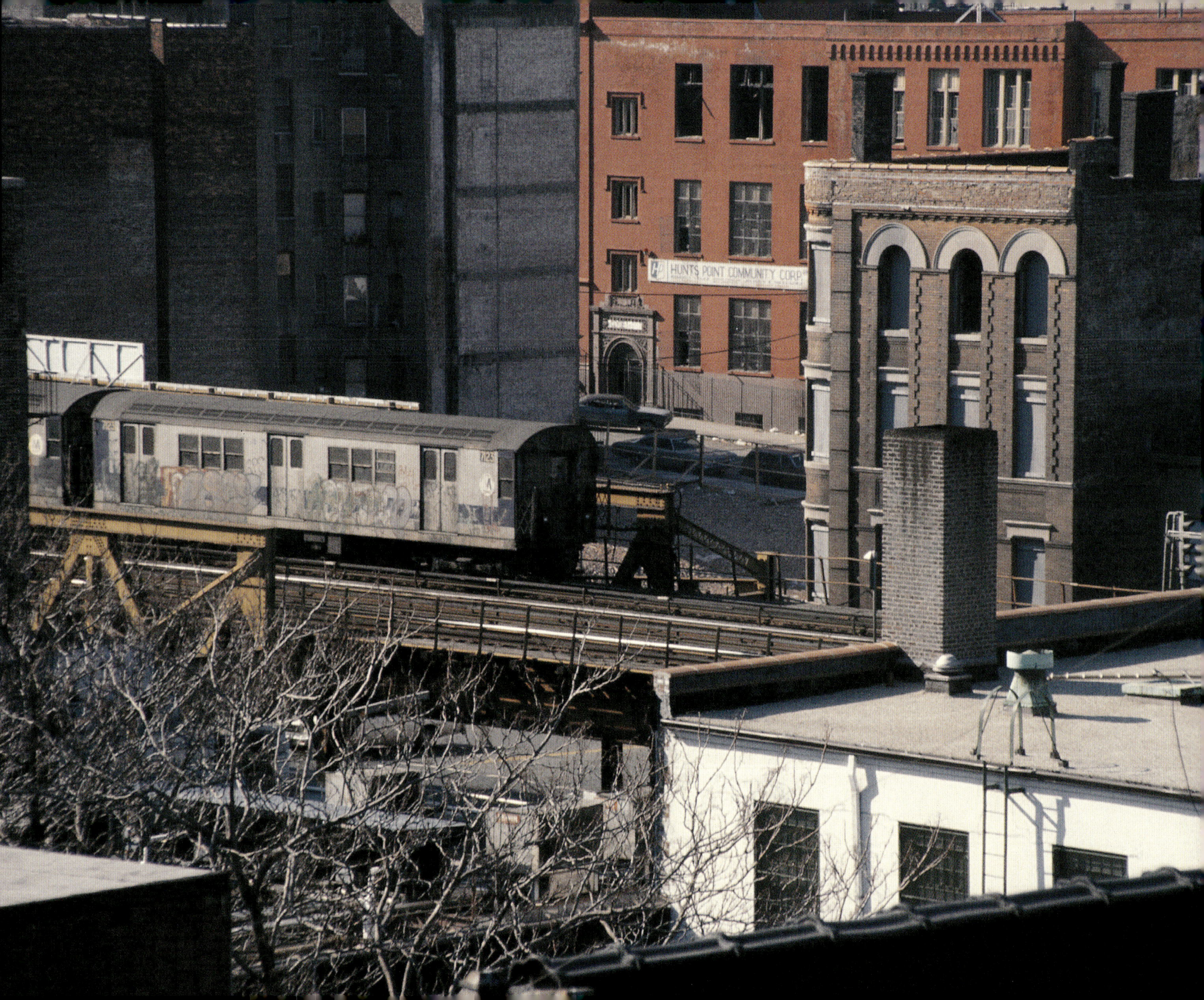

R-21, No. 5 line, South Bronx, 1981

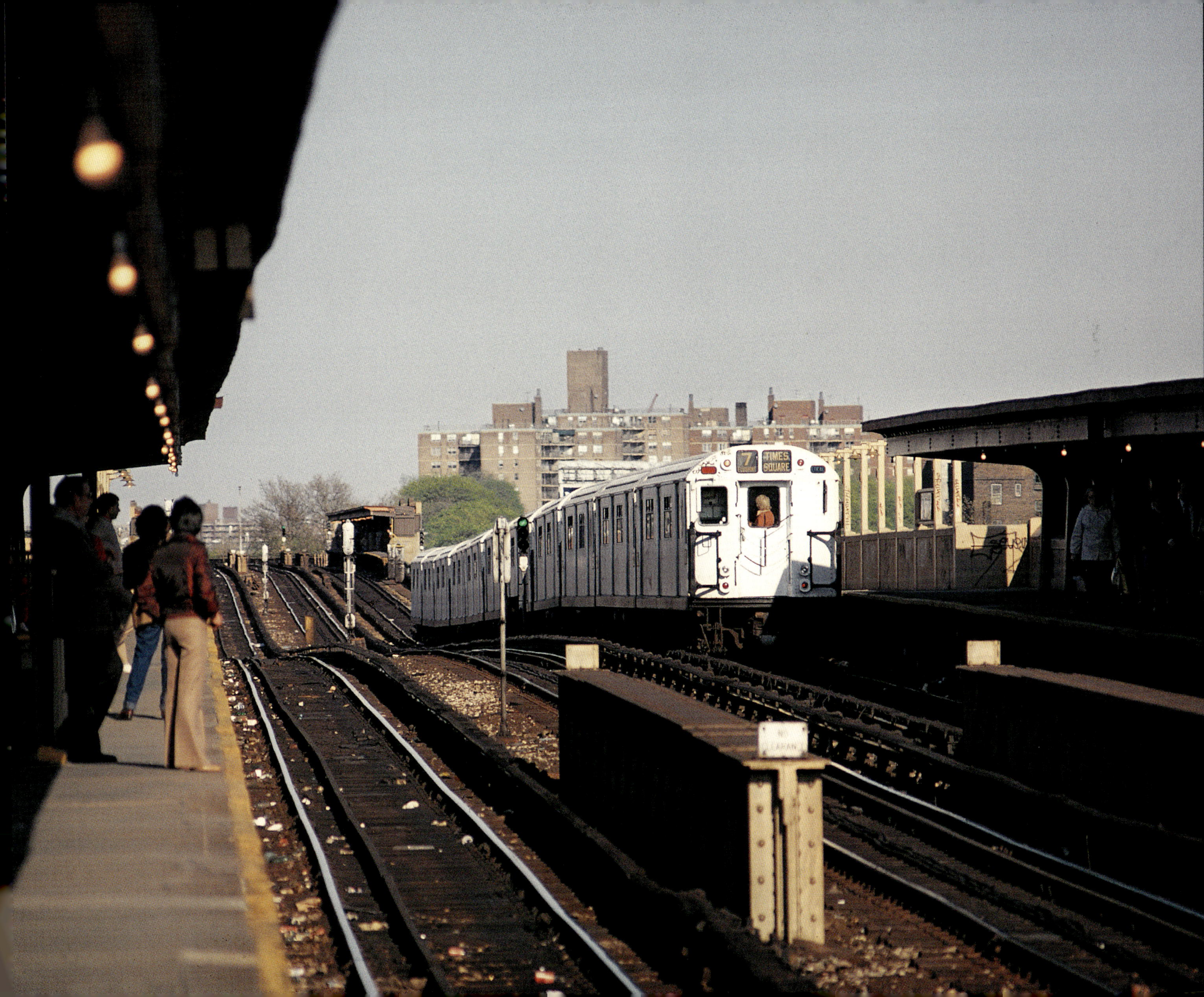

R-33/R-36s, No. 7 Flushing line, 40th St.–Lowery St., Queens, 1982

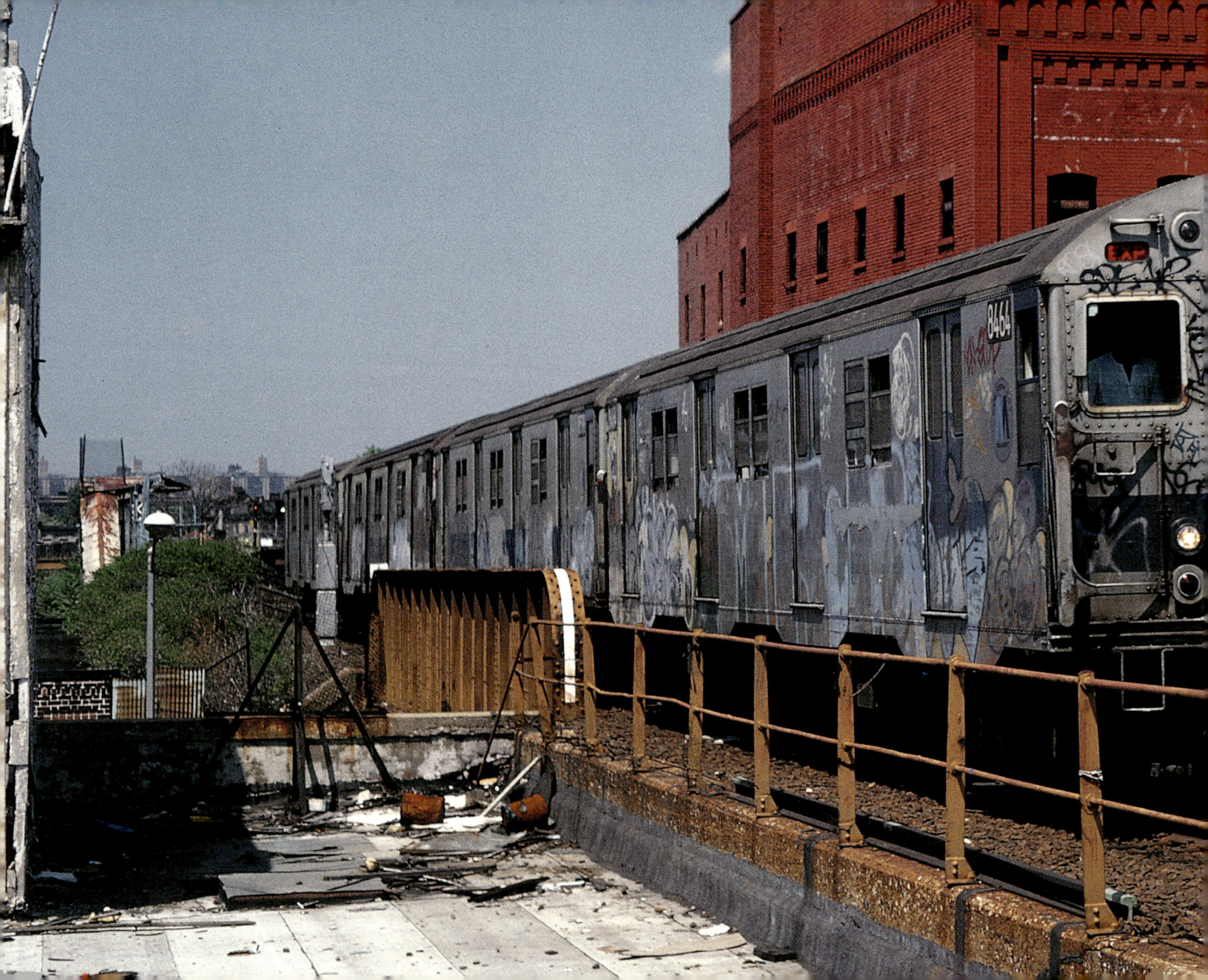
EXP
8464

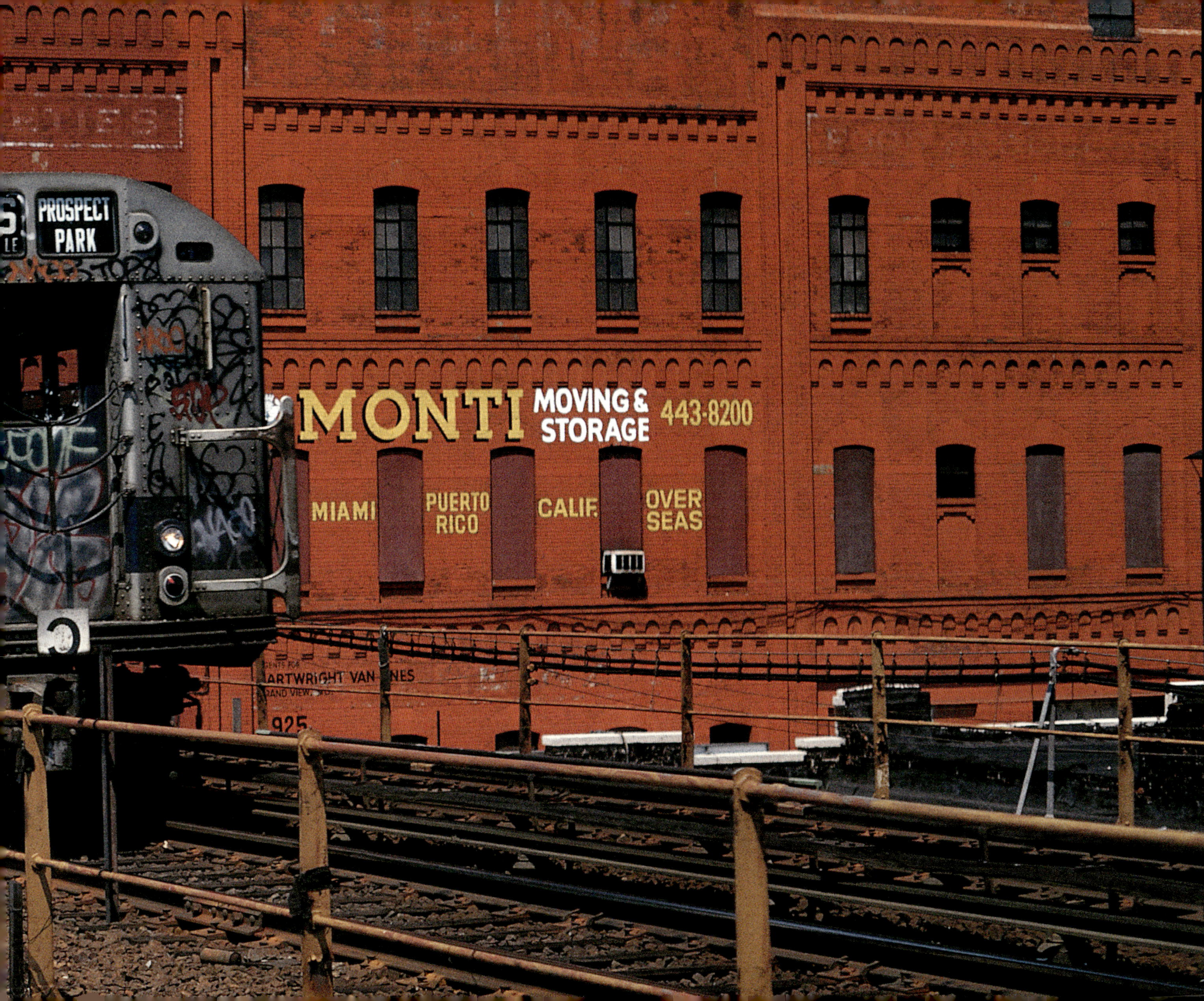

R-30s, Franklin Ave. Shuttle, between Dean St. & Park Place, Brooklyn, 1982

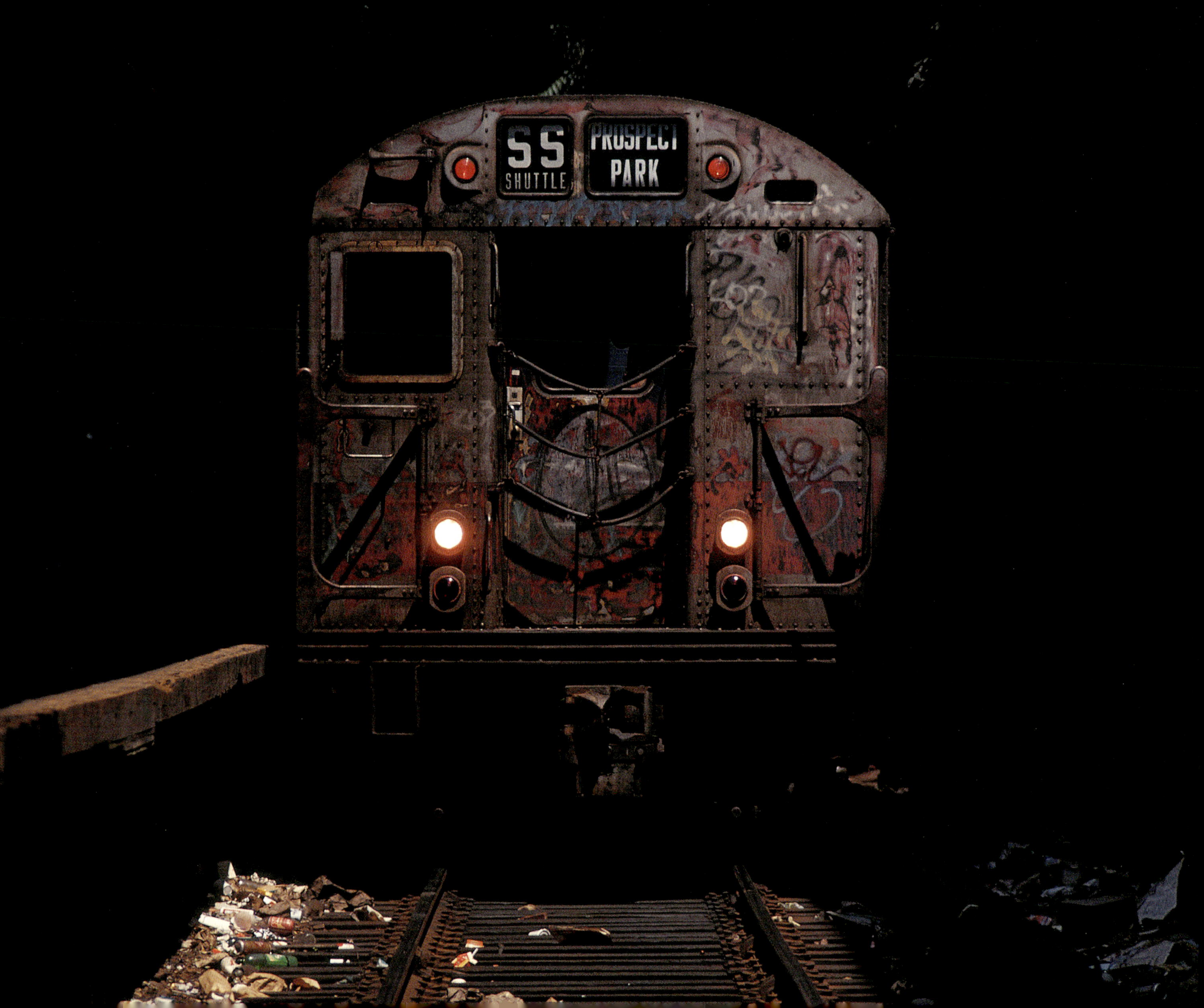

R-27s, Franklin Ave. Shuttle, Prospect Park, Brooklyn, 1982

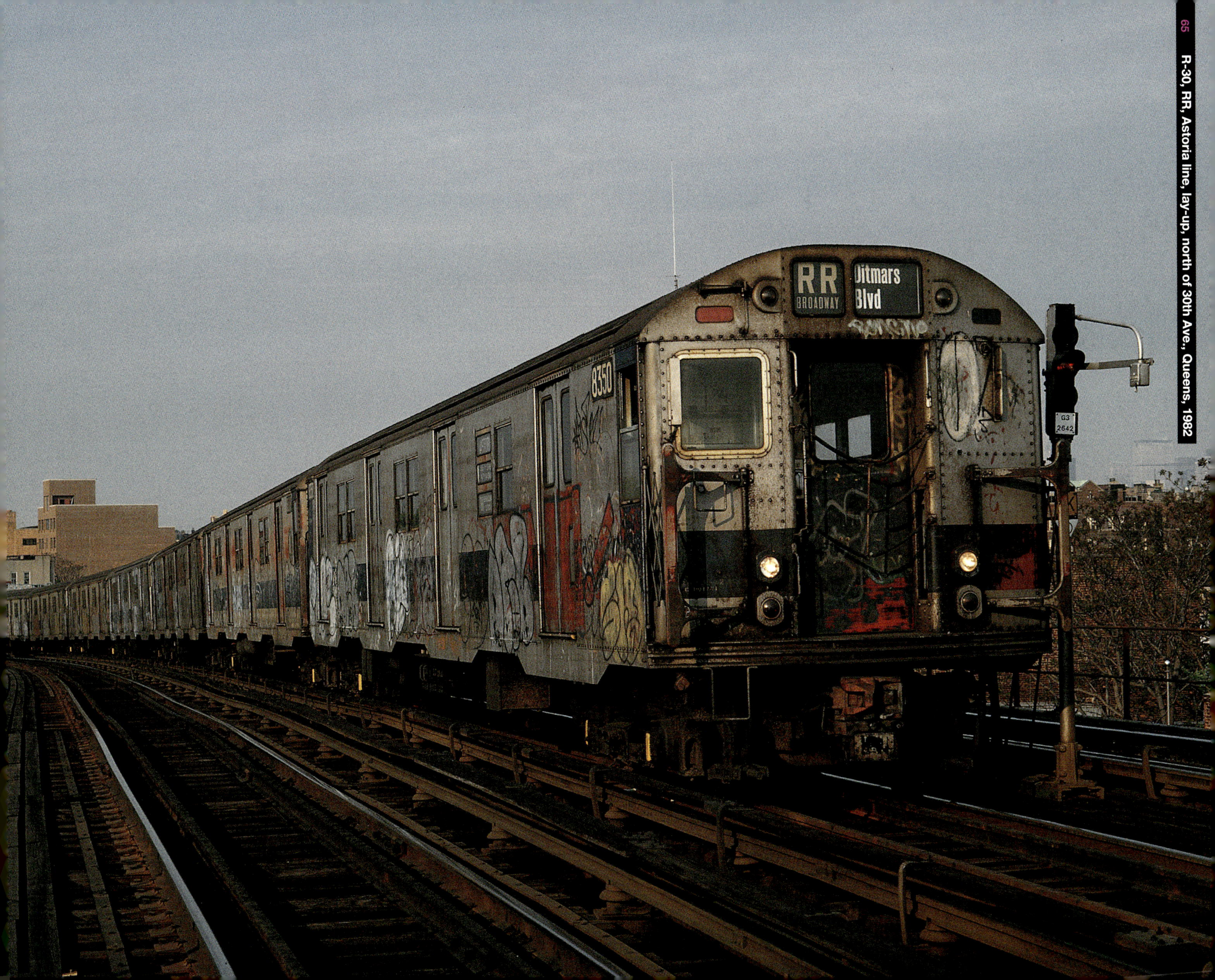

R-30, RR, Astoria line, lay-up, north of 30th Ave., Queens, 1982

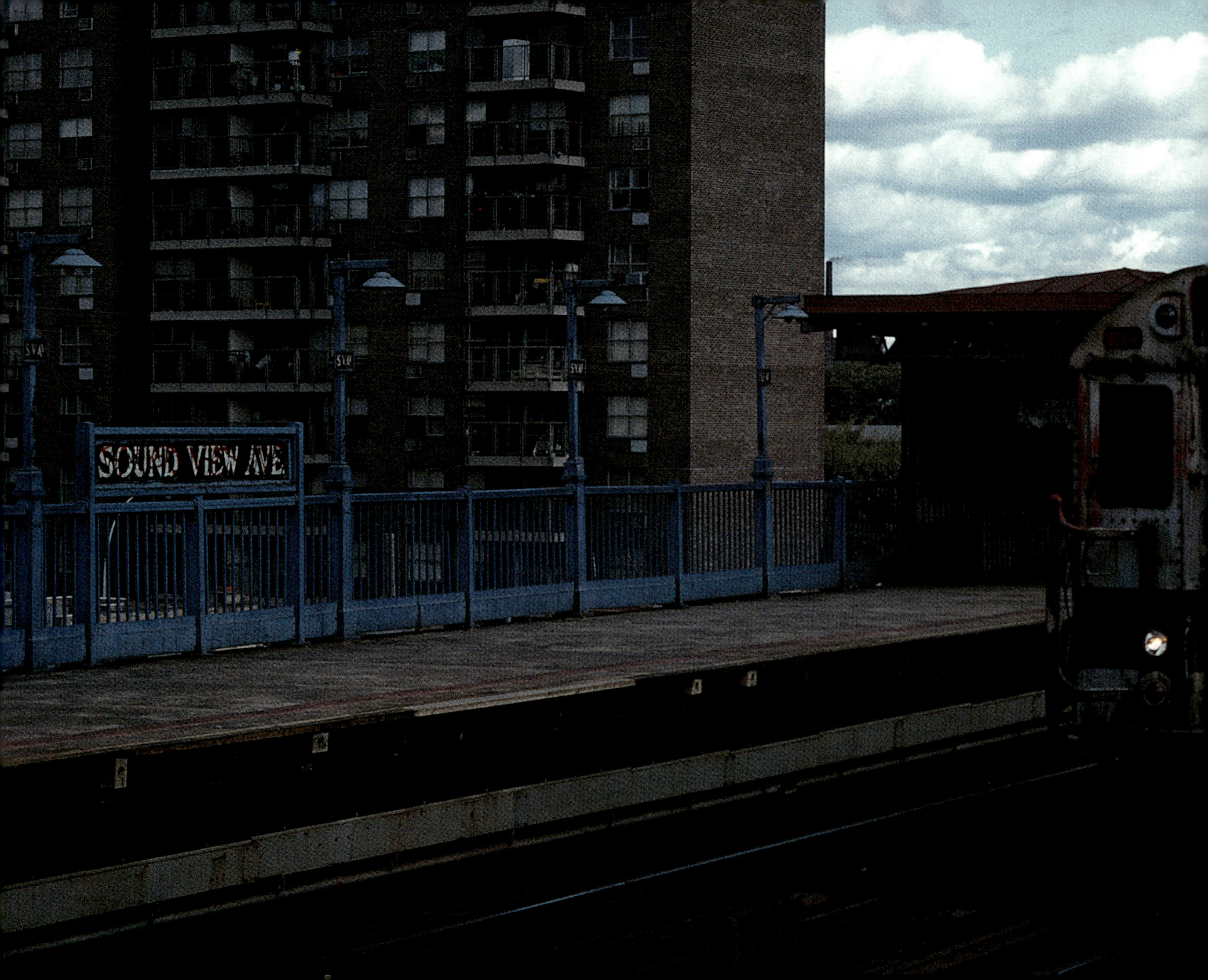
SOUND VIEW AVE.

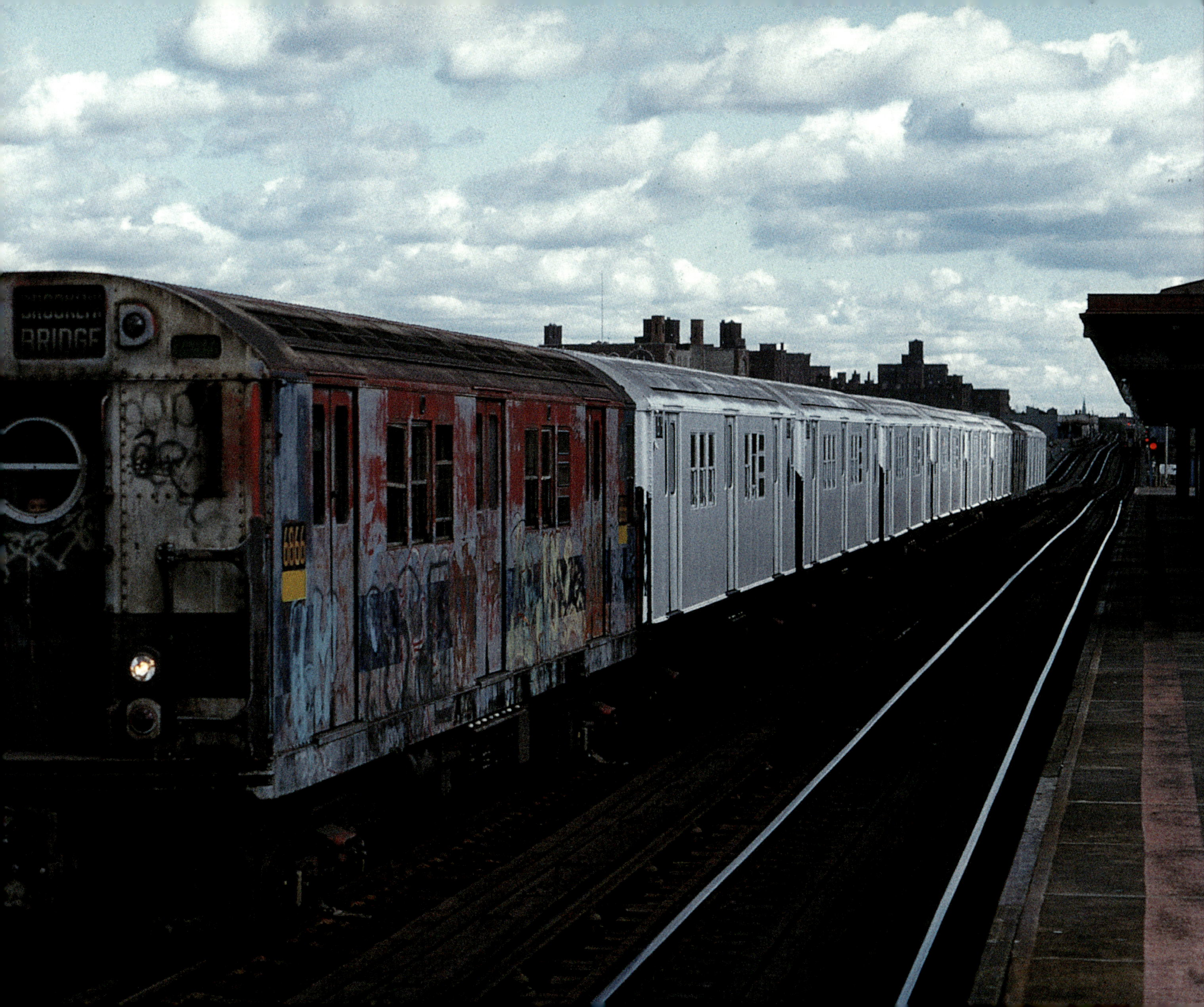

R-17, No. 6 Pelham line, Sound View Ave., Bronx, 1982

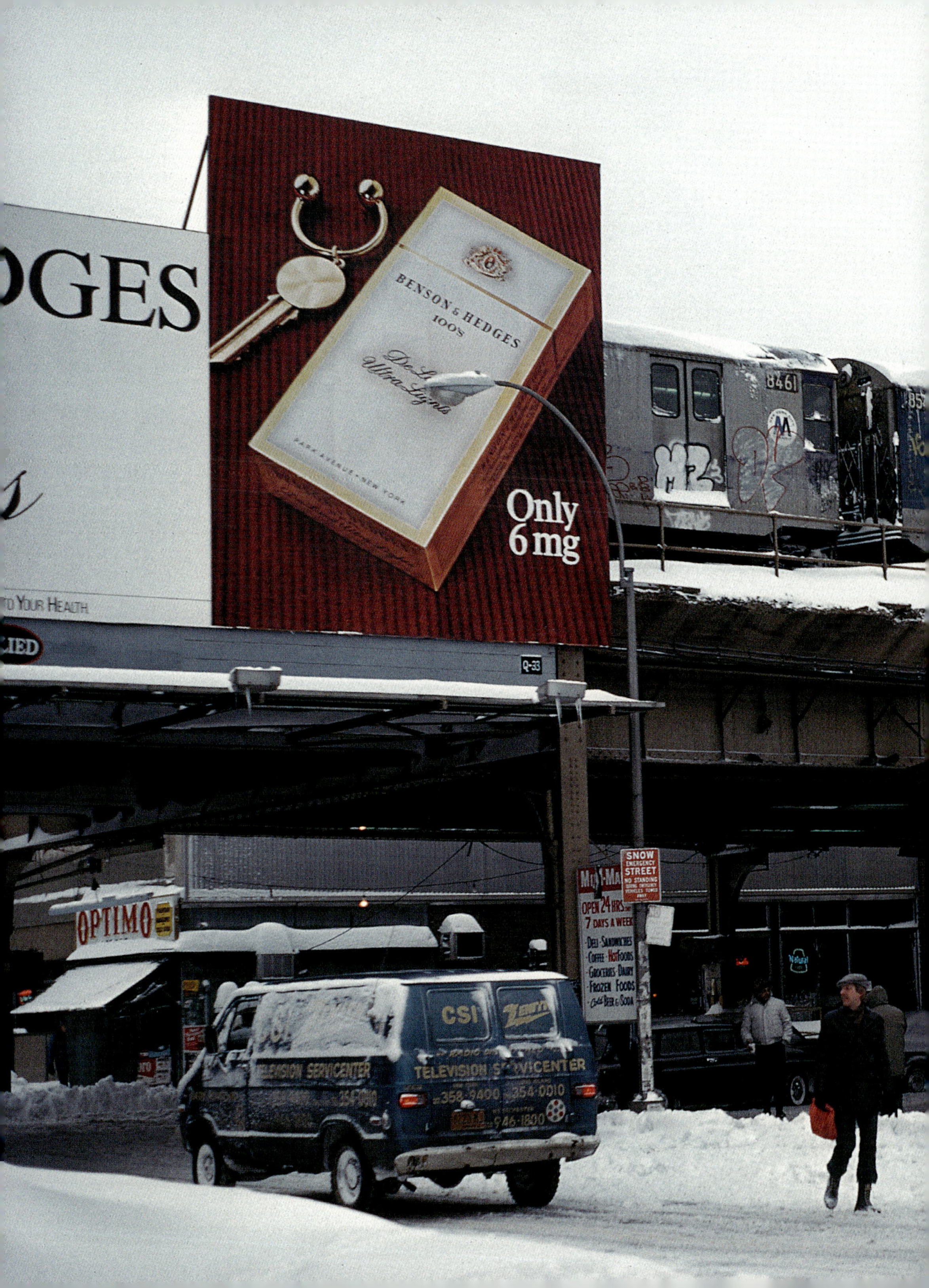
OGES
BENSON & HEDGES
100'S
PARK AVENUE · NEW YORK
Only
6 mg
8461
OPTIMO
SNOW
EMERGENCY
STREET
NO STANDING
OPEN 24 HRS
7 DAYS A WEEK
DELI-SANDWICHES
COFFEE · HOT FOODS
GROCERIES · DAIRY
FROZEN FOODS
Cold BEER & SODA
CSI
TELEVISION SERVICENTER
358-9400
354-0010
946-1800

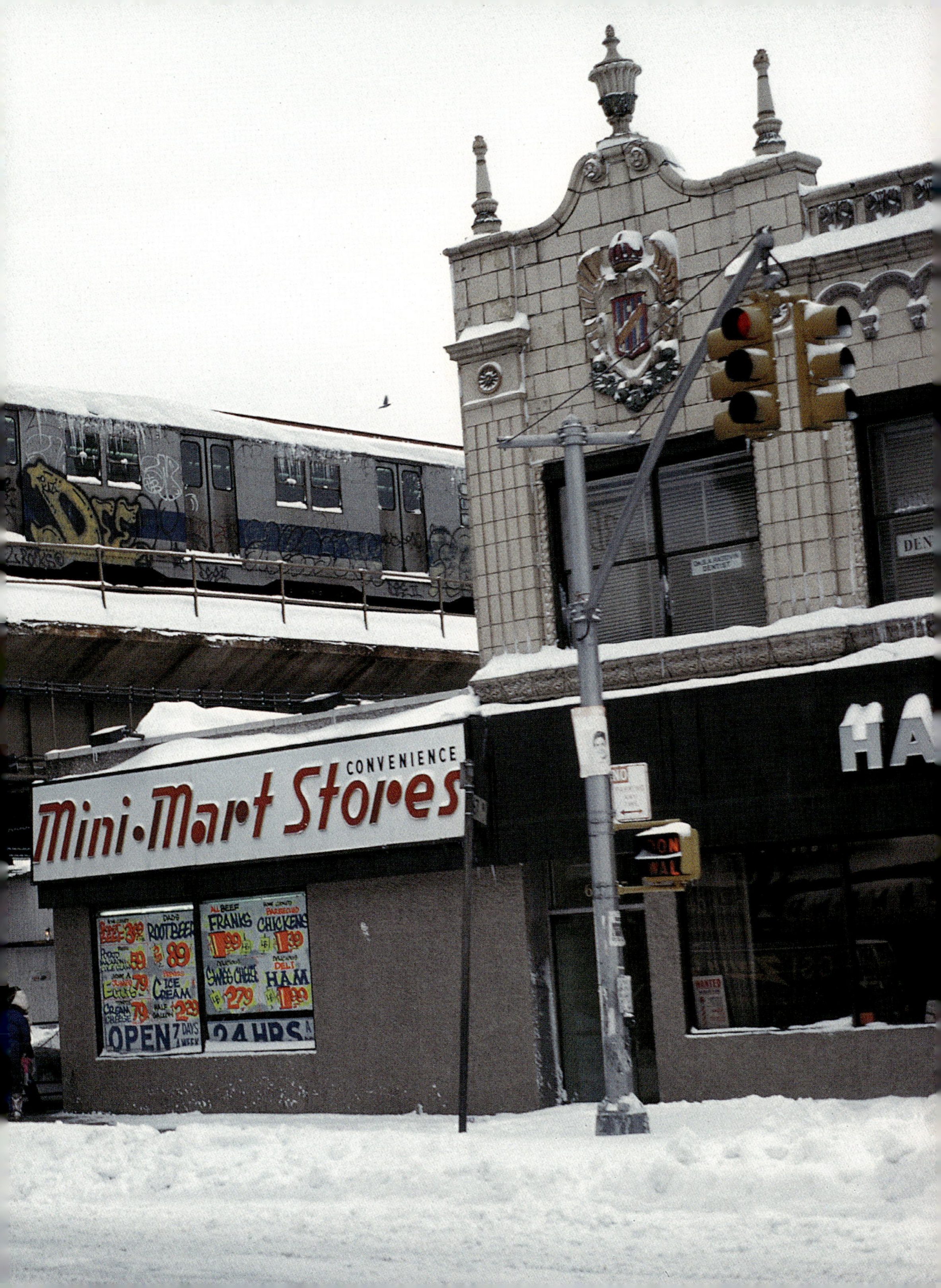
CONVENIENCE
Mini·Mart Stores
ROOTBEER
89
ICE CREAM
ALL BEEF
FRANKS
CHICKENS
DELI
HAM
OPEN
24 HRS
DEN
HA

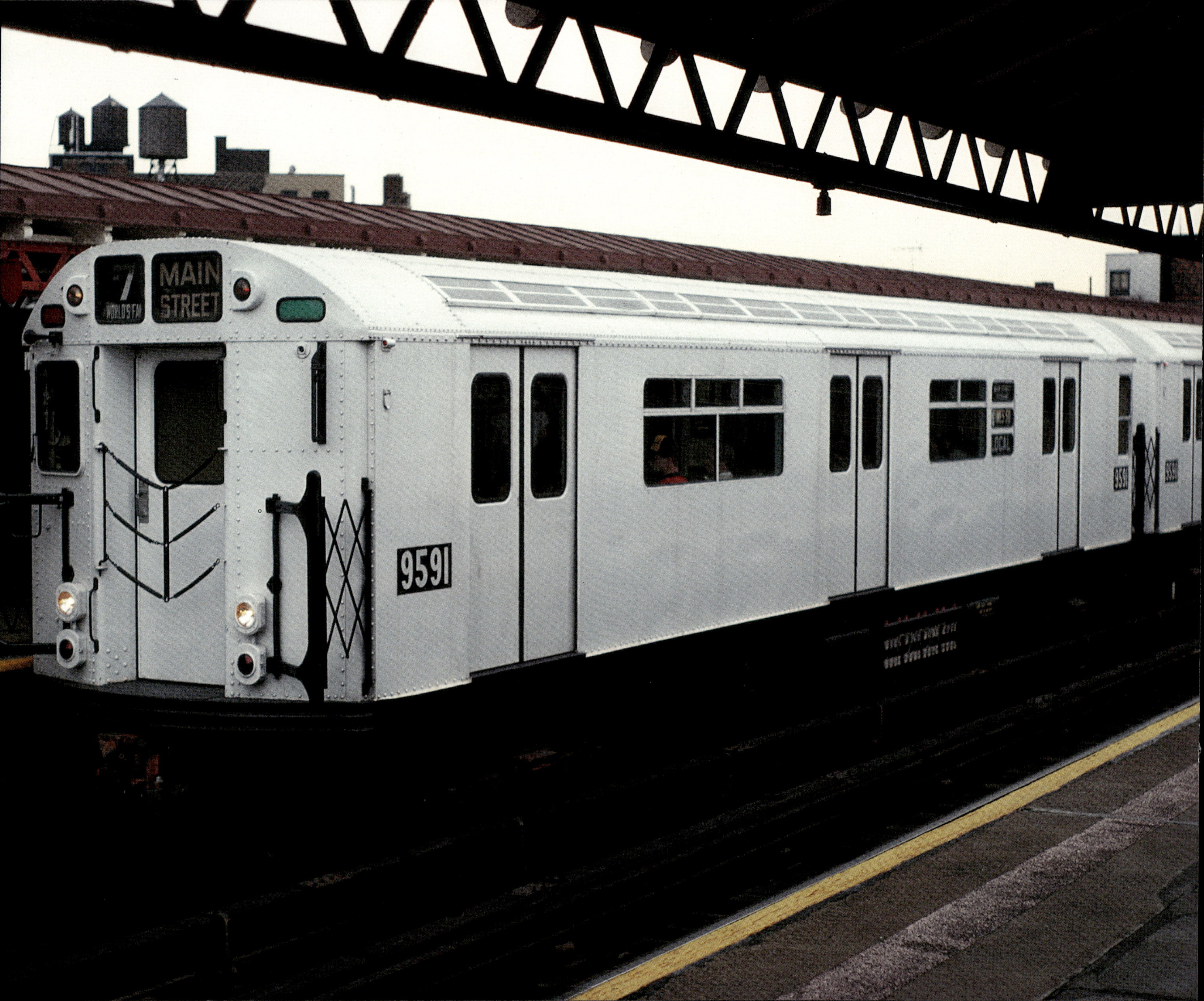

R-36s, No. 7 Flushing line, 45th Rd.–Court House Sq., Queens, 1983

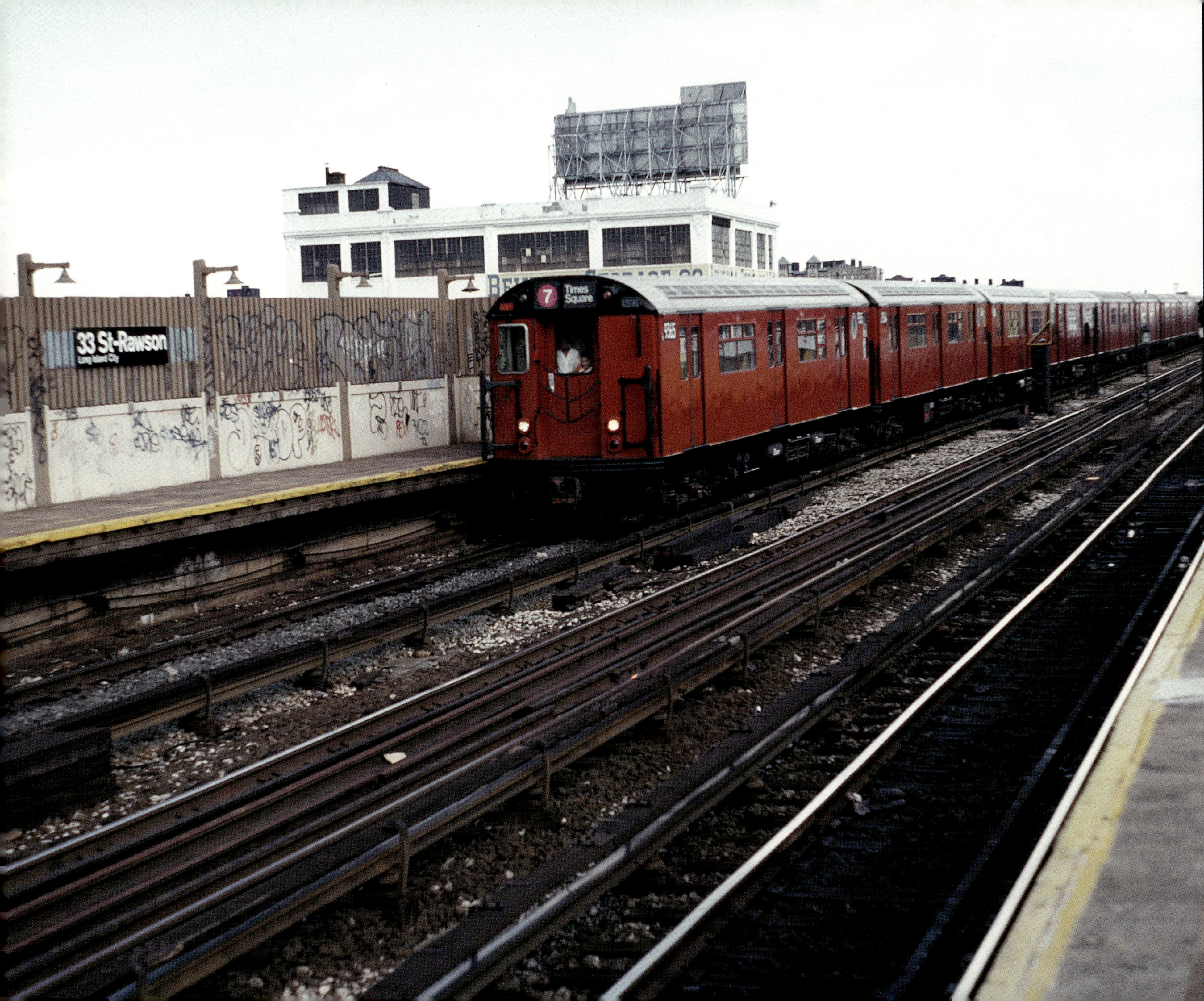

R-36s, No. 7 Flushing line, 33rd St.–Rawson St., Queens, 1984

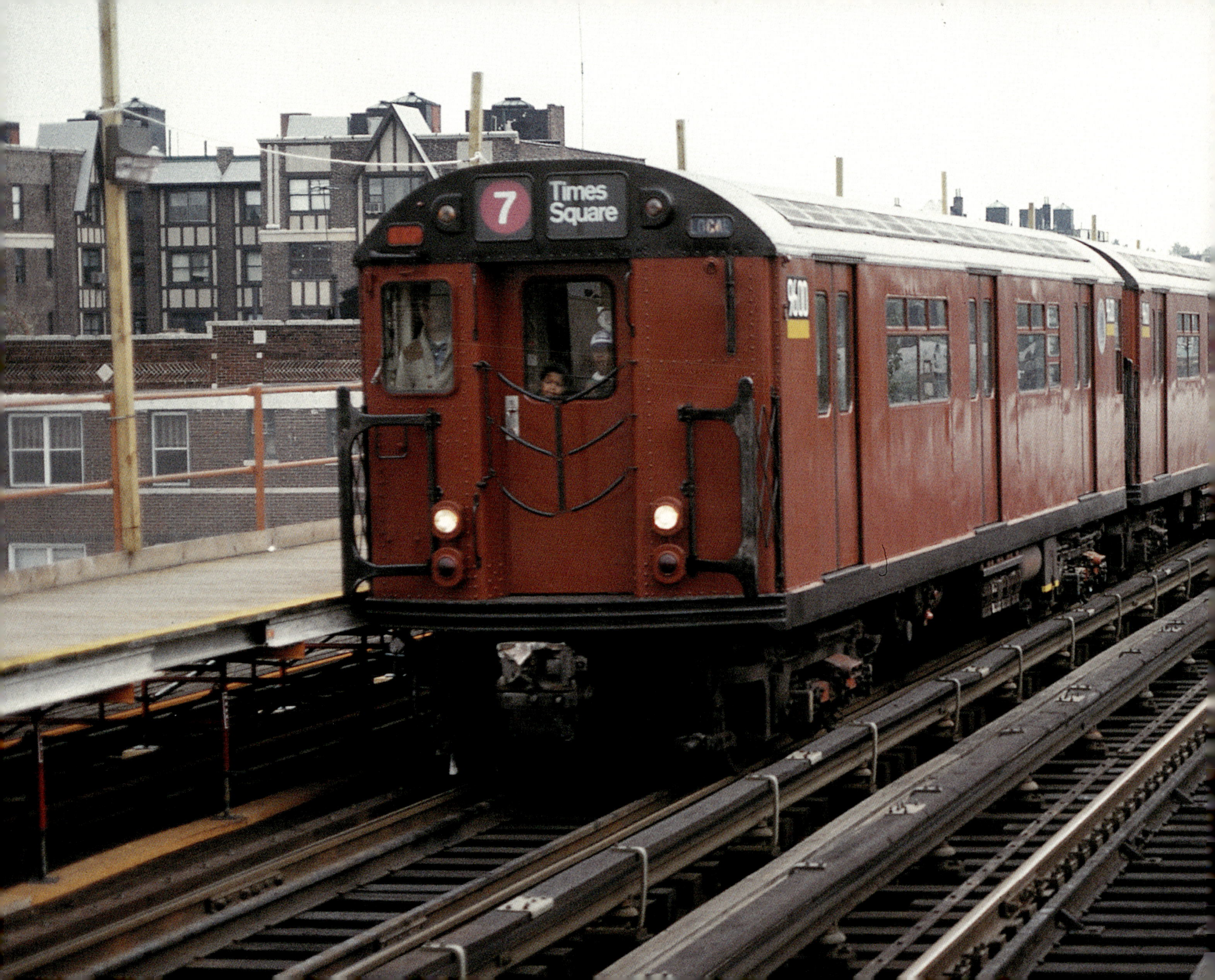
7
Times Square

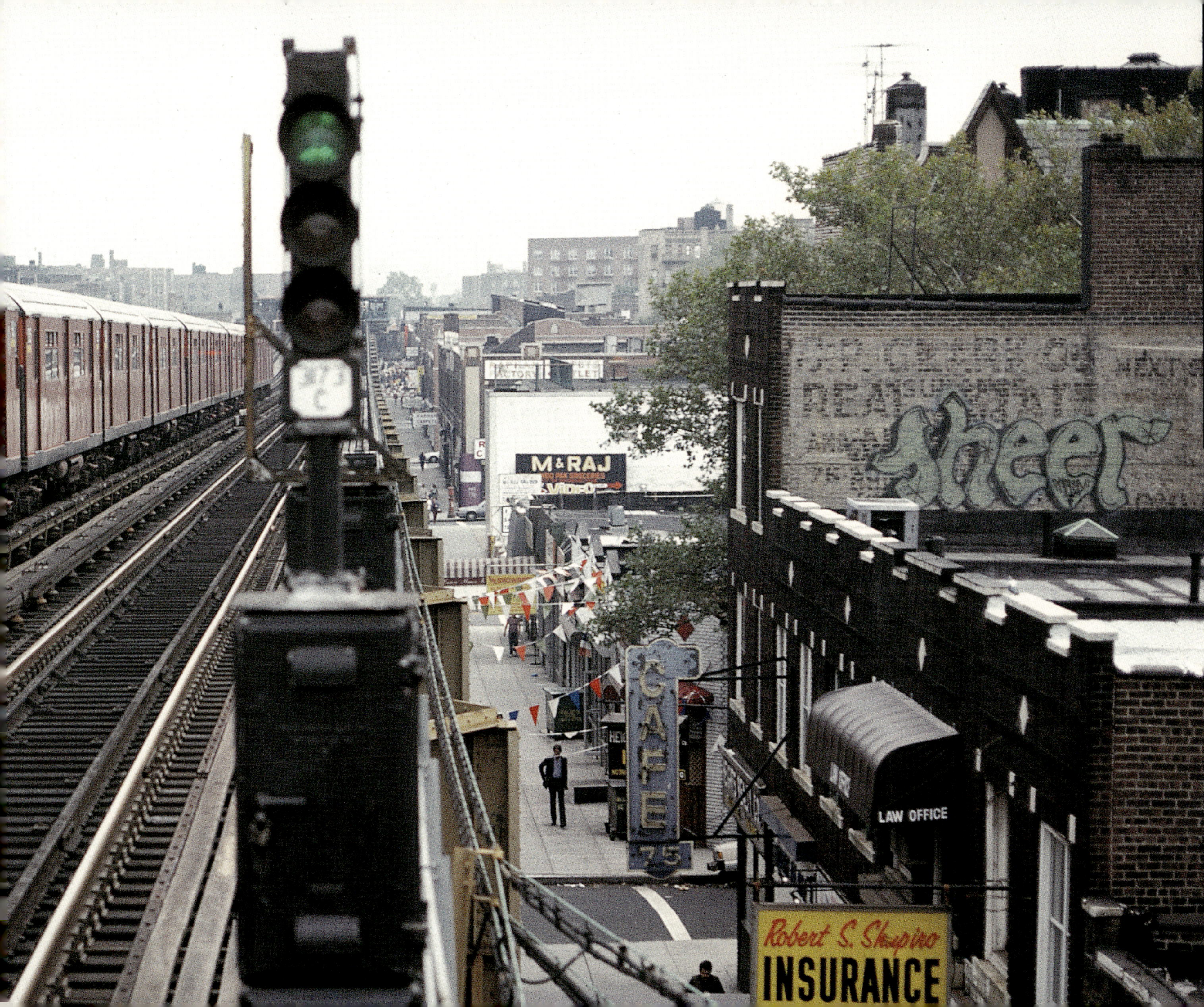

R-36s, No. 7 Flushing Line, 74th St.–Broadway, Queens, 1985

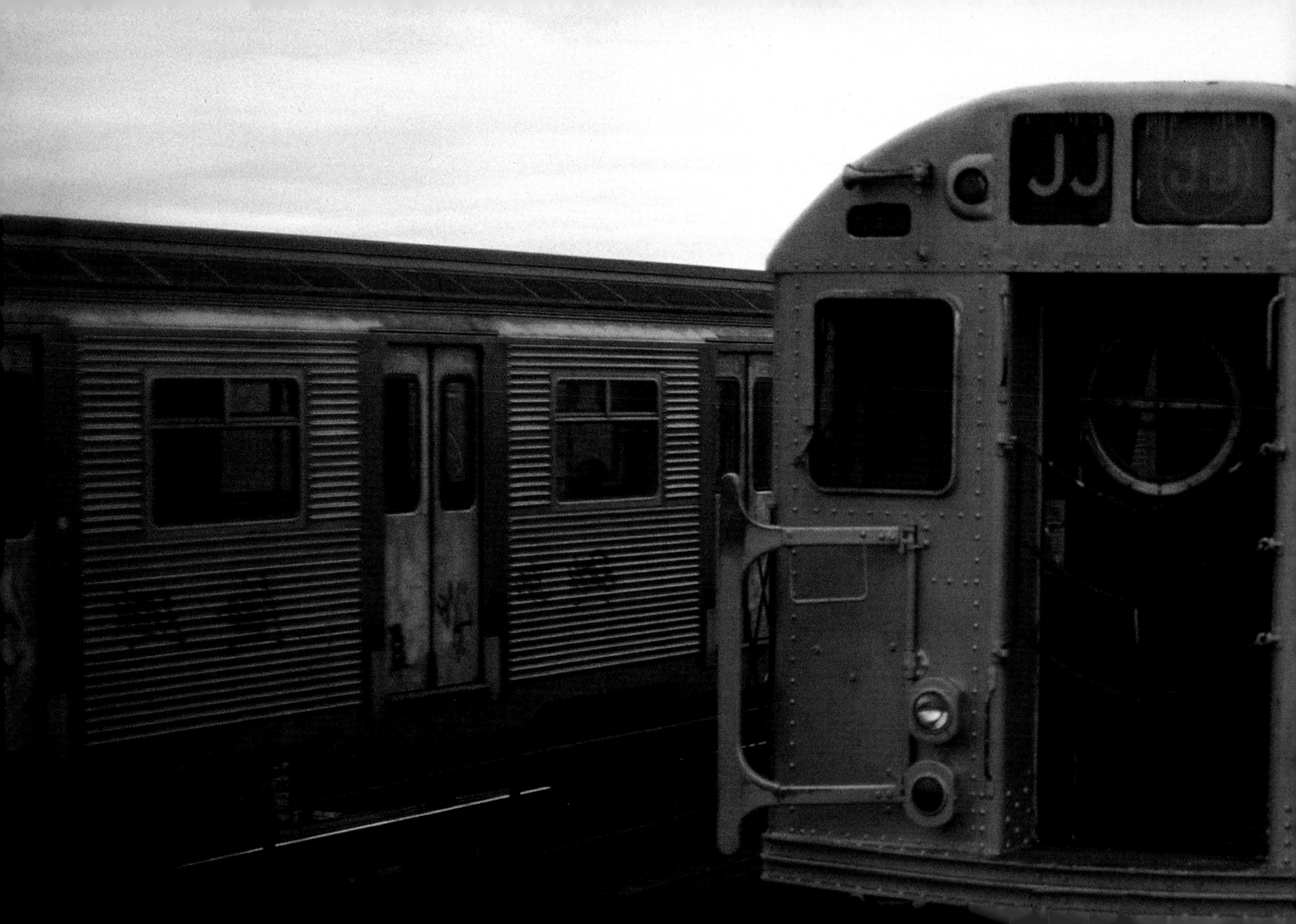
JJ

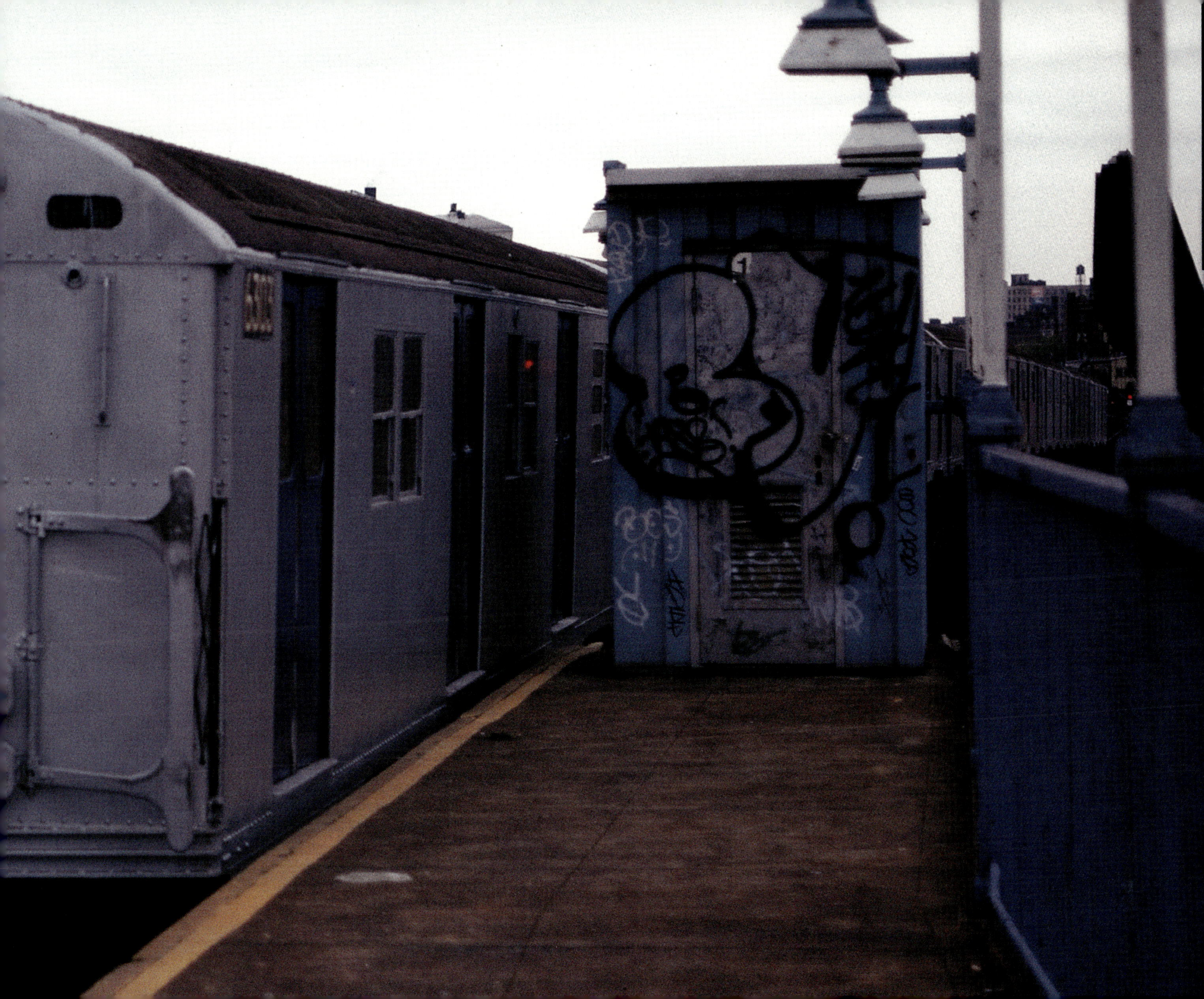

R-32s, R-16s, Jamaica line, 1984

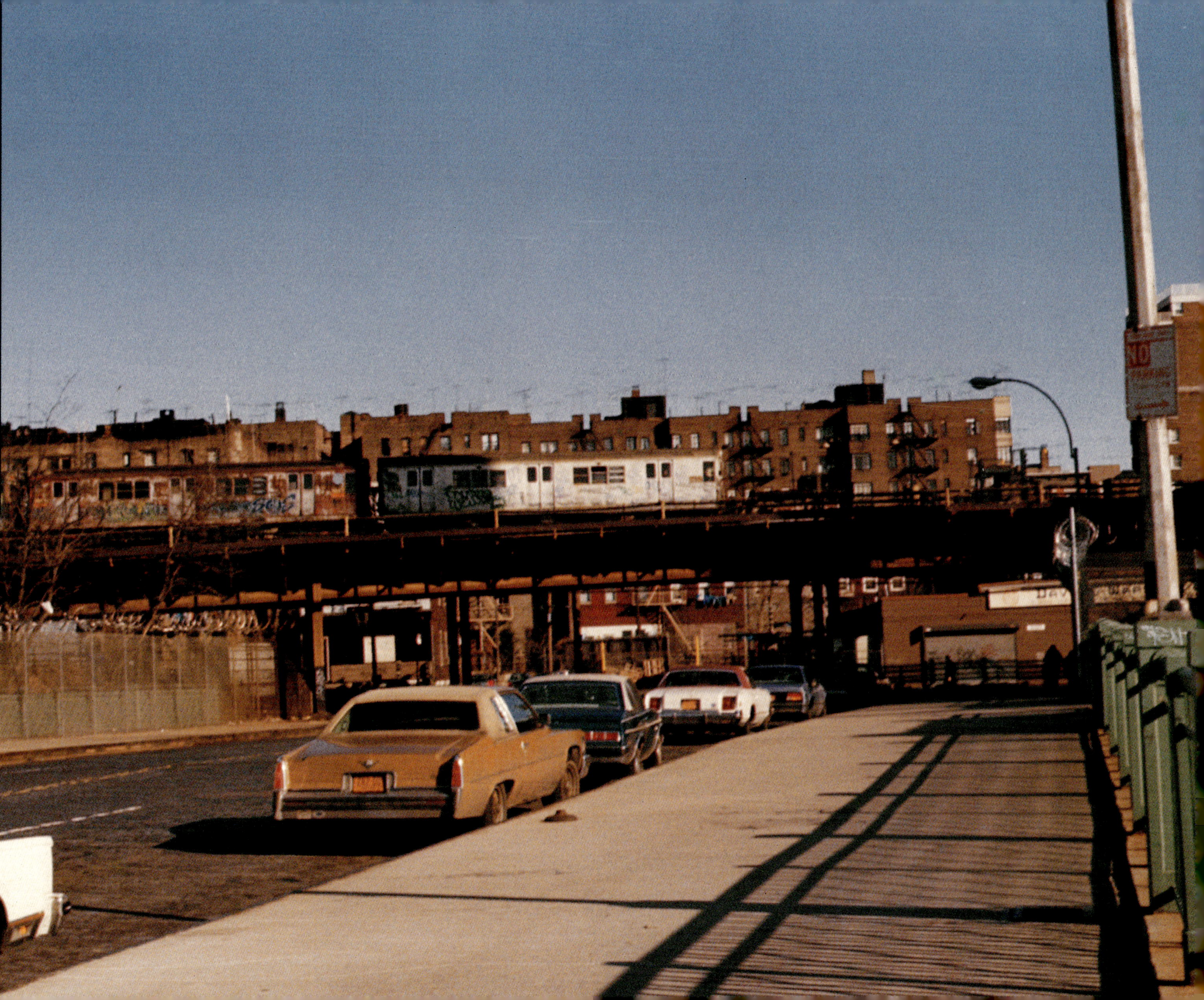

R-17s, No. 4 Jerome Ave. line, north of Bedford Park Blvd., Bronx, 1985

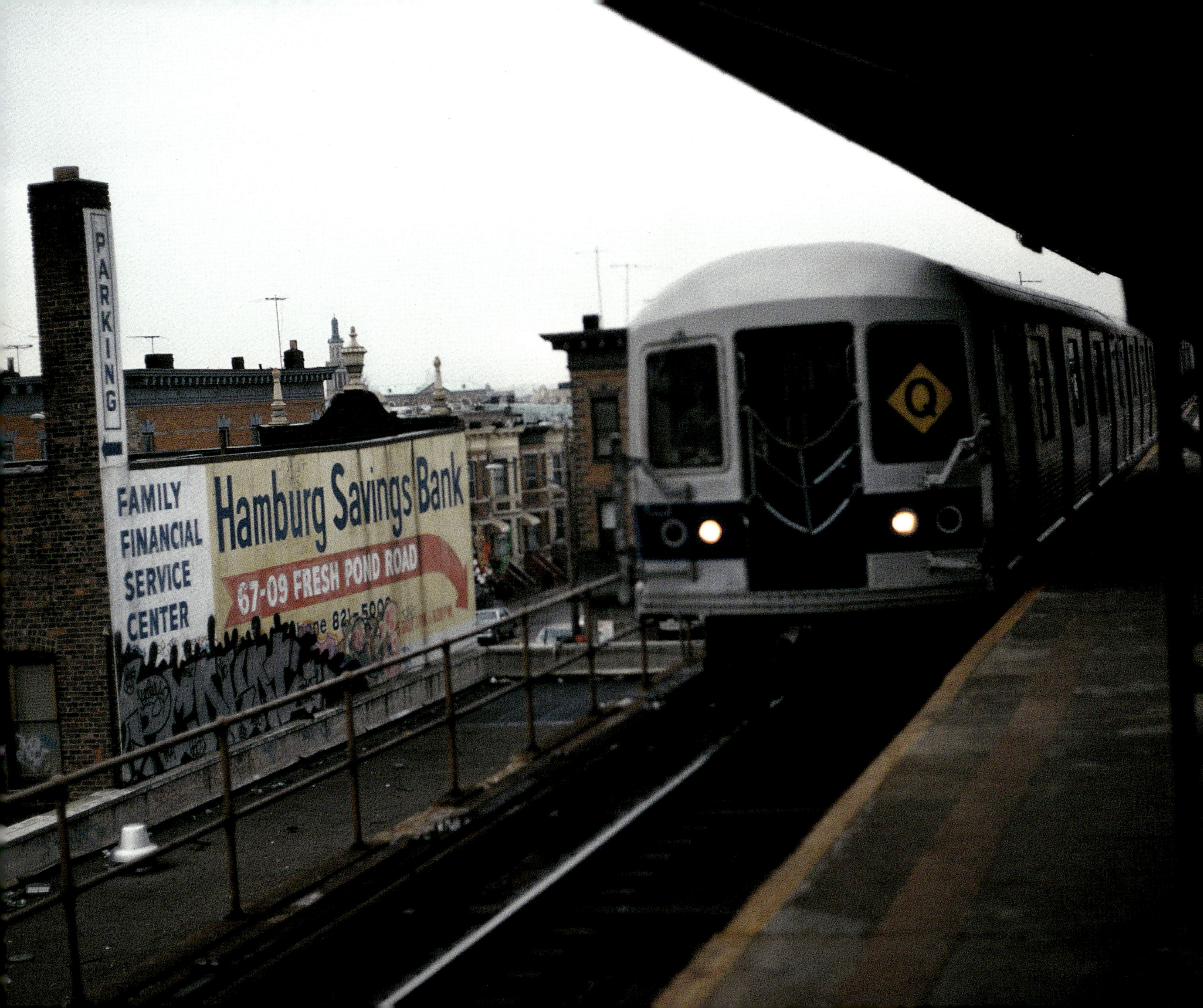

R-42s, Myrtle Ave. line, Fresh Pond Rd., Queens, 1985

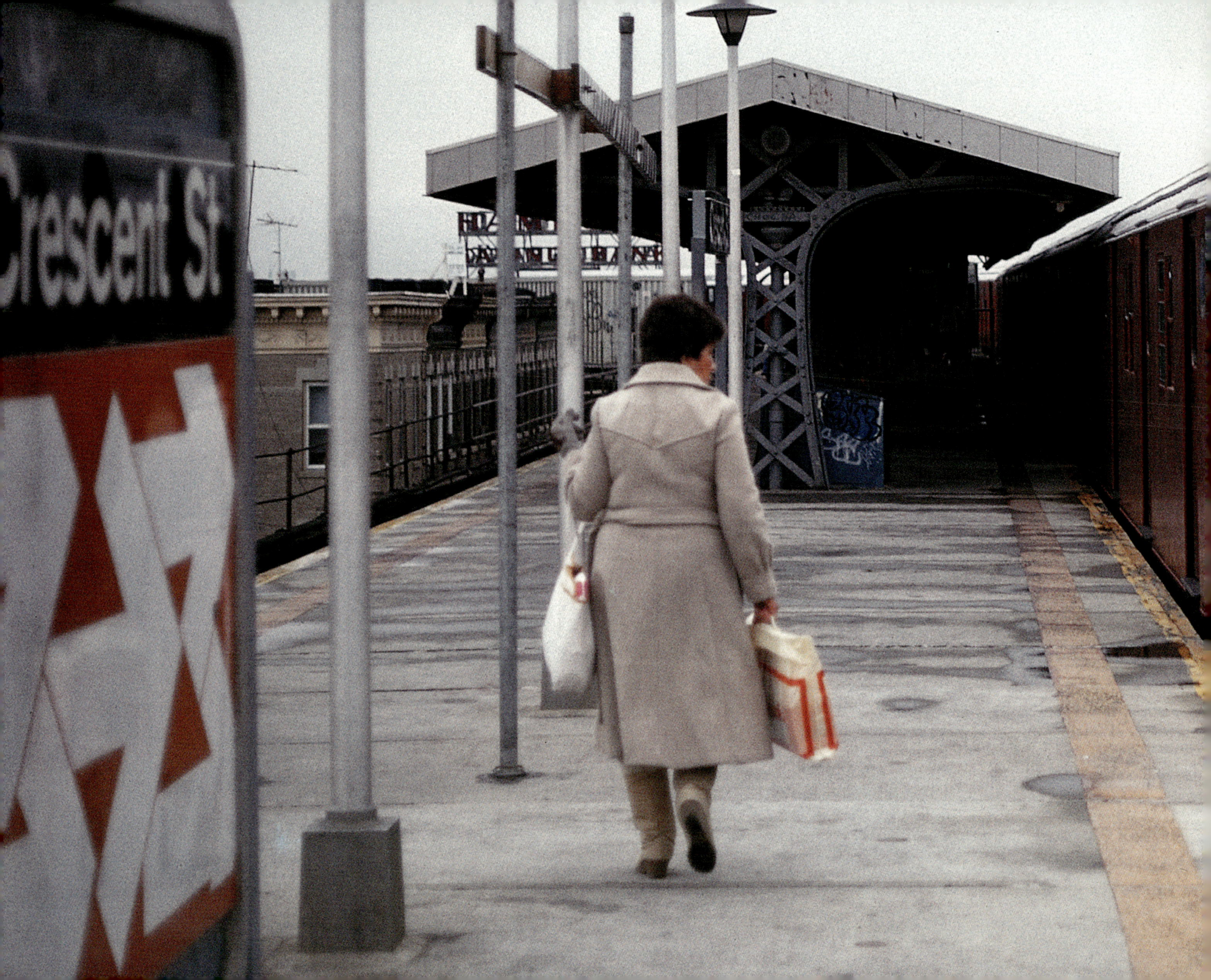
Crescent St

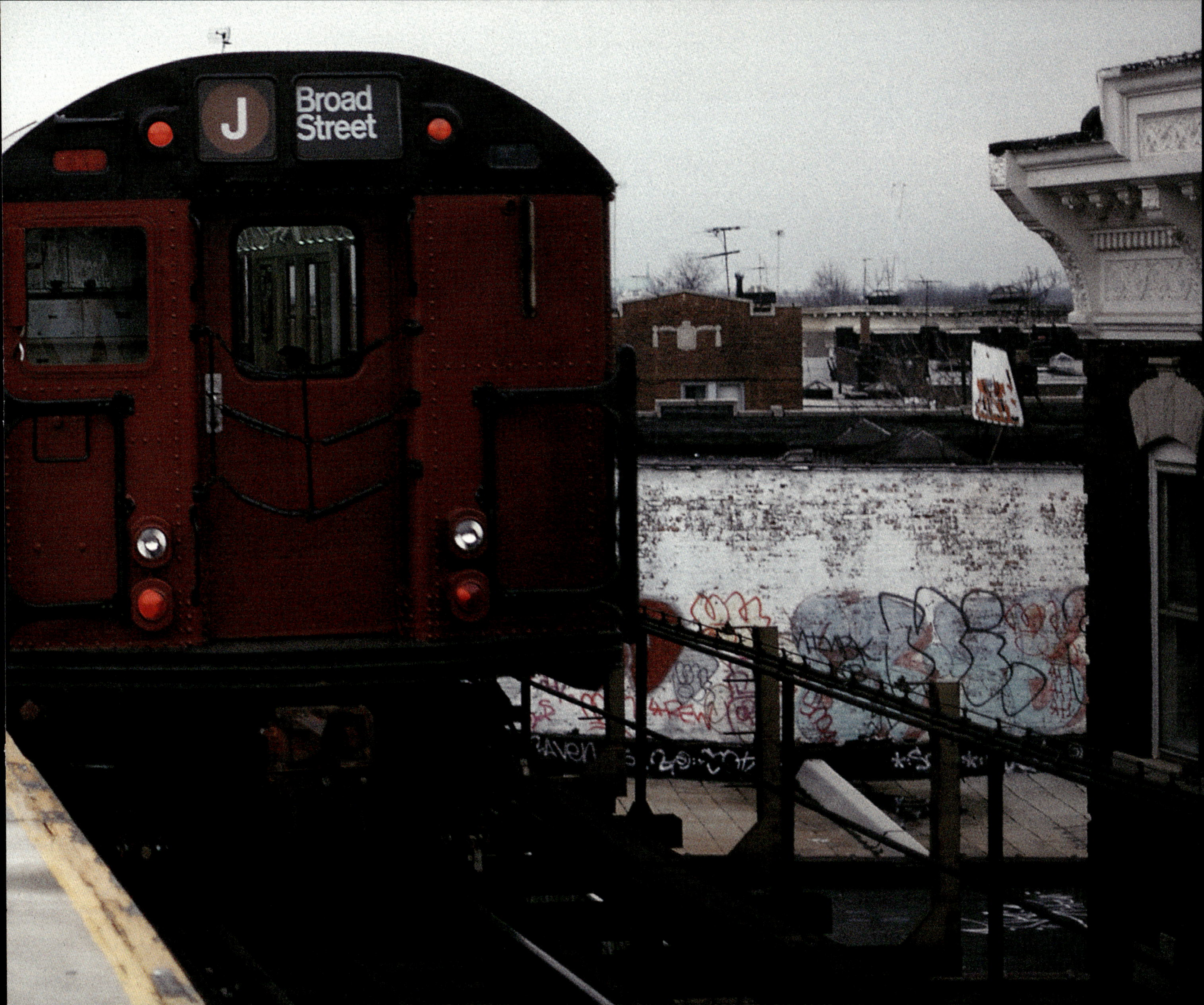

R-30s, Jamaica line, Crescent St., Brooklyn, 1985

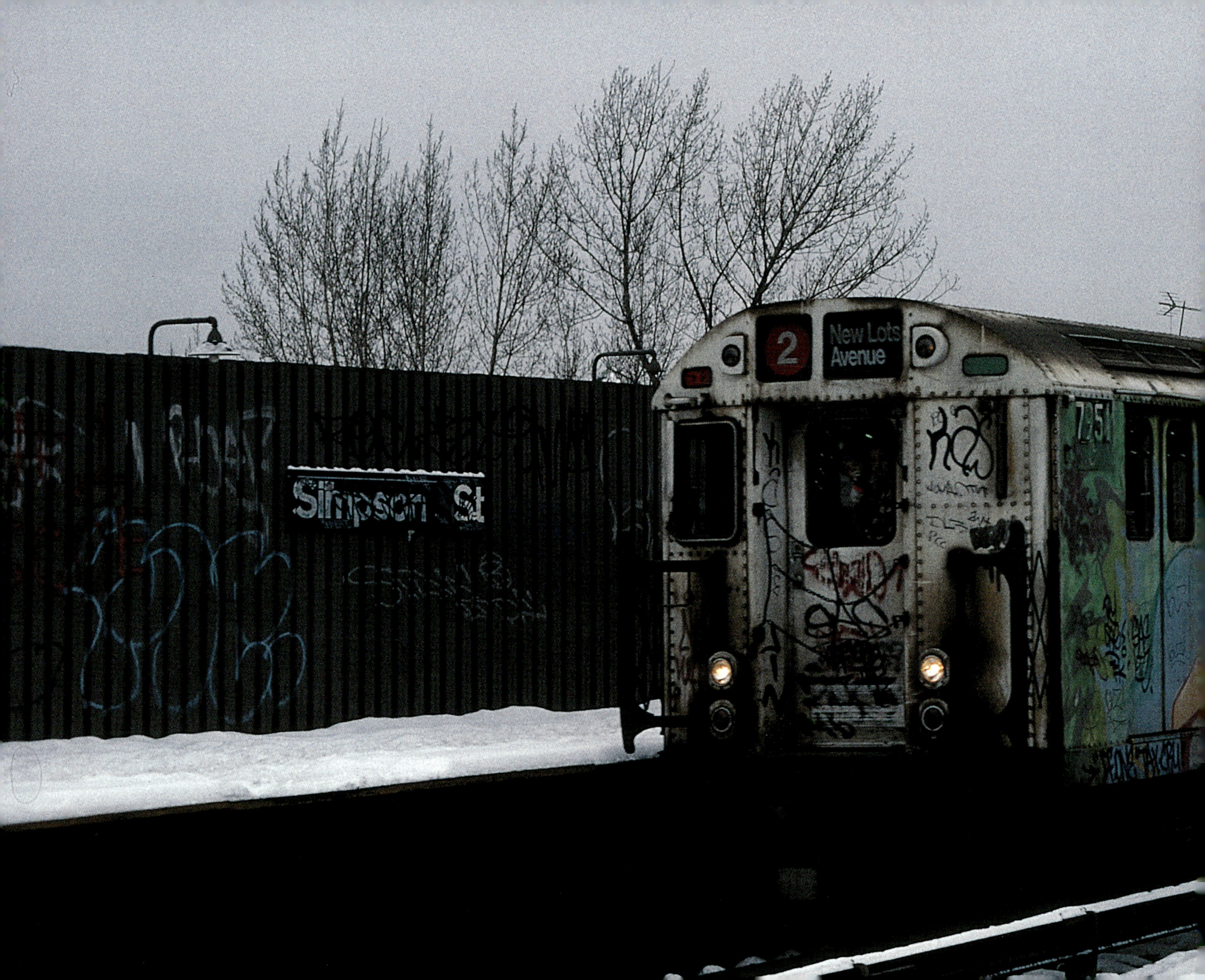
Simpson St
2
New Lots
Avenue

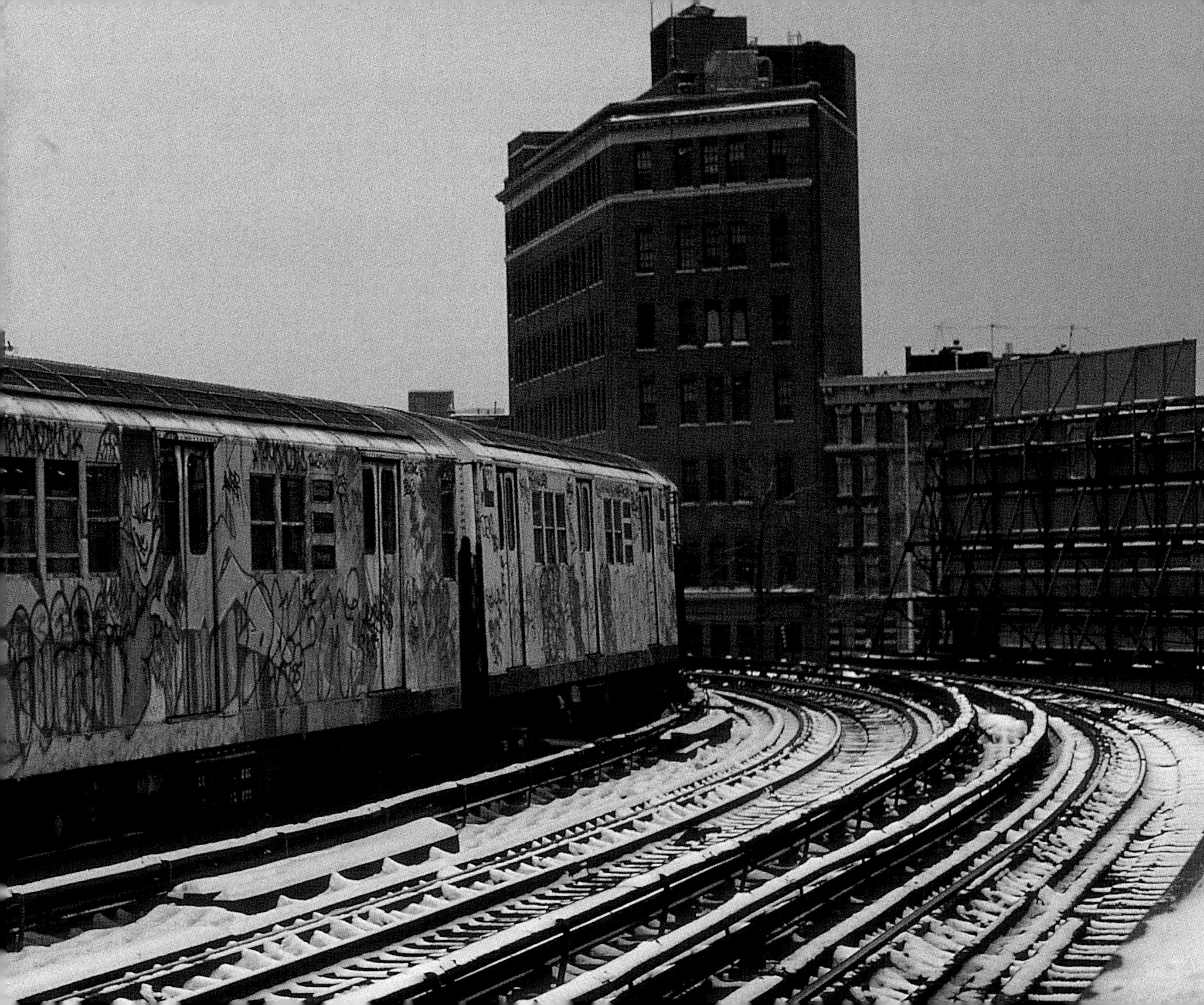

R-28s, No. 2 West Farms line, Simpson St., Bronx, 1986

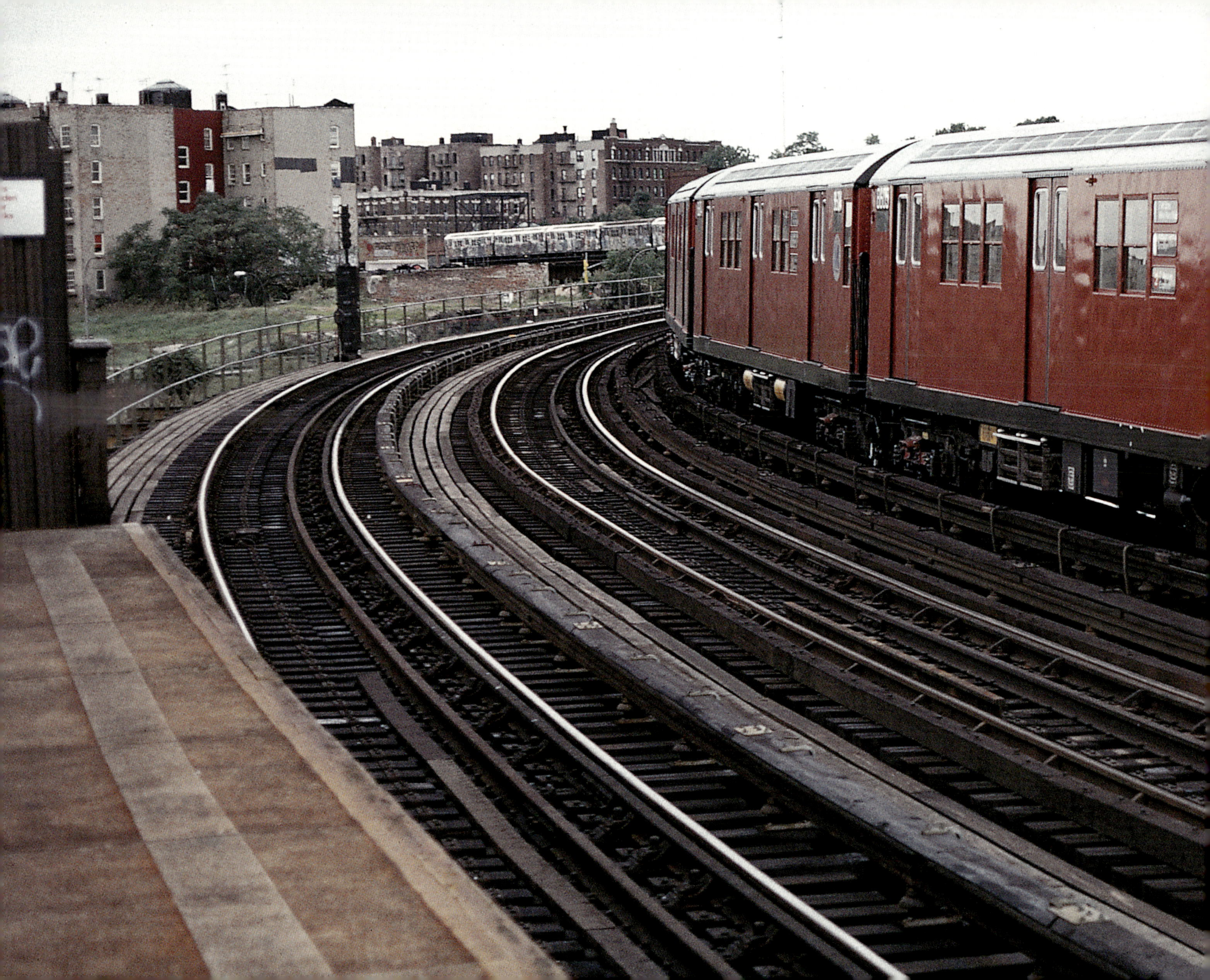

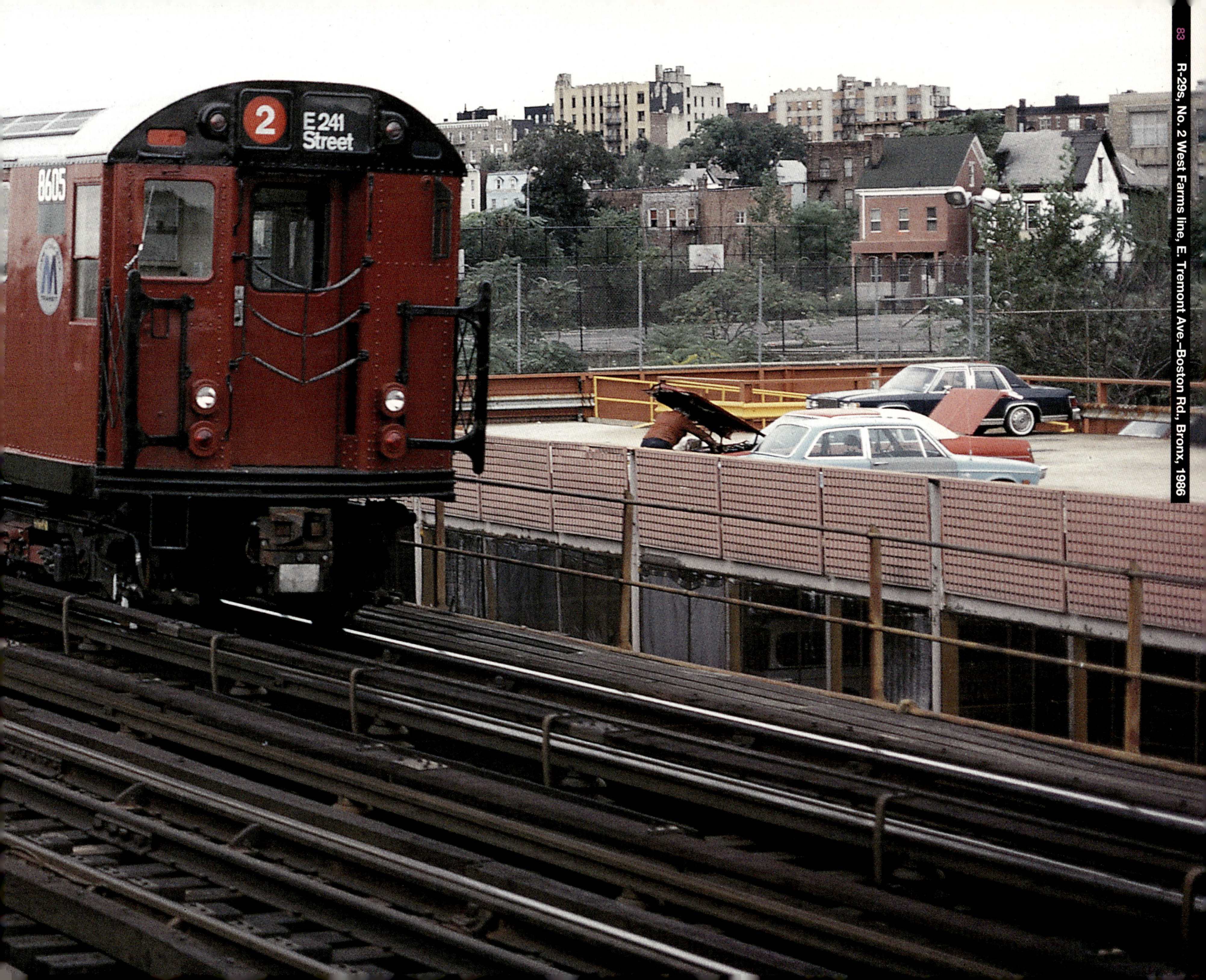

R-29s, No. 2 West Farms line, E. Tremont Ave.–Boston Rd., Bronx, 1986

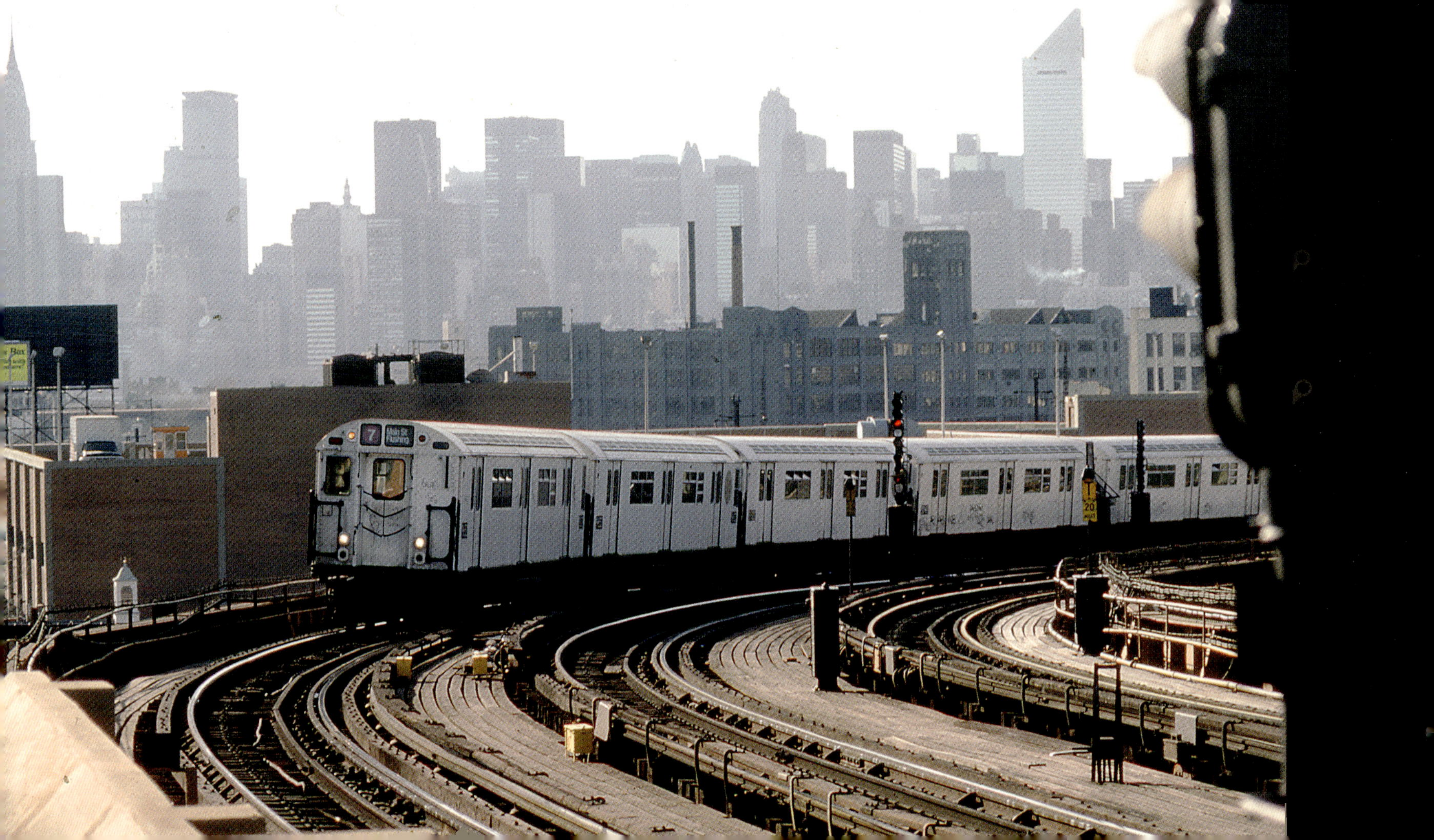
7

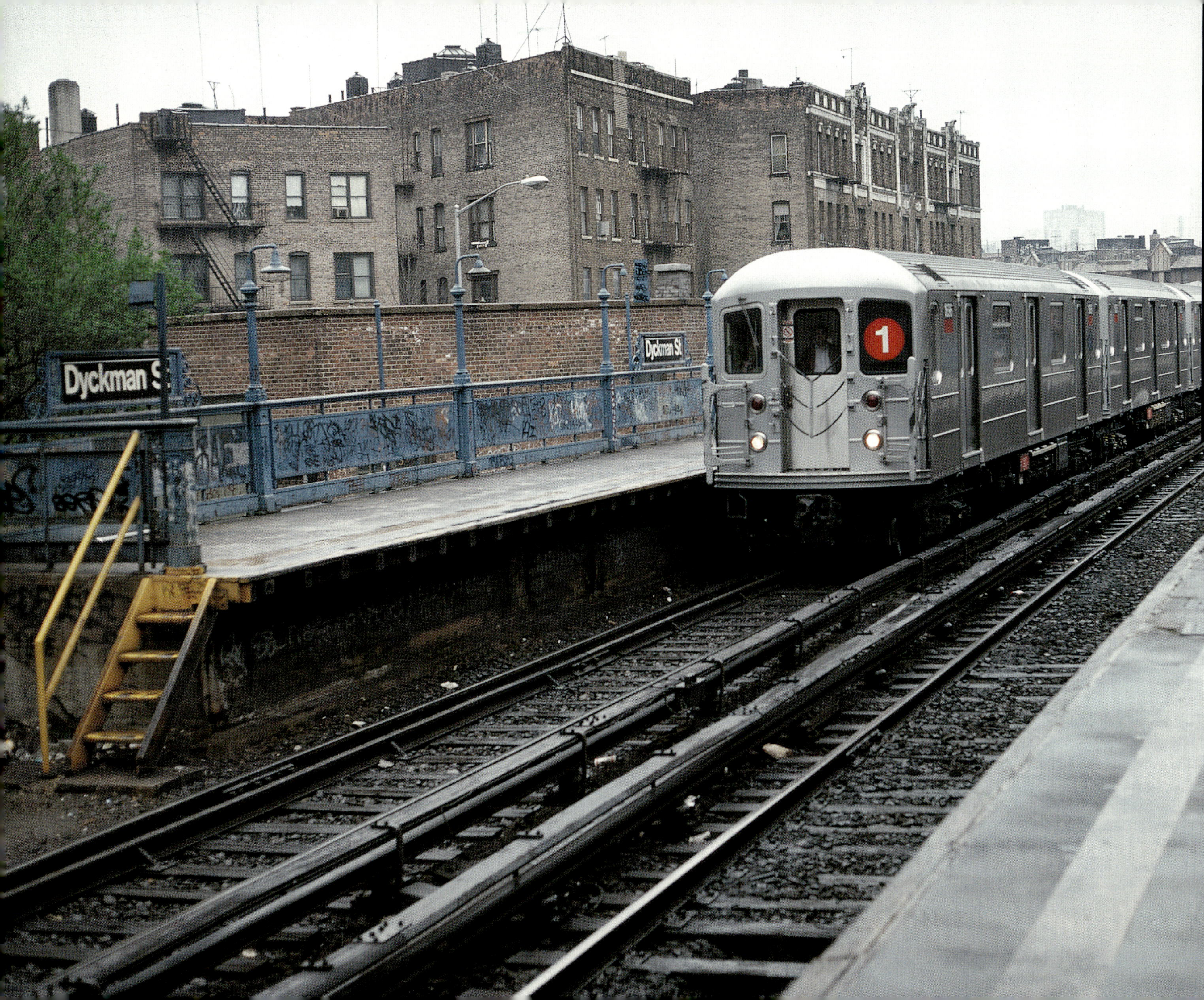

R-62As, No. 1 Broadway line, Dyckman St, Manhattan, 1986

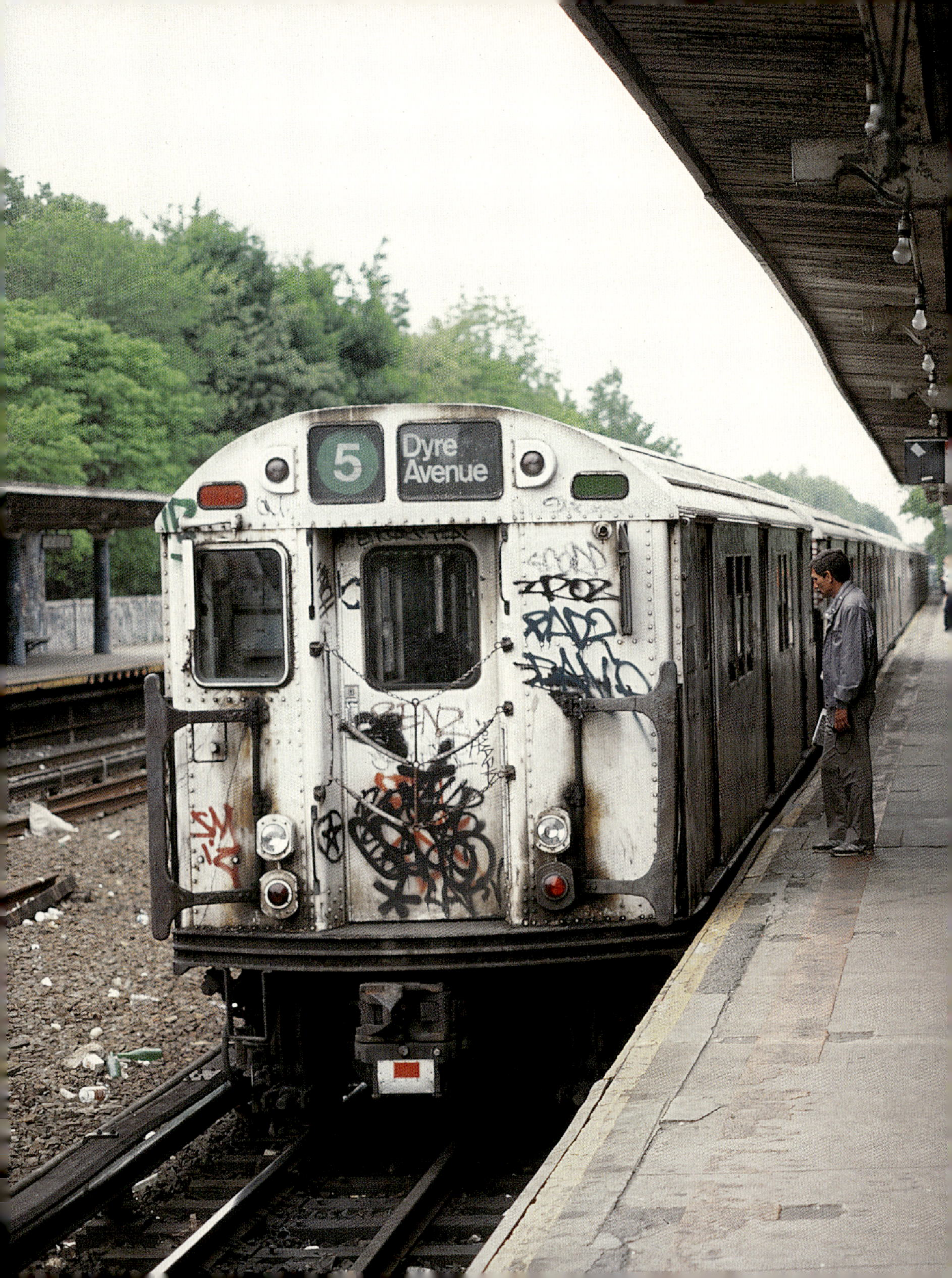
5
Dyre
Avenue

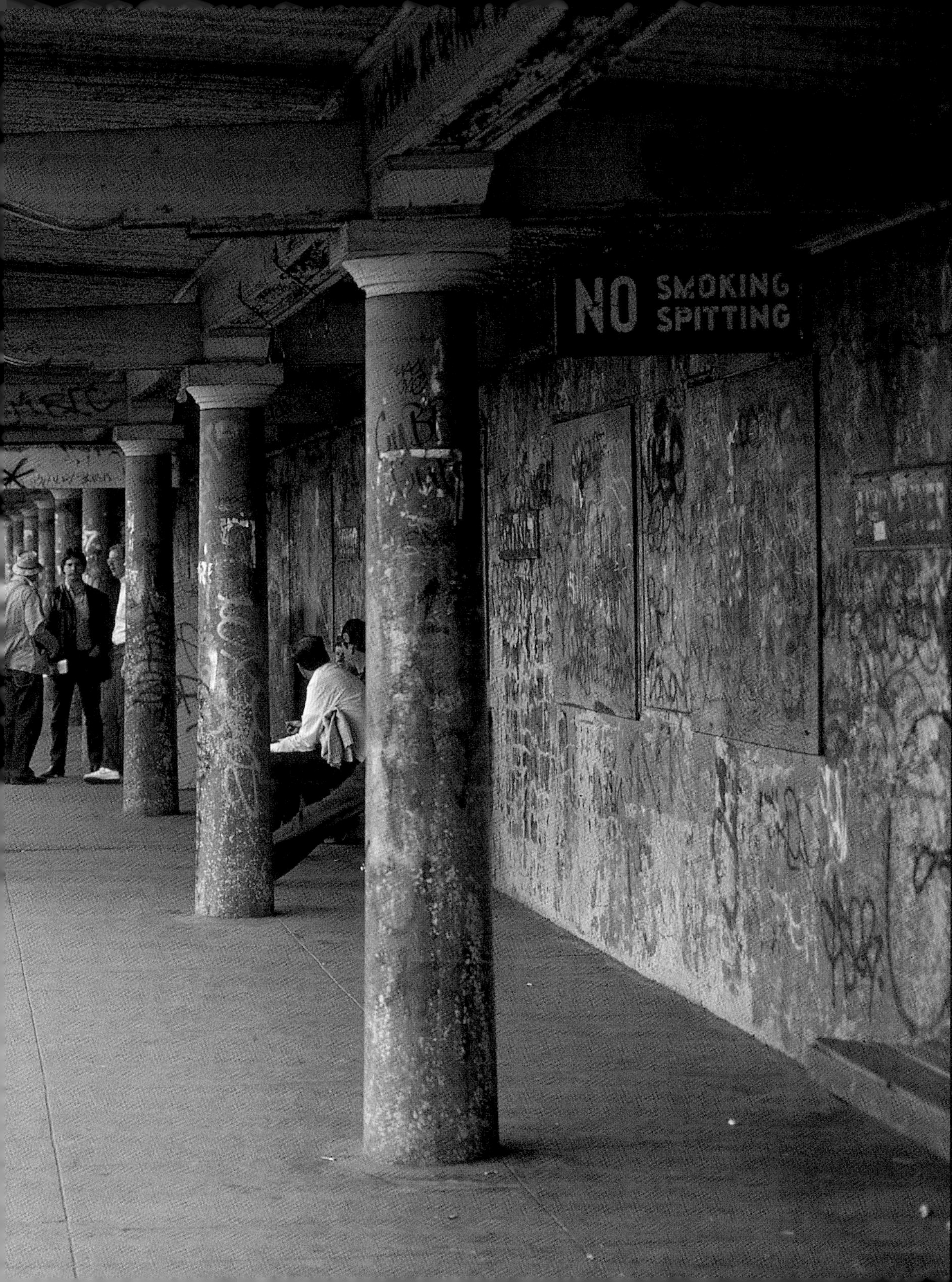

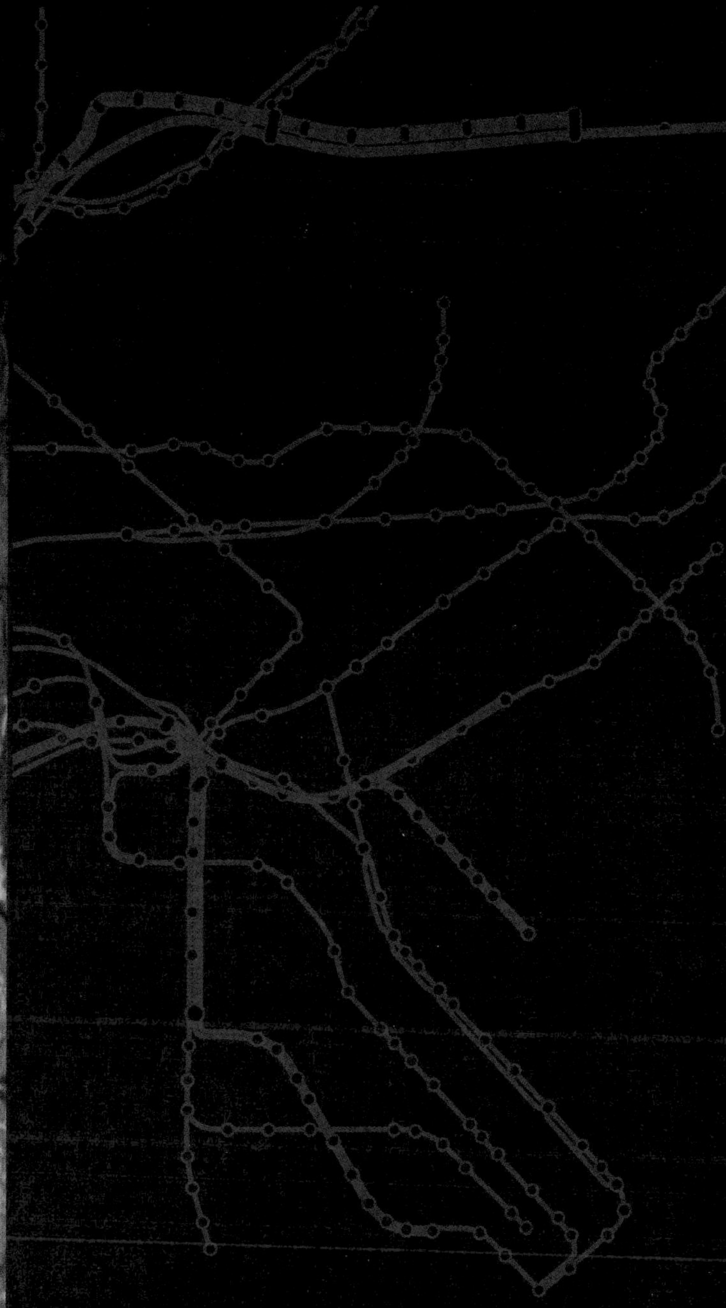

No. 5 Dyre Ave. line, Baychester Ave., Bronx, 1986

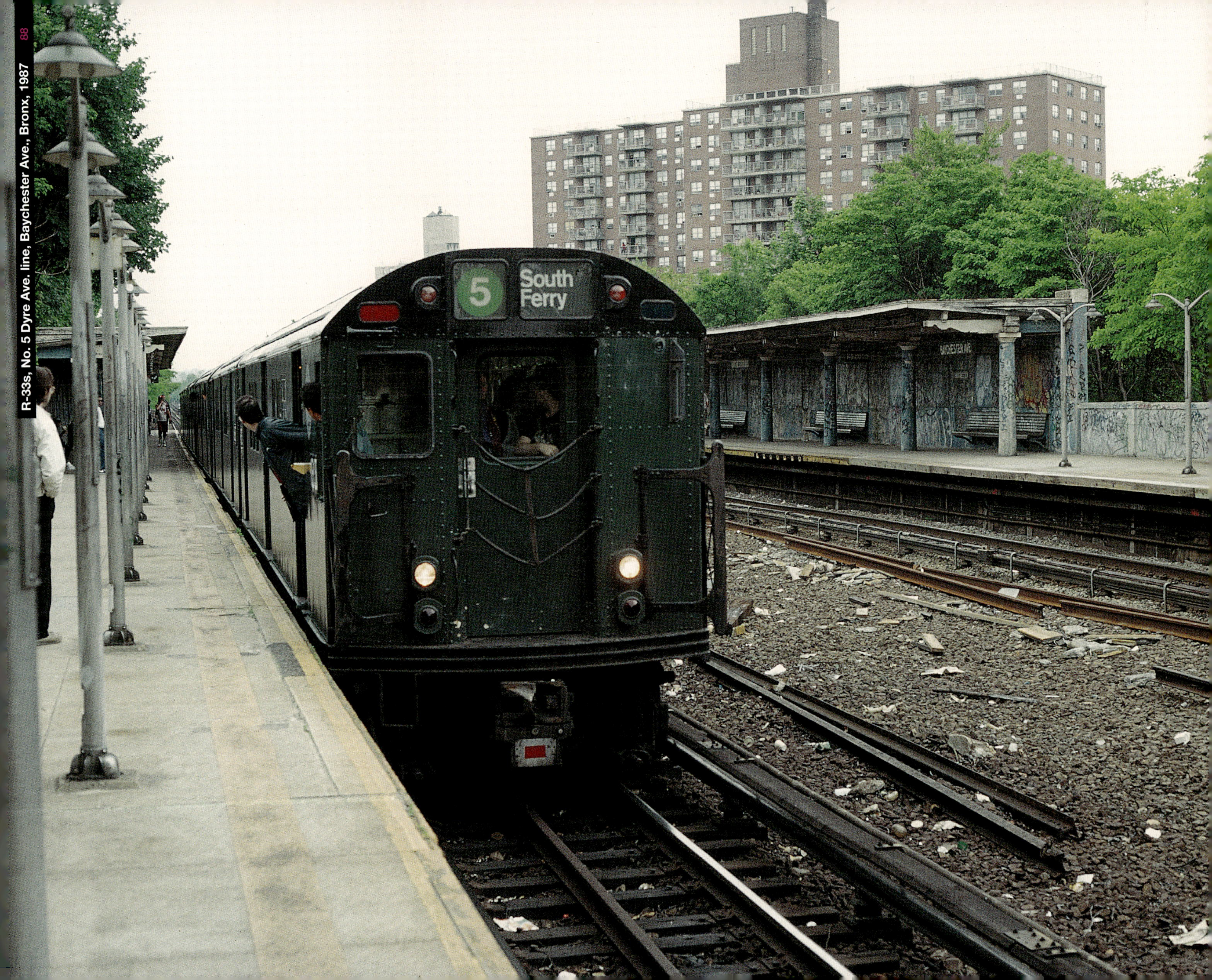

R-33s, No. 5 Dyre Ave. line, Baychester Ave., Bronx, 1987

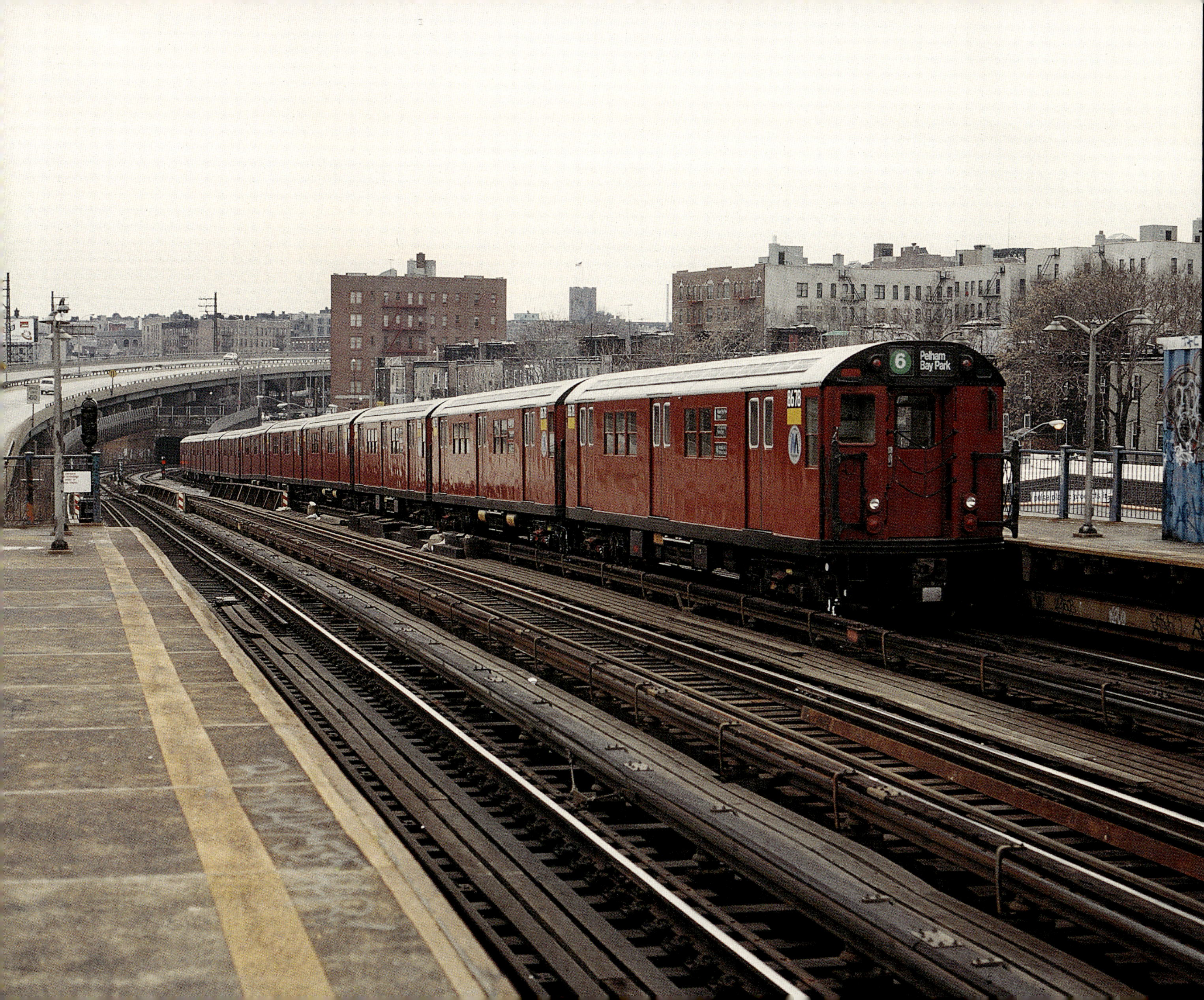

R-29s, No. 6 Pelham Bay line, Whitlock Ave., Bronx, 1987

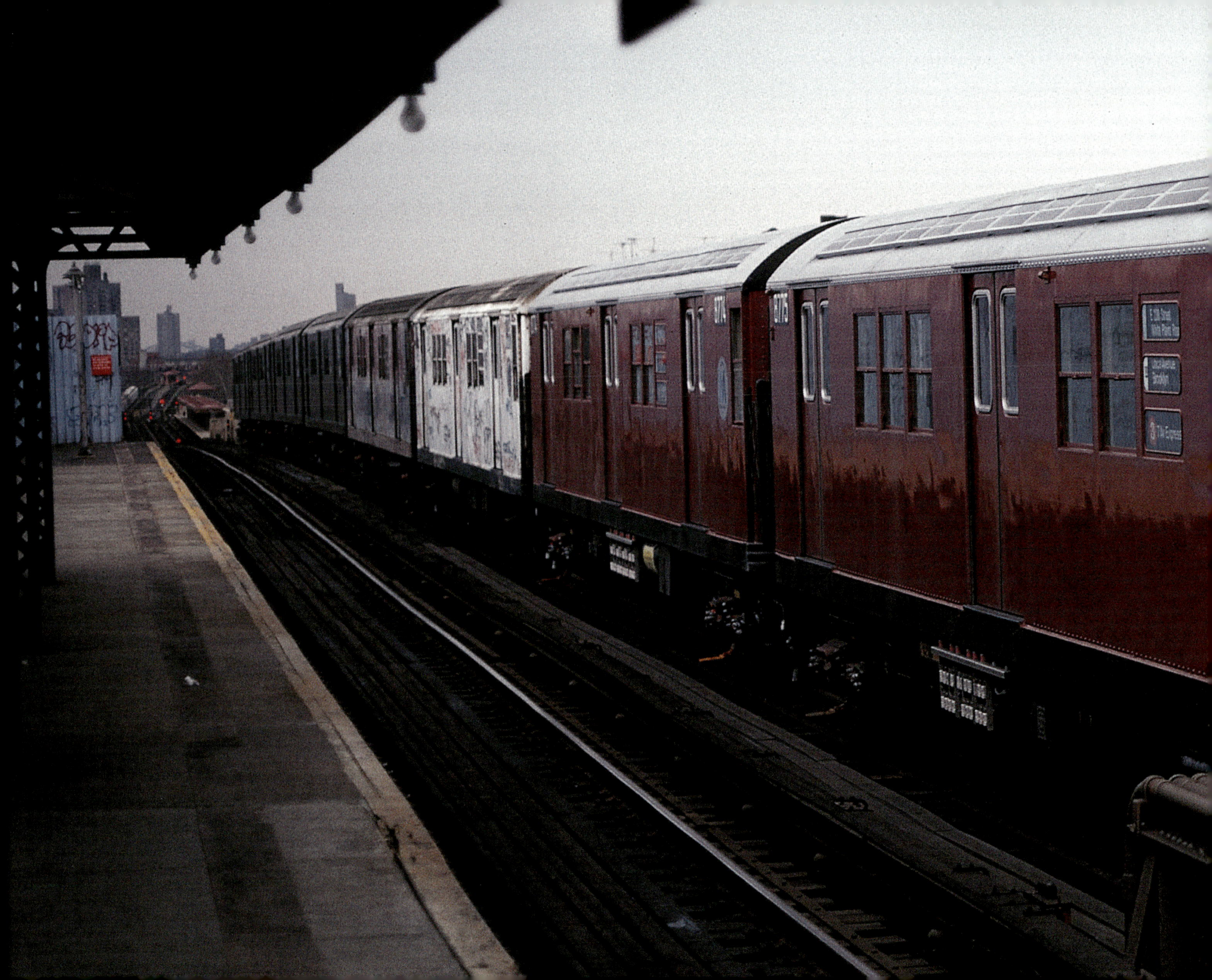
6774
6775

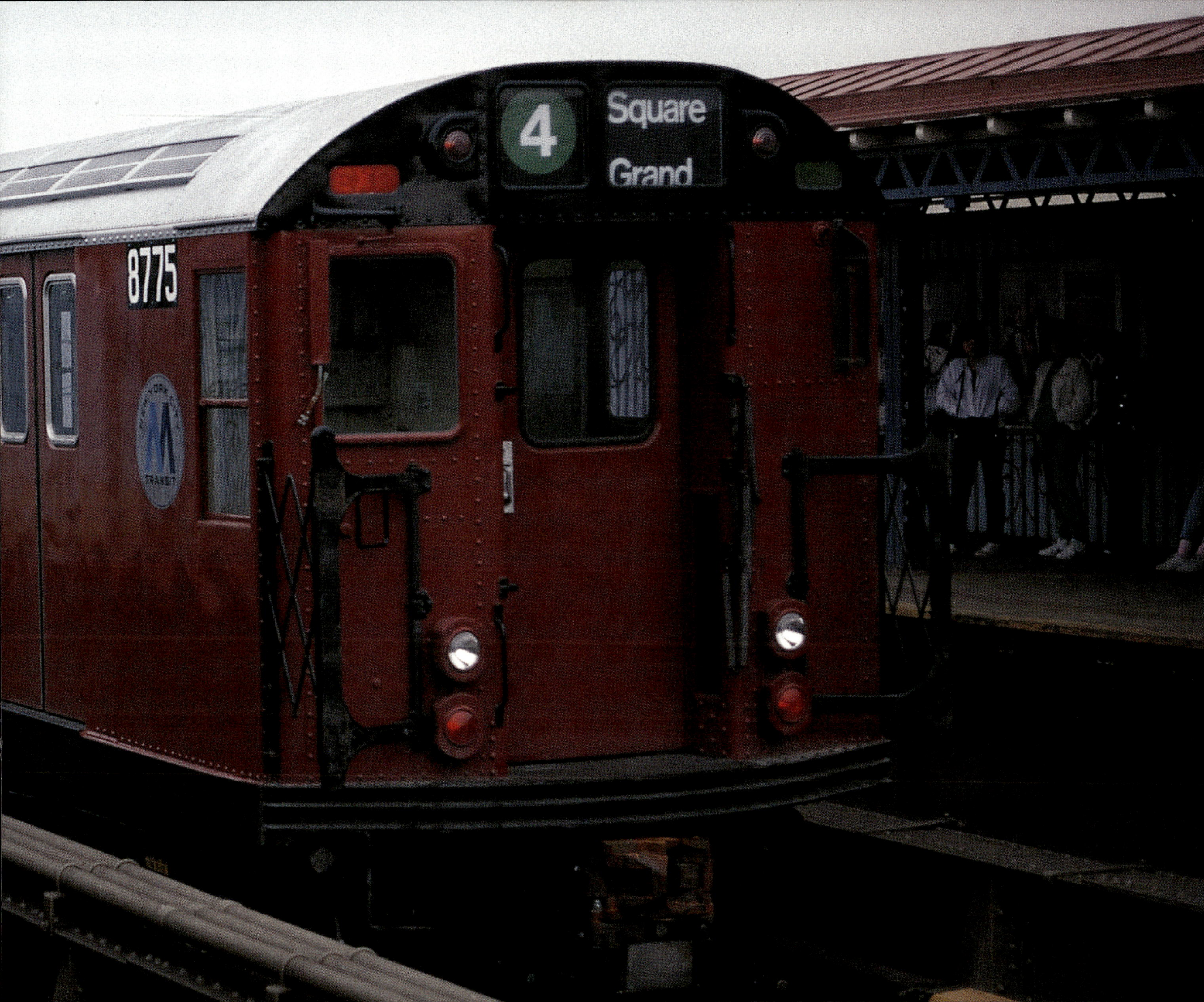

R-29s, White Plains Rd. line, 225th St., Bronx, 1986

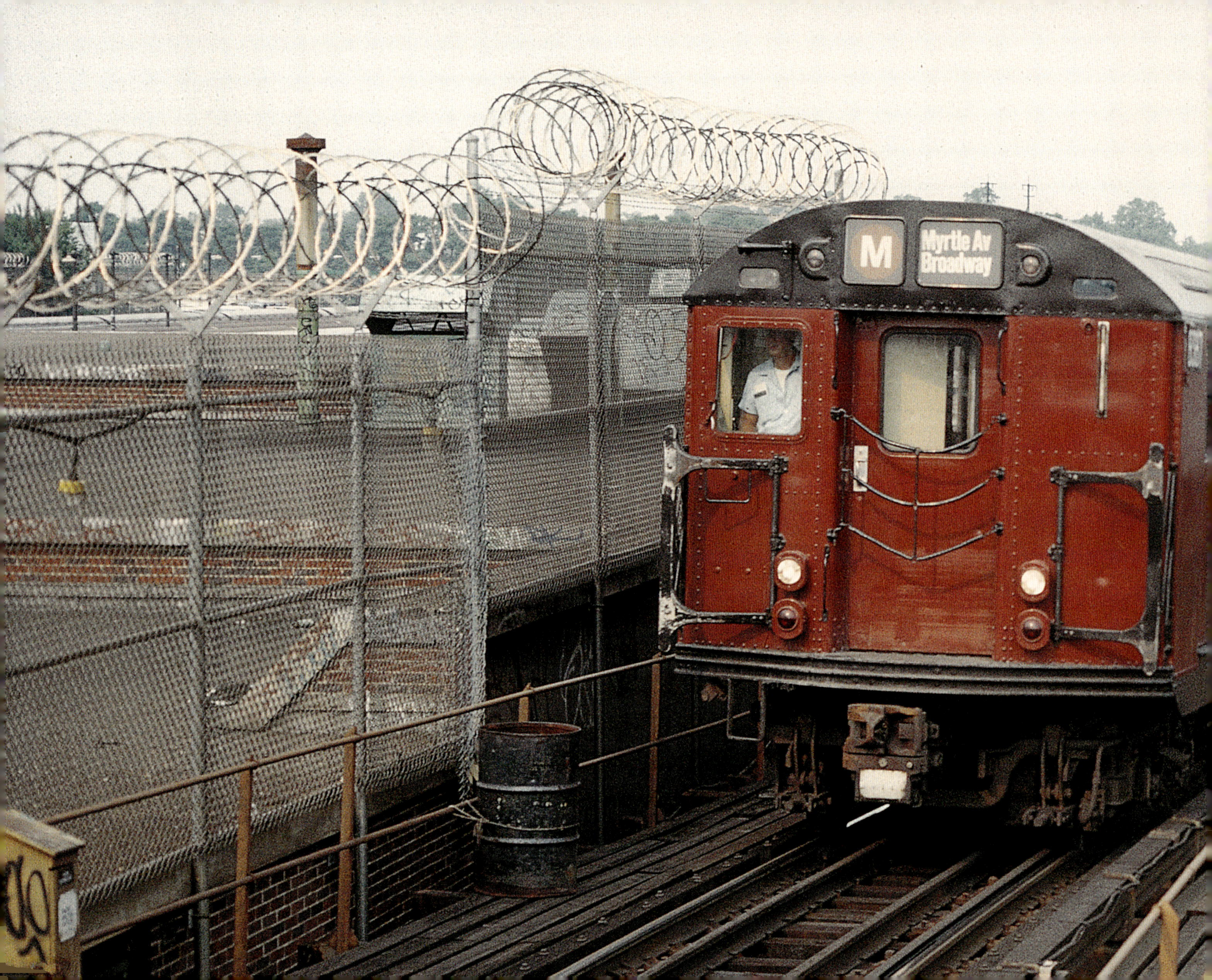
M
Myrtle Av
Broadway

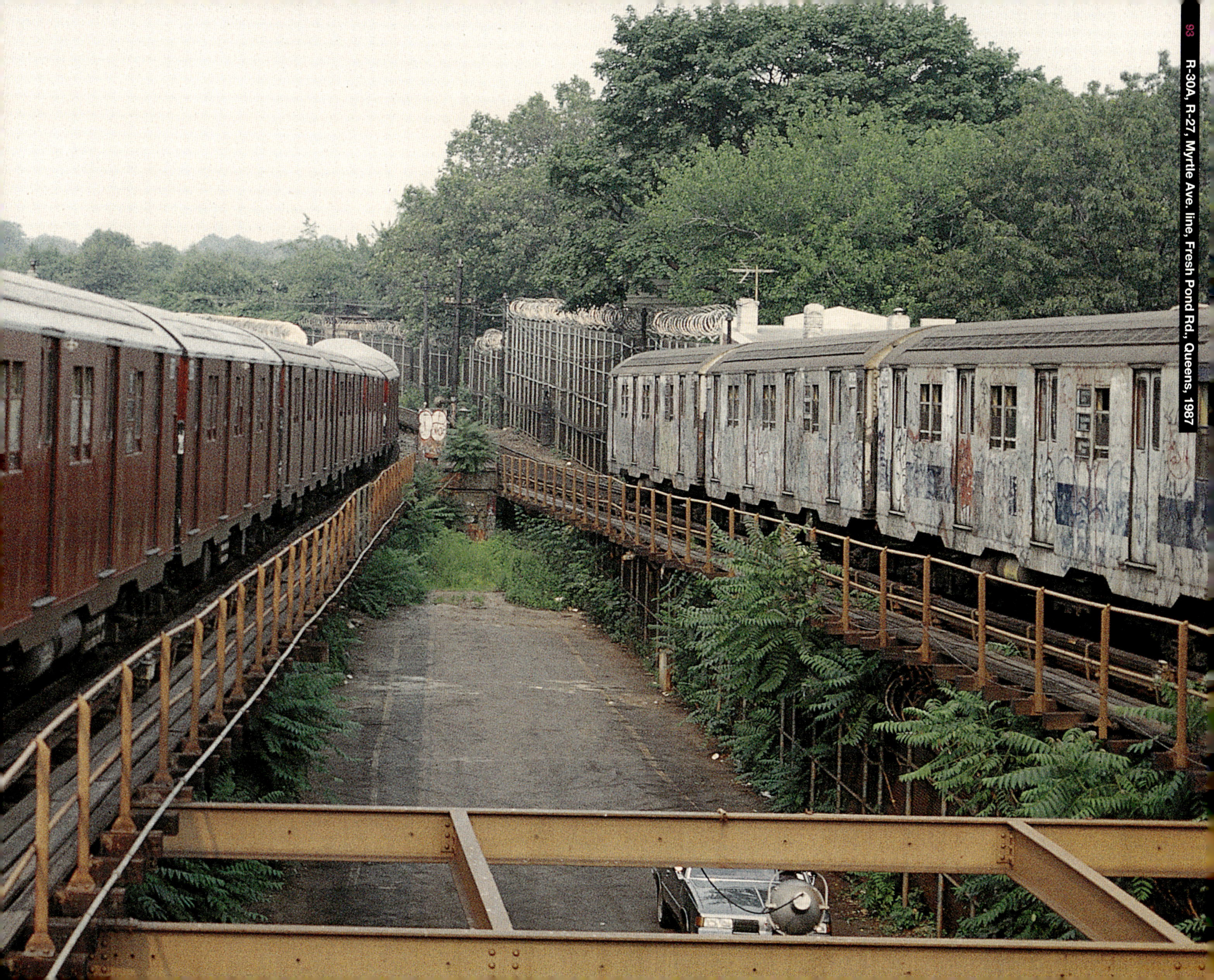

R-30A, R-27, Myrtle Ave. line, Fresh Pond Rd., Queens, 1987

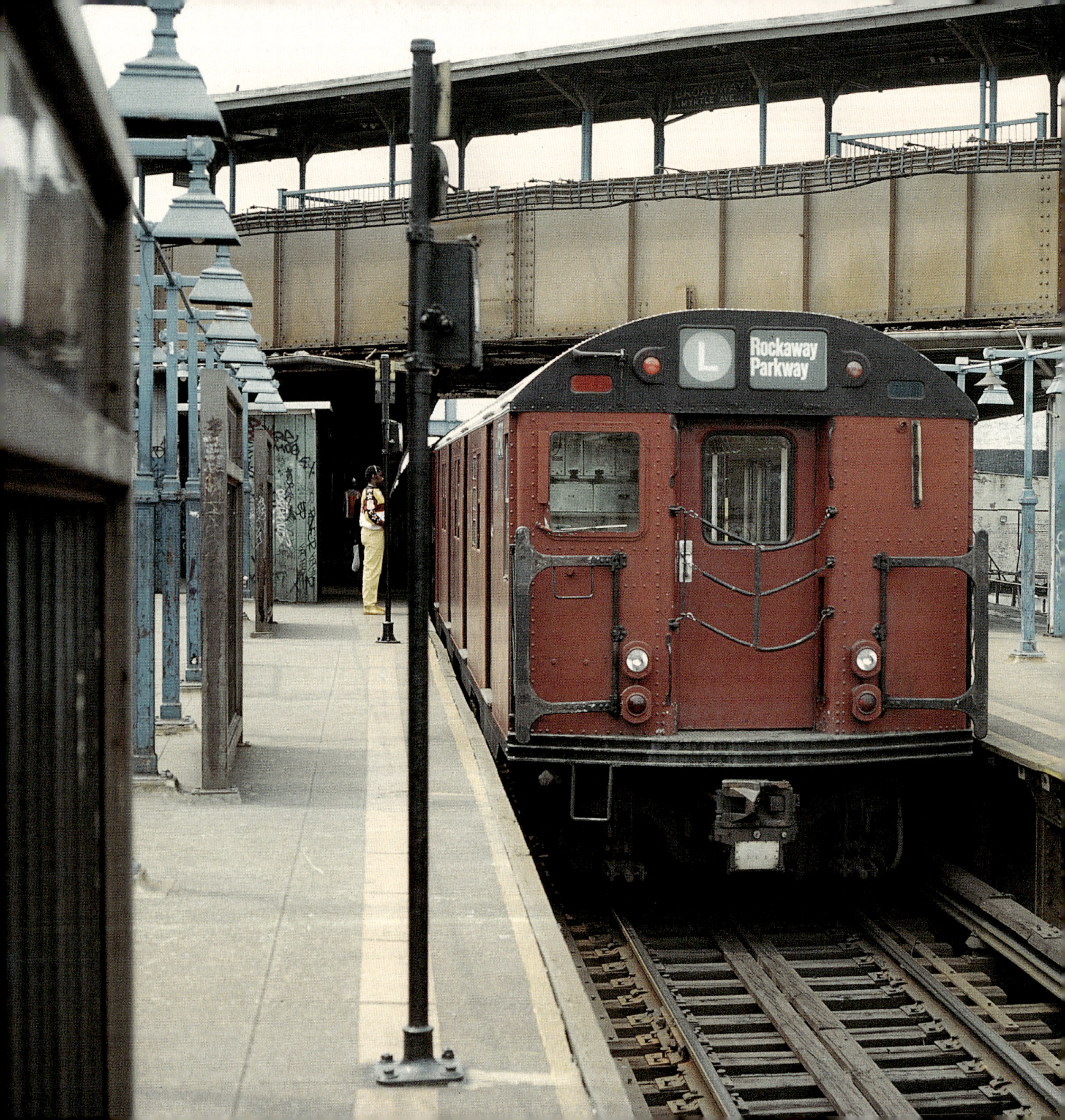
L
Rockaway Parkway

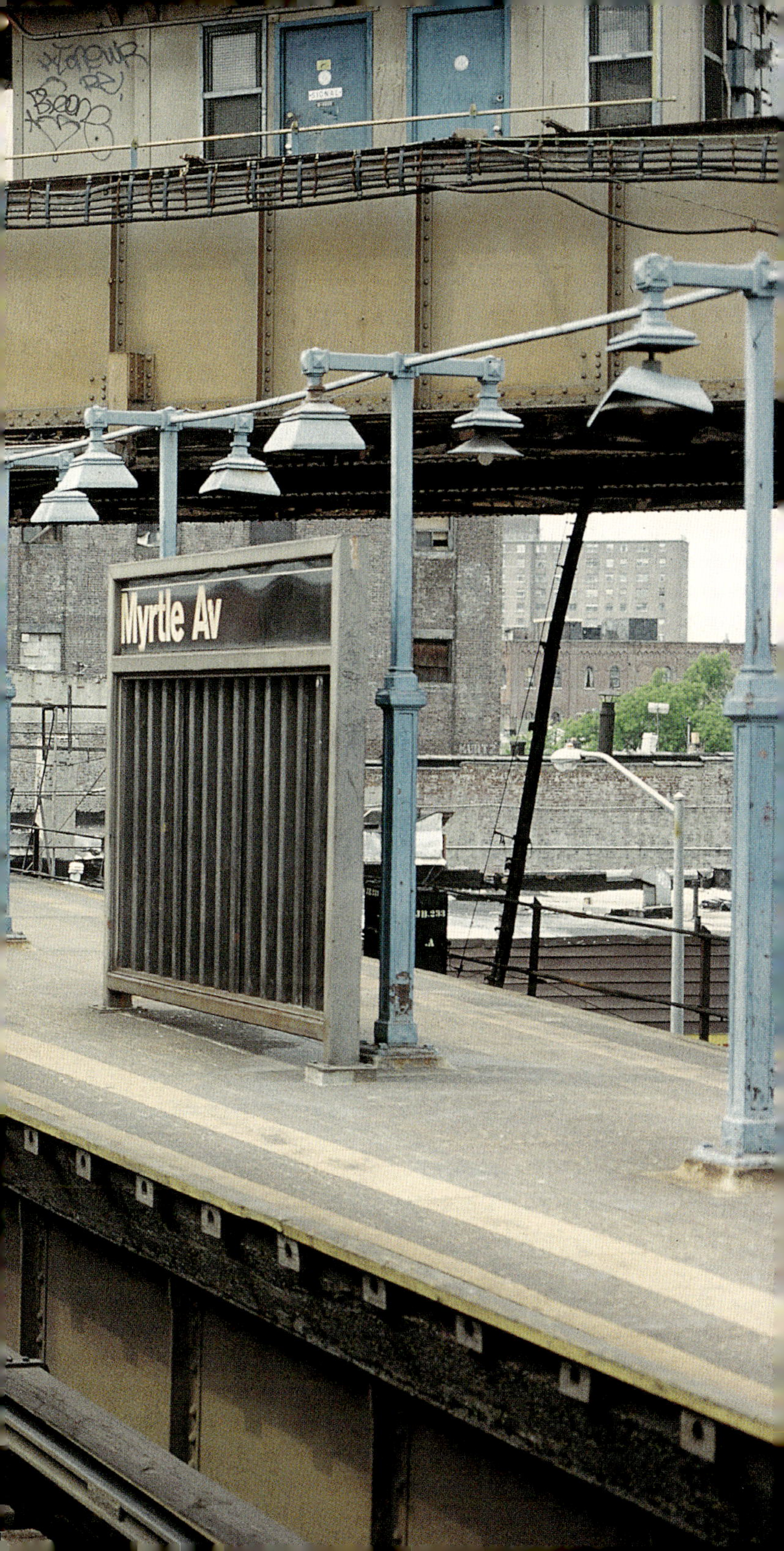
SIGNAL
Myrtle Av

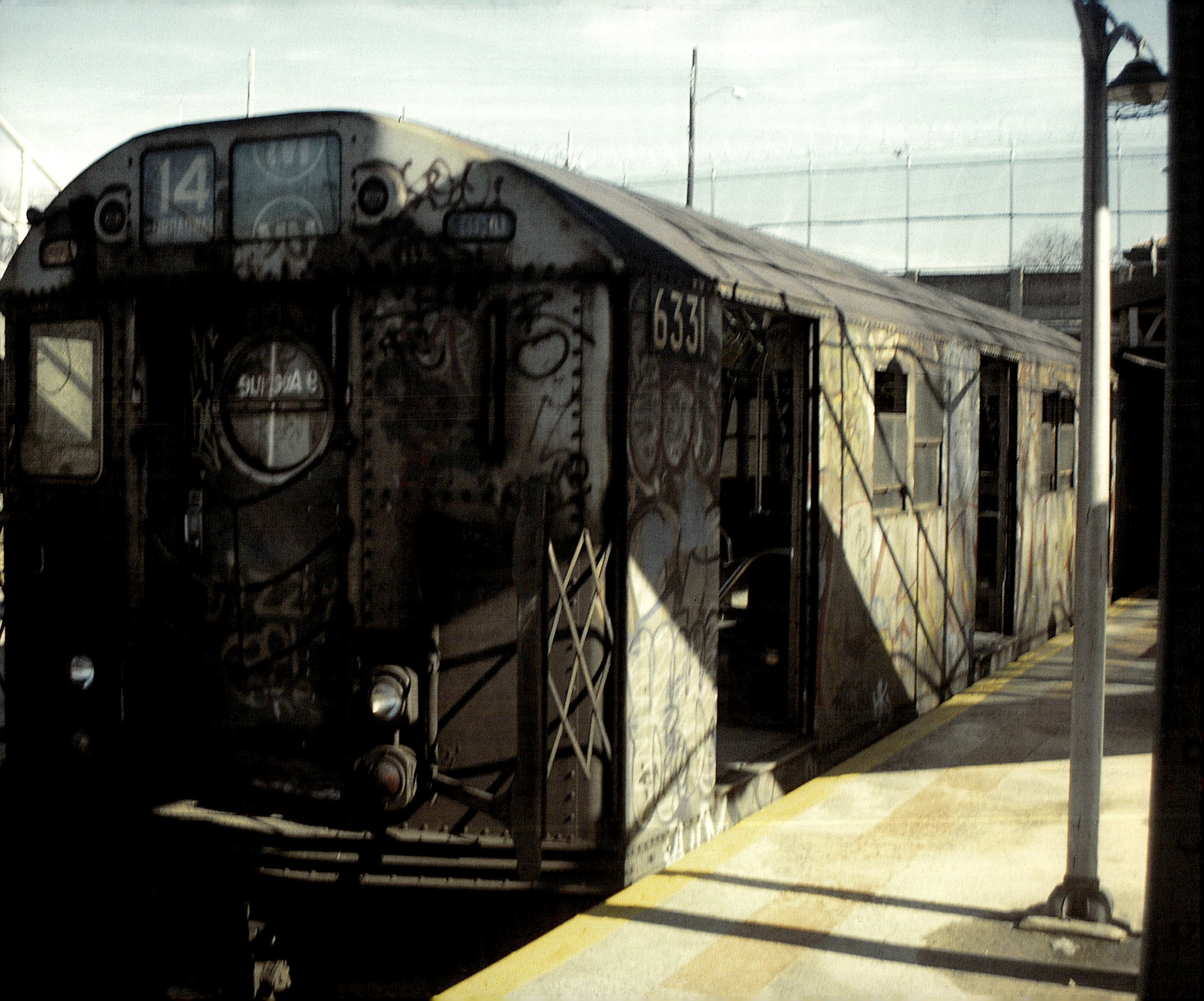

R-16, M, West End line, 9th Ave., Brooklyn, 1987

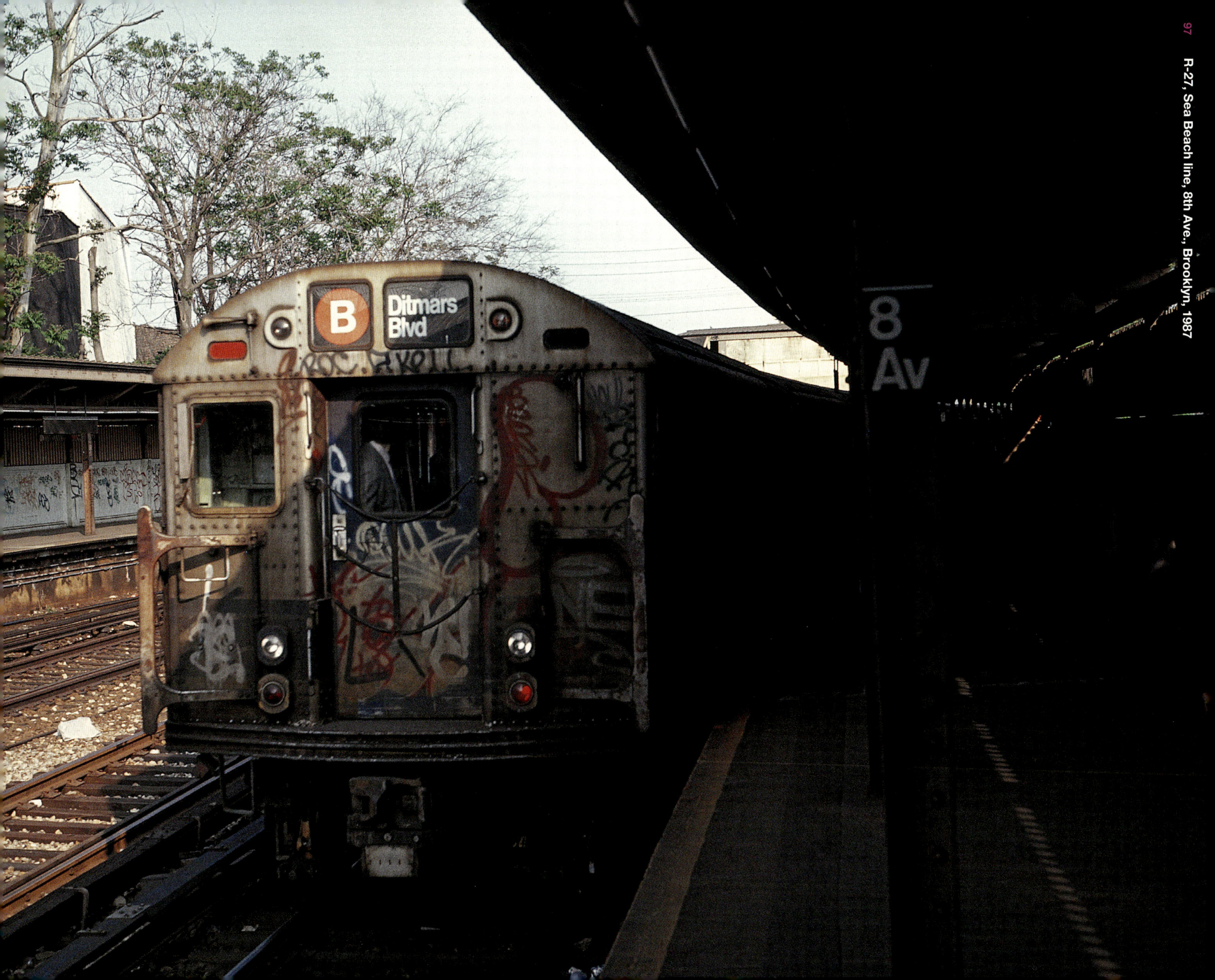

R-27, Sea Beach line, 8th Ave., Brooklyn, 1987

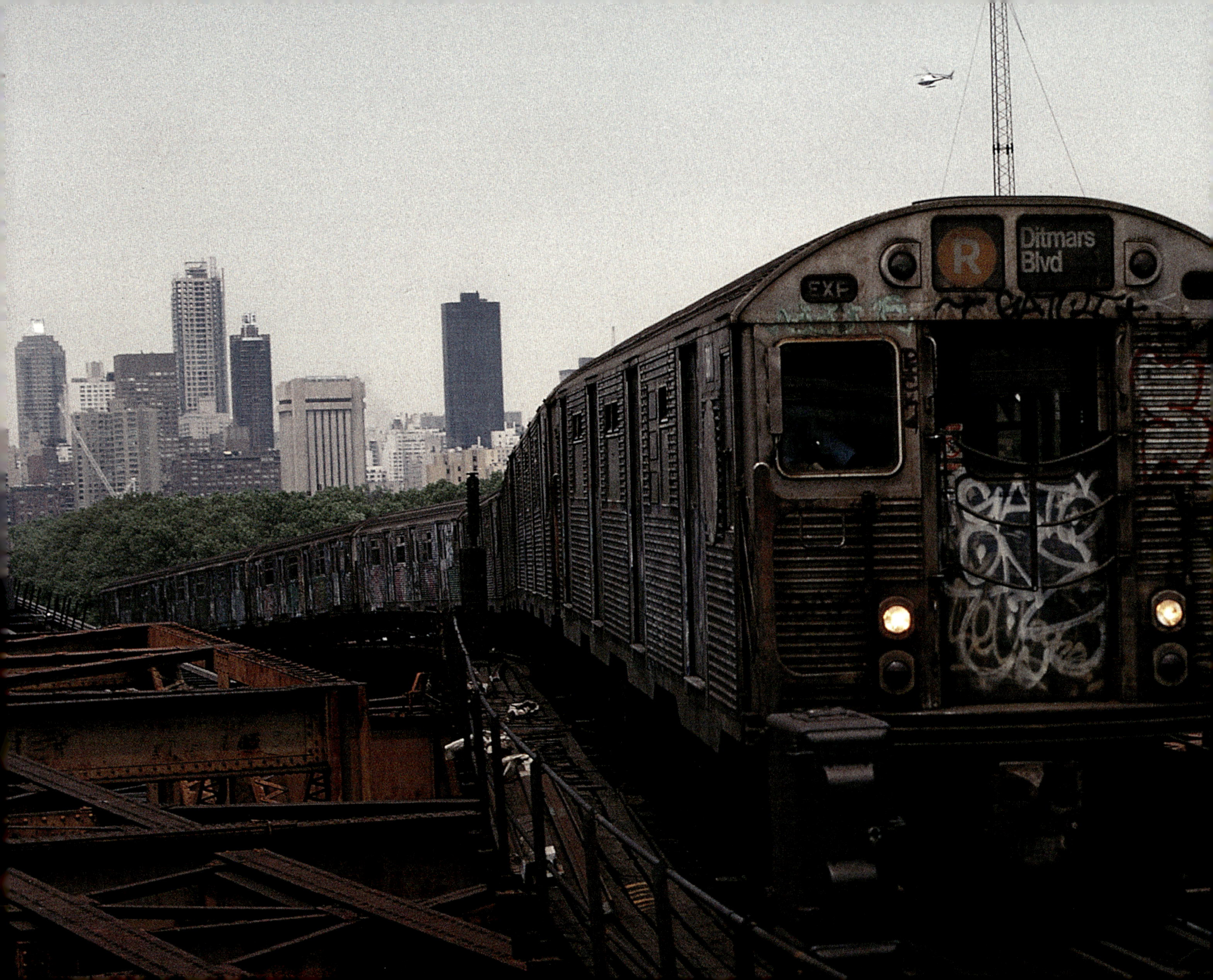
R
Ditmars
Blvd
EXP

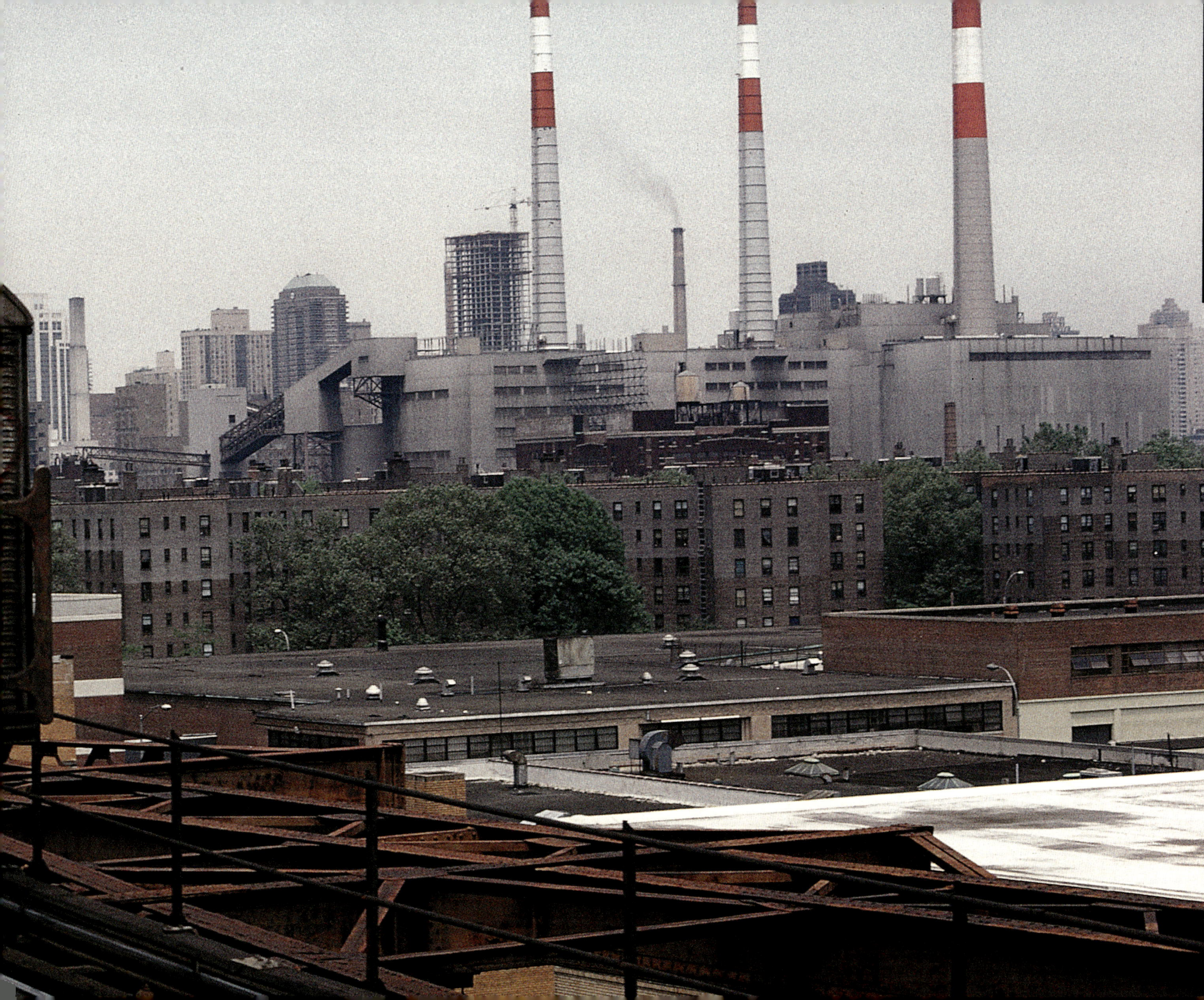

R-32s, R line, Queensboro Plaza, 1987

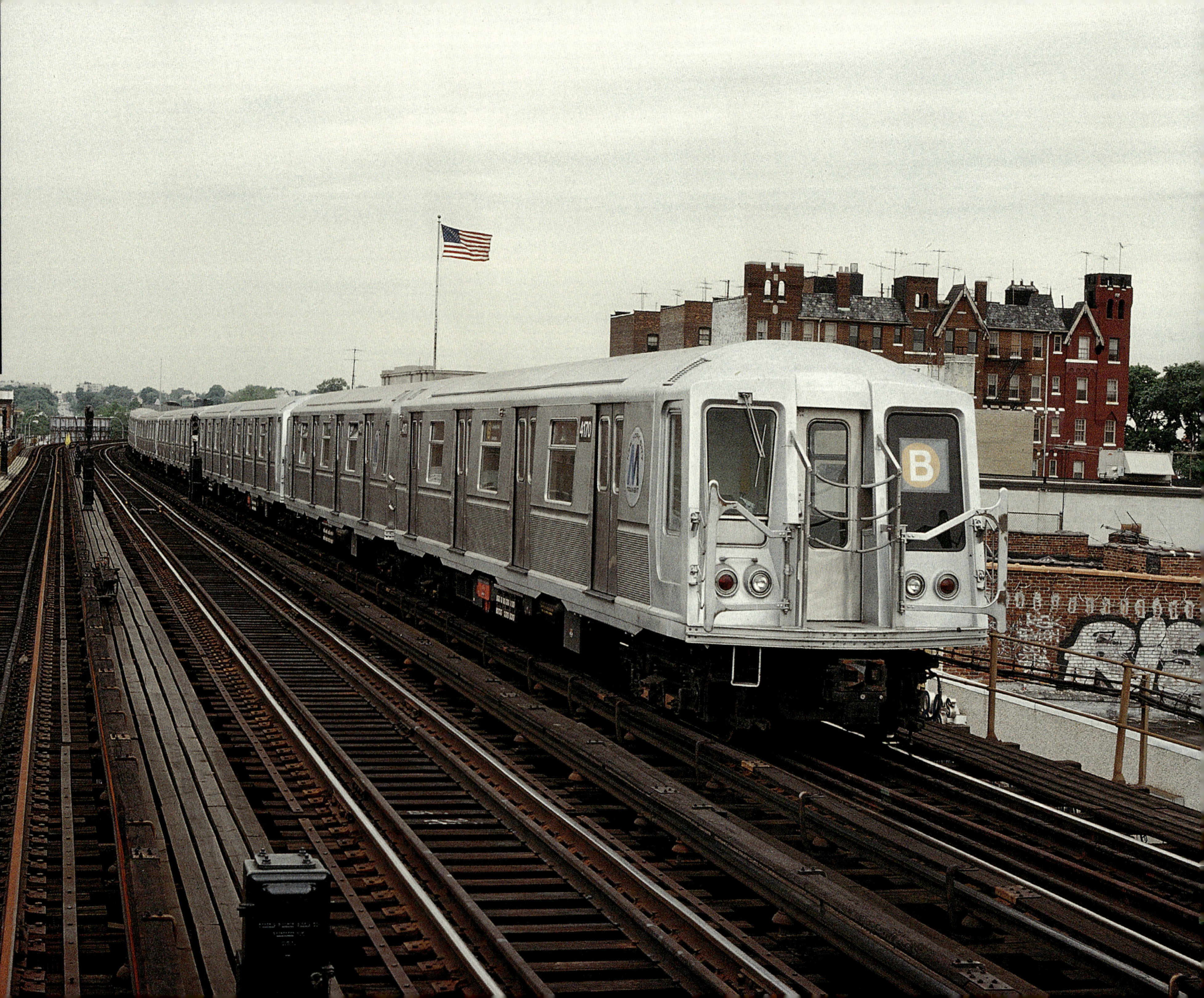

R-40s, B, West End line, 20th Ave., Brooklyn, 1988

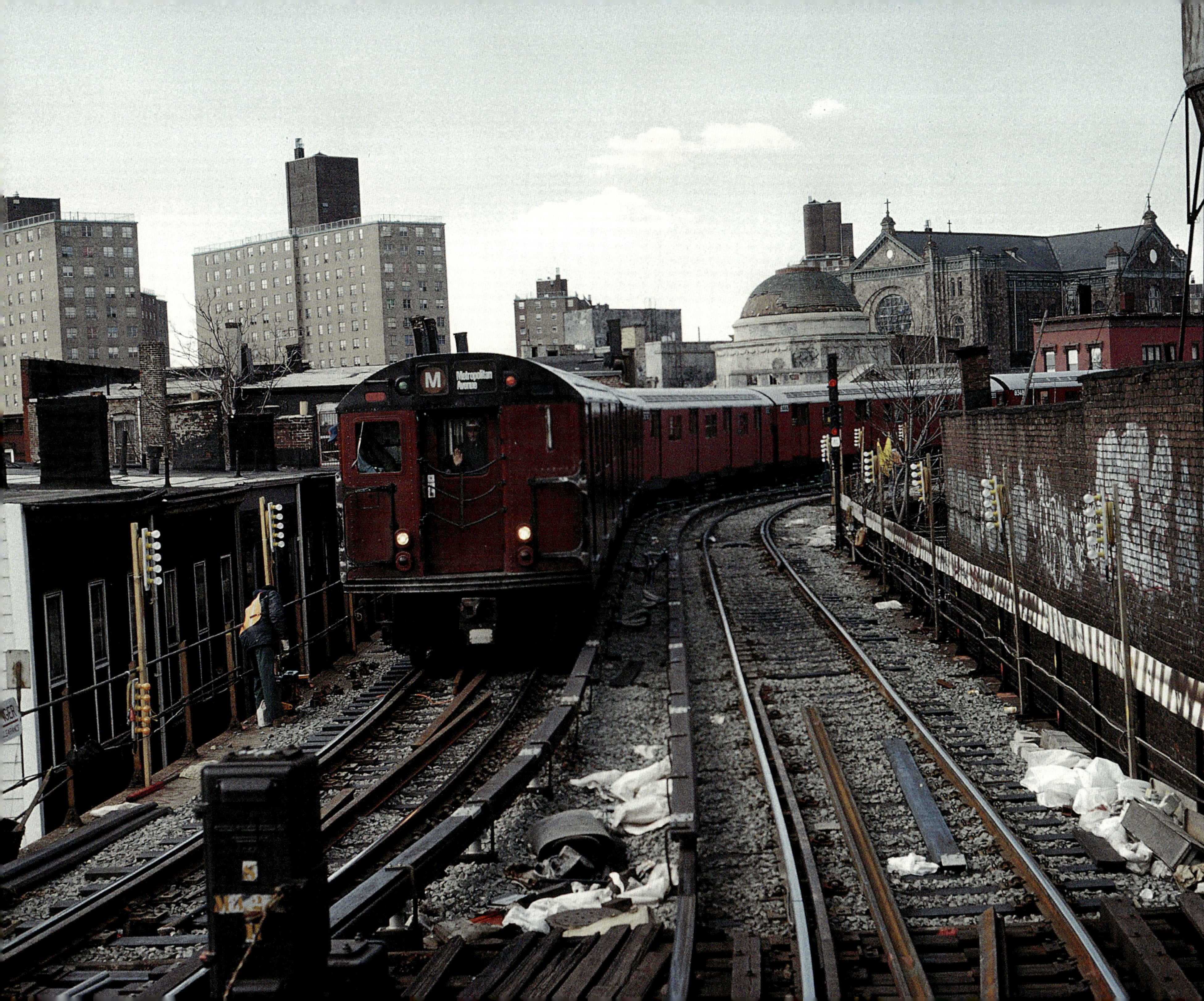

R-30s, Myrtle Ave. line, near Central Ave., Brooklyn, 1988

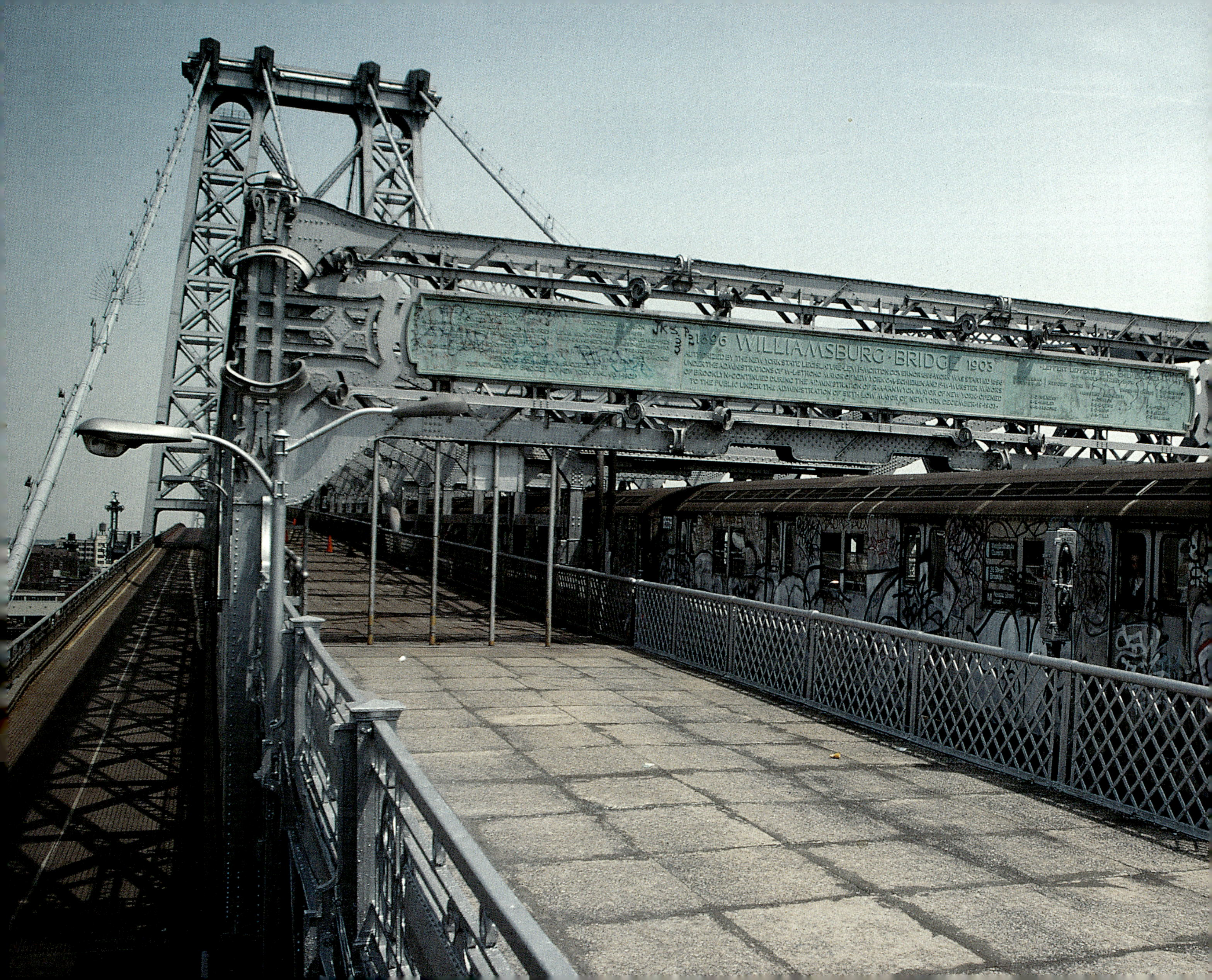
WILLIAMSBURG · BRIDGE 1903

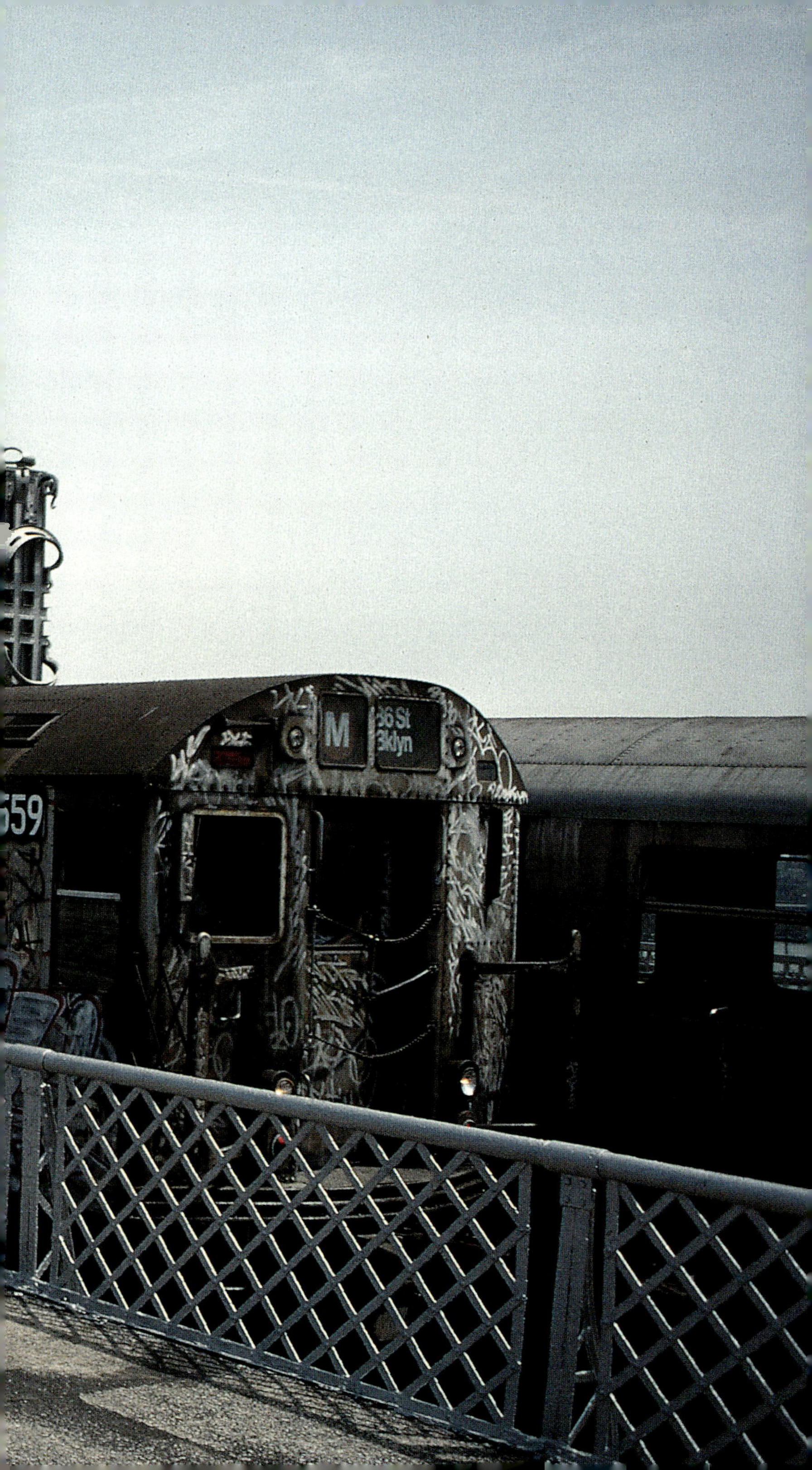
M
36 St
Bklyn
659

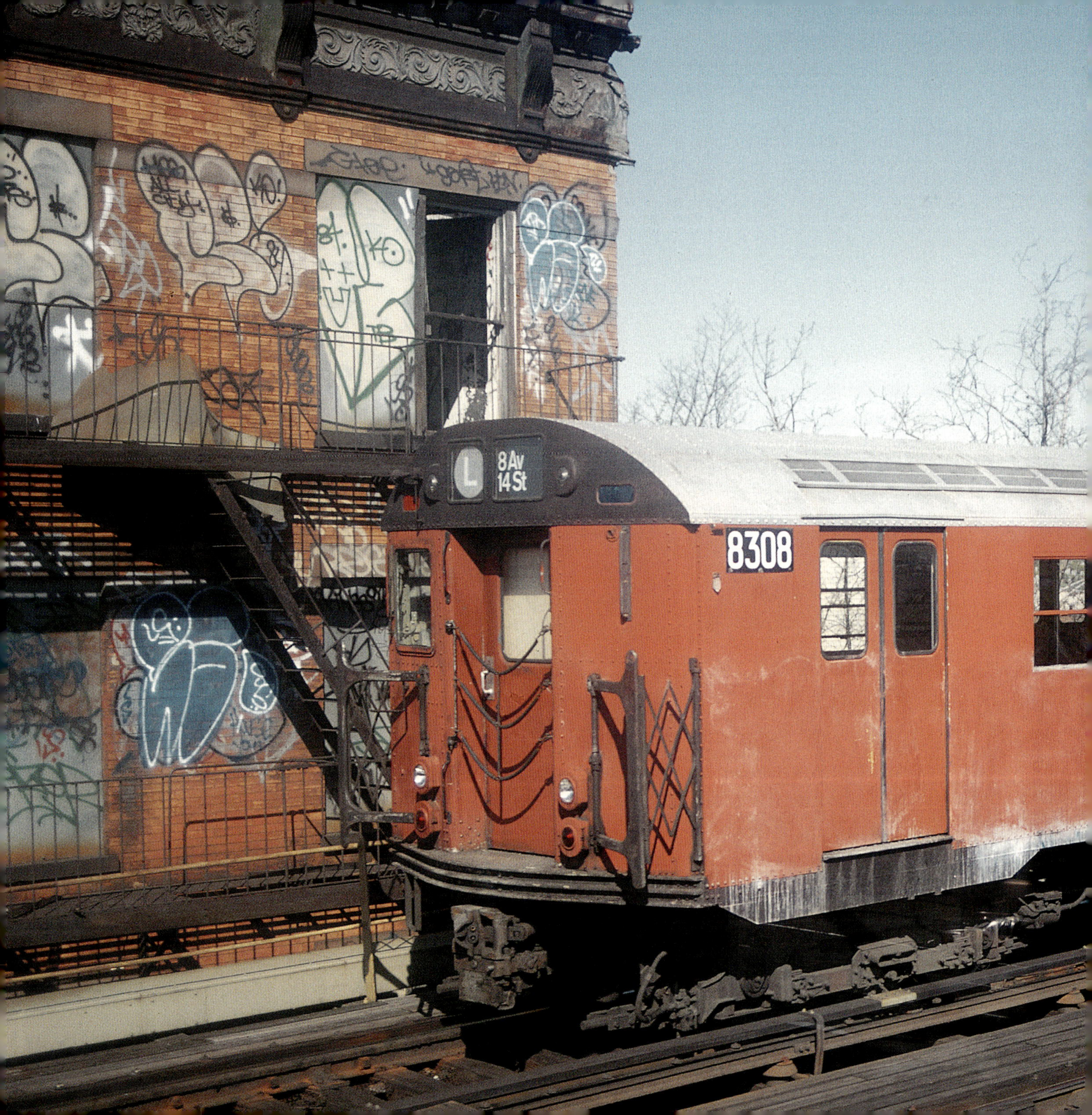
L
8 Av
14 St
8308

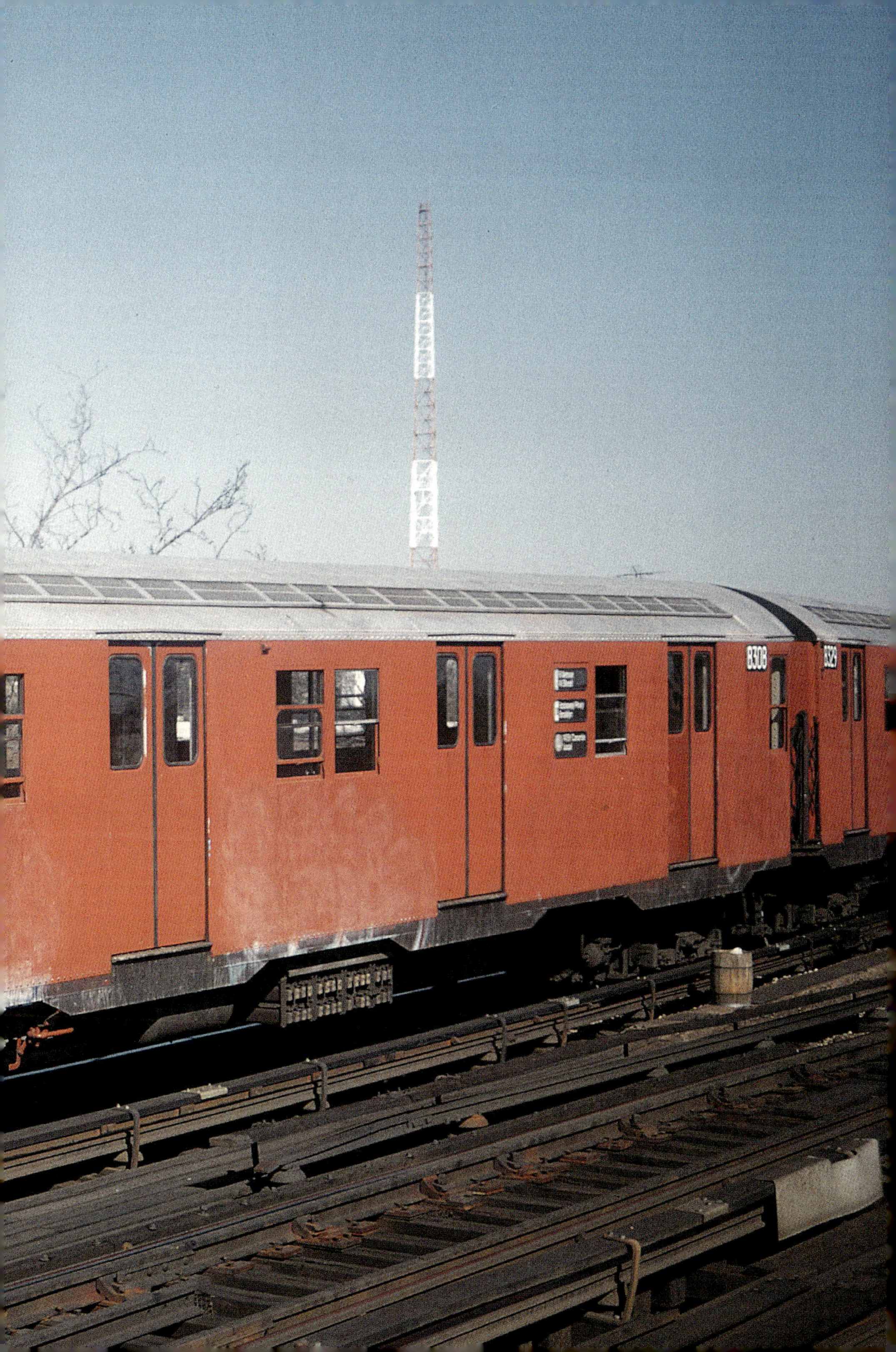
8308

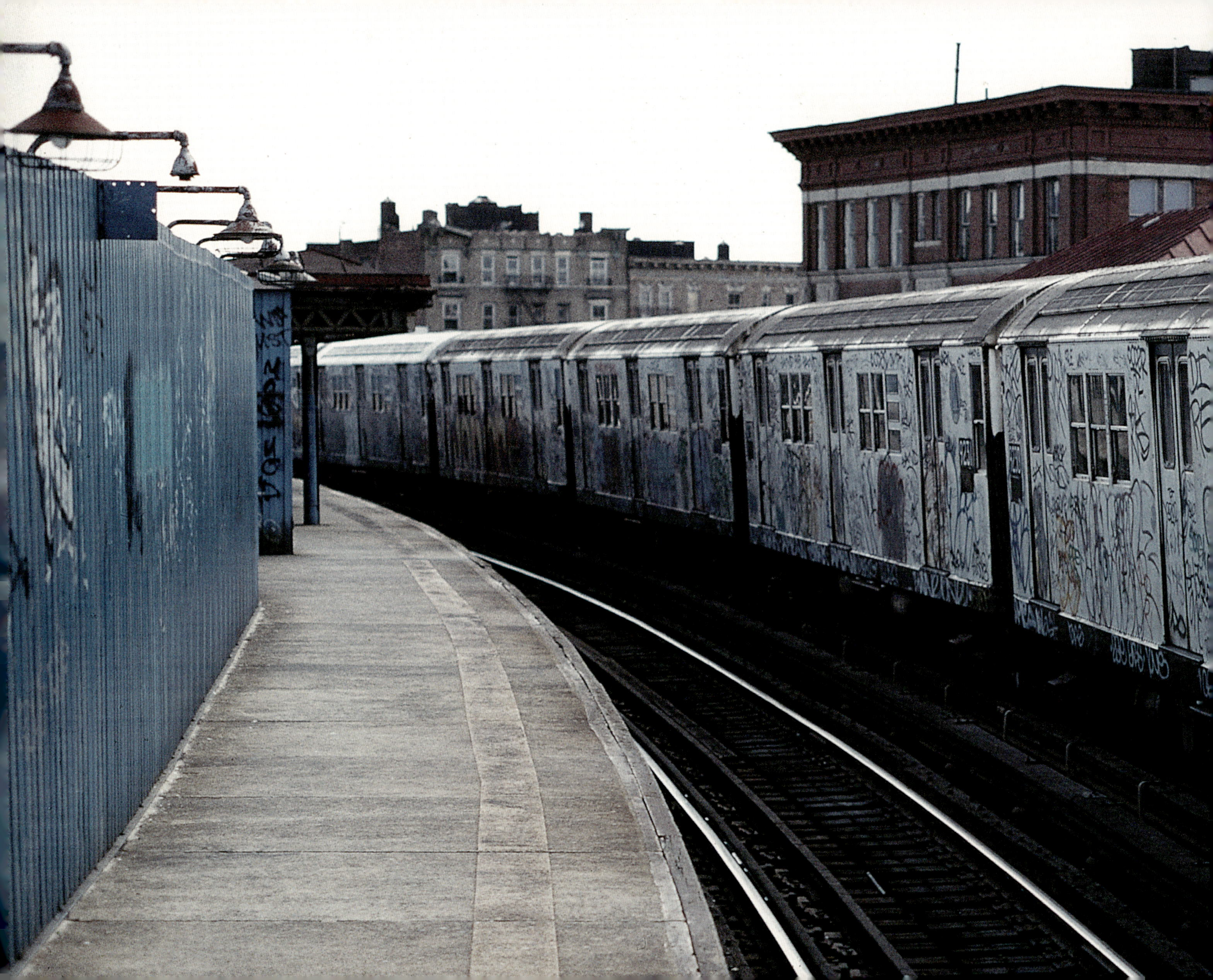

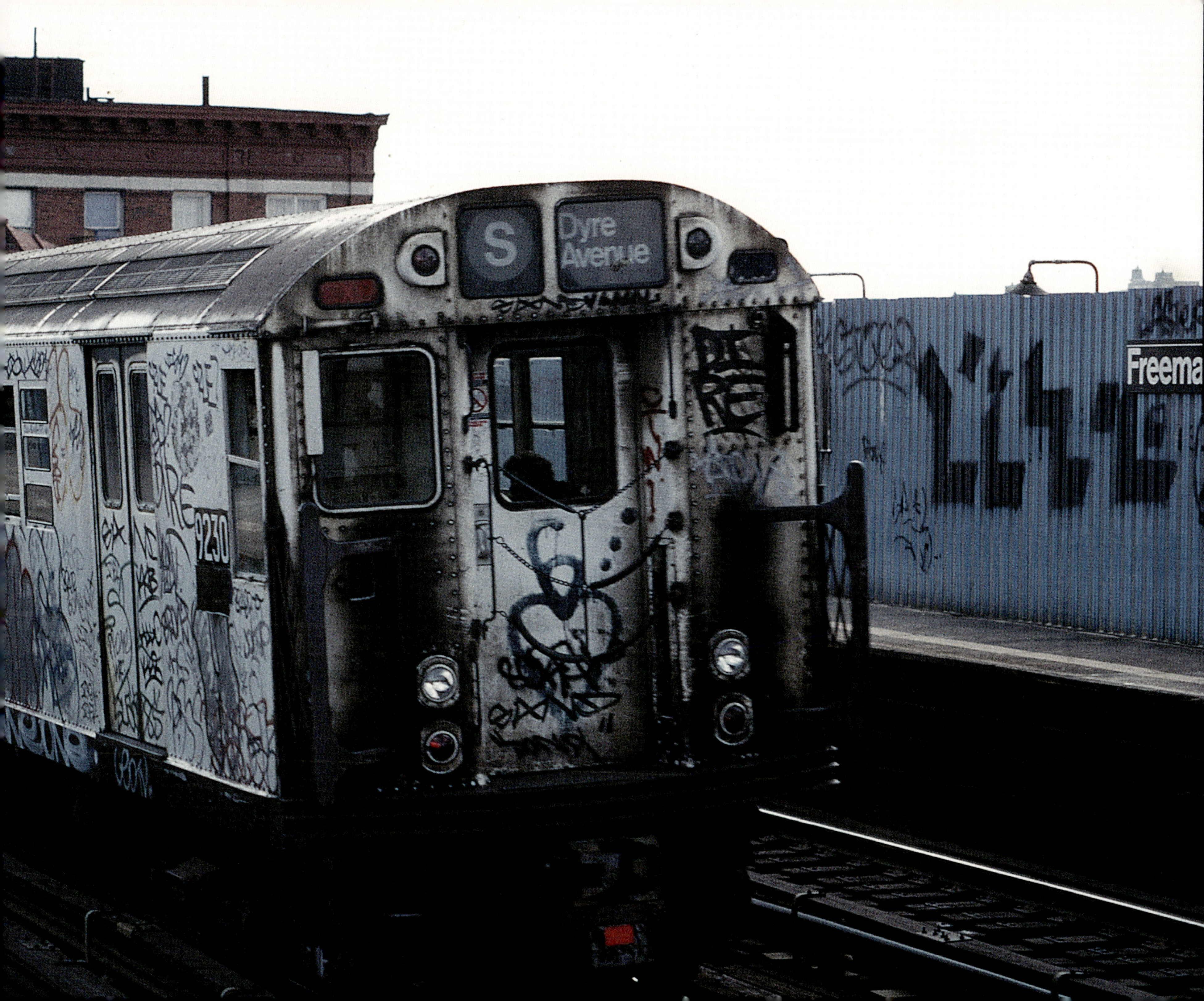

R-33s, No. 5 West Farms line, Freeman St., Bronx, 1988

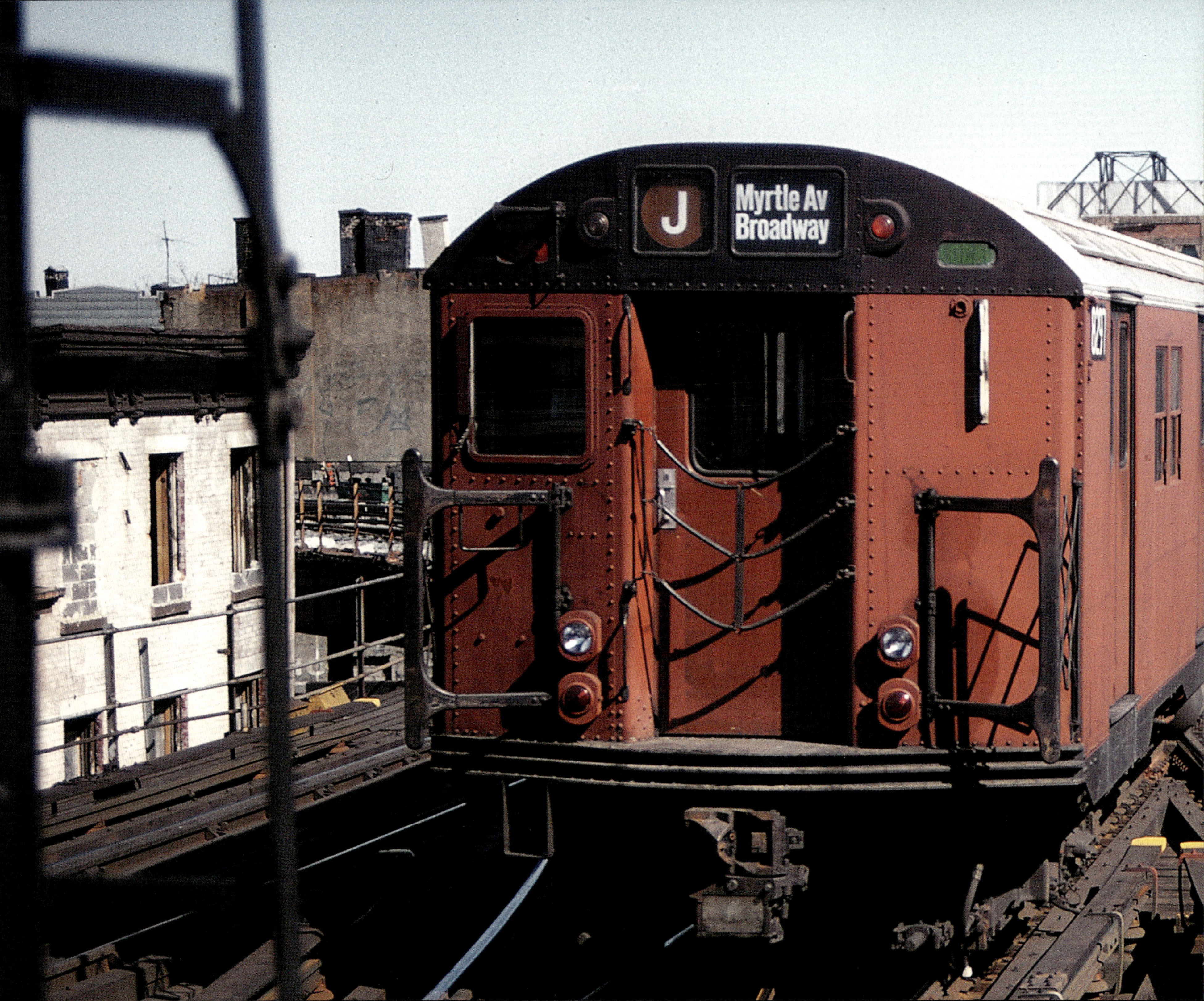
J
Myrtle Av
Broadway

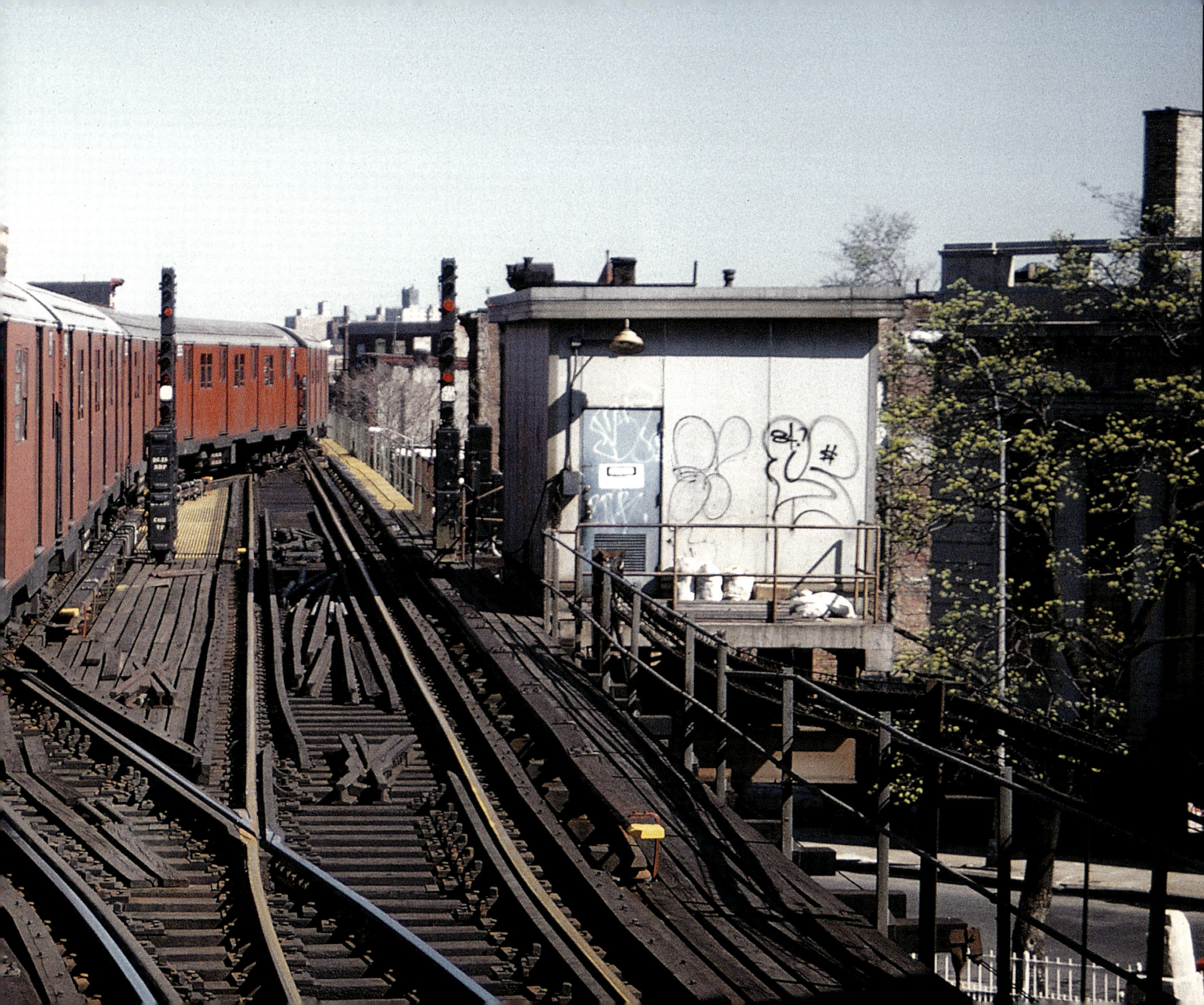

R-30, J line, Myrtle Ave.–Broadway, Brooklyn, 1988

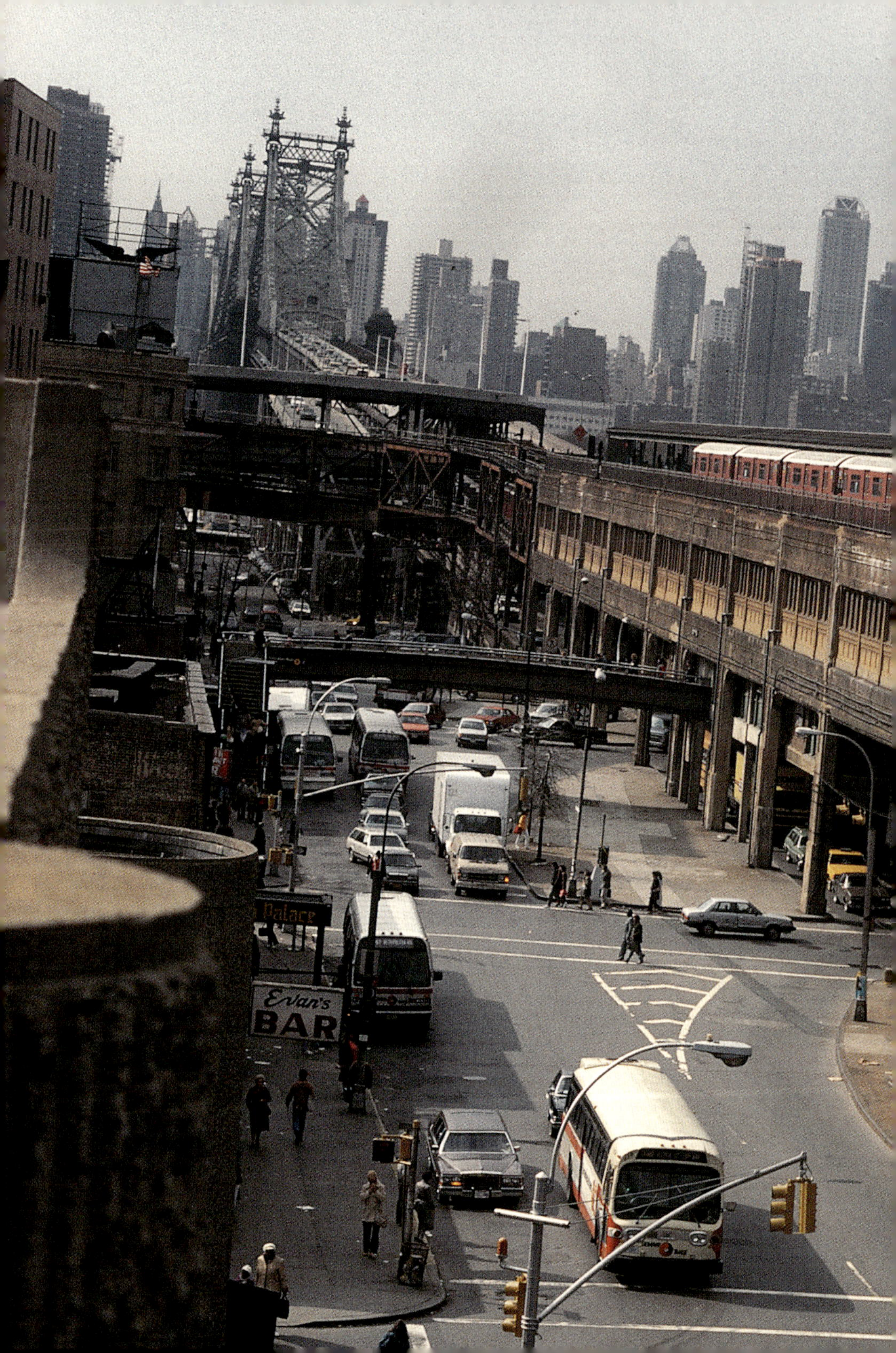
Palace
Evan's
BAR

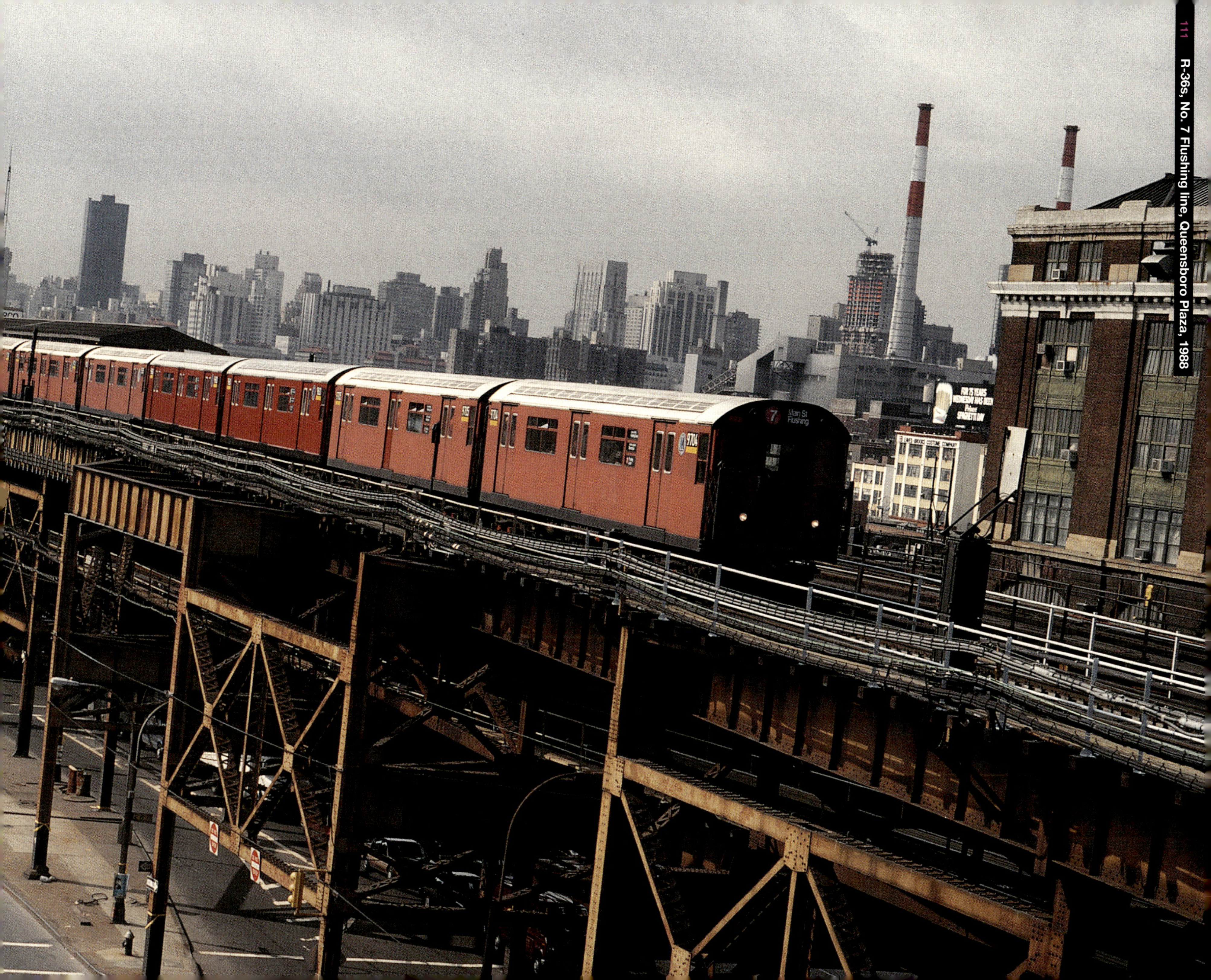

R-36s, No. 7 Flushing line, Queensboro Plaza, 1988

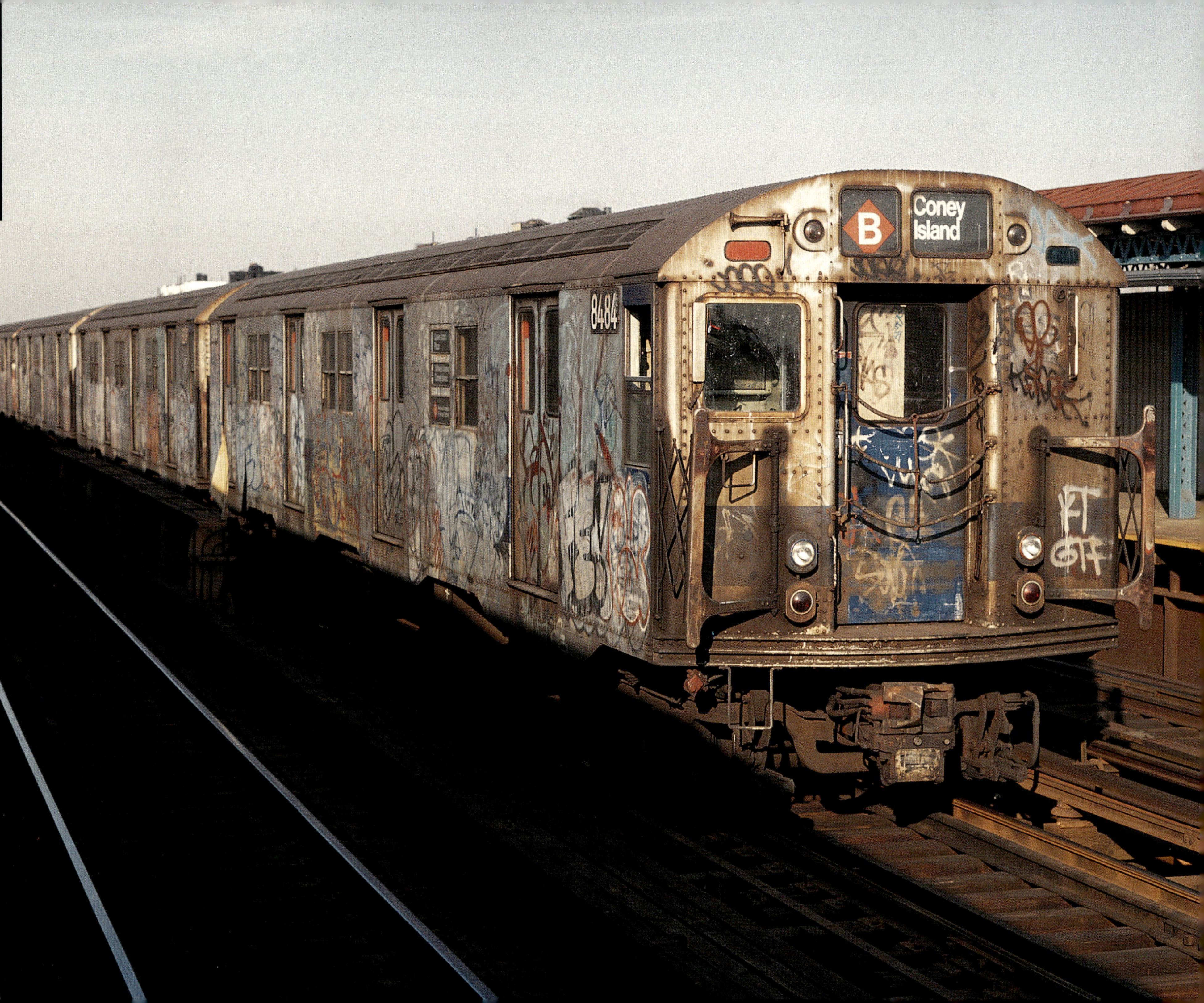

R-30, B line, lay-up, 1988

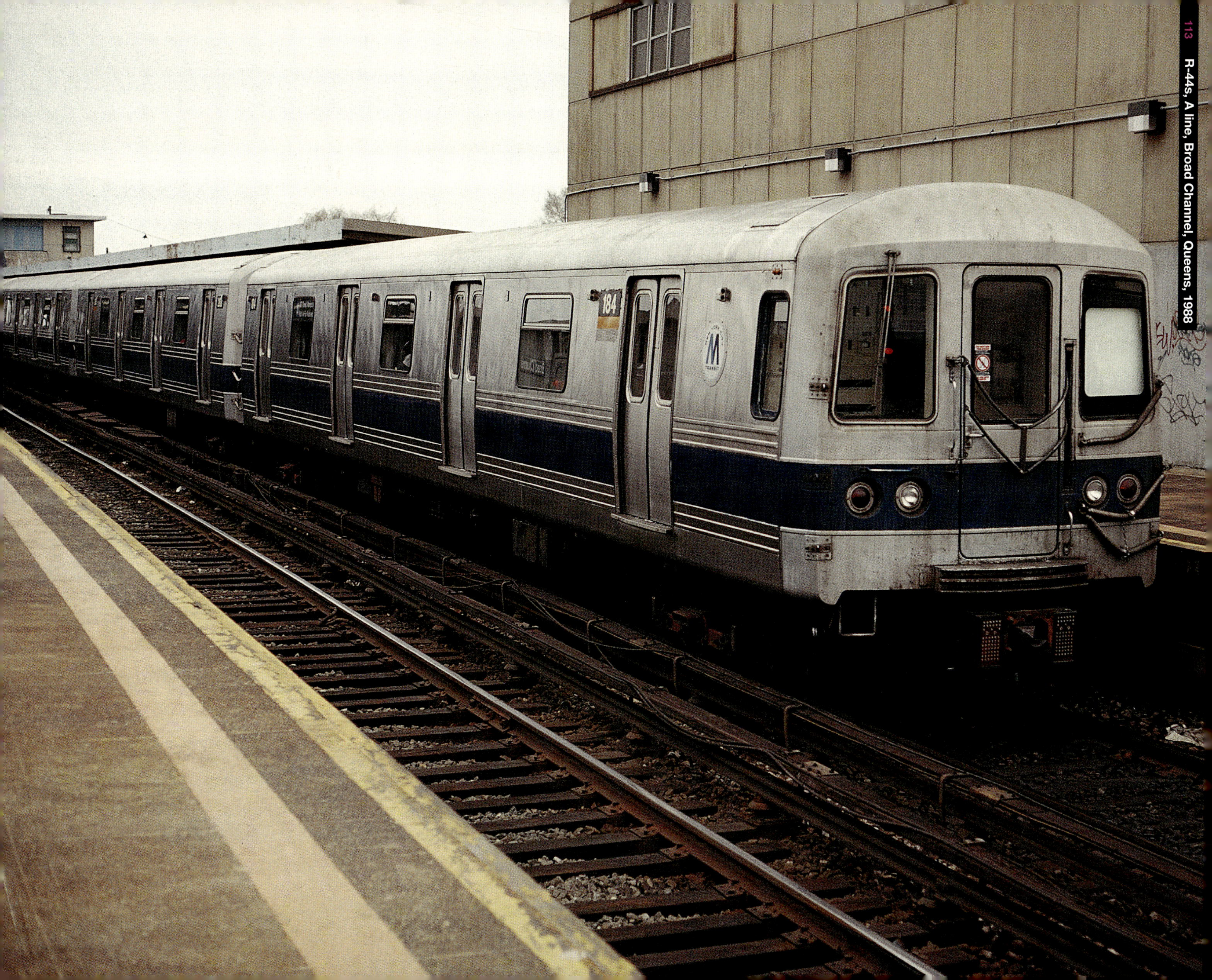

R-44s, A line, Broad Channel, Queens, 1988

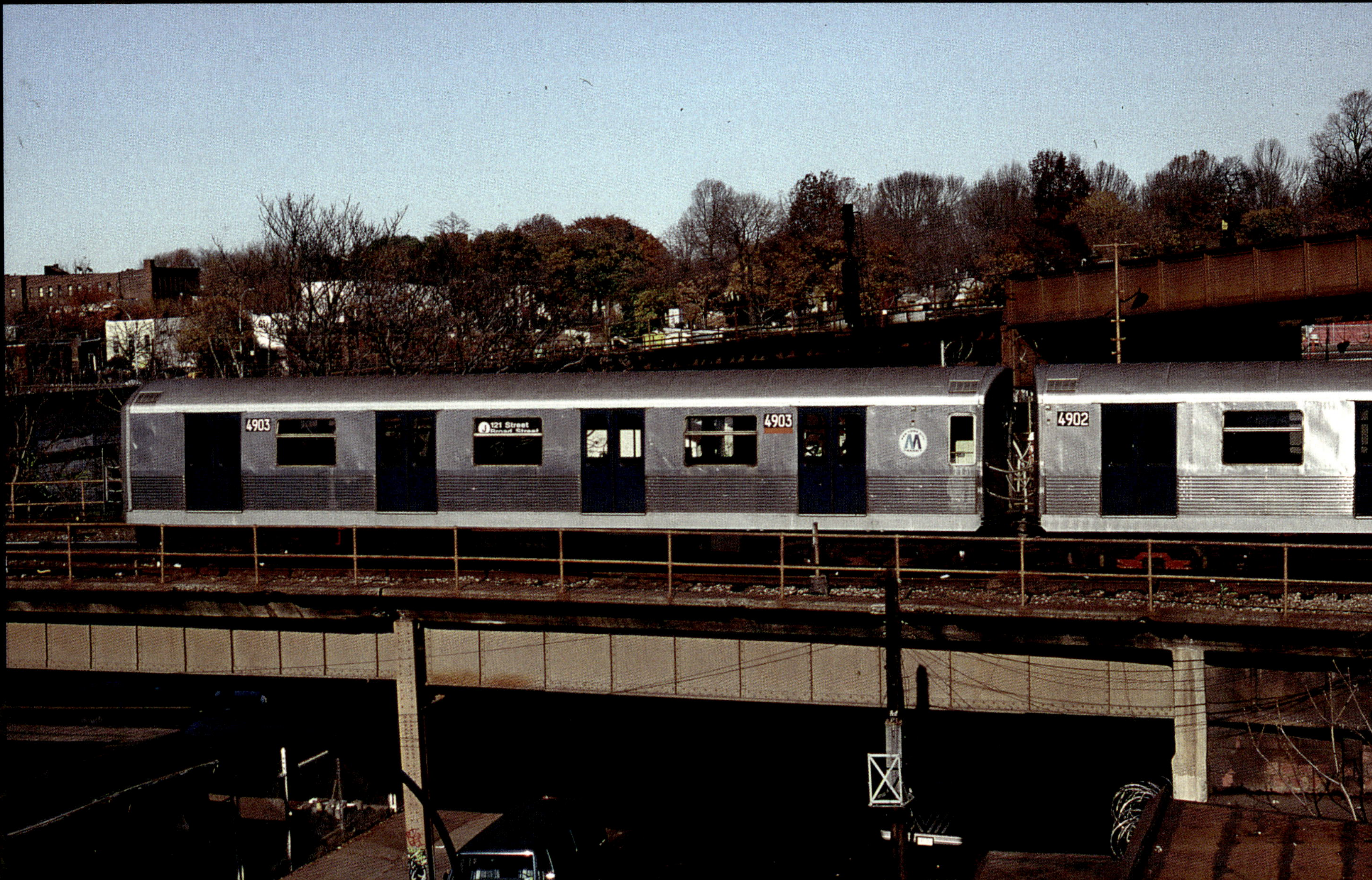

R-42, E. New York Yard lead track, Brooklyn,

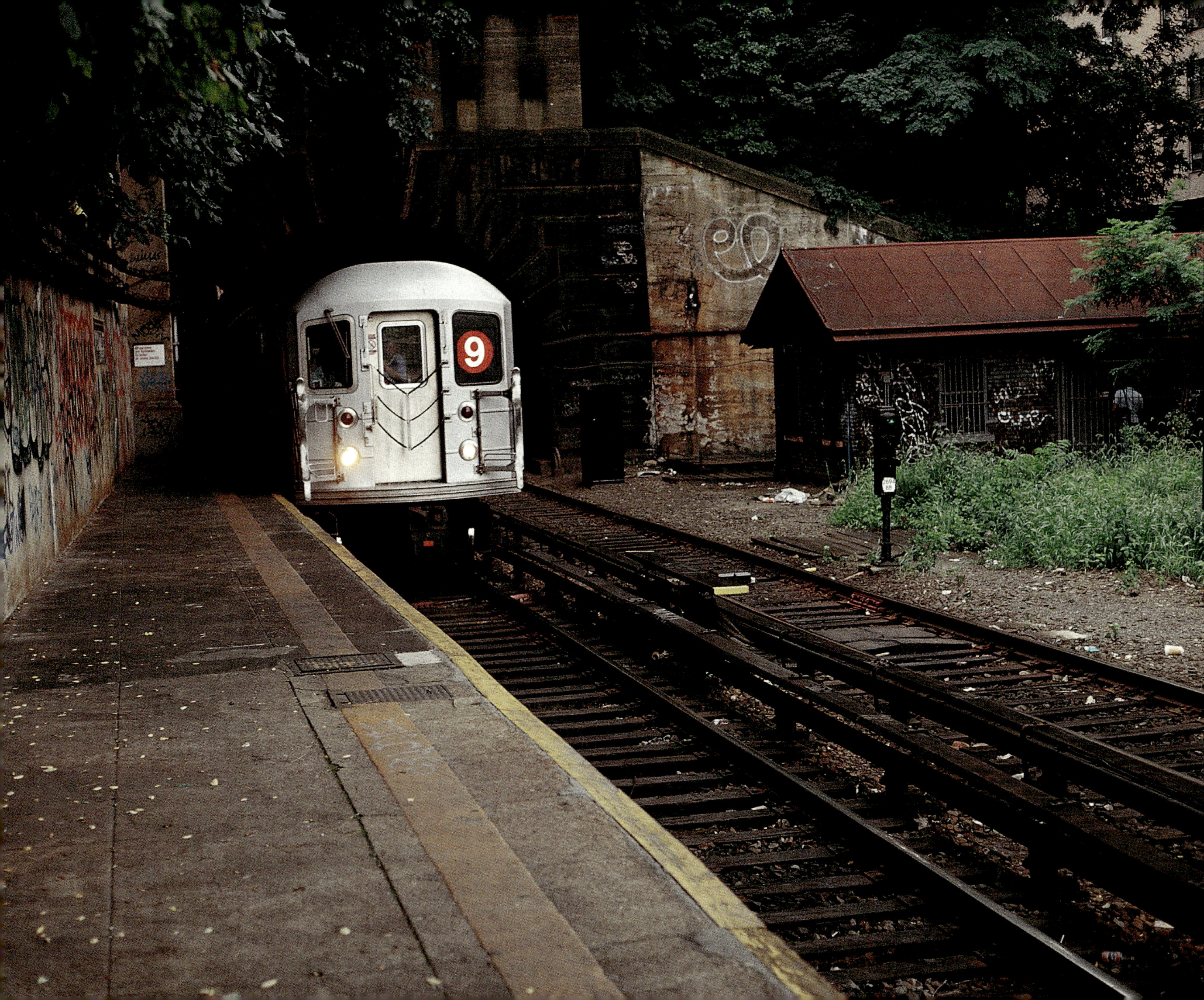

R-62As, No. 9 skip-stop, Broadway line, Dyckman St., Manhattan, 1989

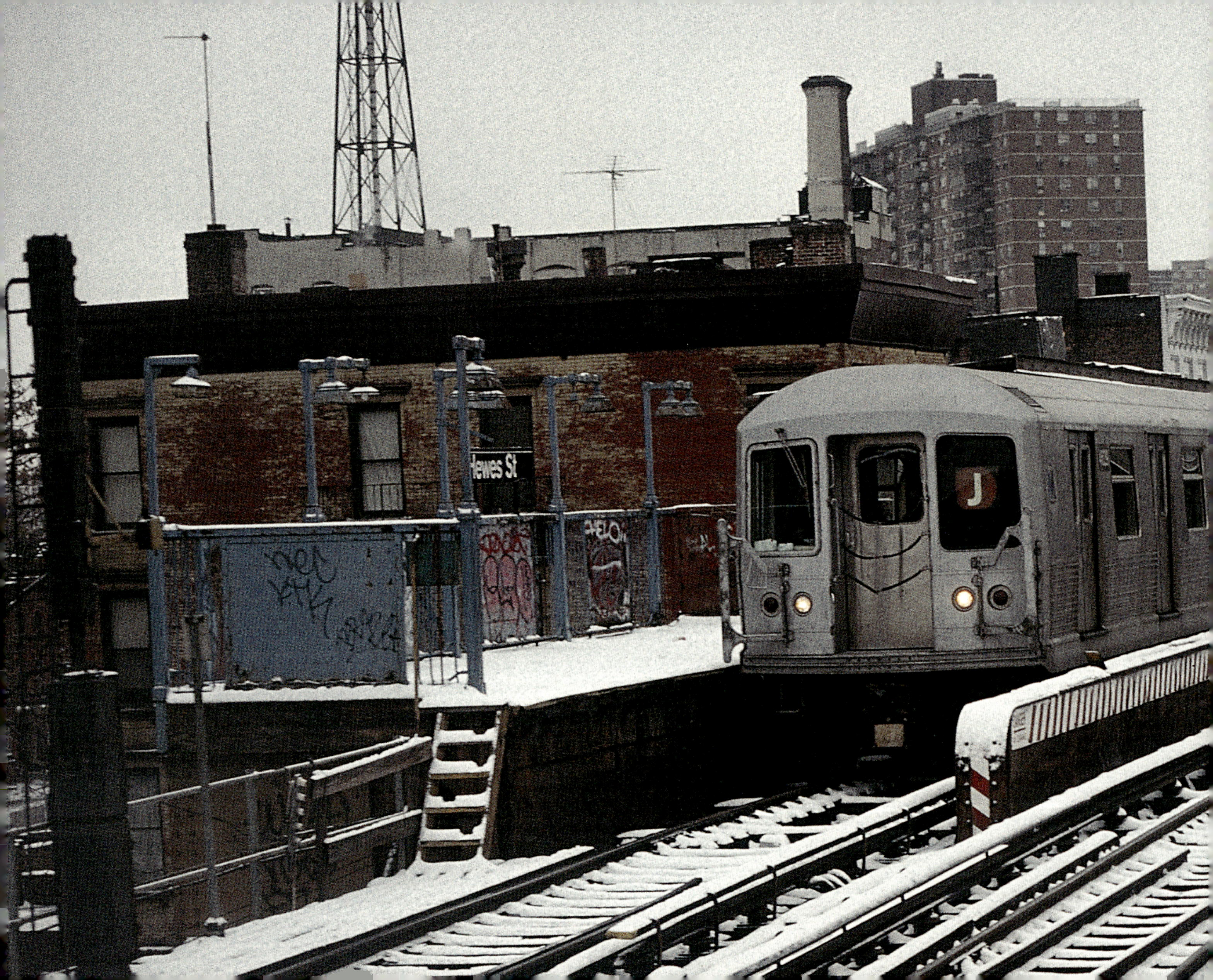
Hewes St
J

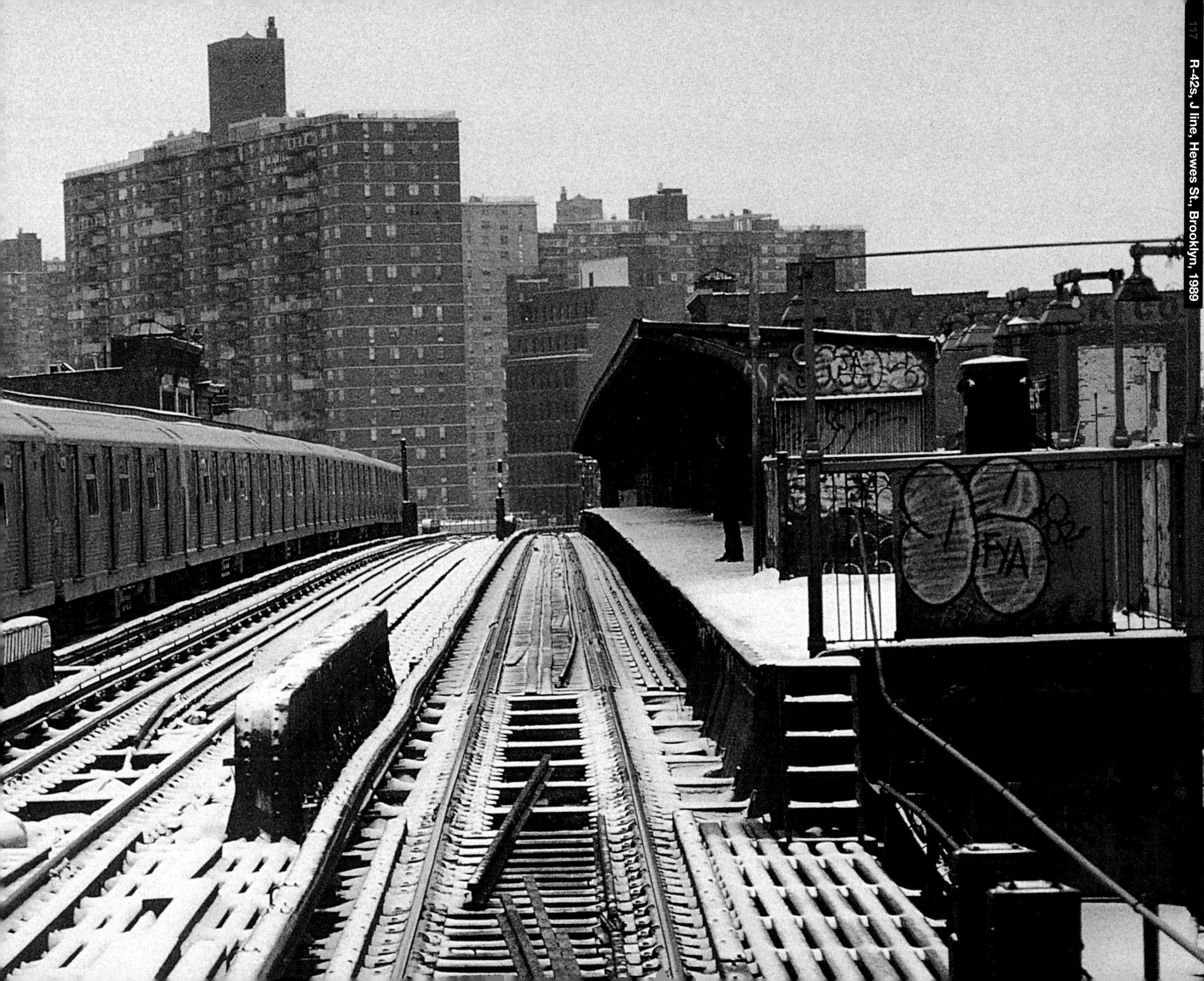

R-42s, J line, Hewes St., Brooklyn, 1989

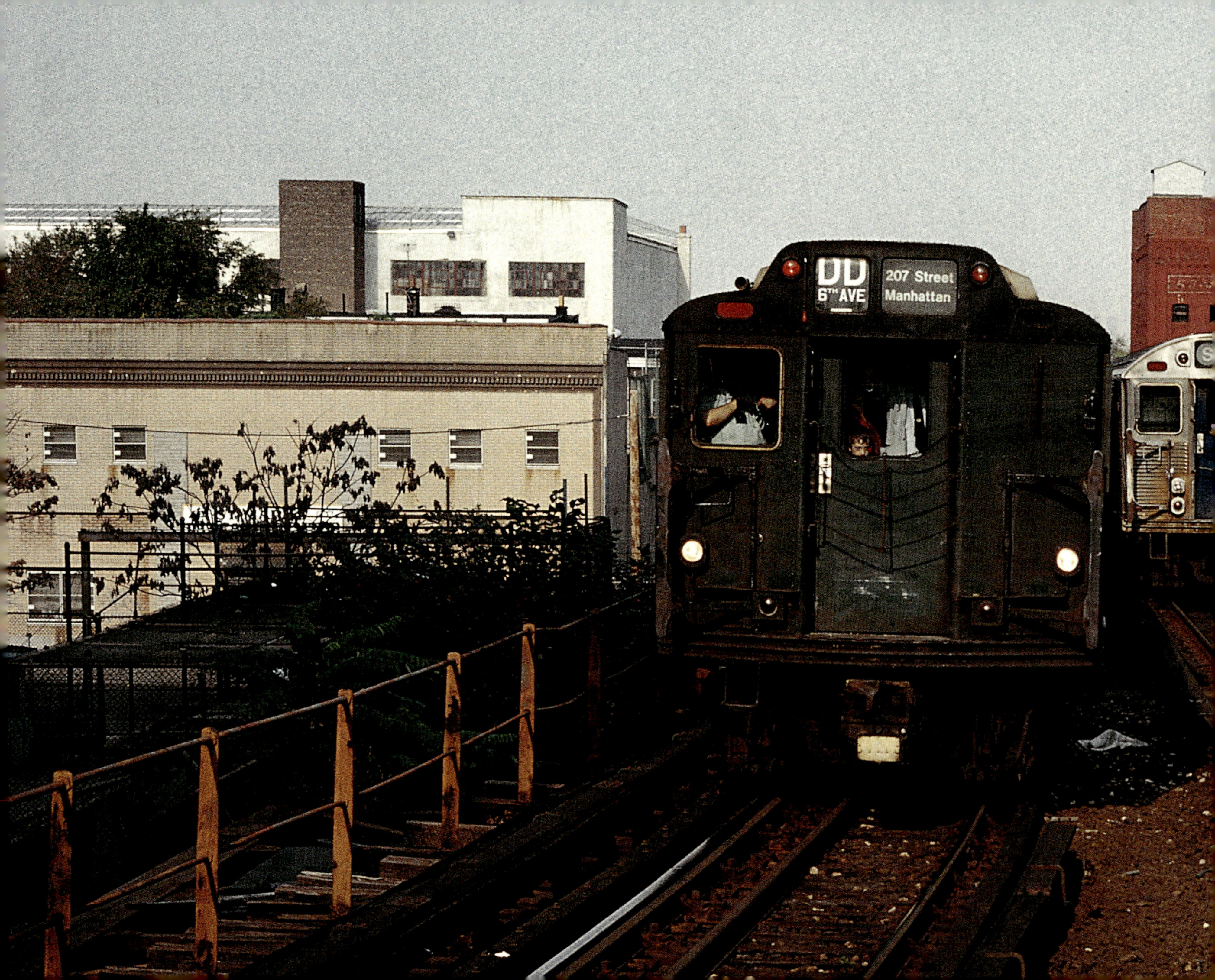
DD
6TH AVE
207 Street
Manhattan

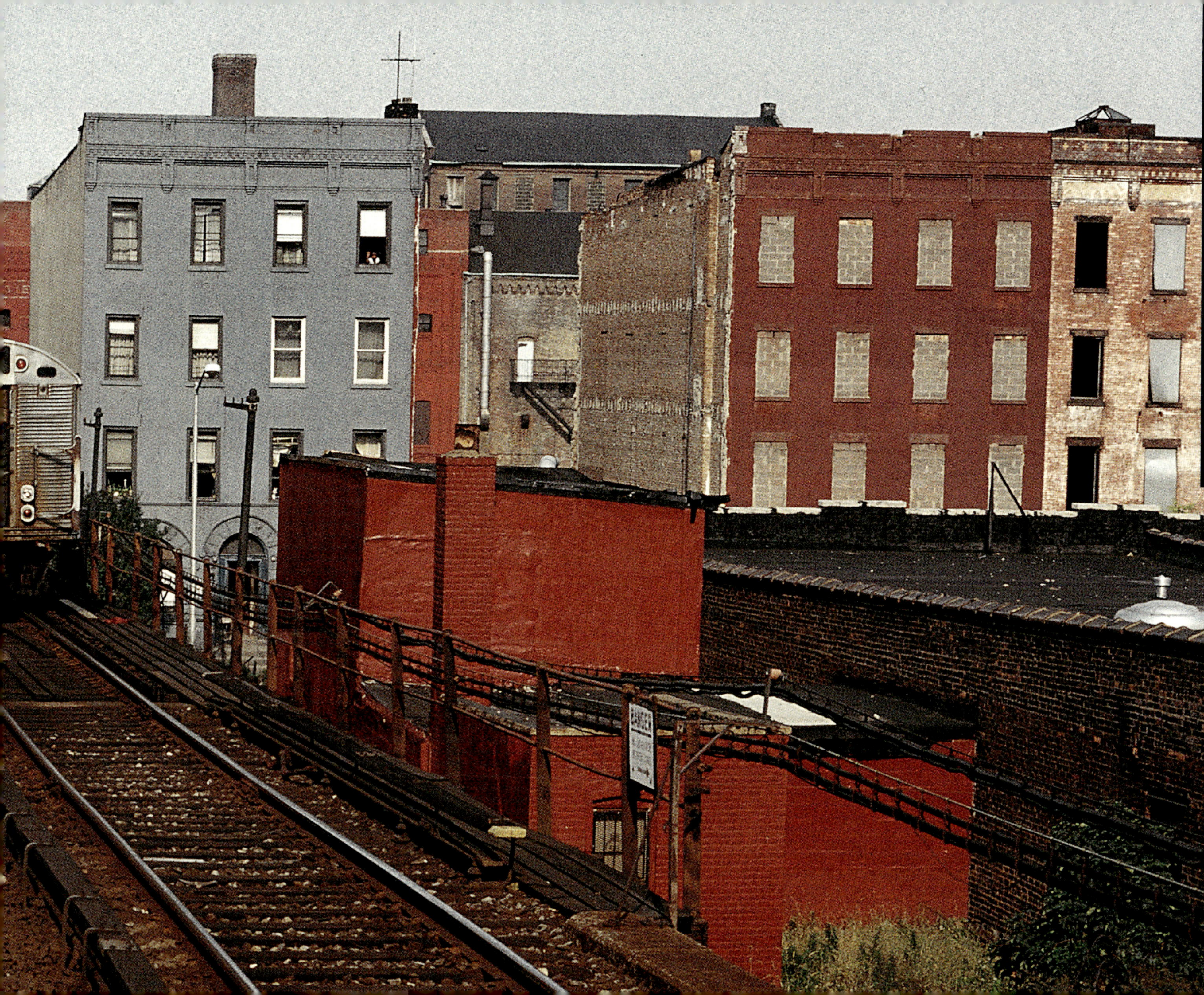

R-10s fan trip, Franklin Ave. Shuttle line, Park Place, Brooklyn, 1989

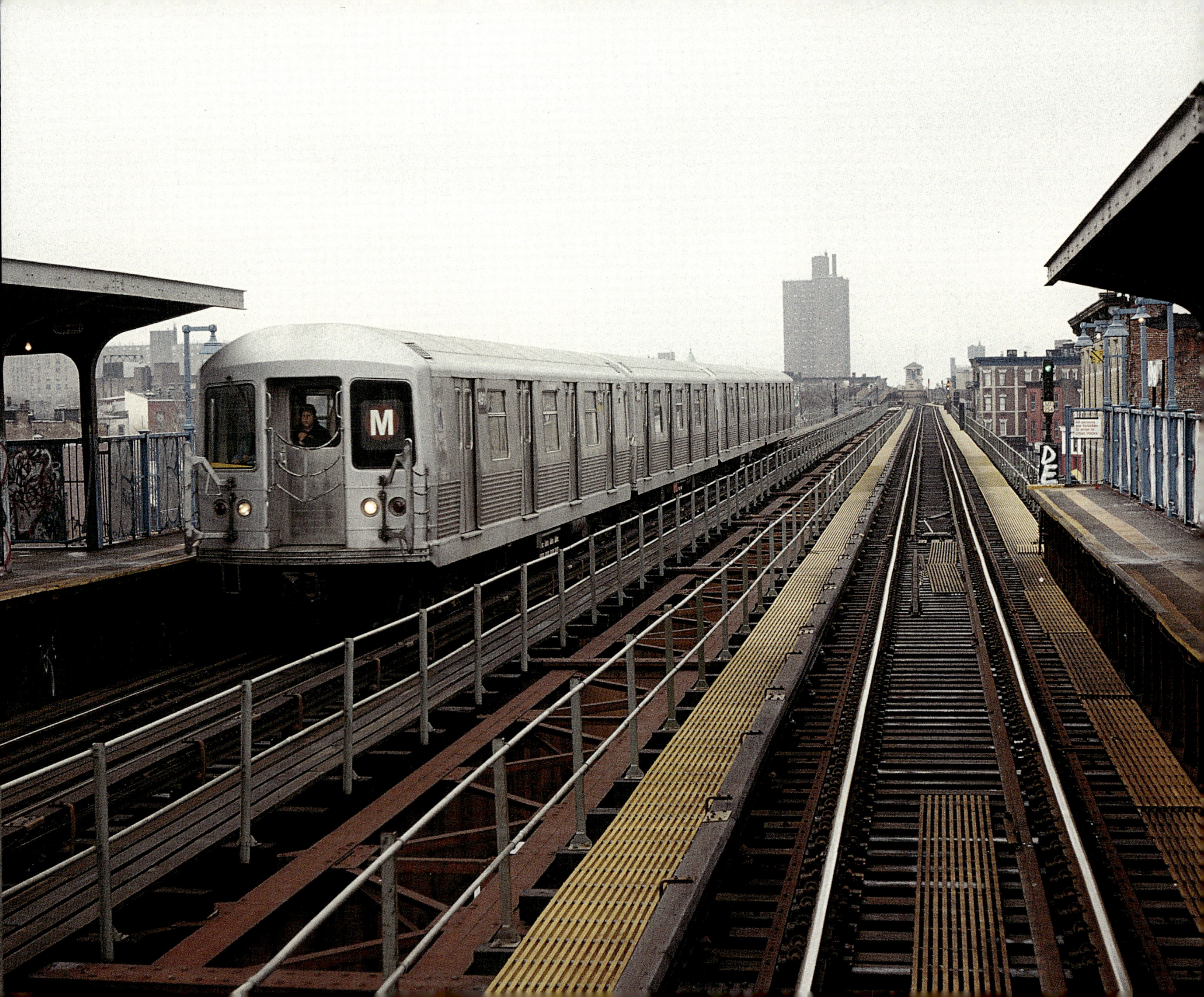

R-42s, Myrtle Ave. line, Central Ave., Brooklyn, 1989

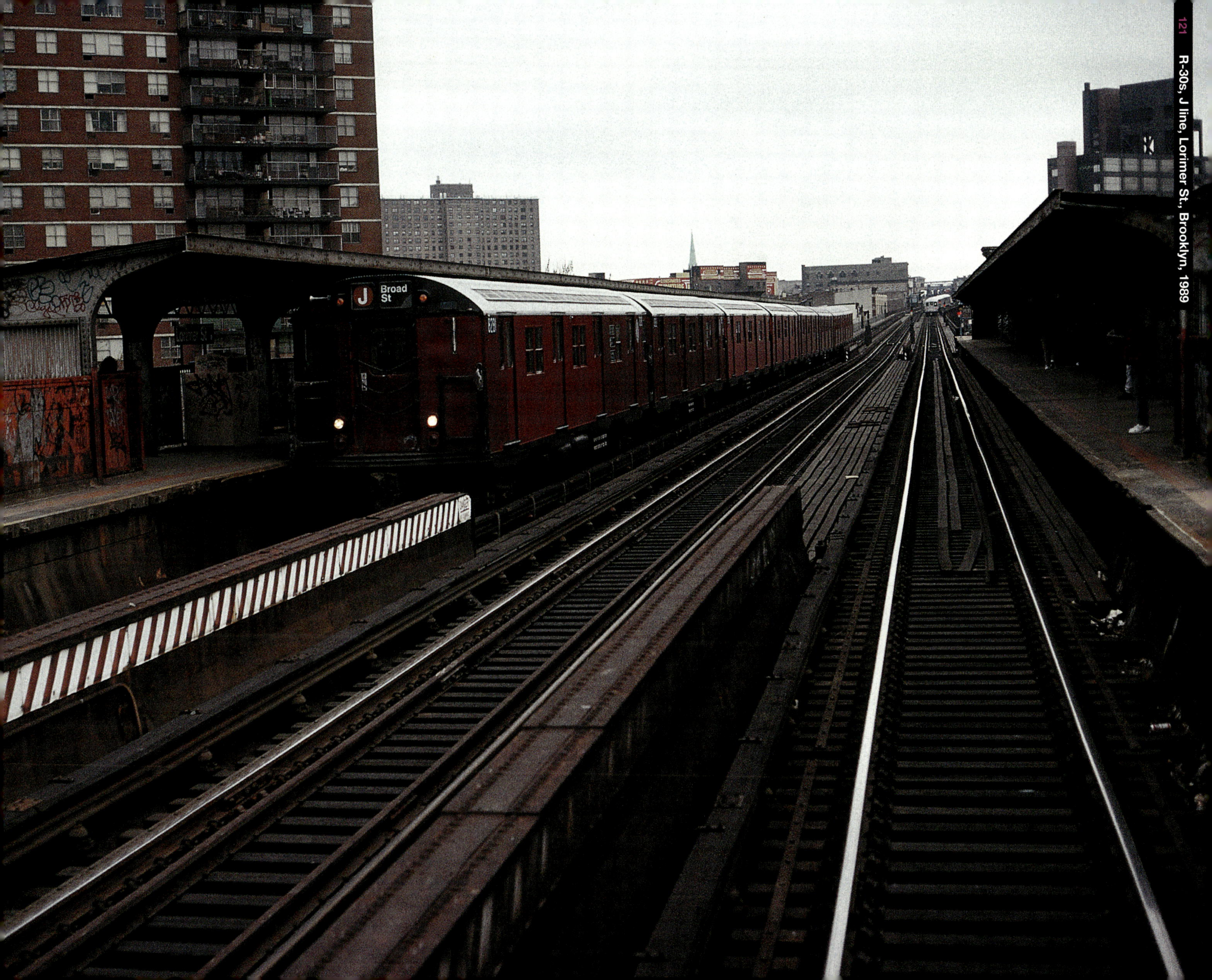

R-30s, J line, Lorimer St., Brooklyn, 1989

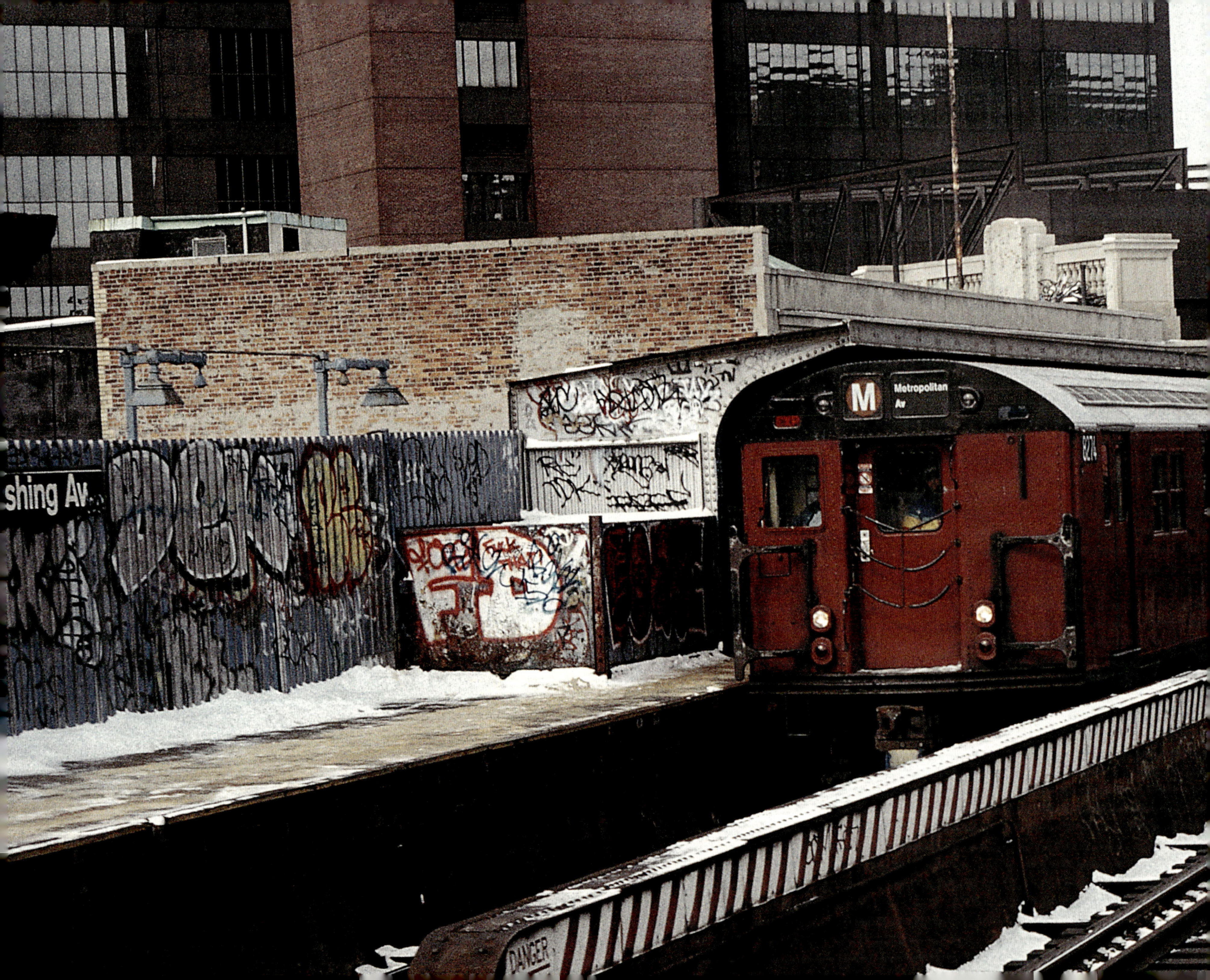

shing Av
M
Metropolitan
Av
DANGER

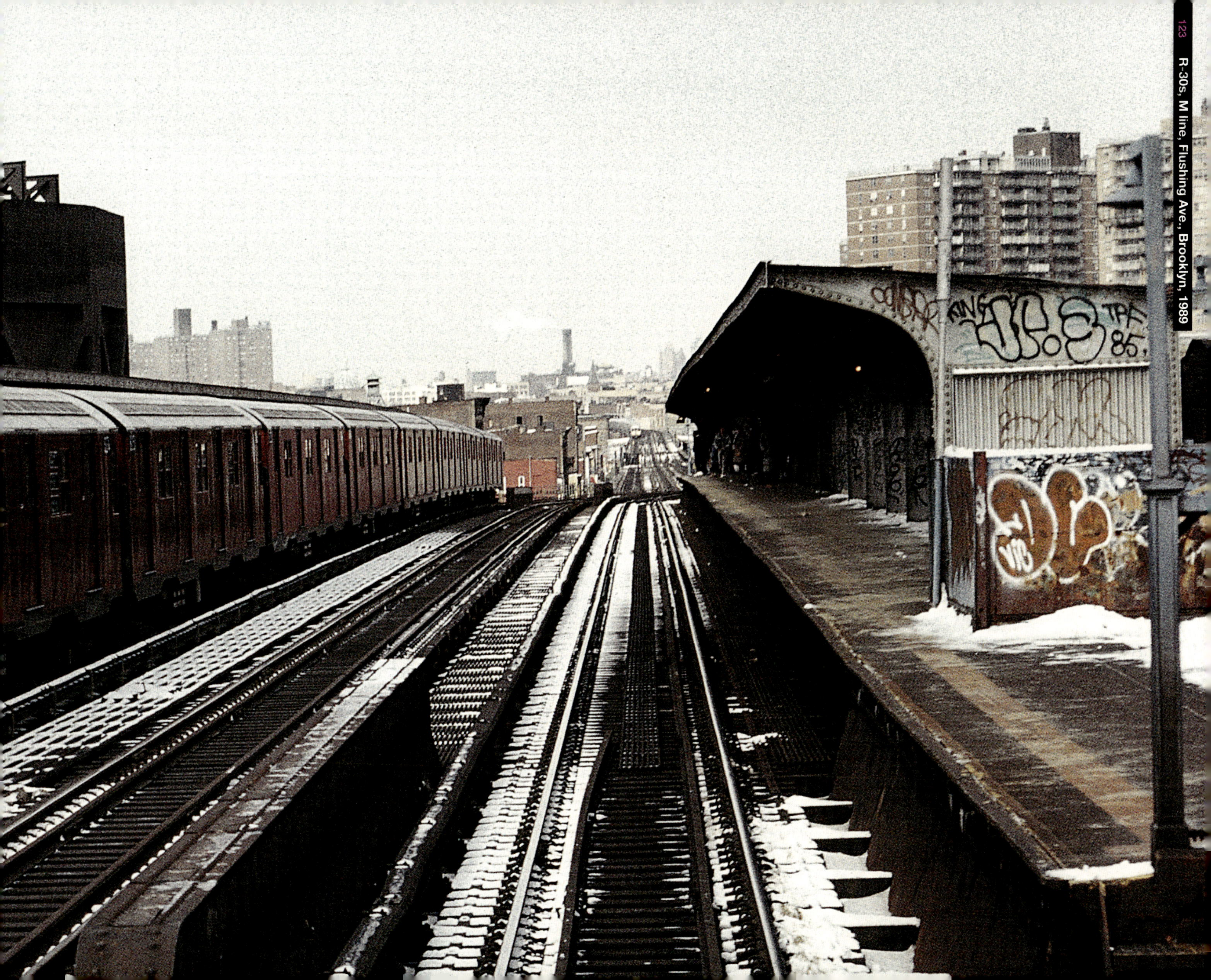

R-30s, M line, Flushing Ave., Brooklyn, 1989

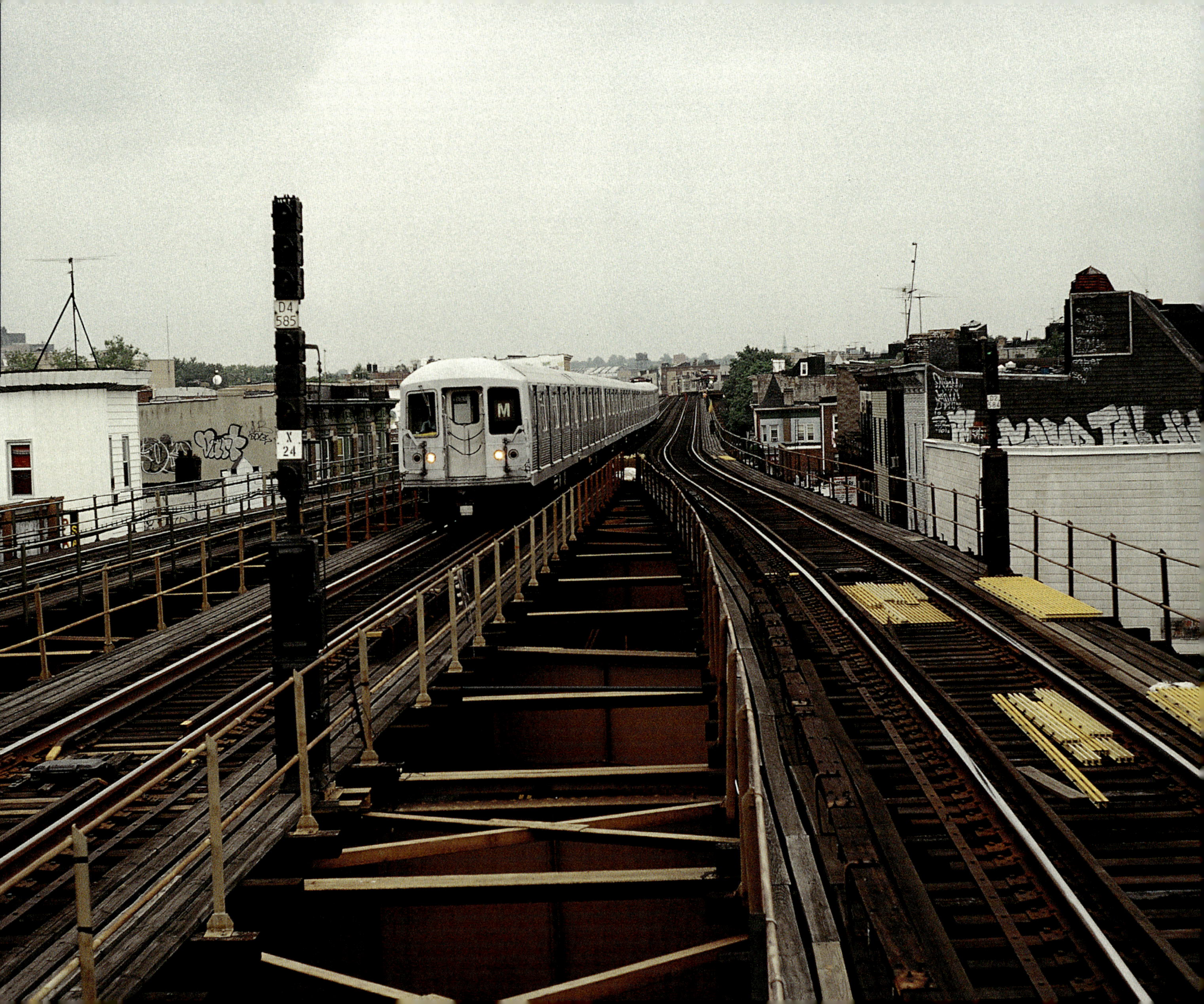

R-42s, M, West End Line, 62nd St., Brooklyn, 1990

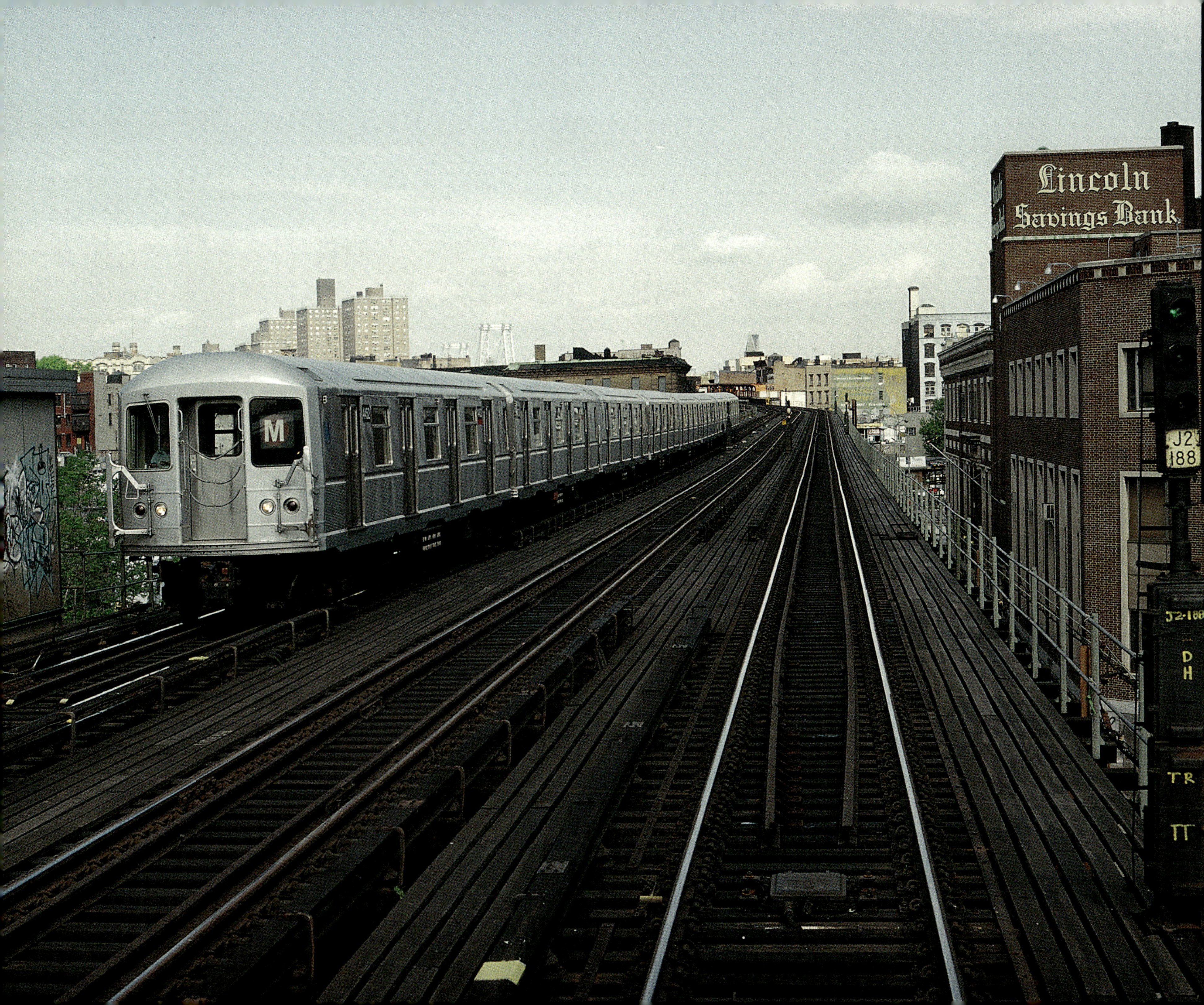

Modified R-40s, M line, between Hewes & Lorimer Sts., Brooklyn, 1990

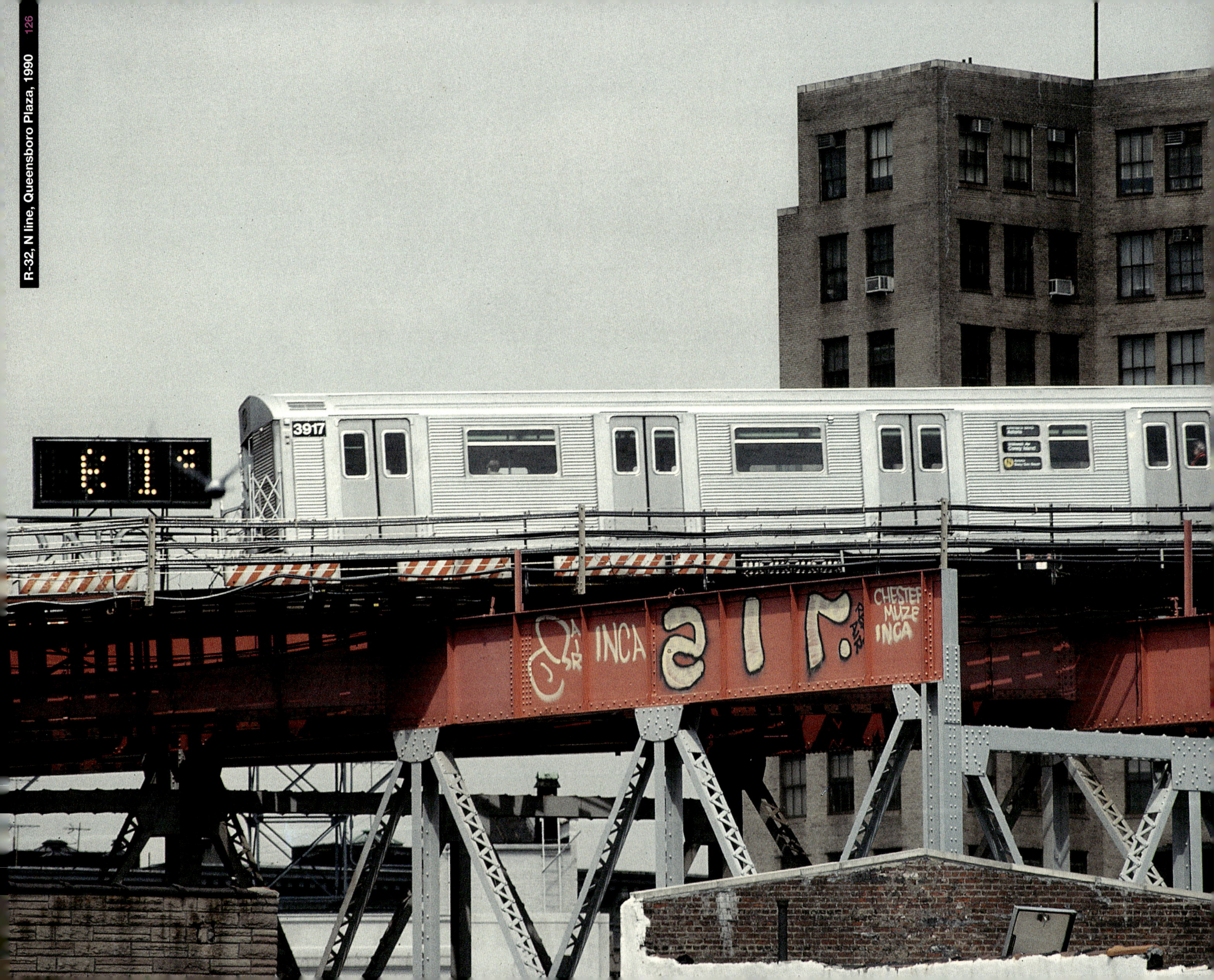

R-32, N line, Queensboro Plaza, 1990

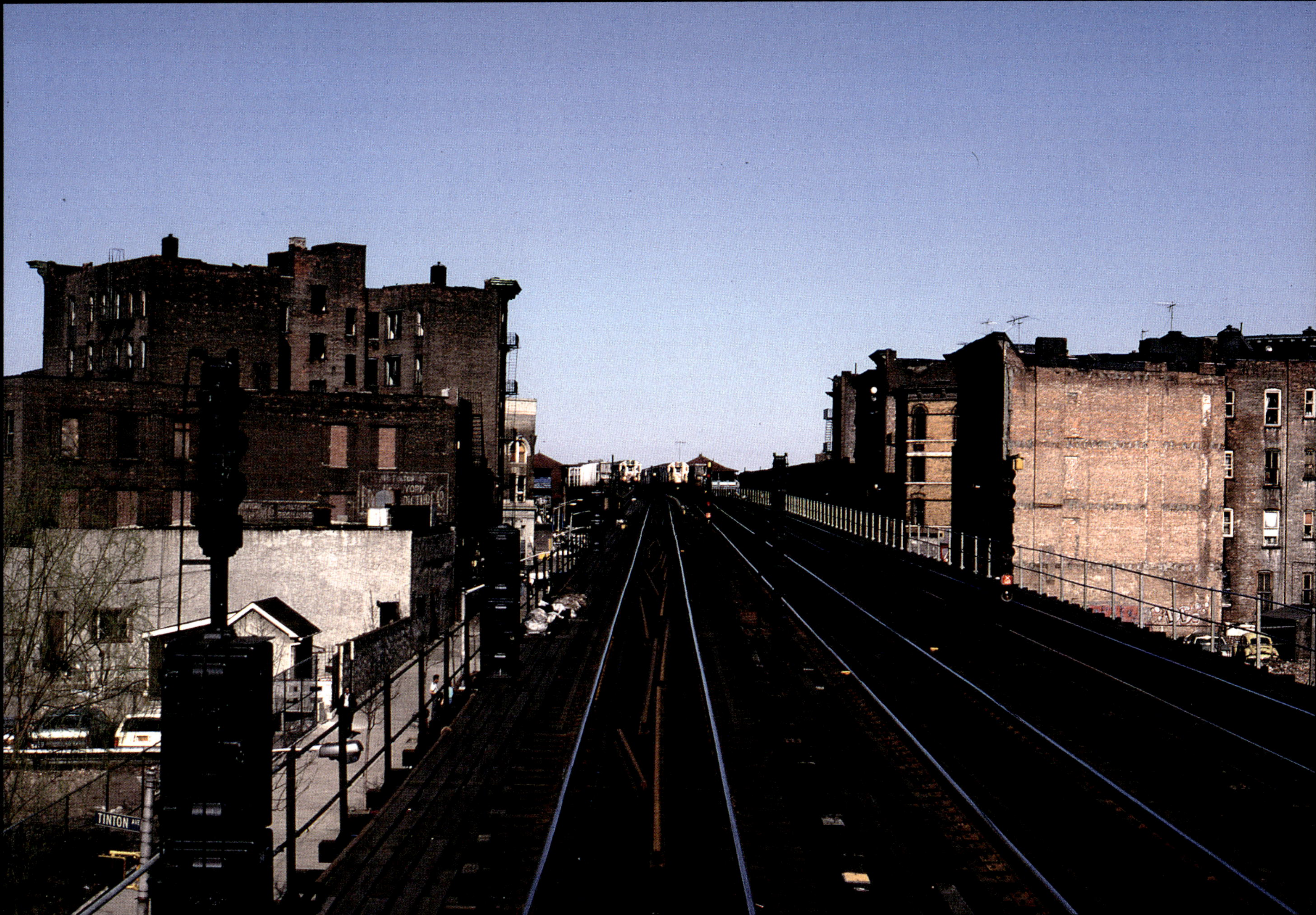

Nos. 2 & 5 West Farms line, near Jackson Ave., Bronx, 1986

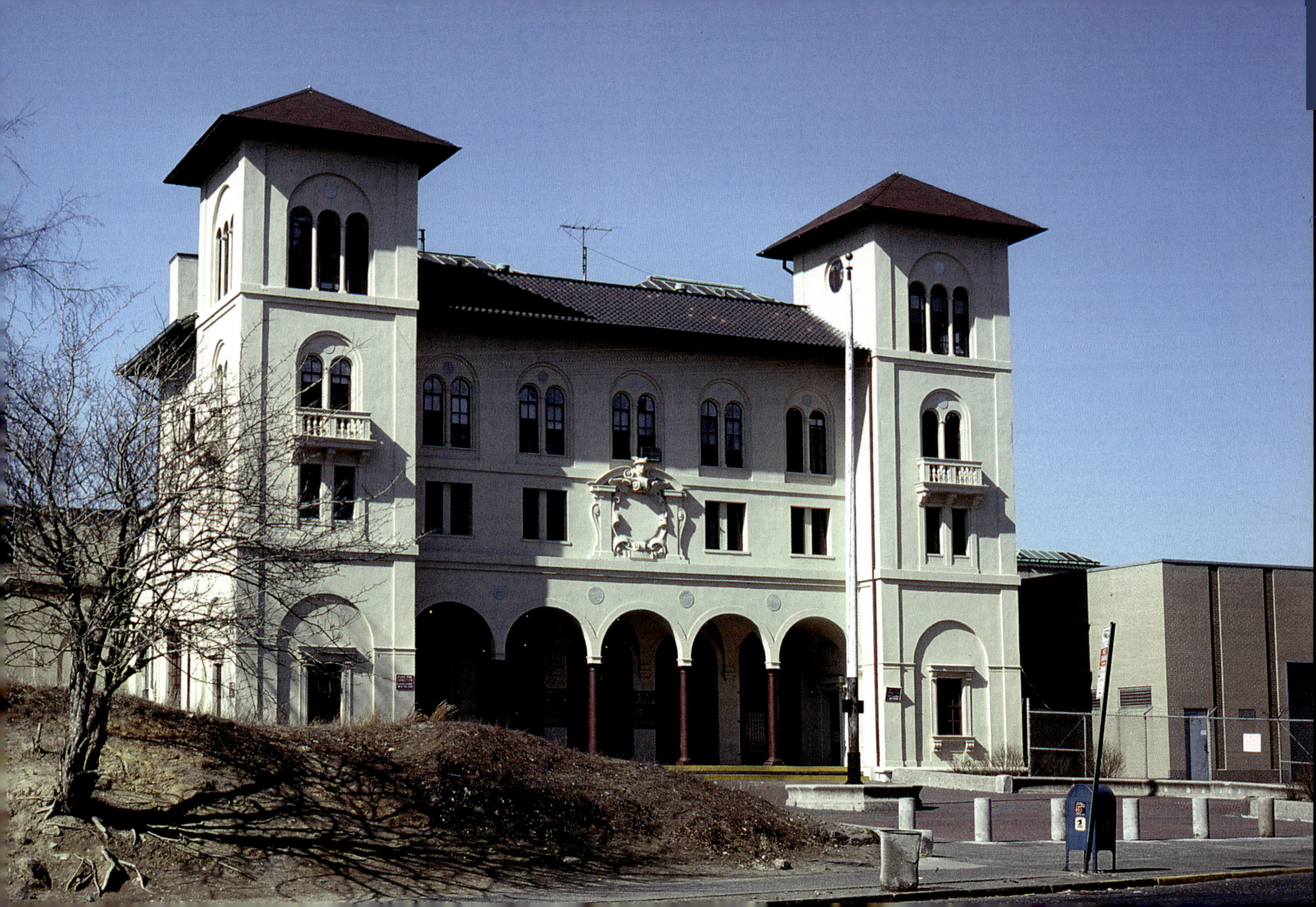

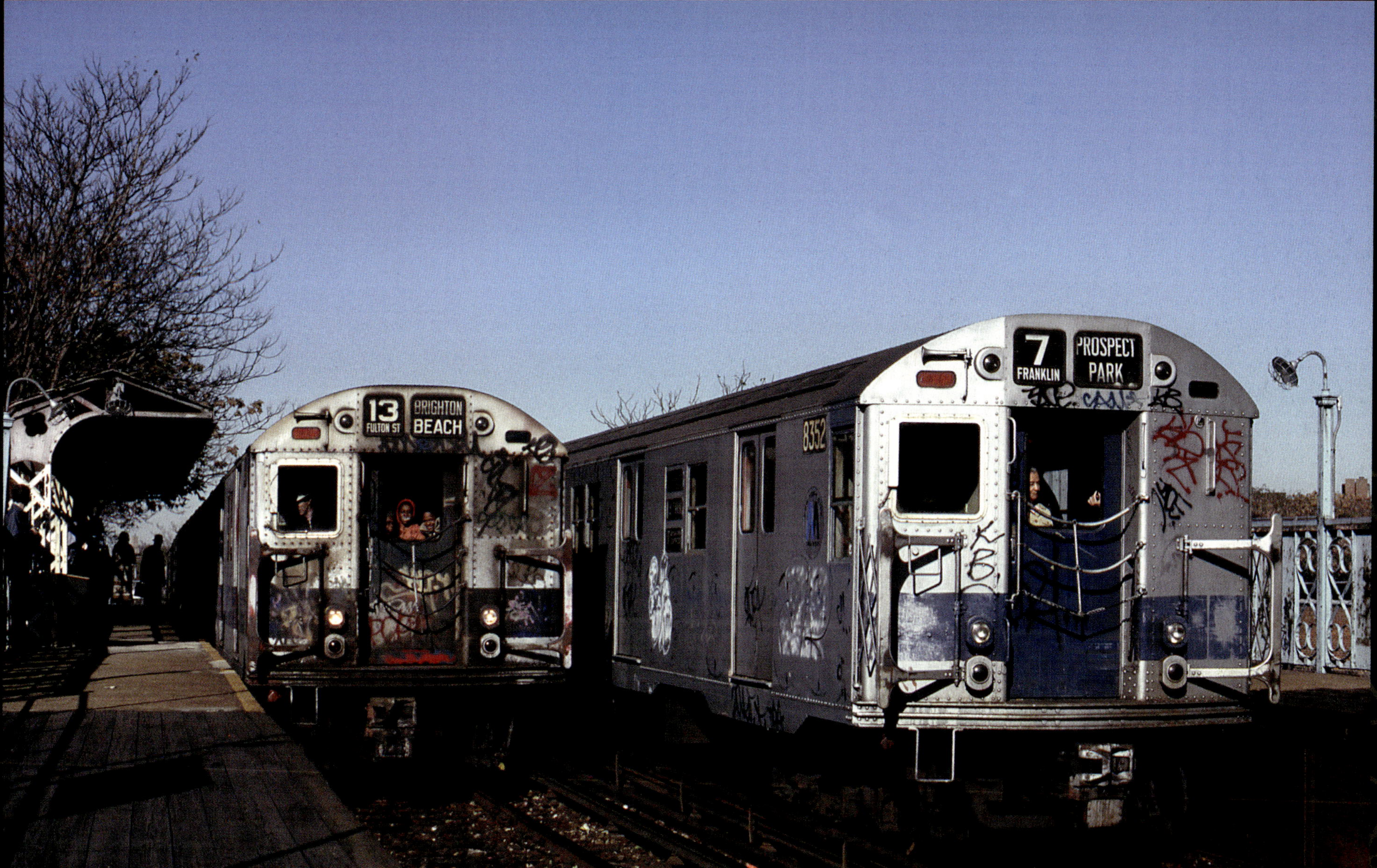

, Franklin Ave. Shuttle, Dean St., Brooklyn, 1981

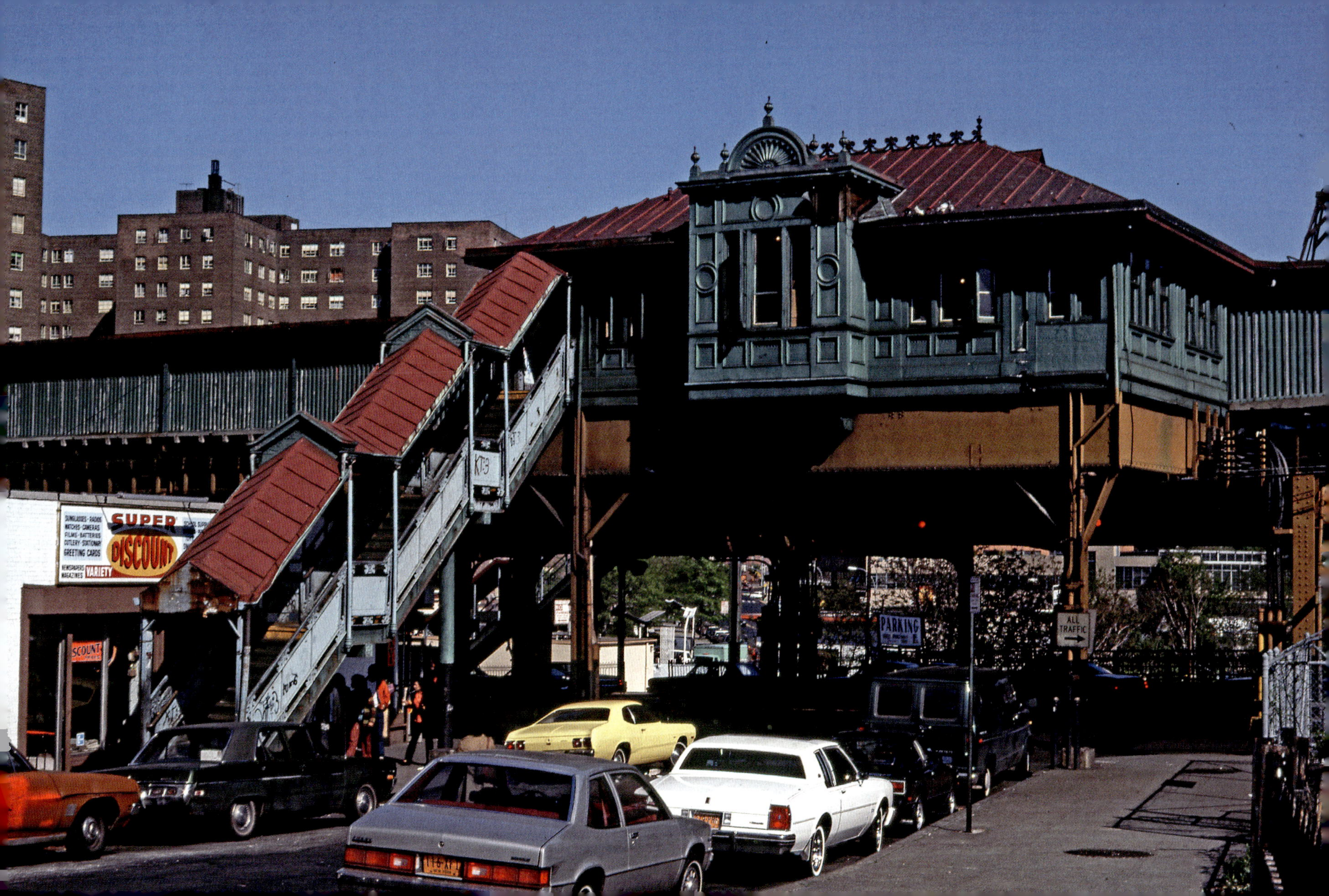
SUPER
DISCOUNT
GREETING CARDS
NEWSPAPERS
MAGAZINES
VARIETY
PARKING
ALL TRAFFIC

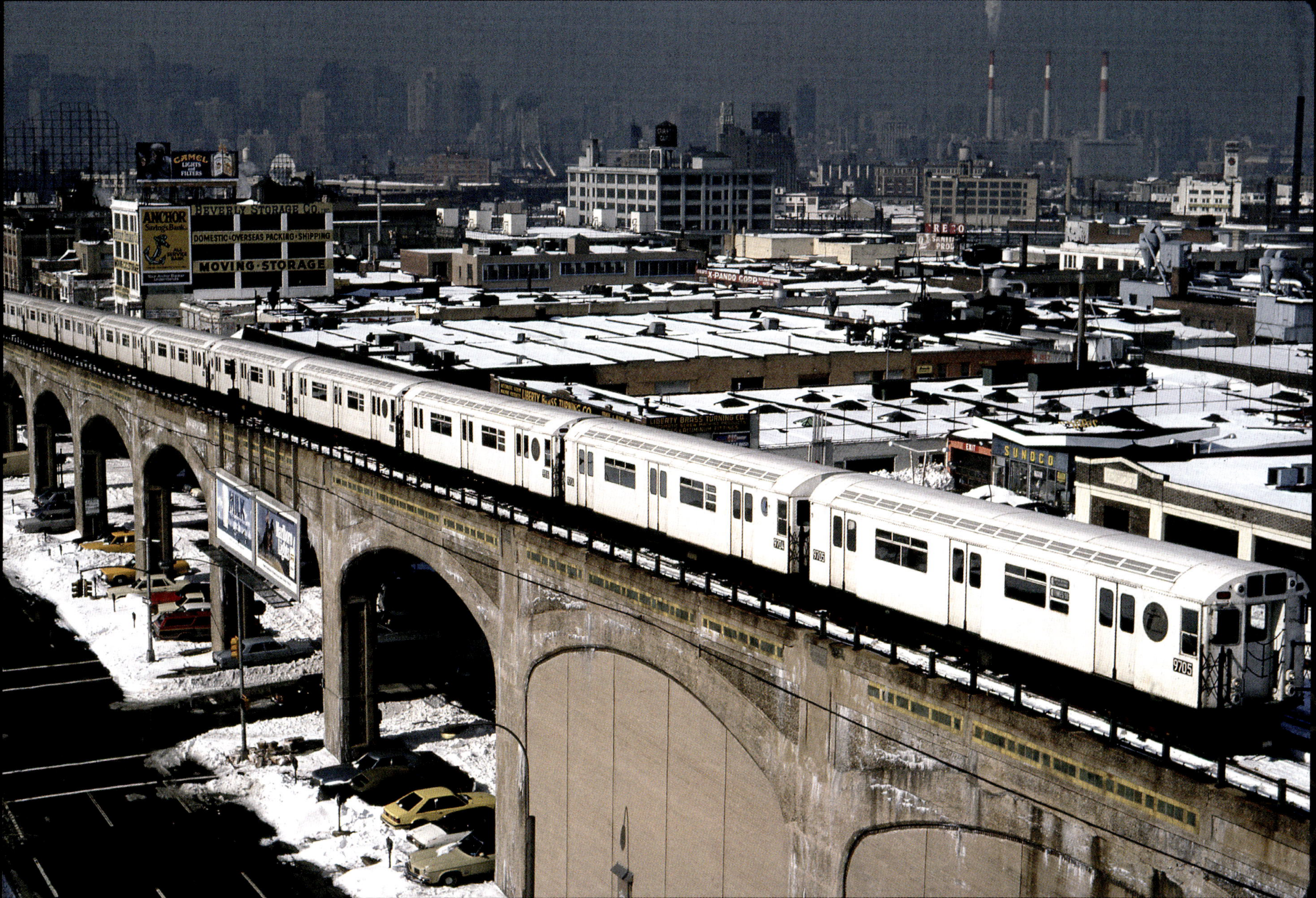
CAMEL
ANCHOR
BEVERLY STORAGE CO.
DOMESTIC • OVERSEAS PACKING • SHIPPING
MOVING • STORAGE
X-PANDO CORP
LIBERTY BRASS TURNING CO.
SUNOCO
9704
9705

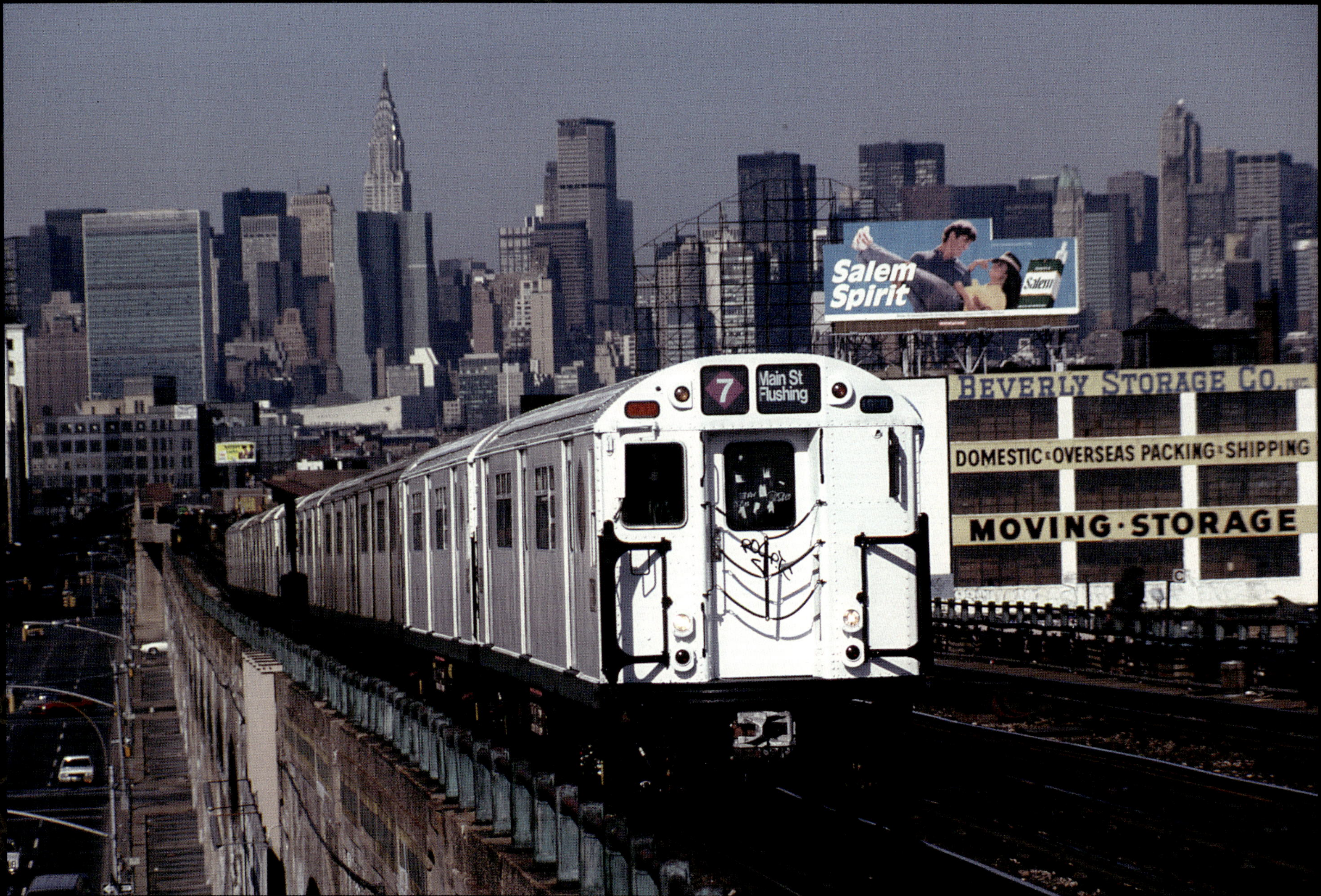

R-36s, No. 7 Flushing line, 40th St.–Lowery St., Queens, 1984

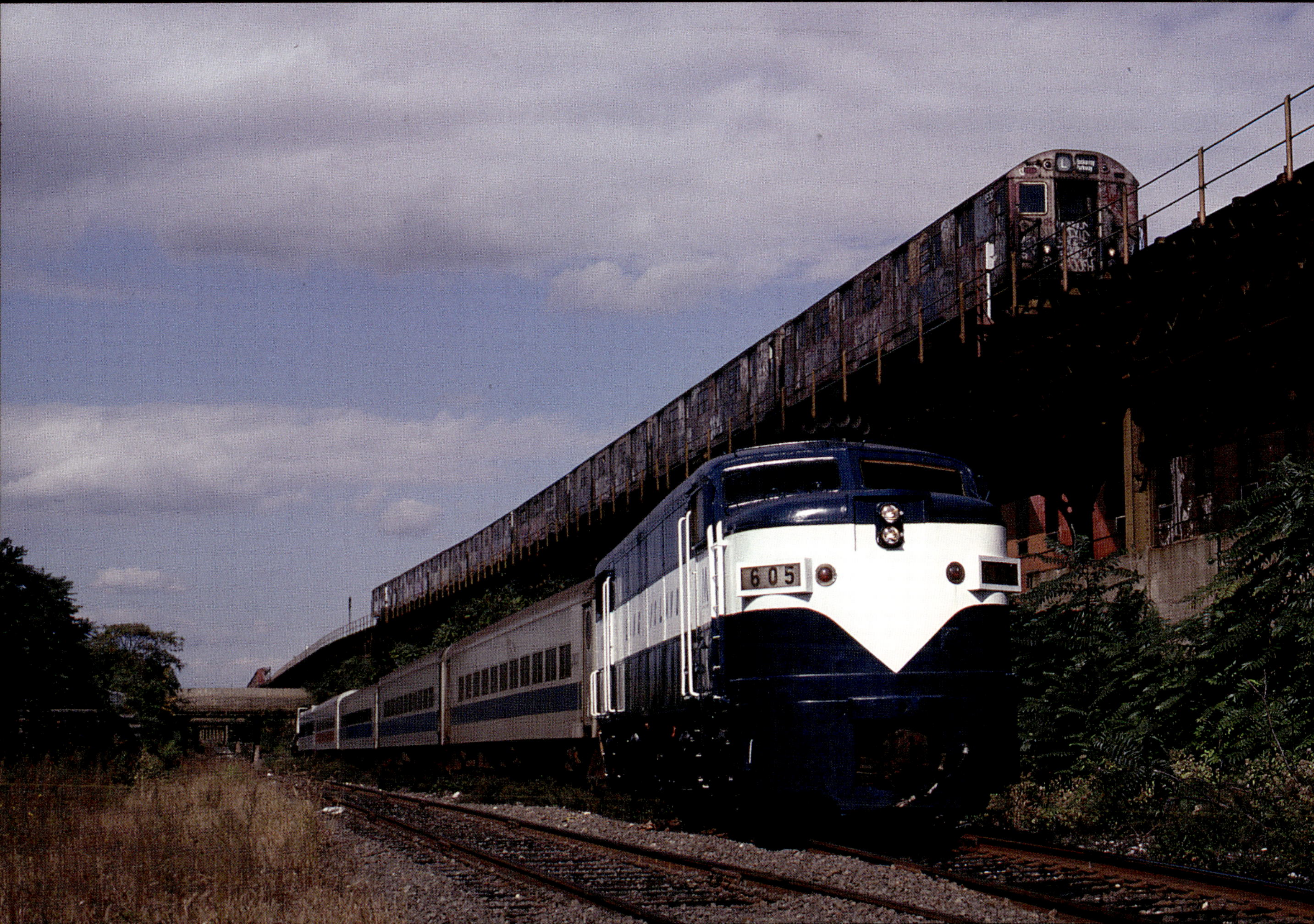

R-30, L, Canarsie line, Livonia Ave., Brooklyn, LIRR fan trip, 1986

R-26, No. 2 line, E. 180th St., Bronx, 1986 | R-40s, R-27s, B line, Queensboro Plaza, 1986

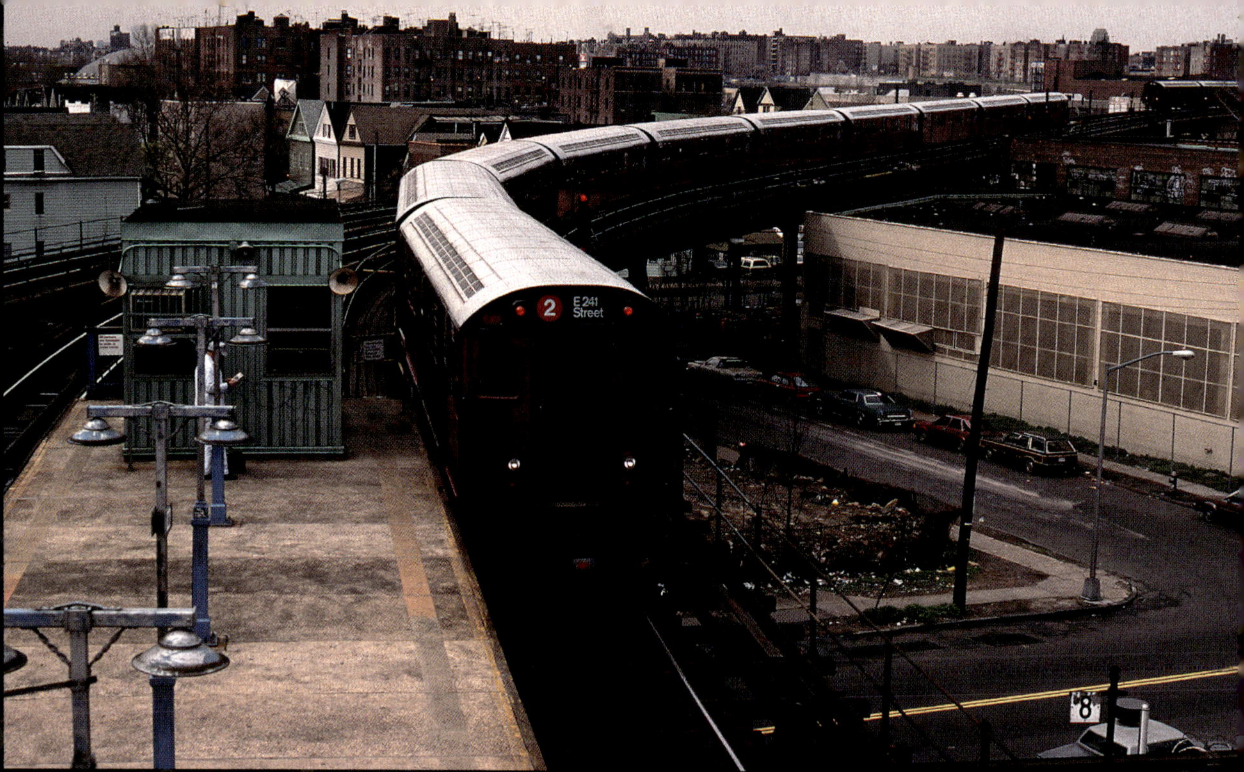

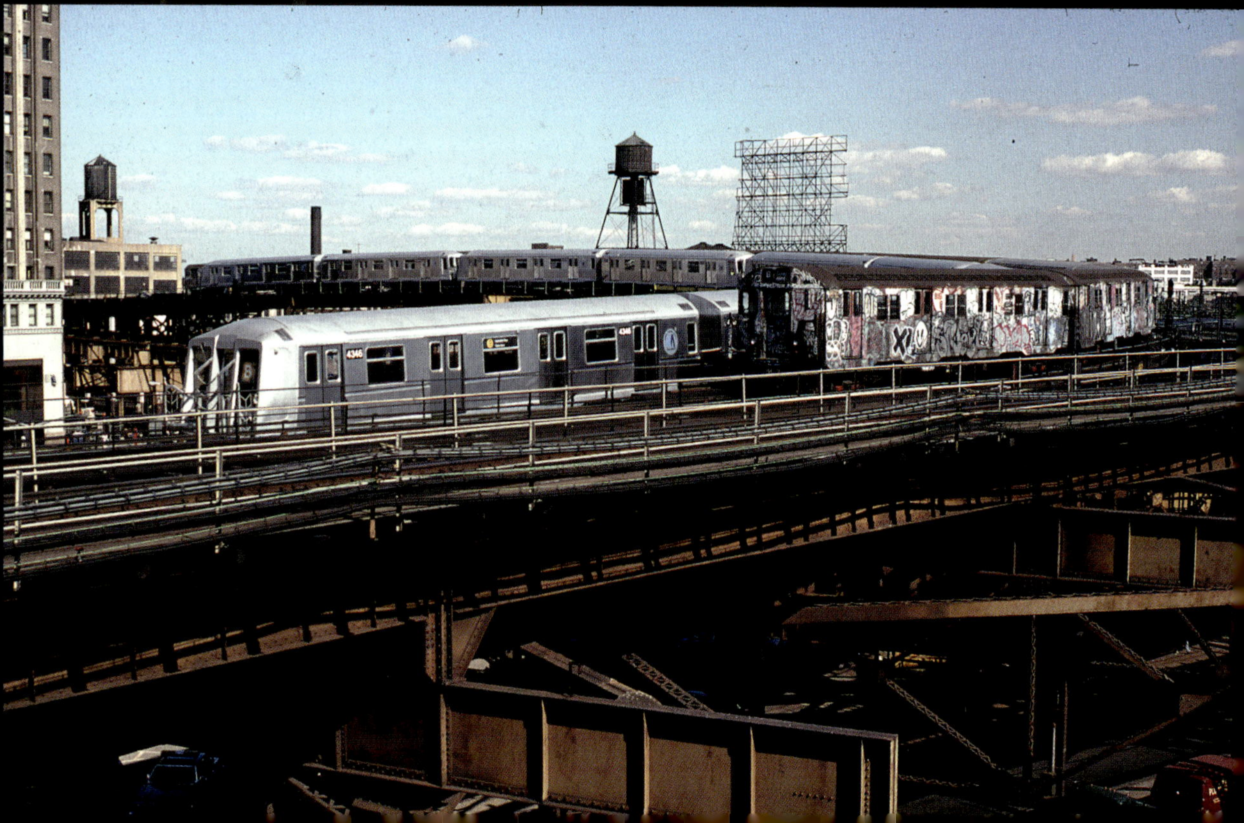

Subway Yards

New York
Subways & Stations
1970–1990

CHAPTER 3

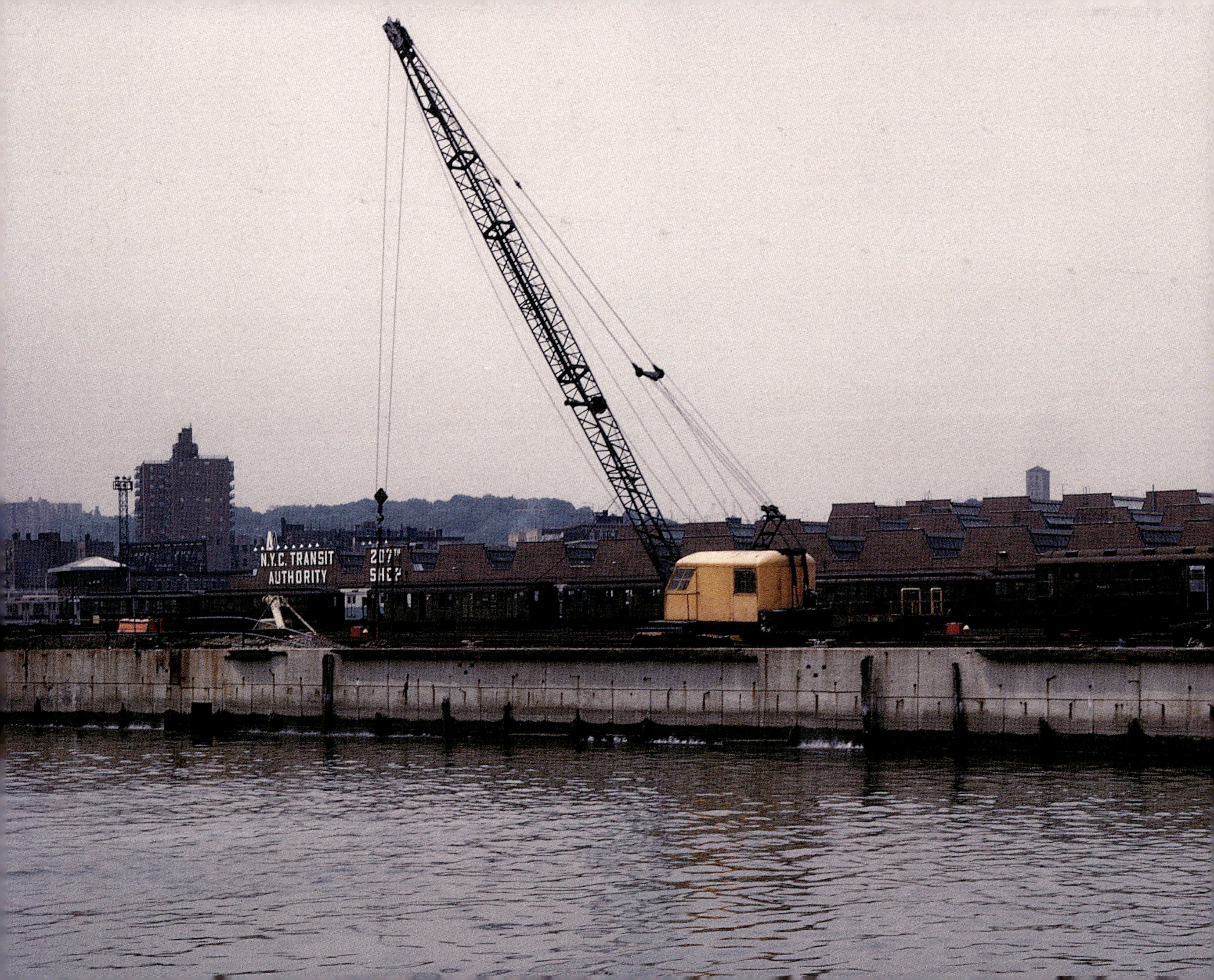
N.Y.C. TRANSIT
AUTHORITY
207TH
SHOP

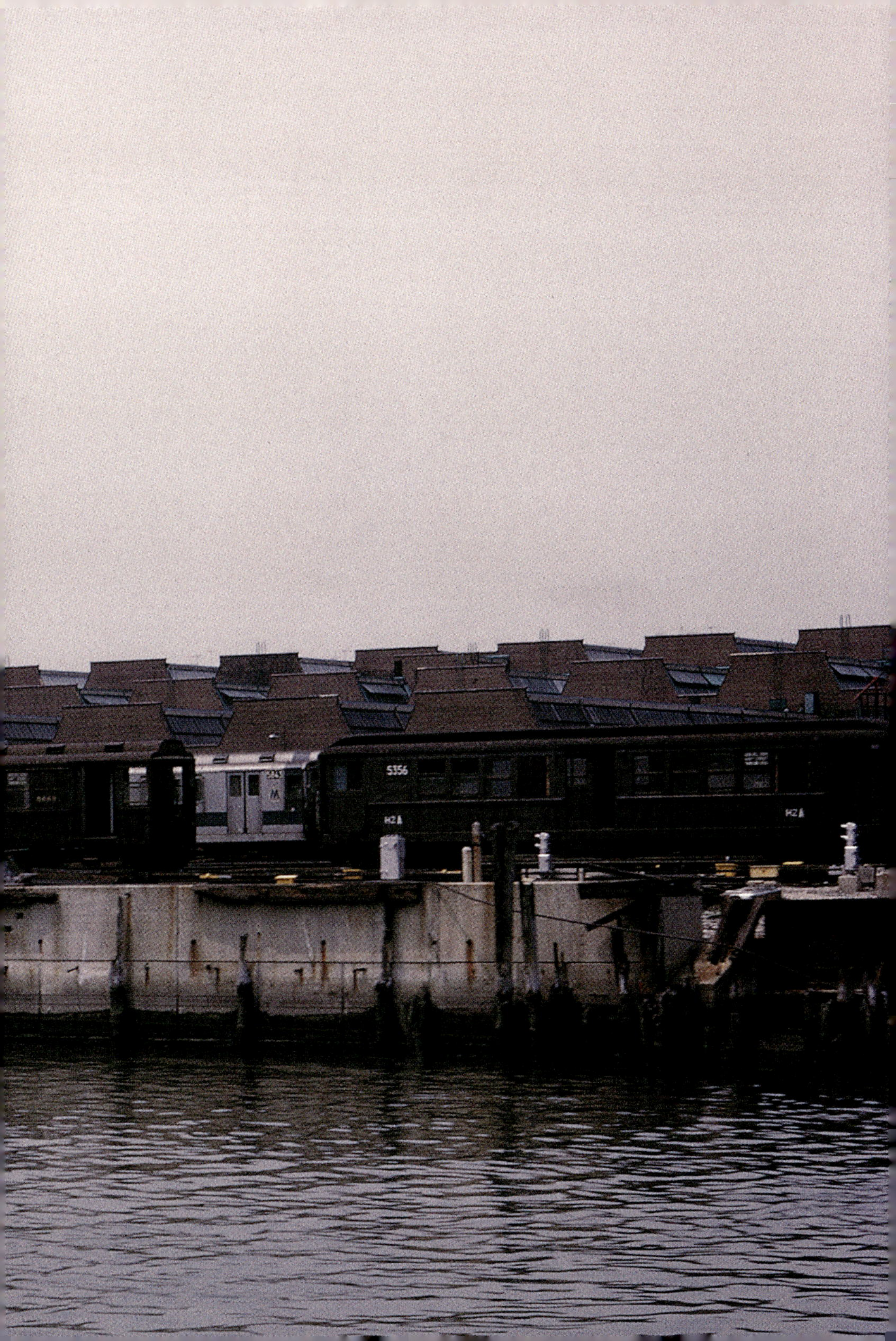
5356

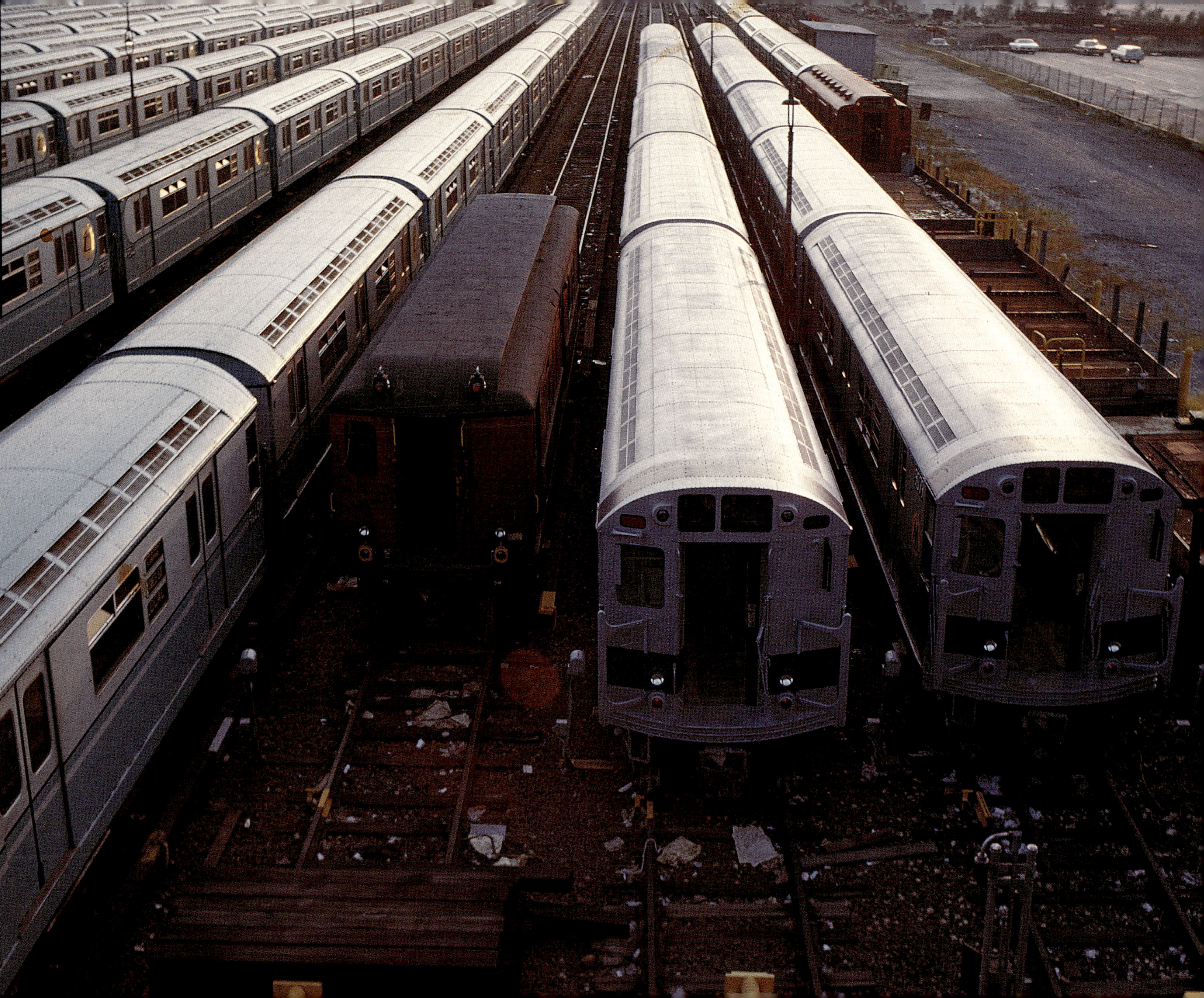

R-33, R-36s, Corona Yard, Queens,1972

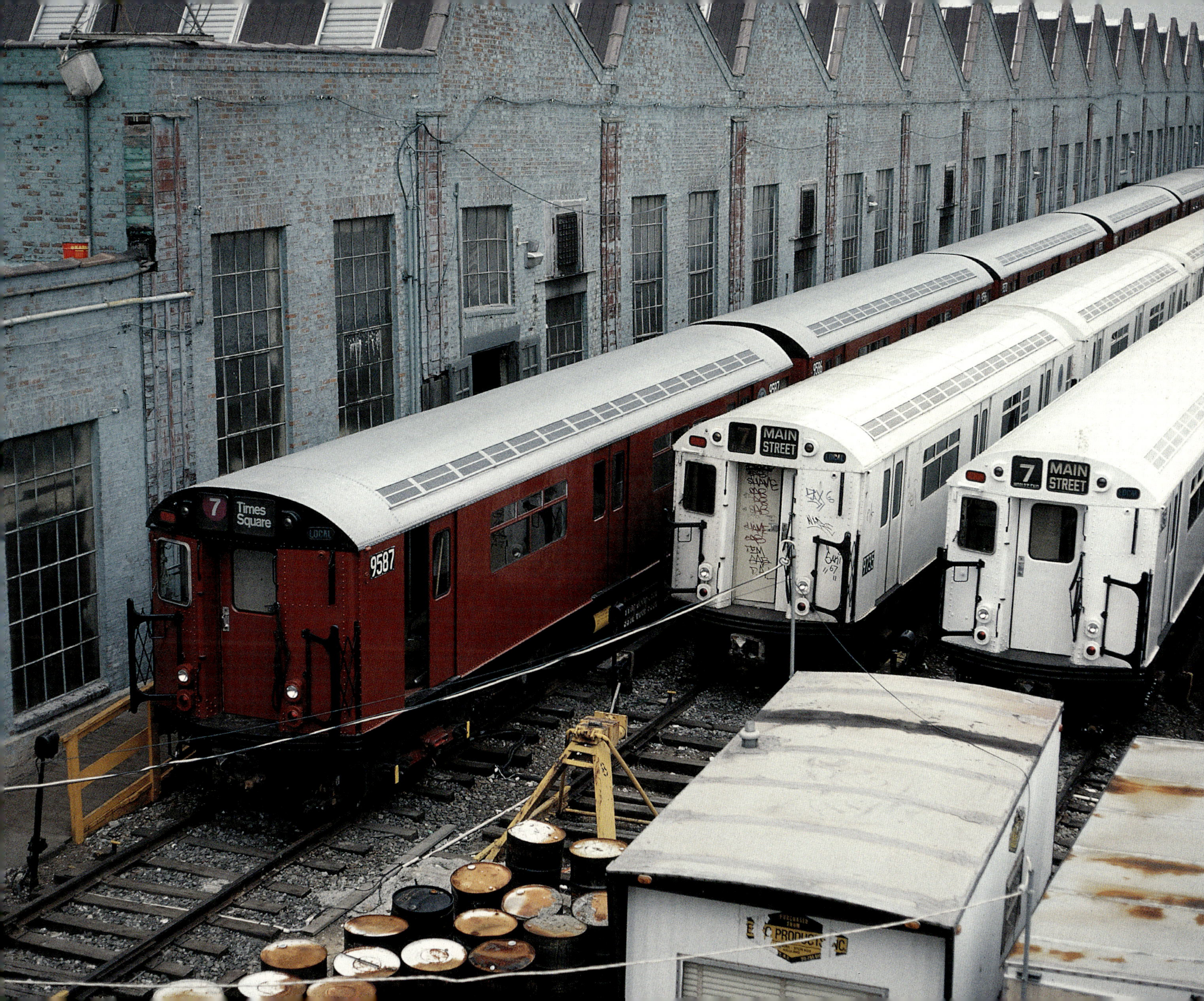

R-36s, Corona Yard, Queens, 1984

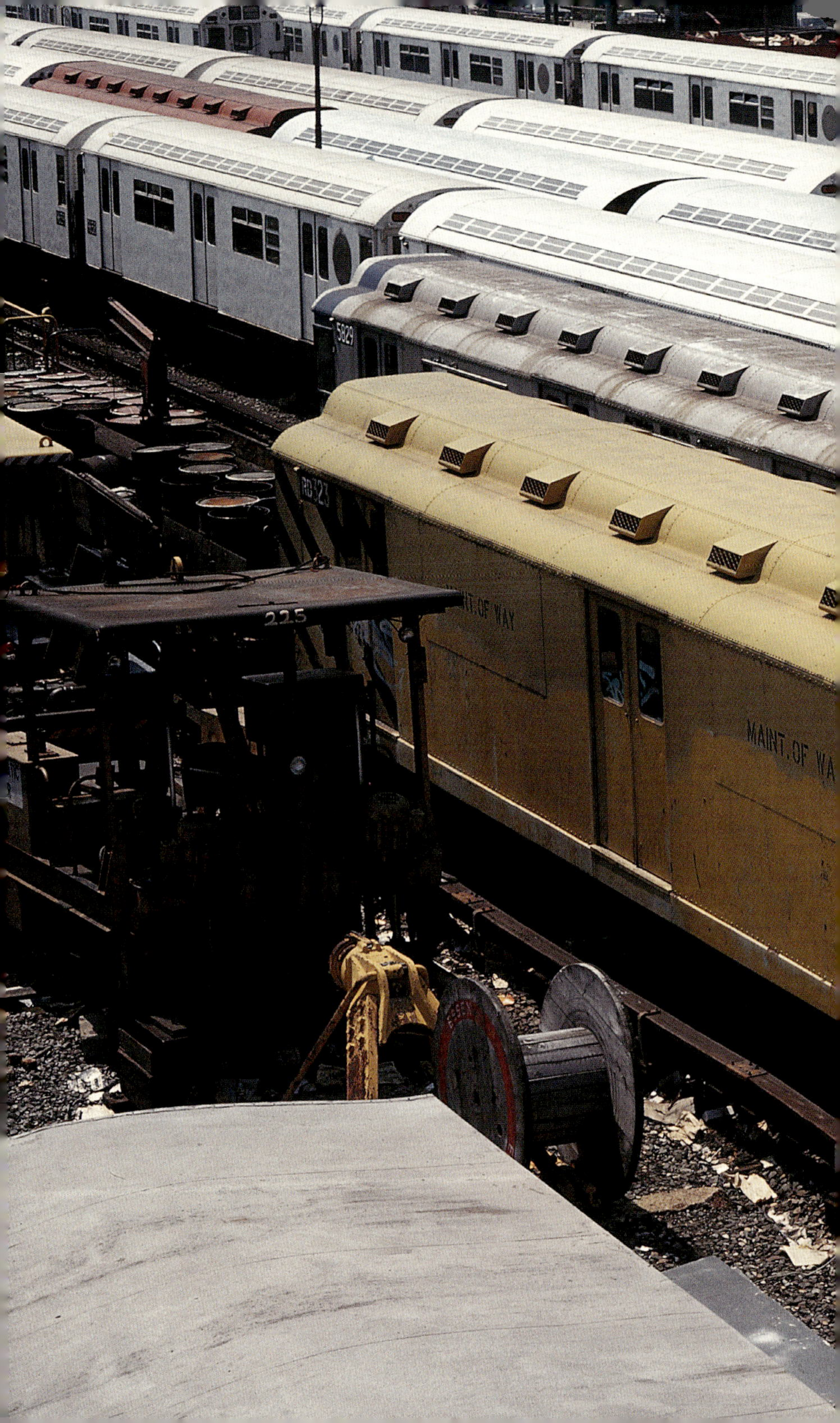
5829
225

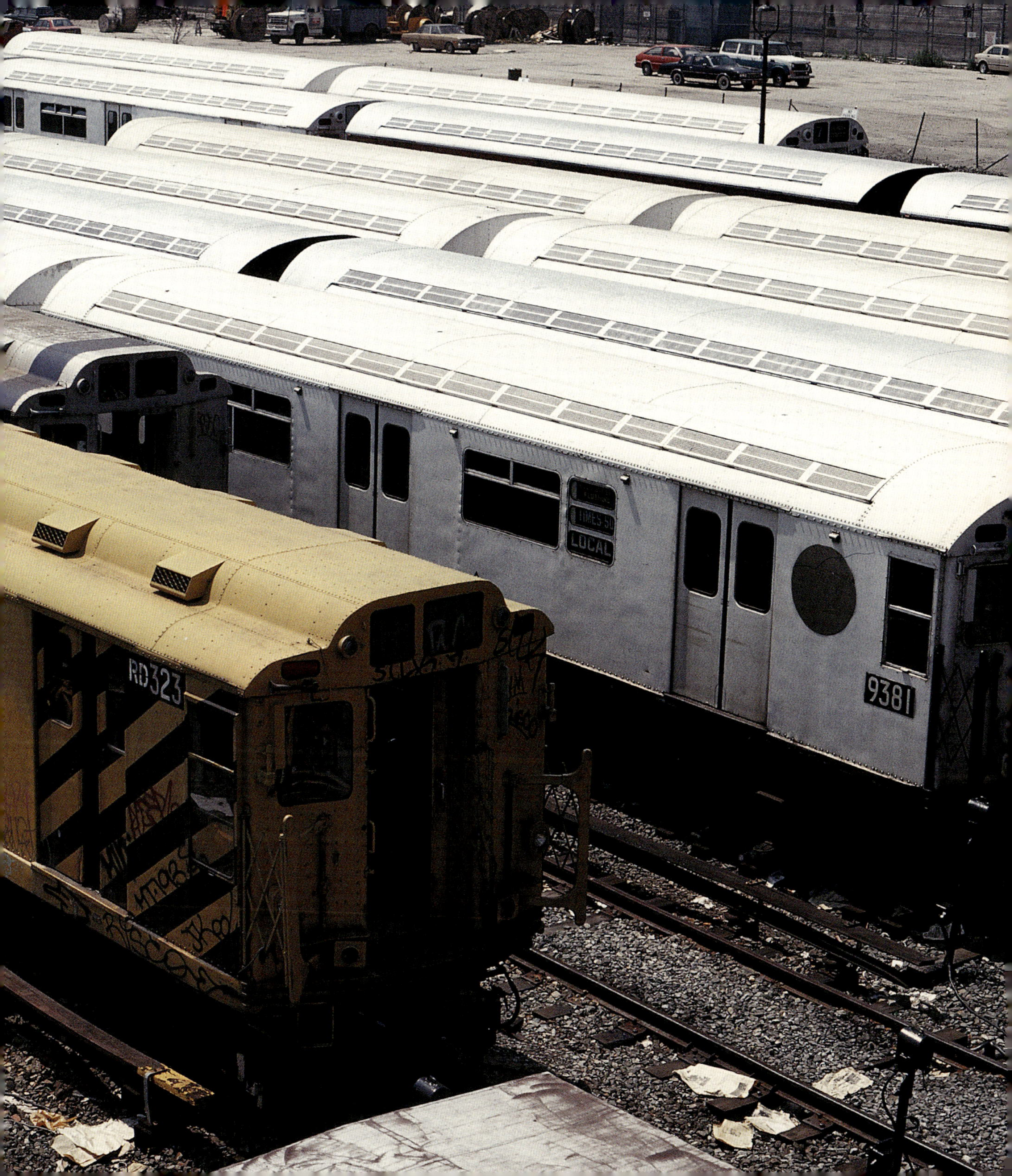
RD323
TIMES SQ
LOCAL
9381

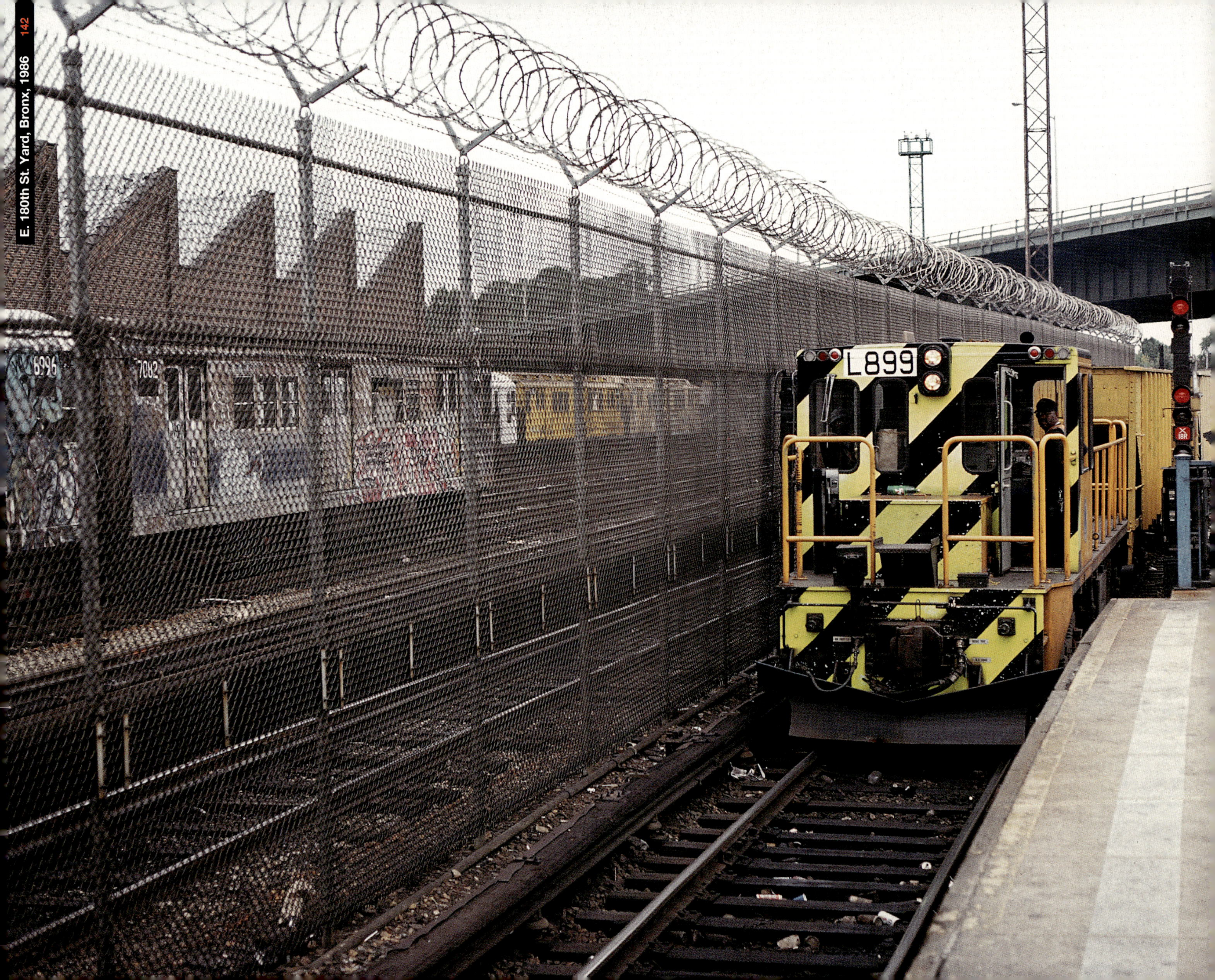

E. 180th St. Yard, Bronx, 1986

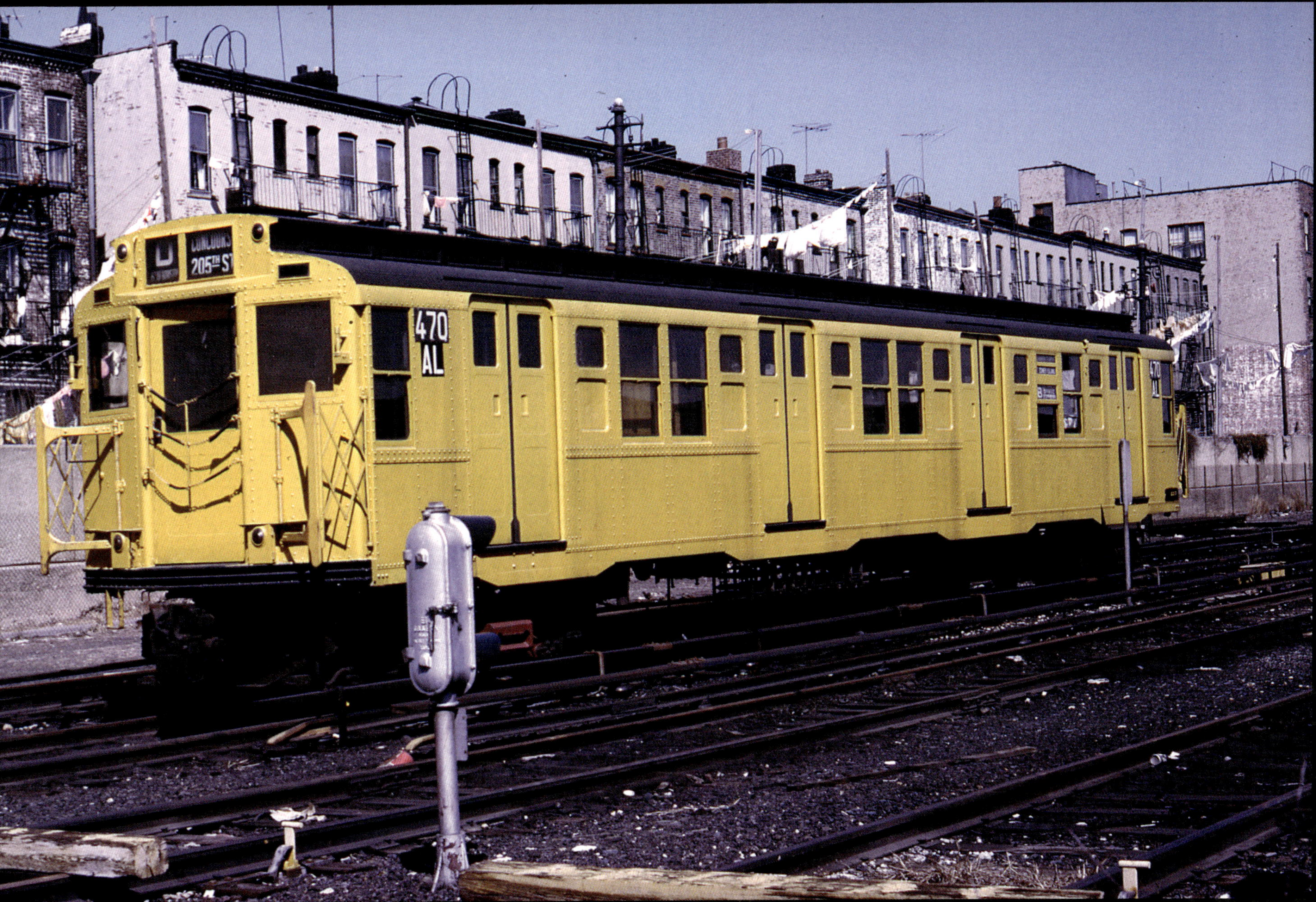

ohol car, Fresh Pond Yard, Queens, 1971

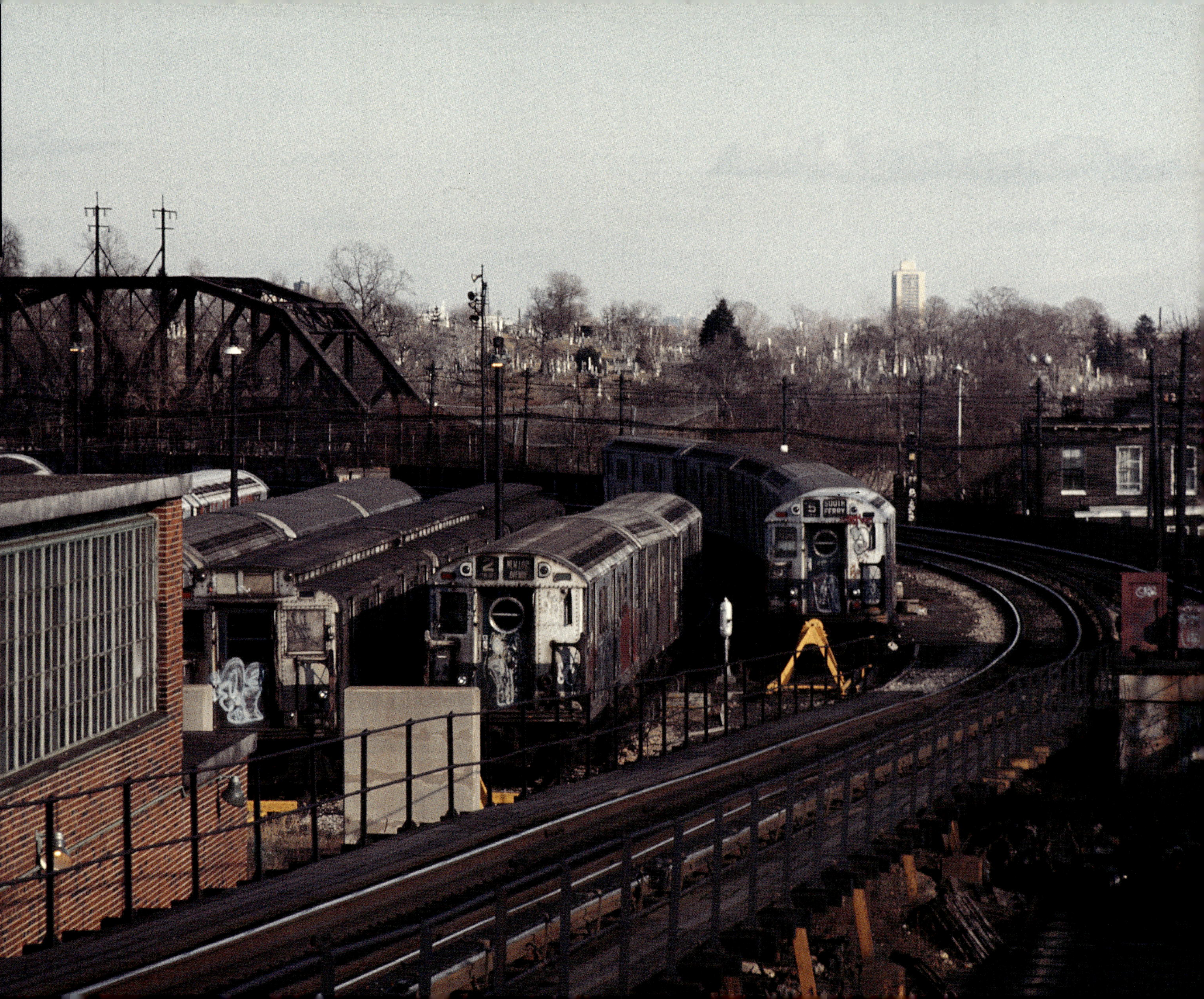

Fresh Pond Yard, Queens, 1976

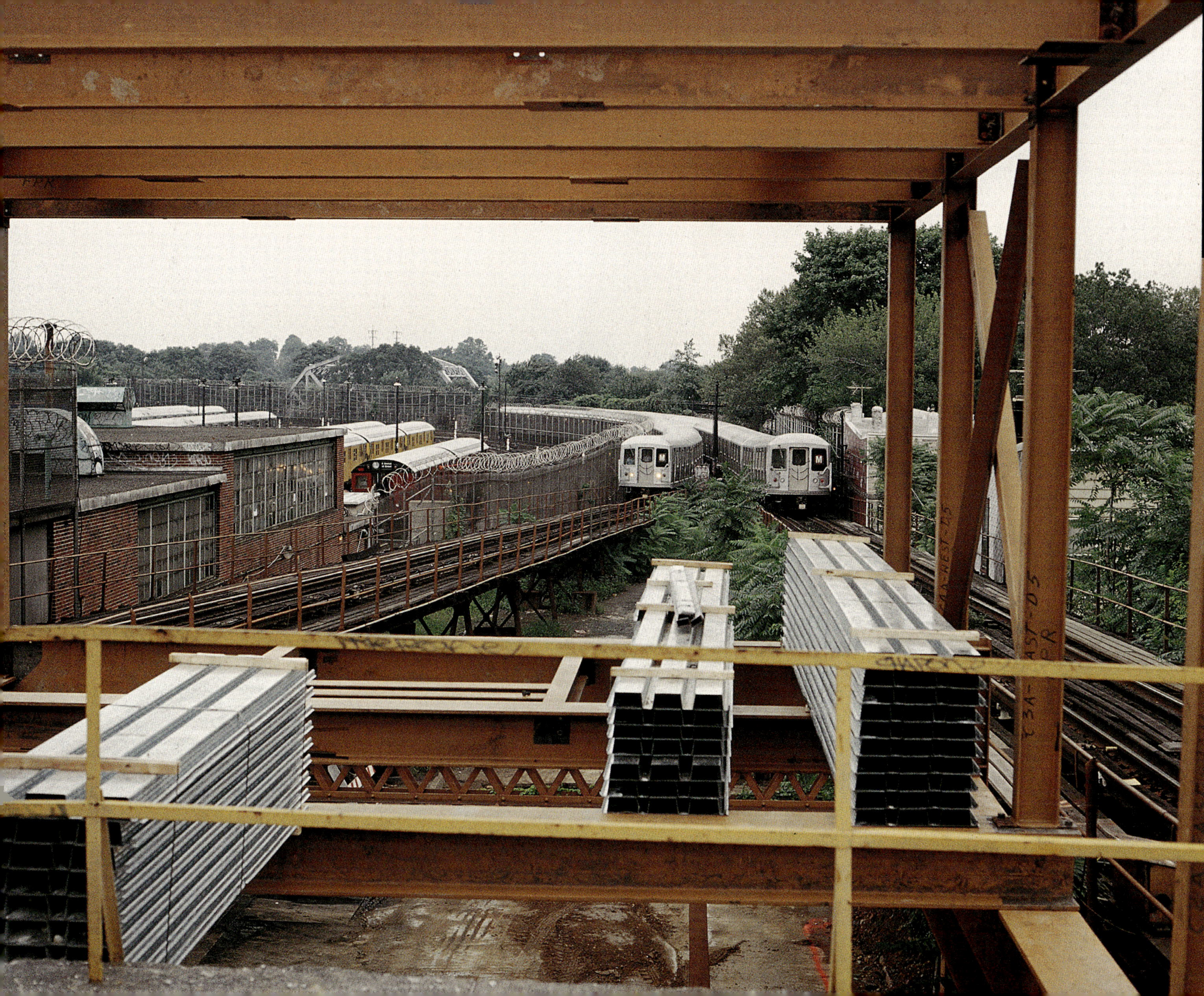

Fresh Pond Yard, Queens, 1989

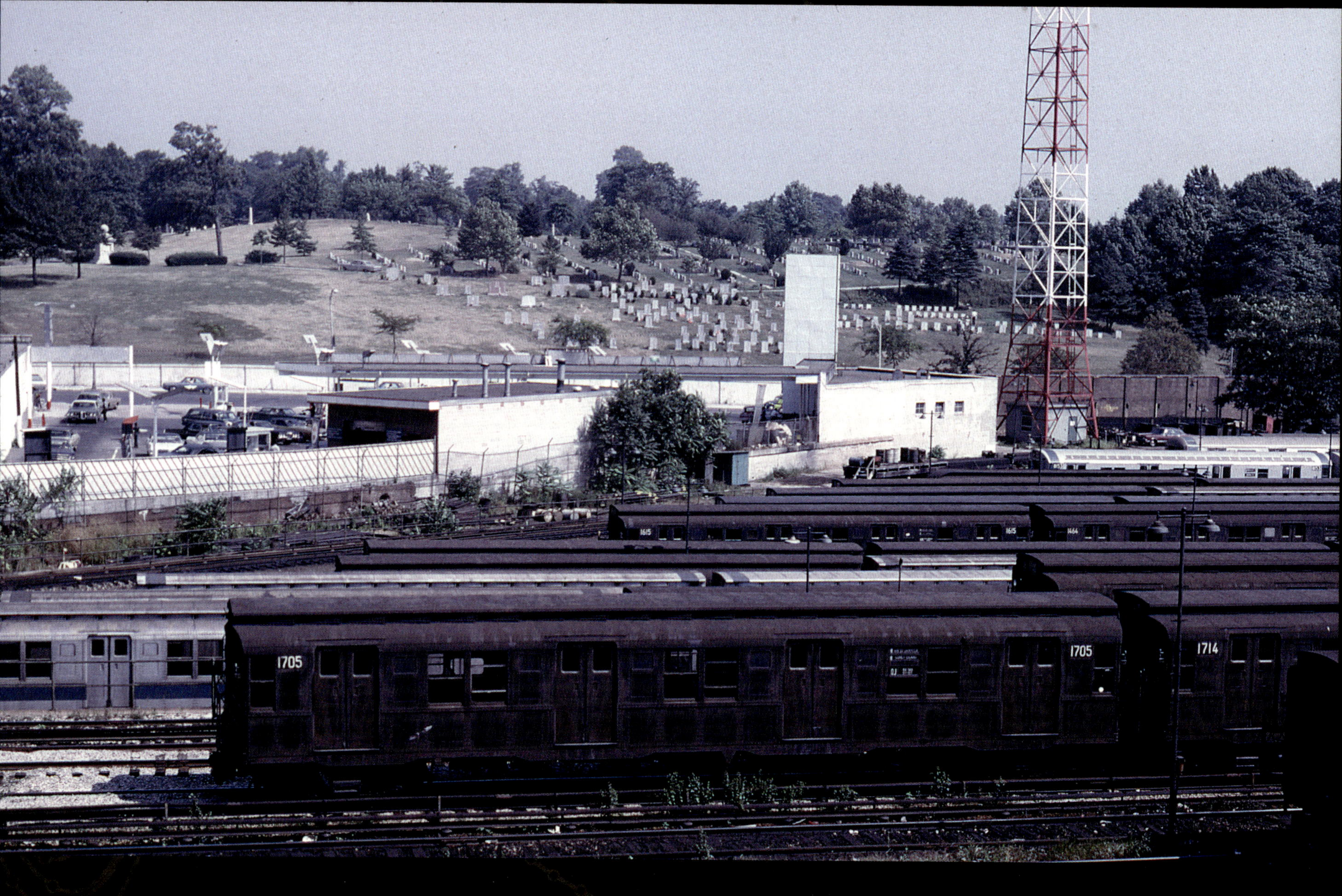
1705
1705
1714
1615
1615
1464

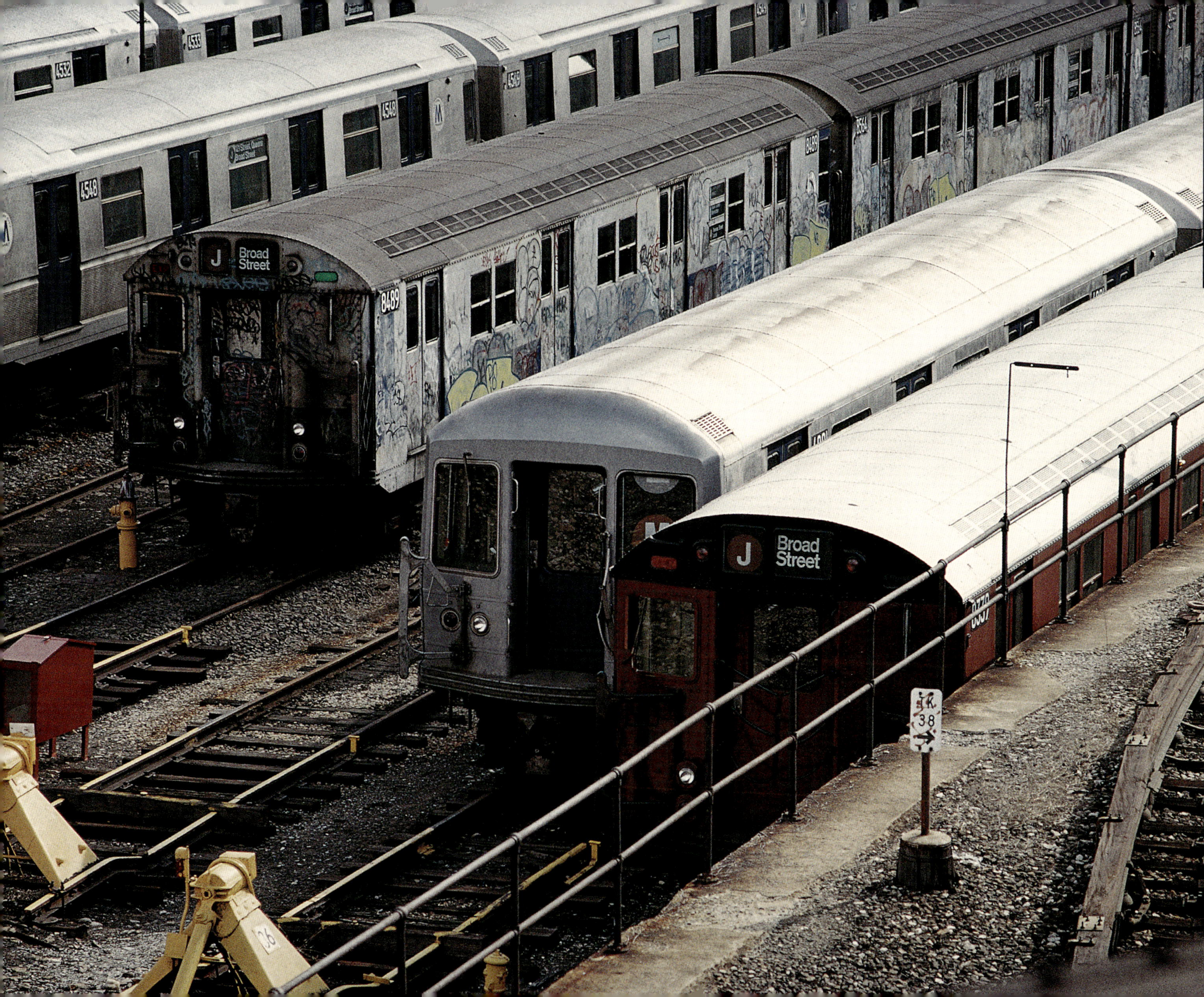

East New York Yard, Brooklyn, 1988

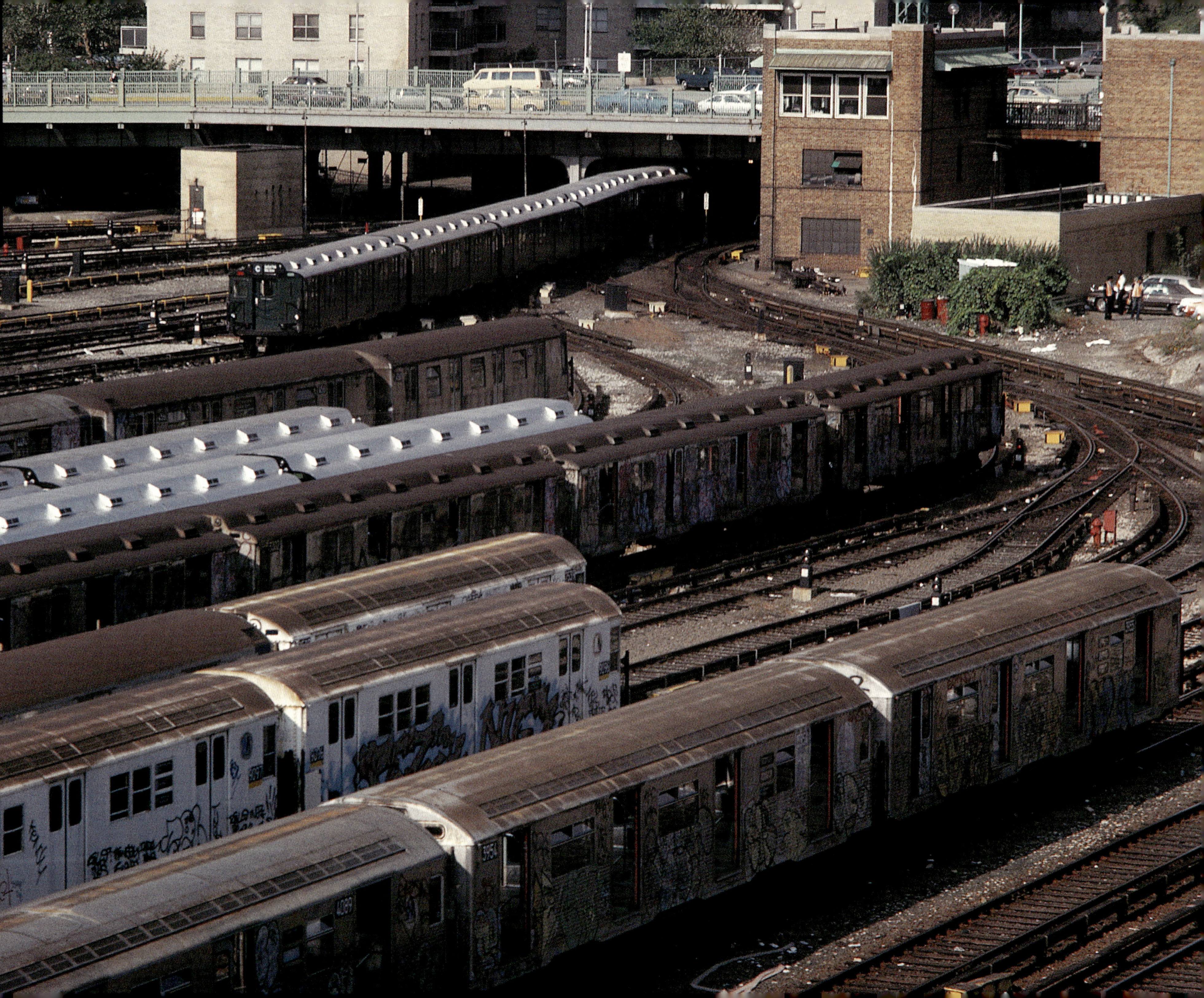

Concourse Yard, Bronx, 1985

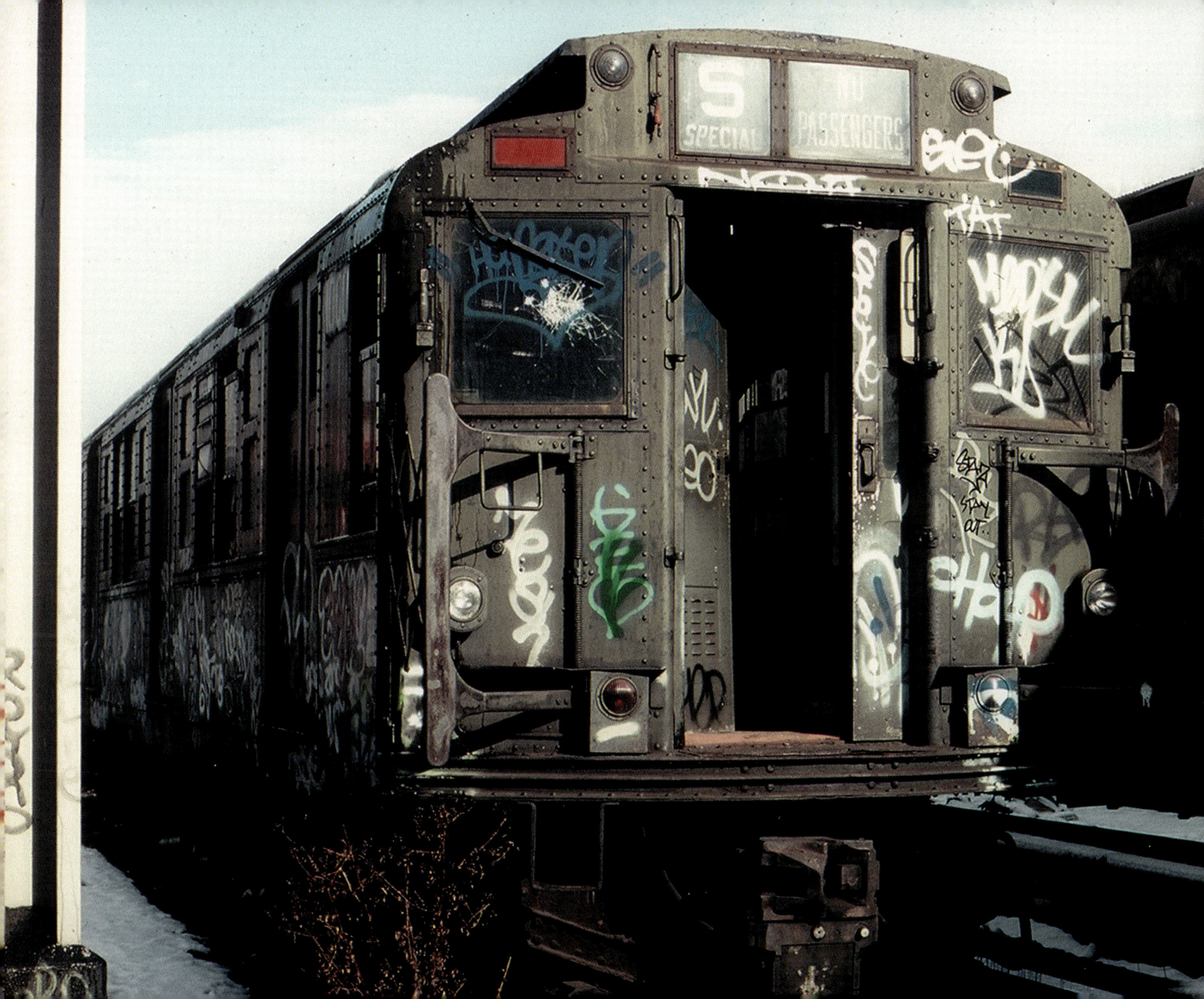

R-6-3, Concourse Yard, Bronx,1988

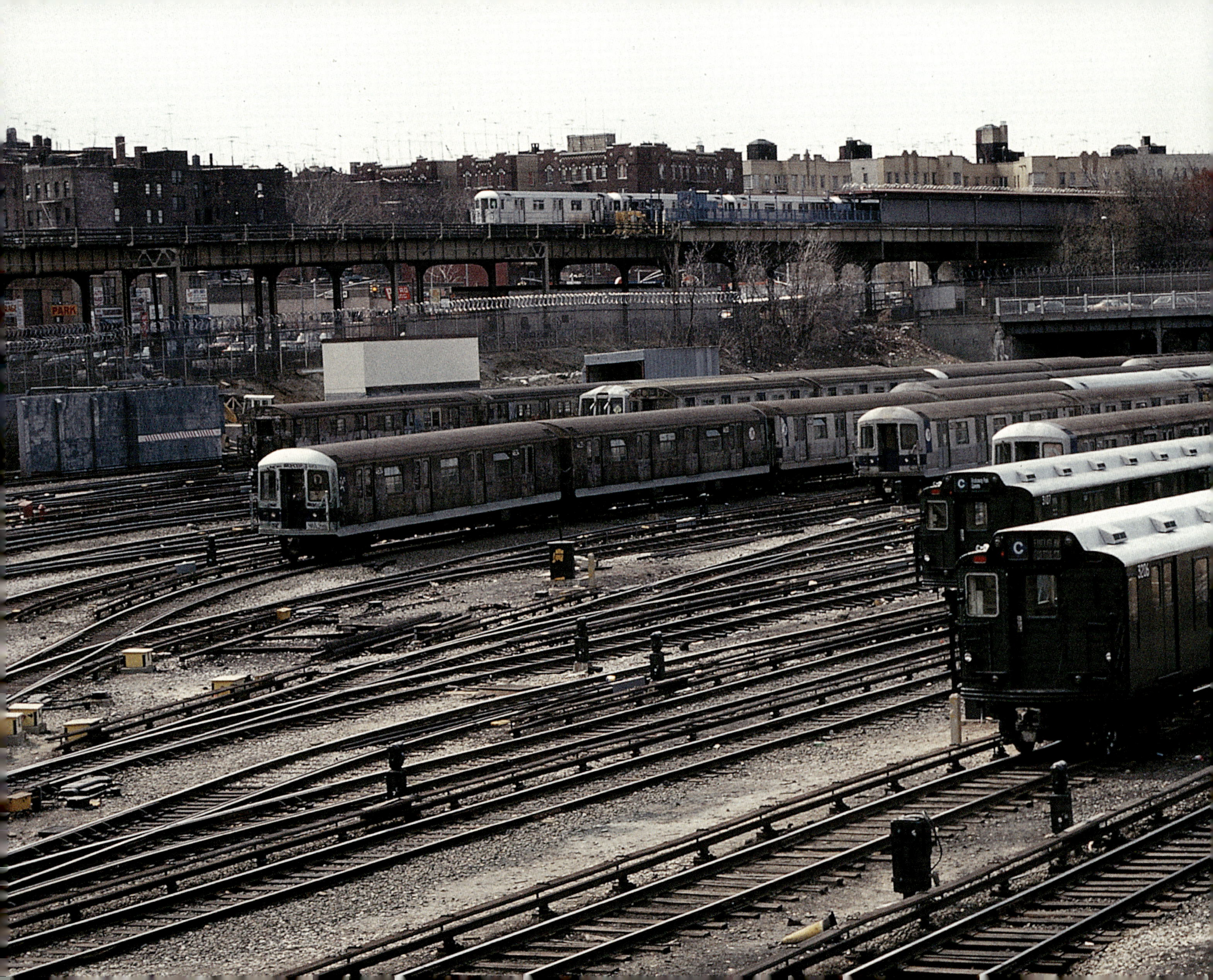
PARK
C
C

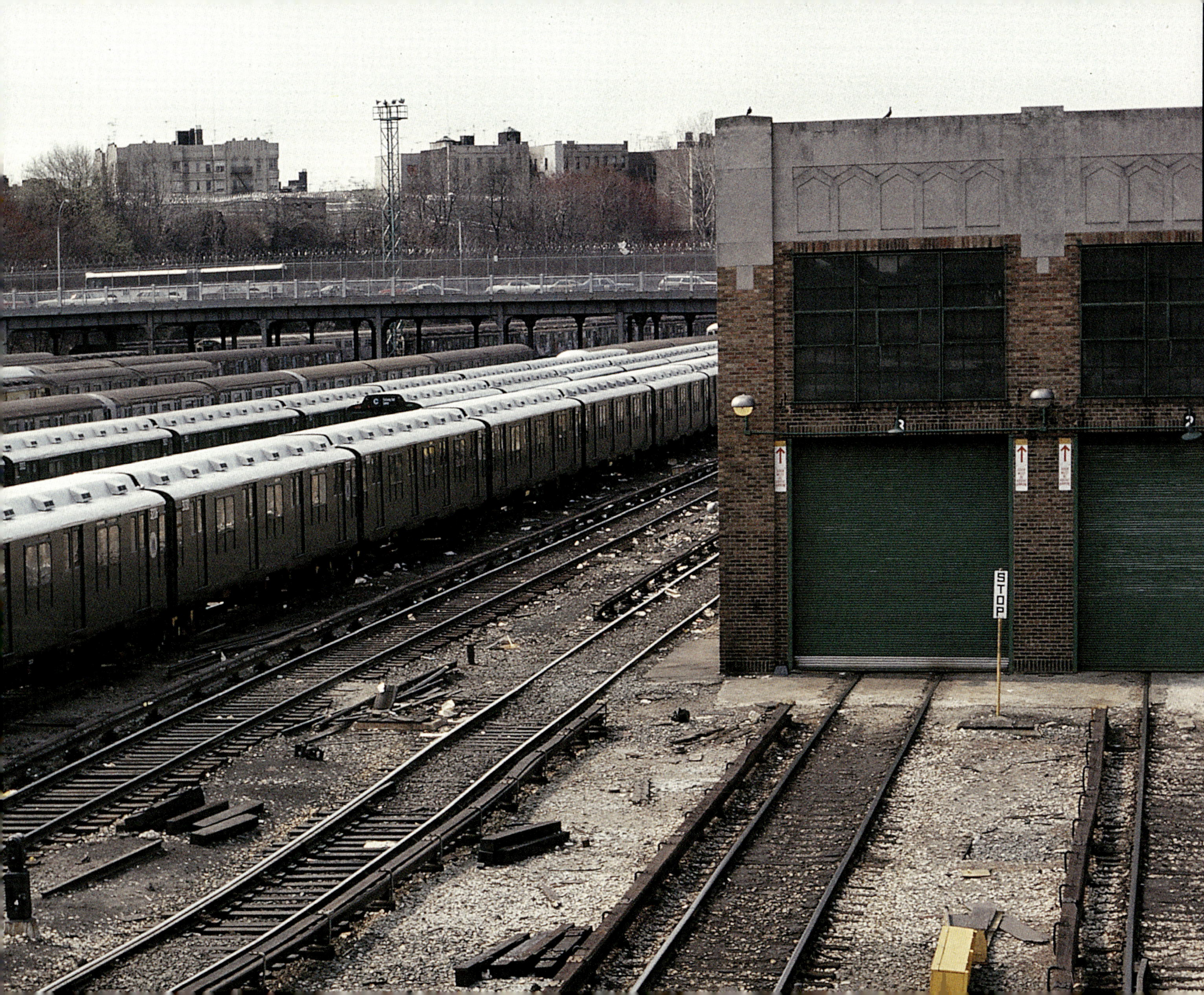

Concourse Yard, Bronx, 1985

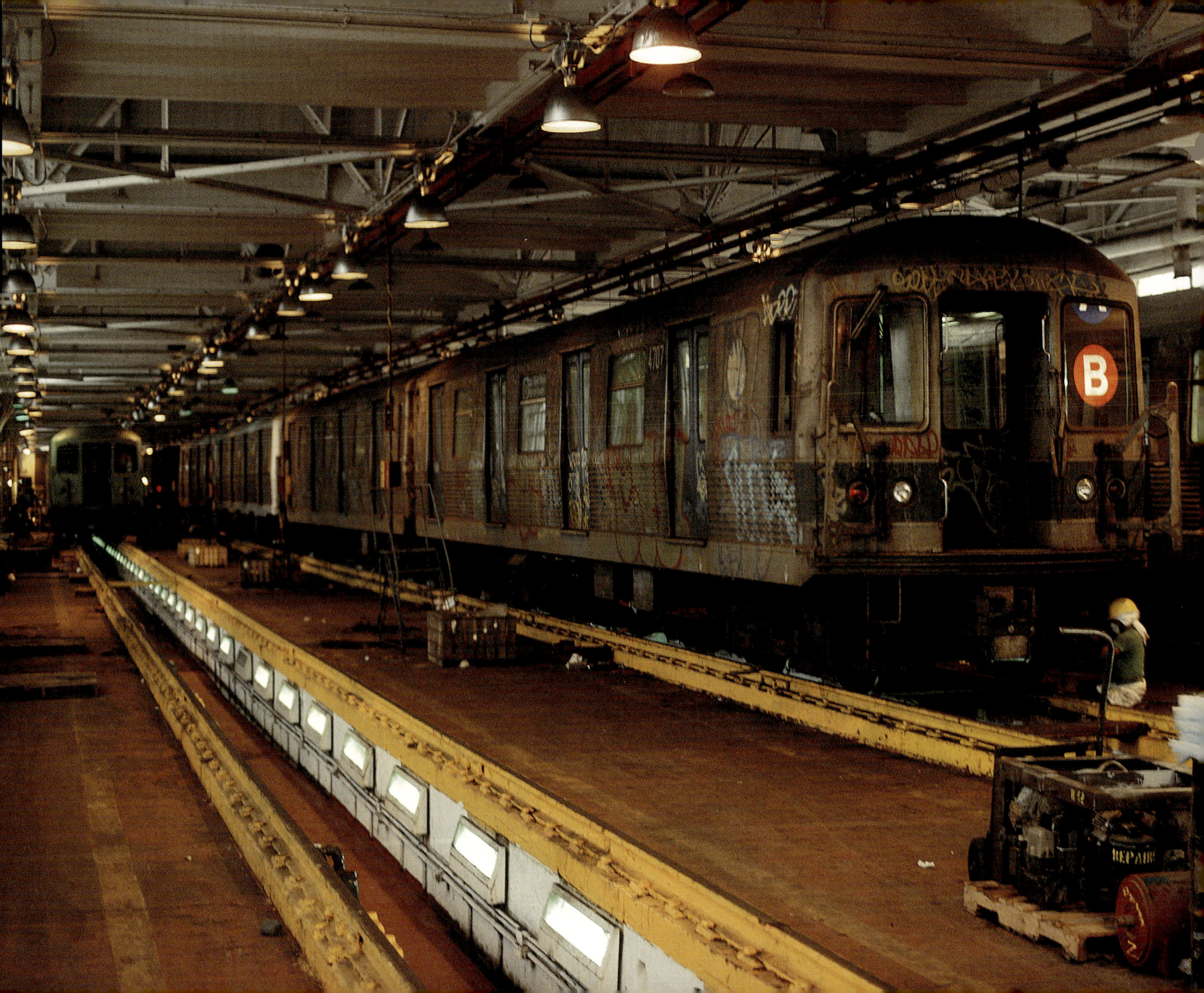

R-42, Concourse Shops, Bronx, 1988

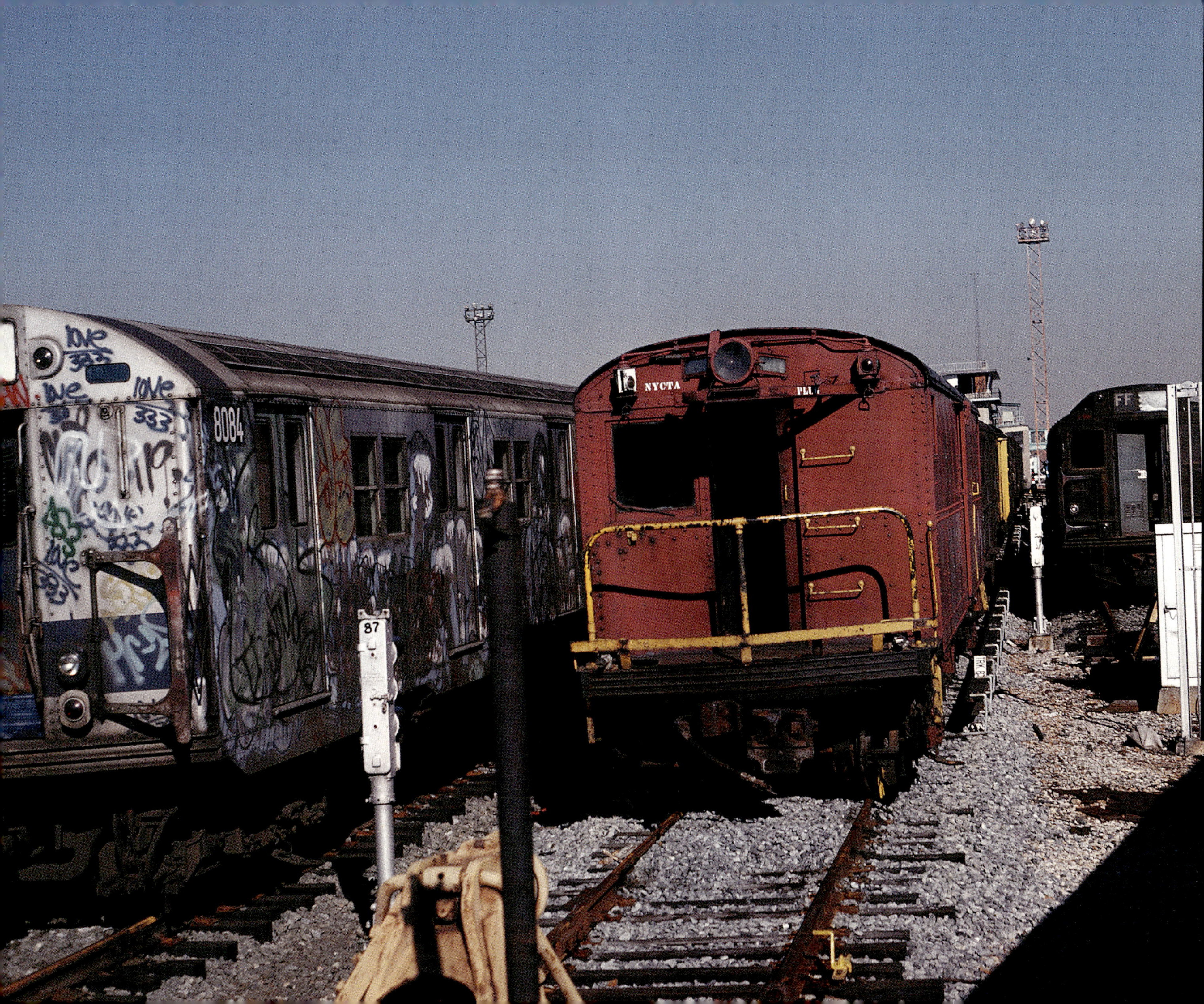

Coney Island Yard, Brooklyn, 1978 . . . Car #8084 *(left)* can be seen in Walter Hill's 1979 movie *The Warriors*.

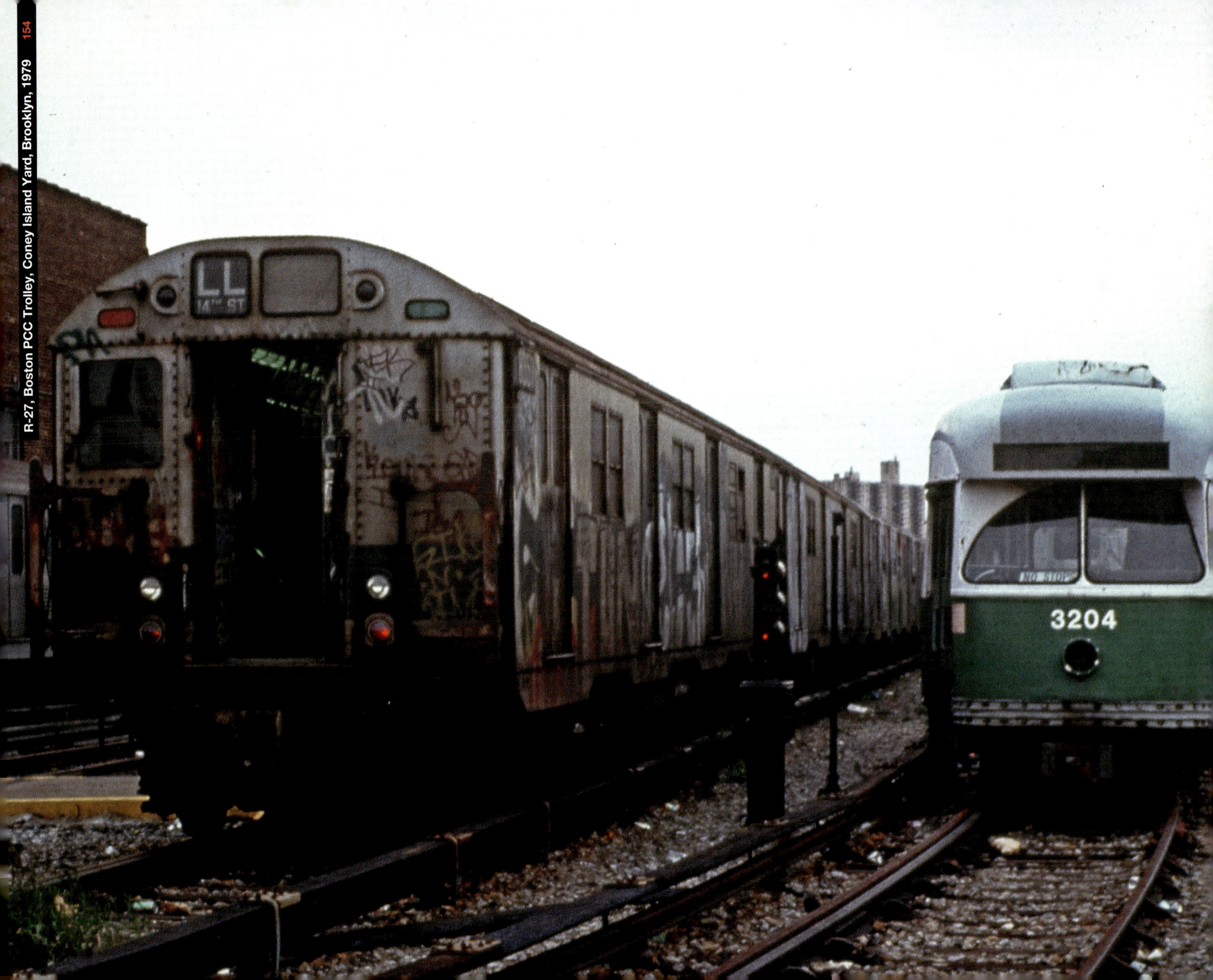

R-27, Boston PCC Trolley, Coney Island Yard, Brooklyn, 1979

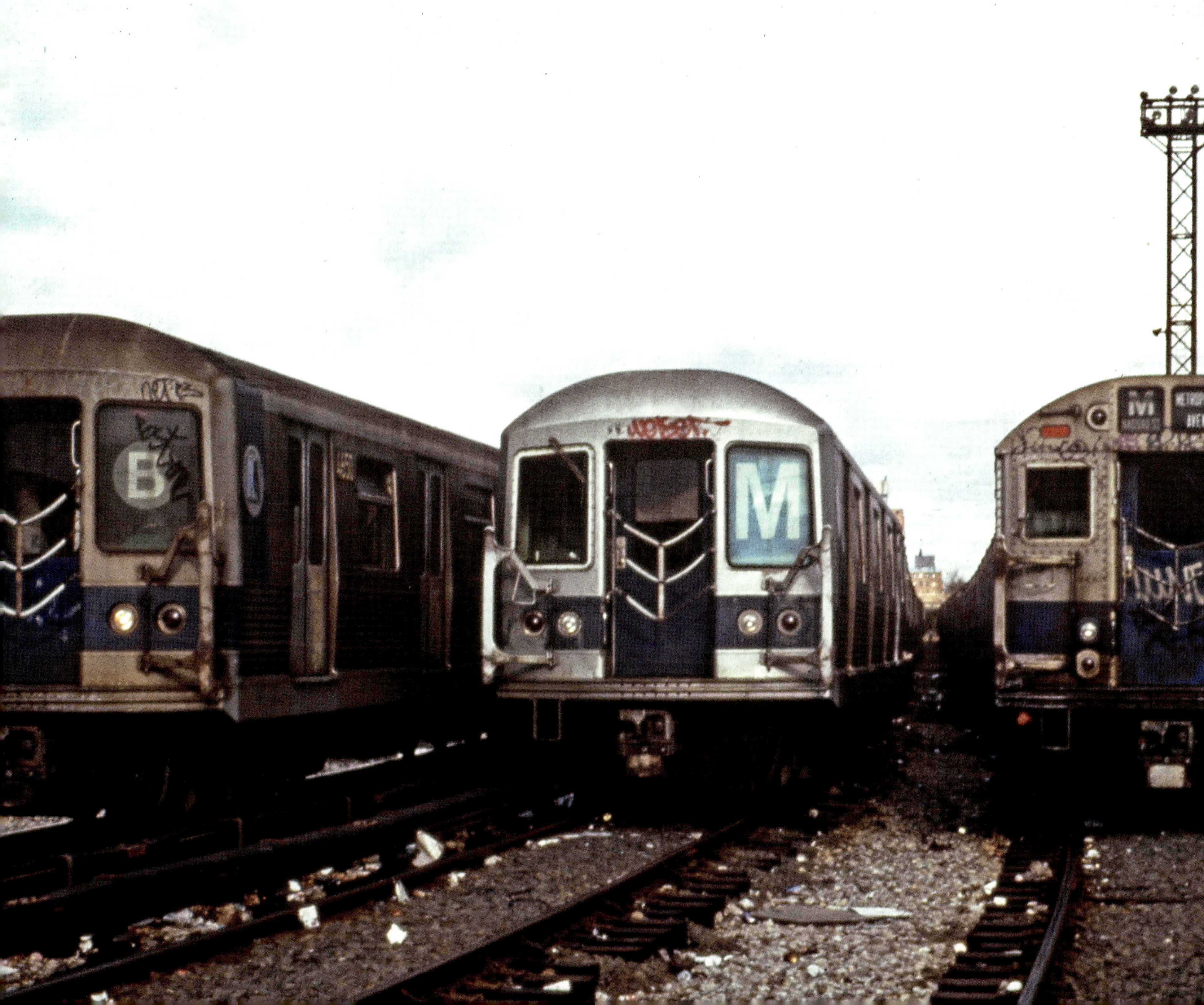

Coney Island Yard, Brooklyn, 1981

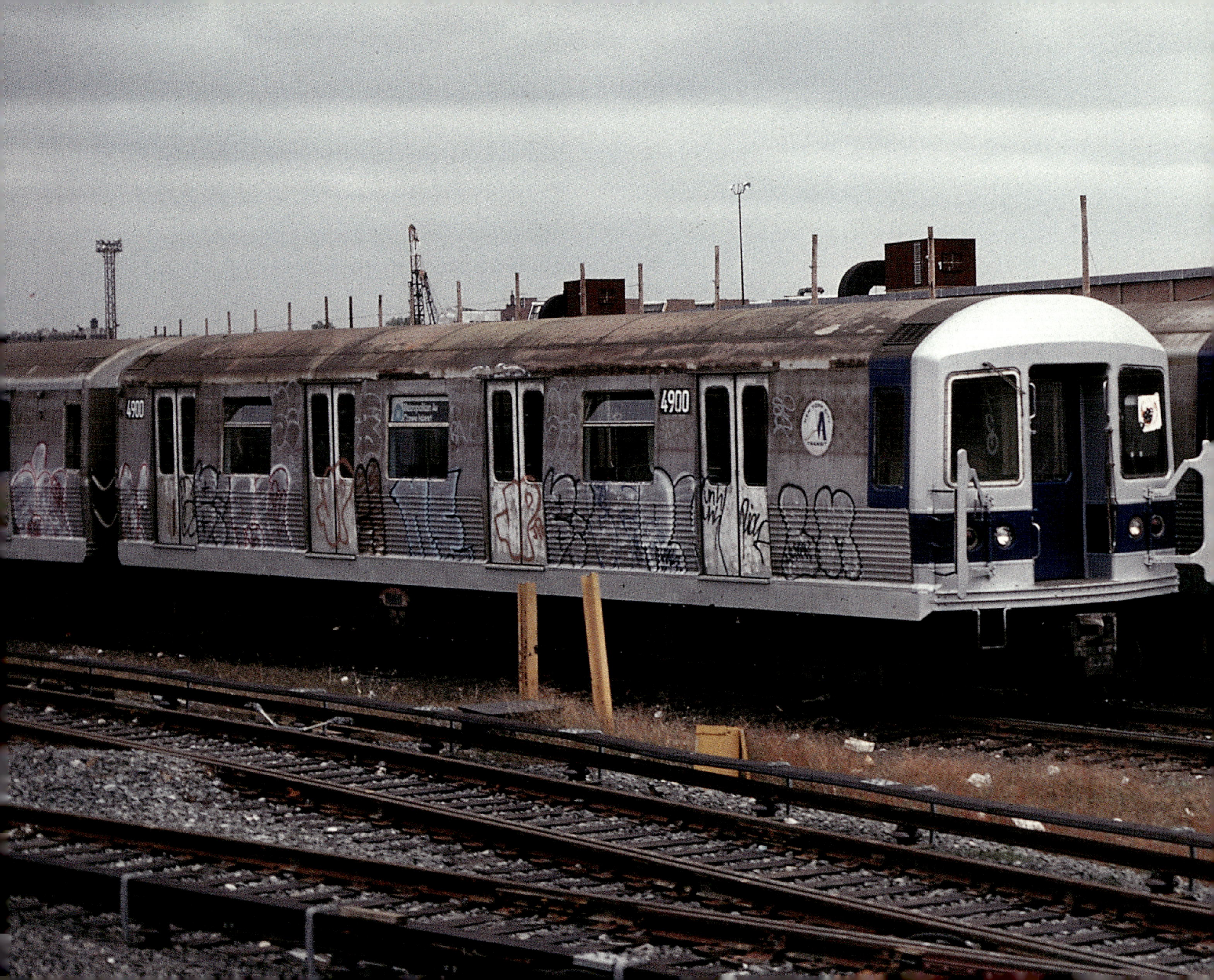
4900
4900

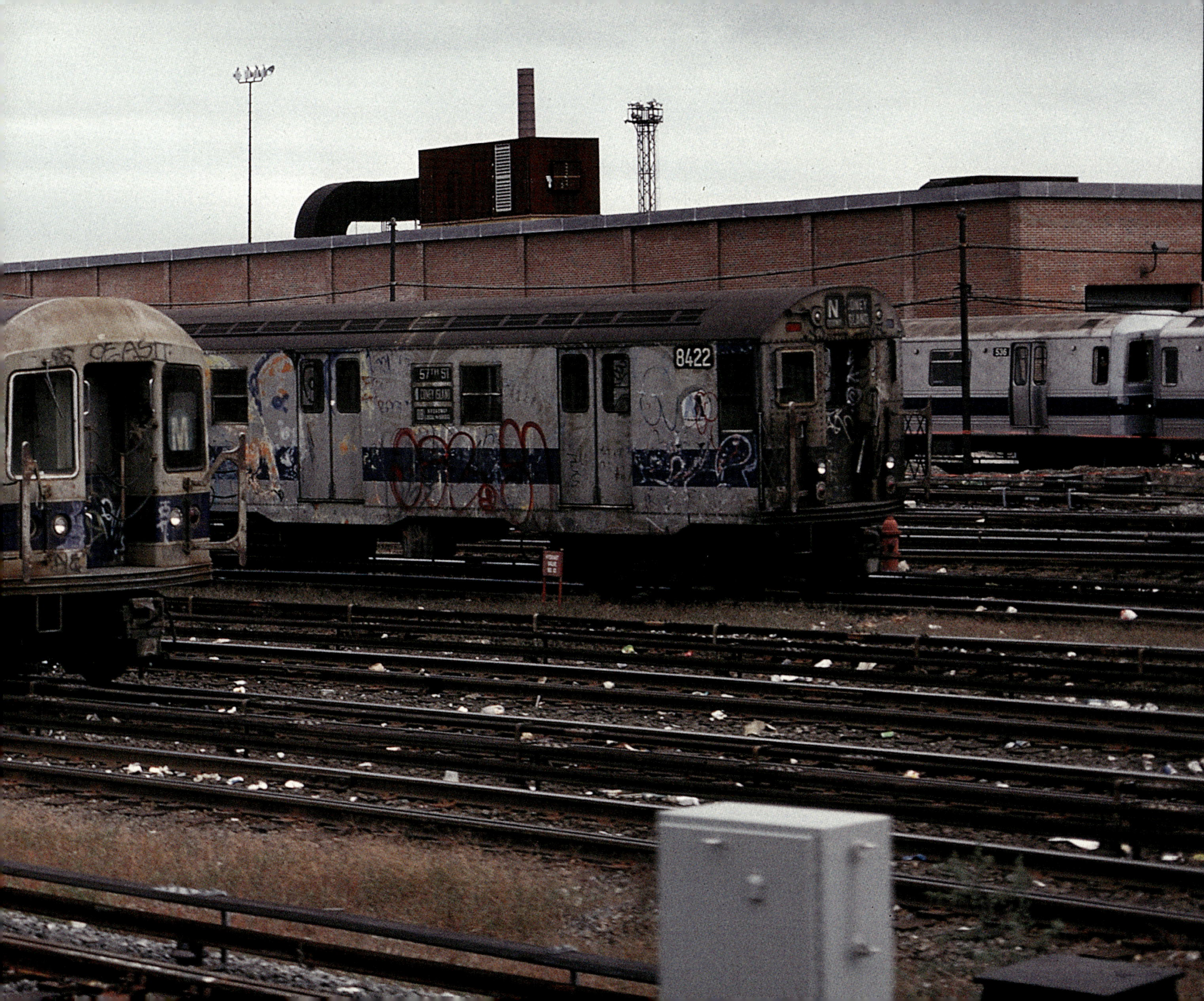

Coney Island Yard, Brooklyn, 1984

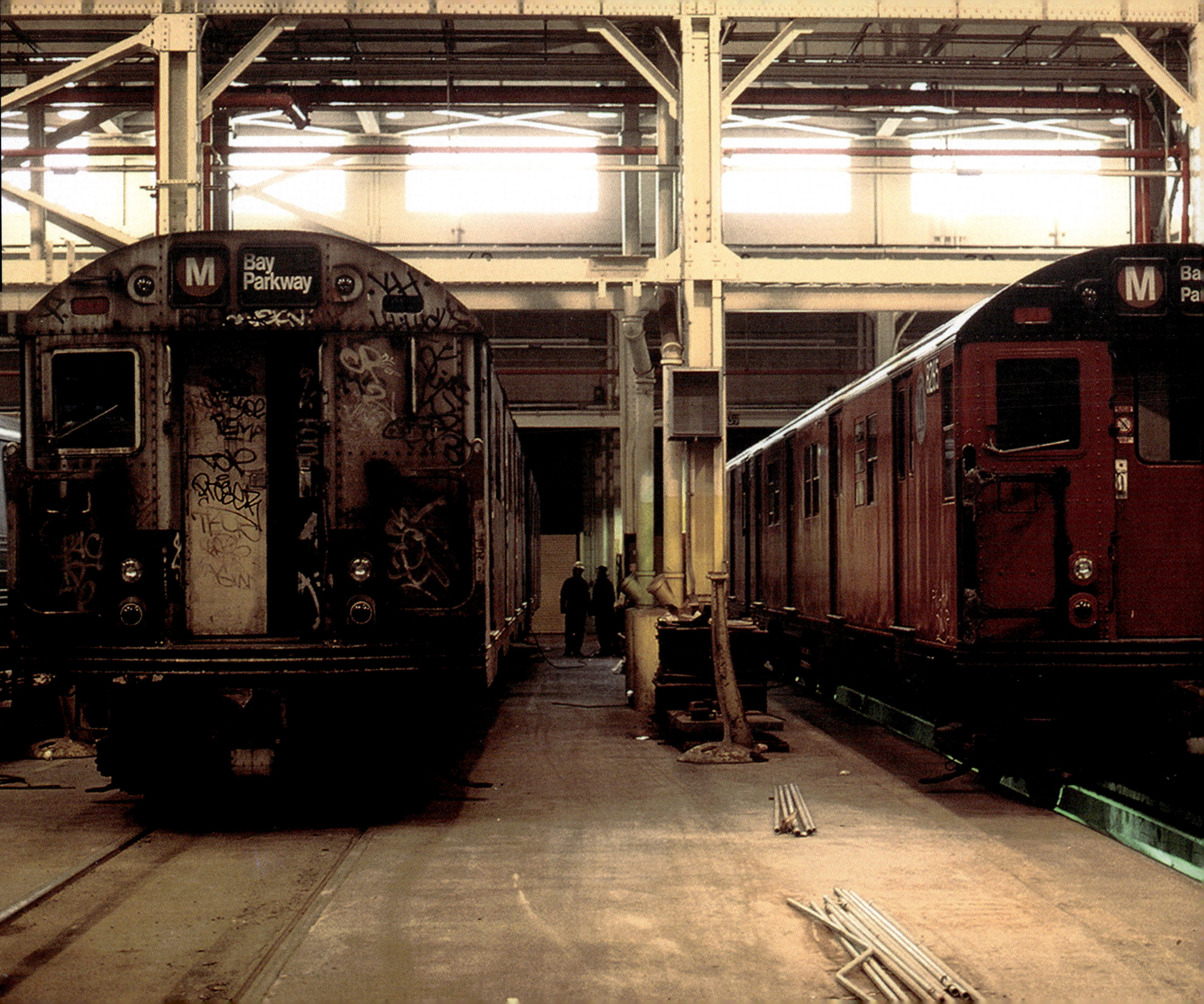

Coney Island Shops, Brooklyn, 1989

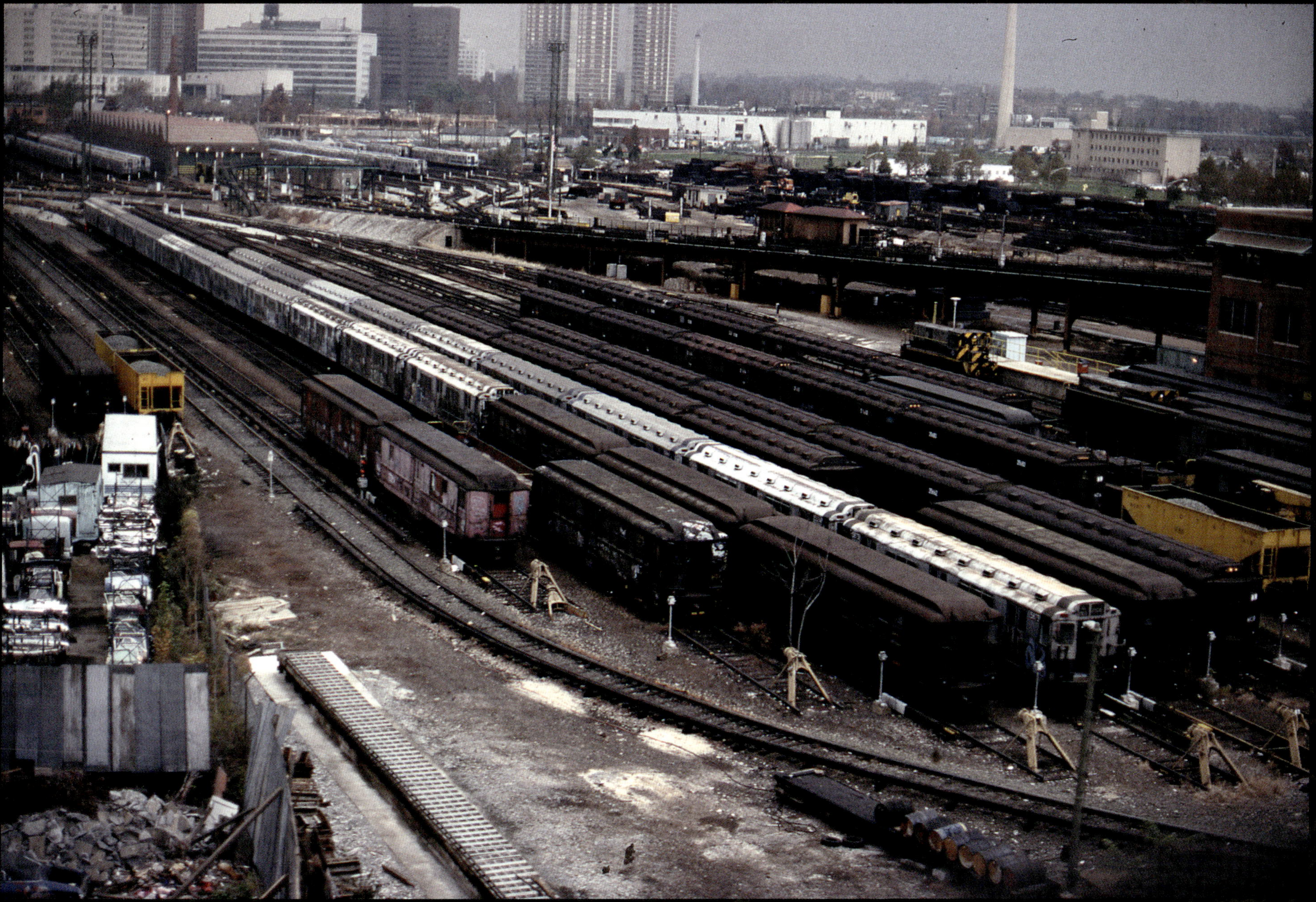

Westchester Yard, No. 6 Pelham line, Bronx, 1976

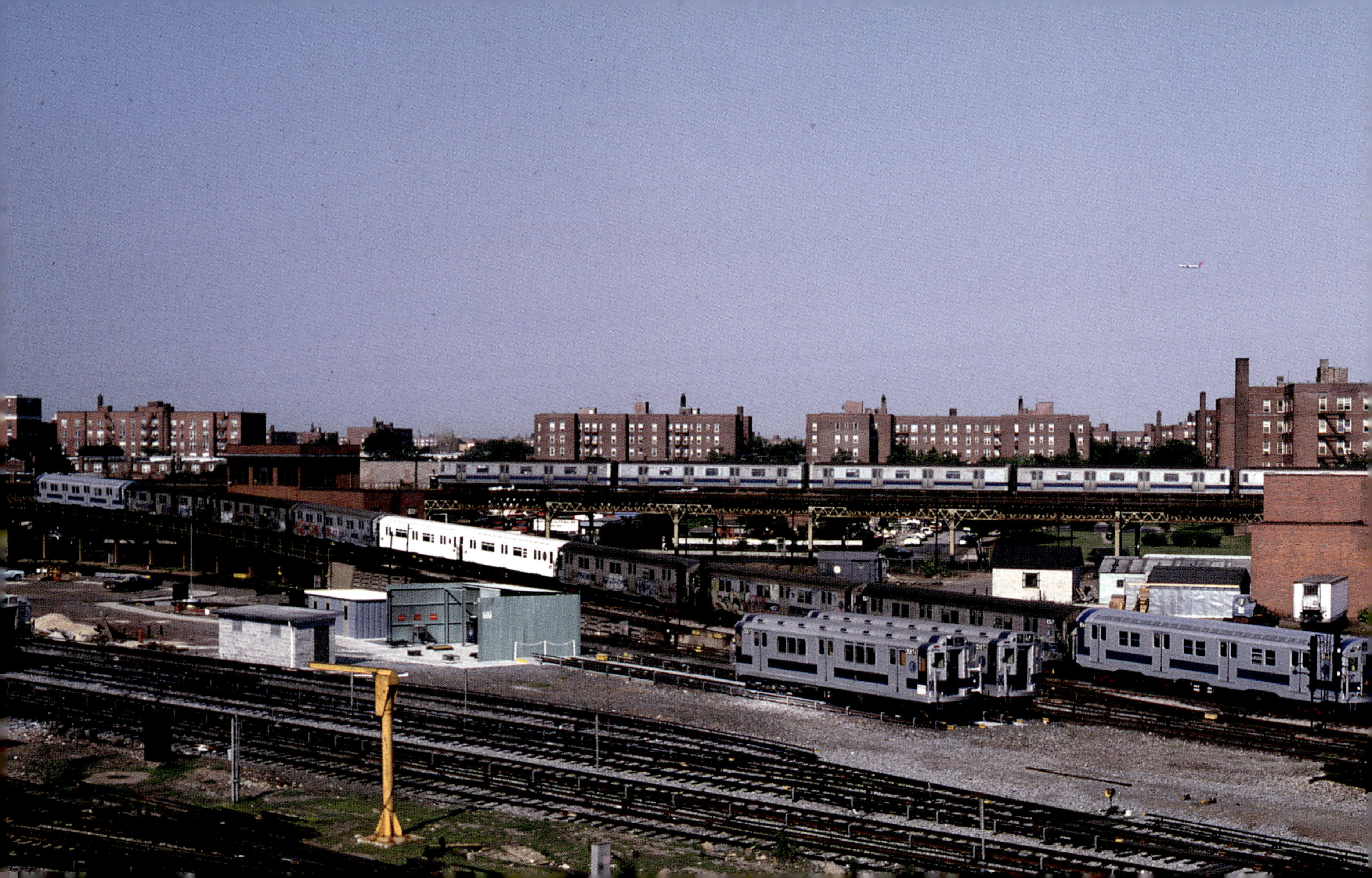

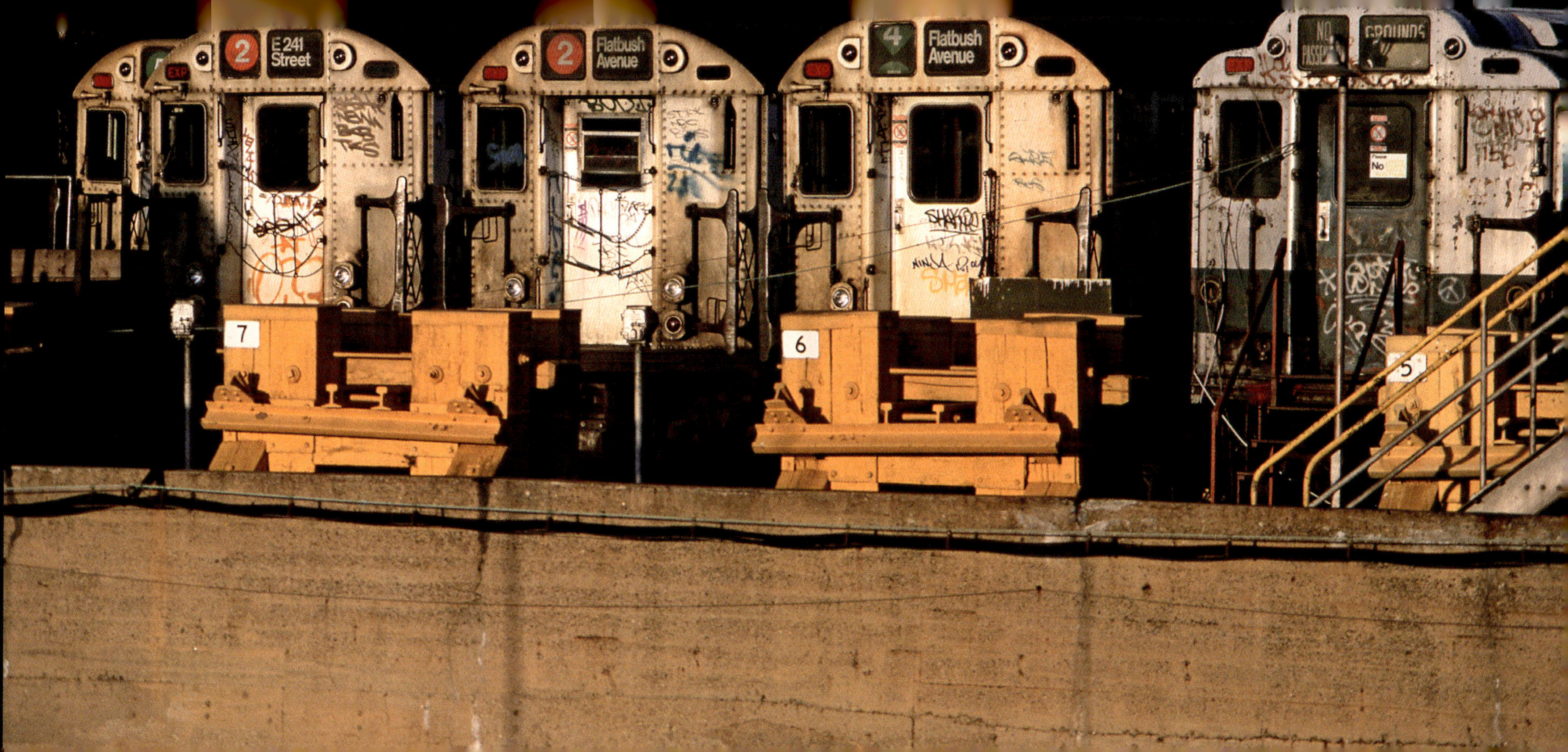
2
E 241 Street
2
Flatbush Avenue
4
Flatbush Avenue
GROUNDS
7
6
5

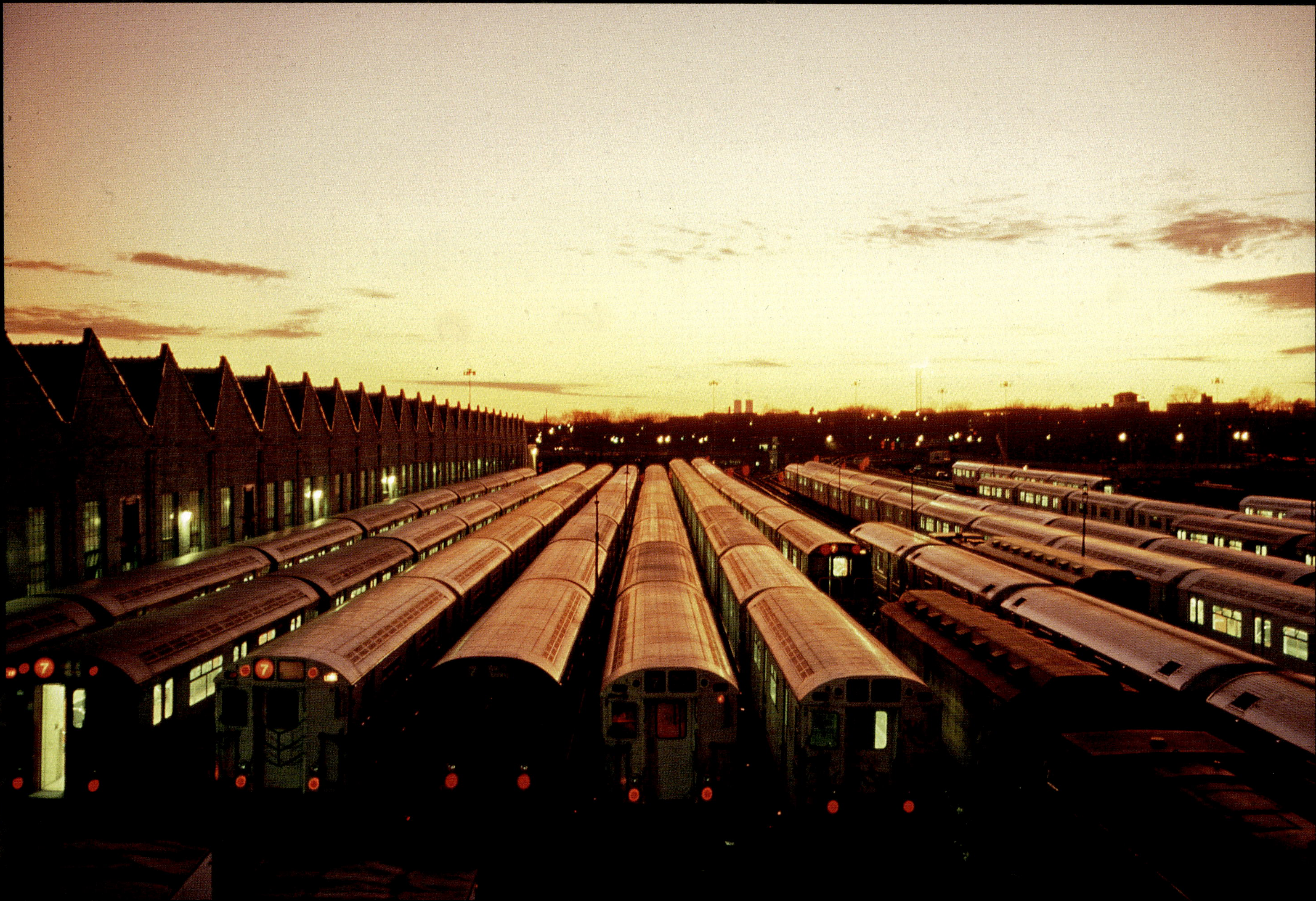

Corona Yard, Queens, 1985

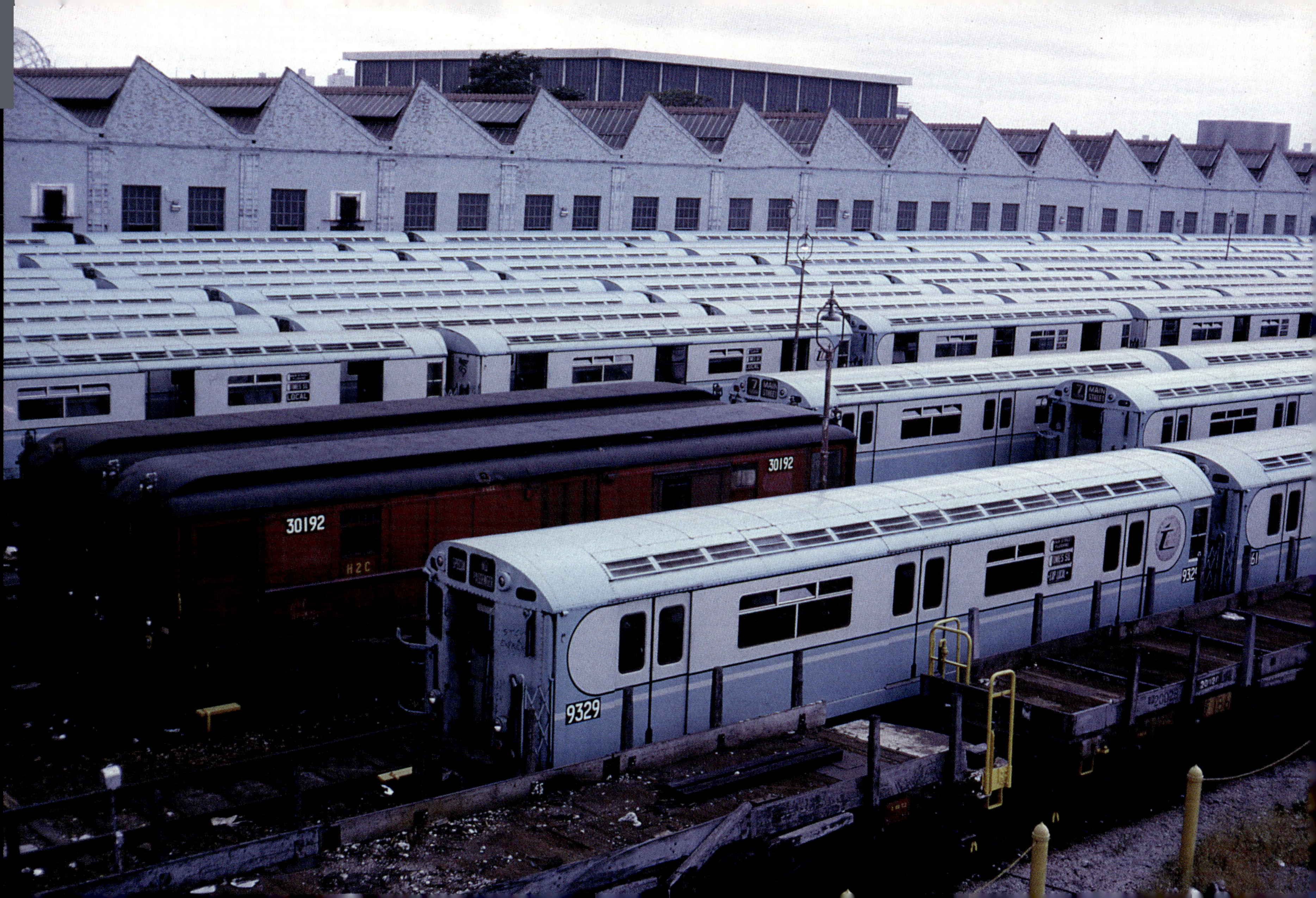
30192
30192
H2C
9329

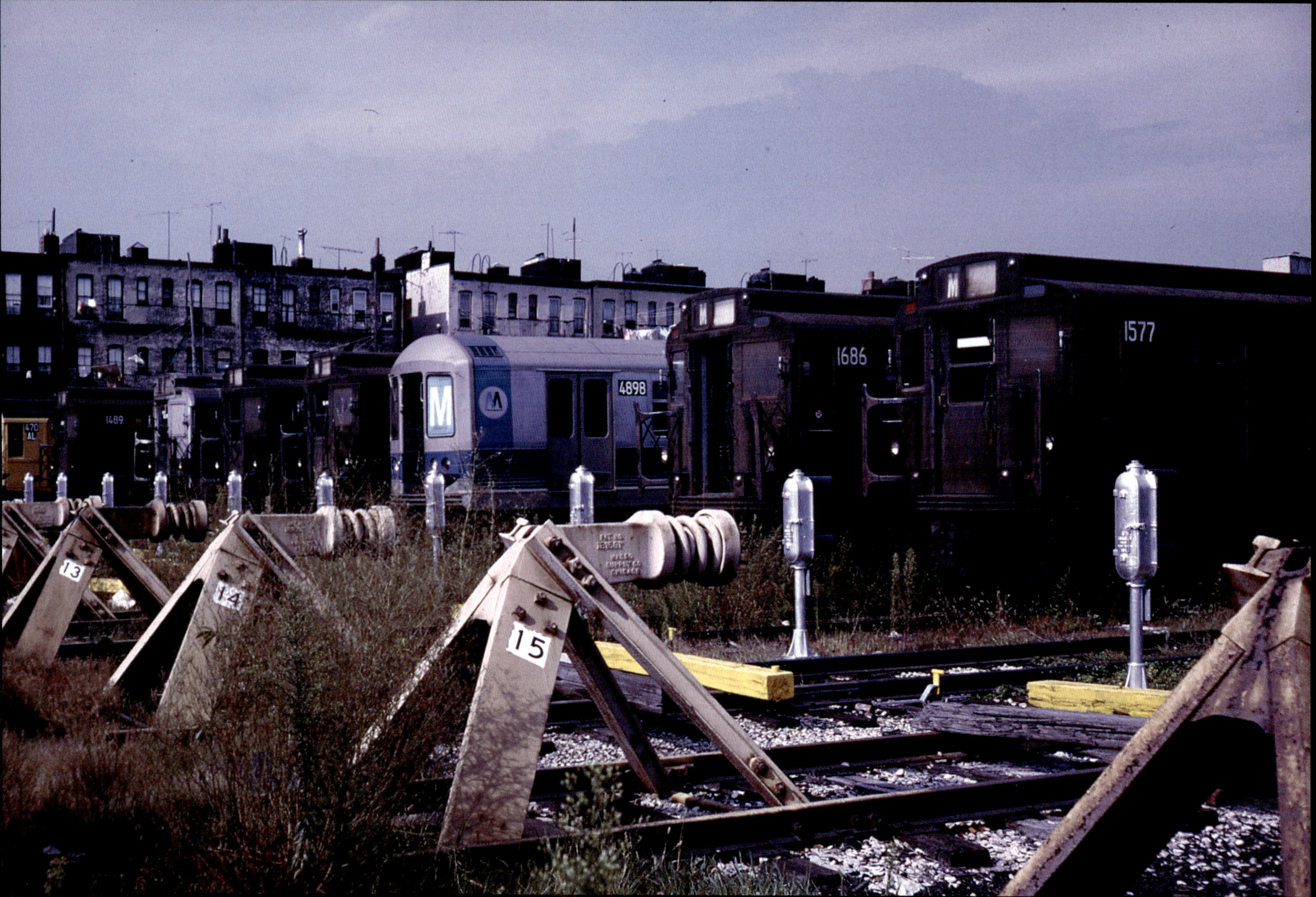

M
4898
1686
1577
1489
13
14
15

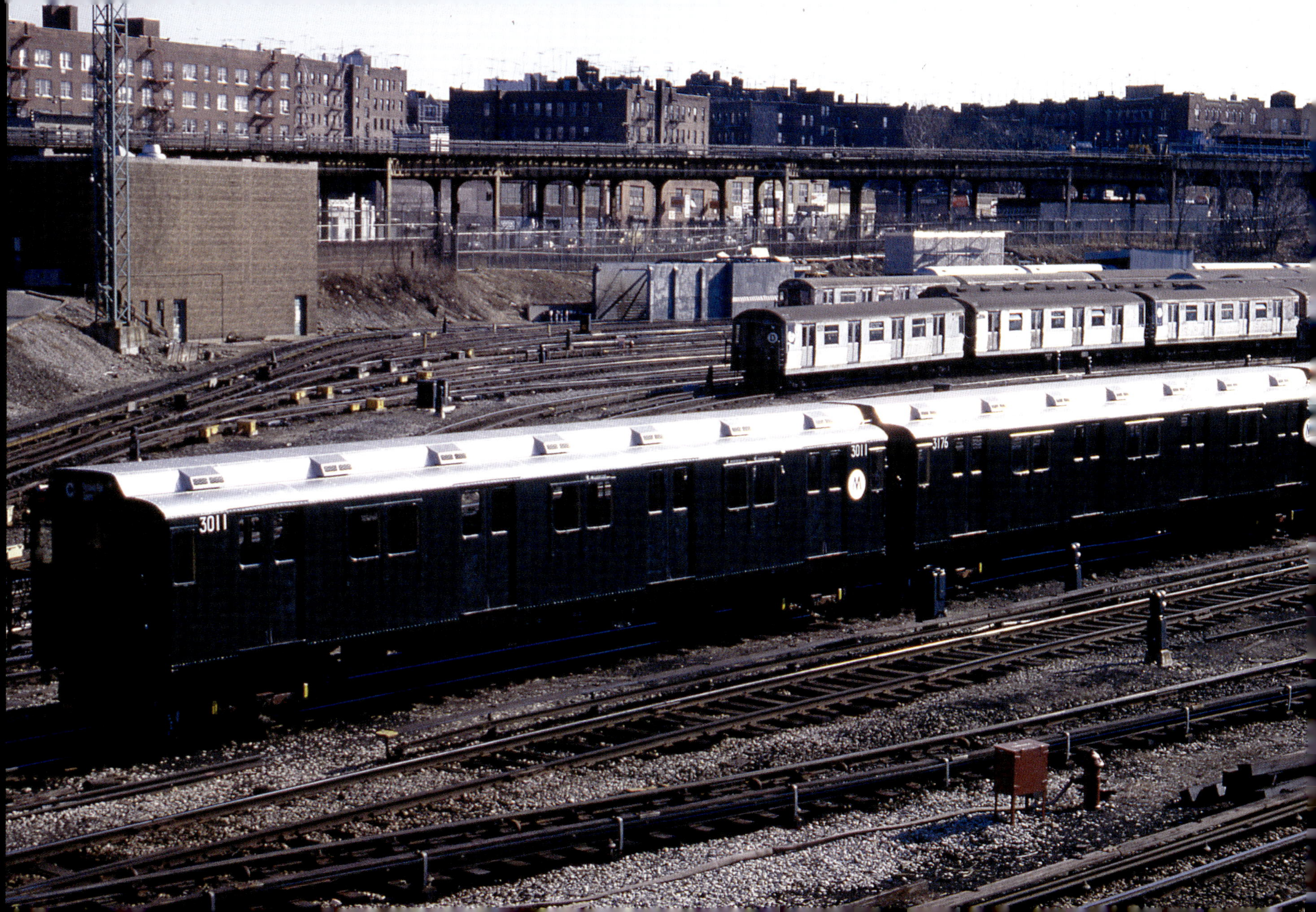
3011
3011
3176

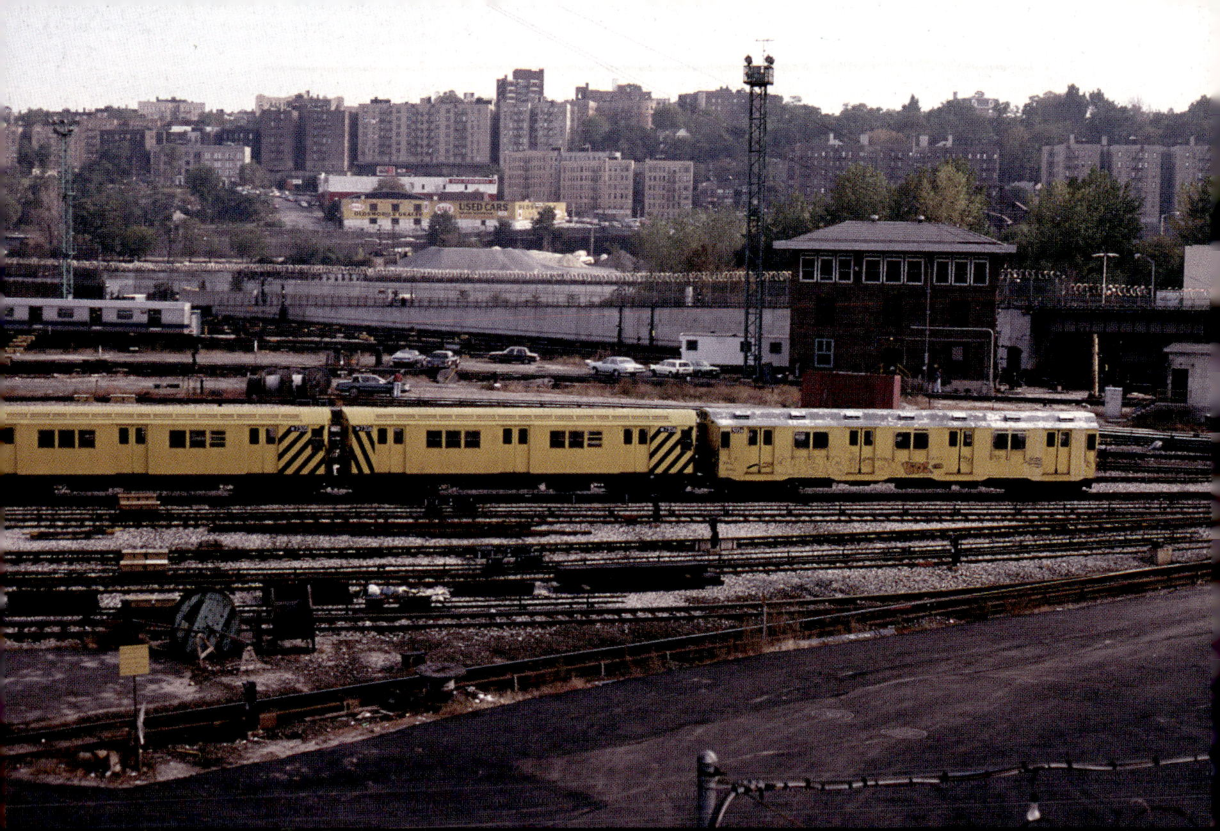
USED CARS

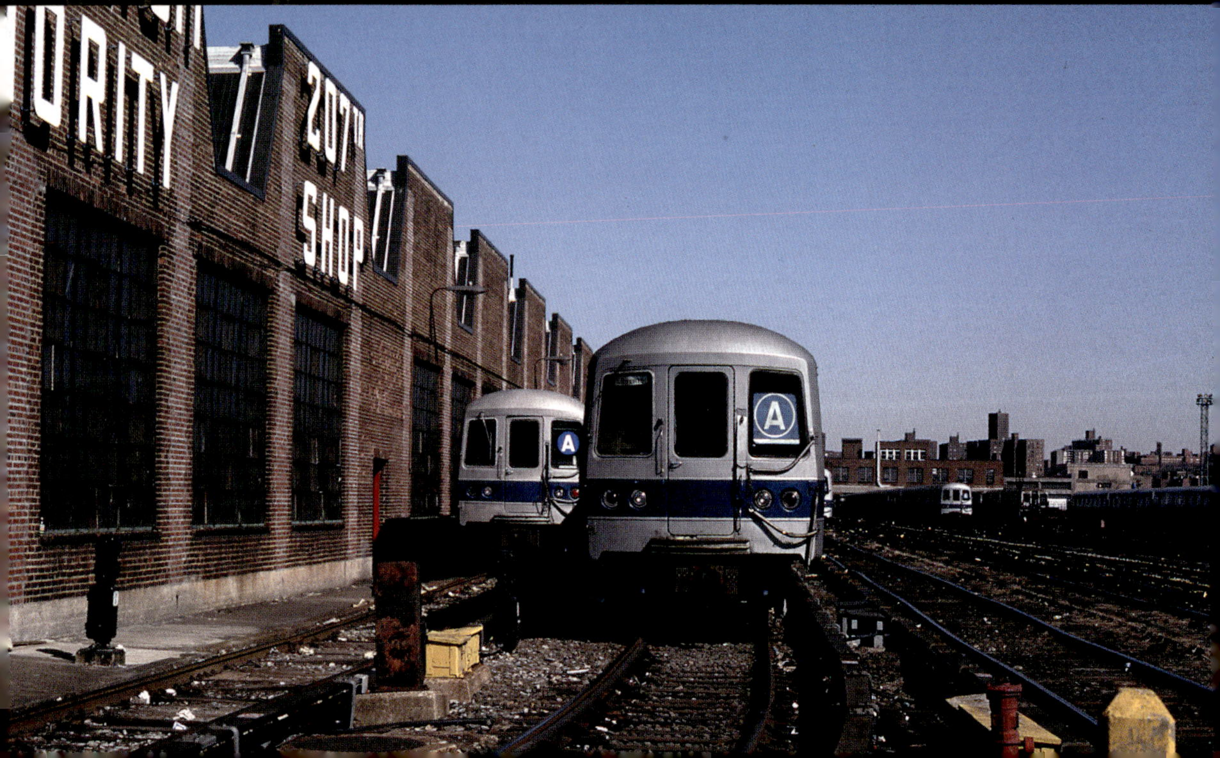
RITY
207TH
SHOP
A
A

The Underground

New York
Subways & Stations
1970–1990

CHAPTER 4

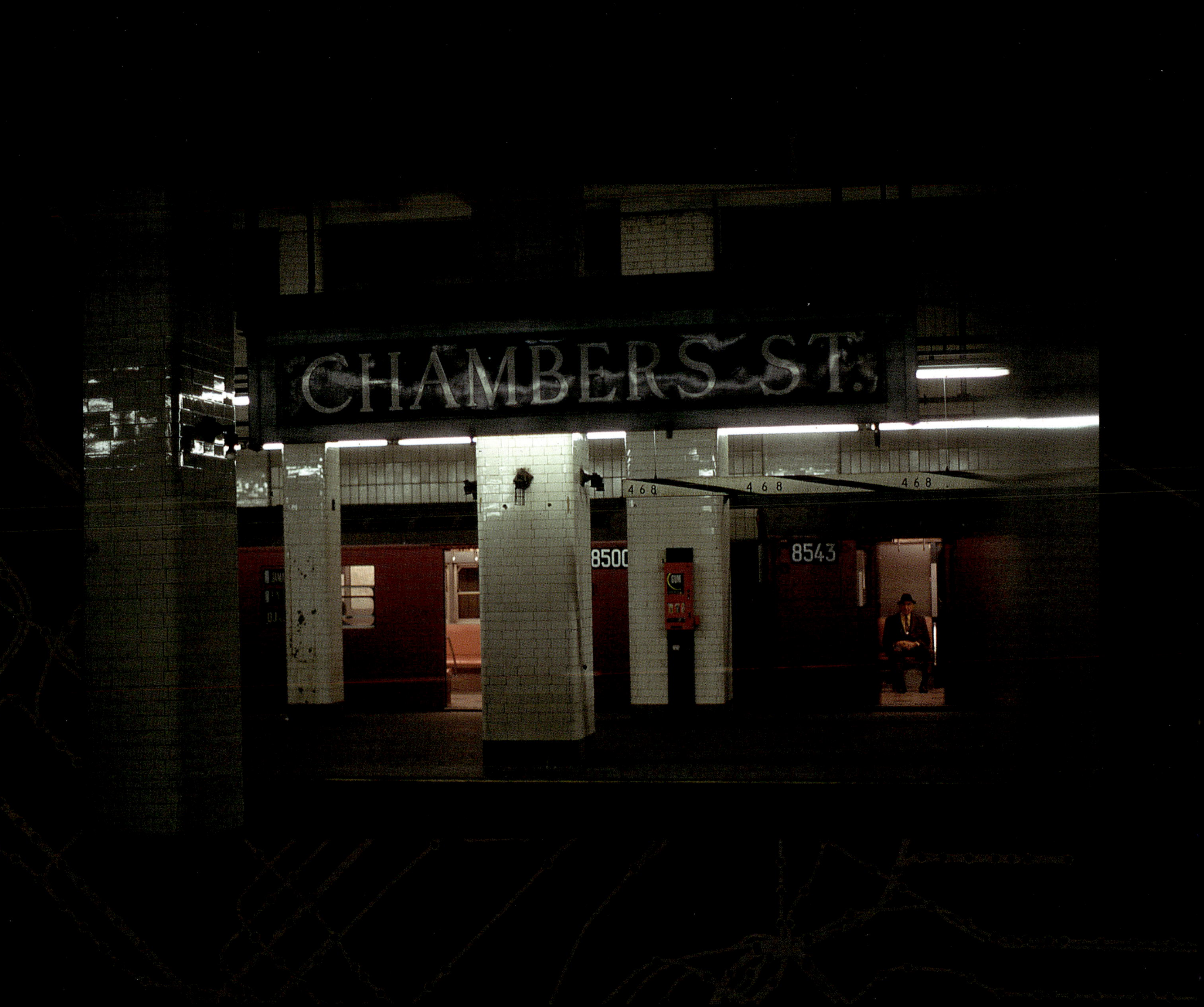

R-30, Chambers St., Manhattan, 1970

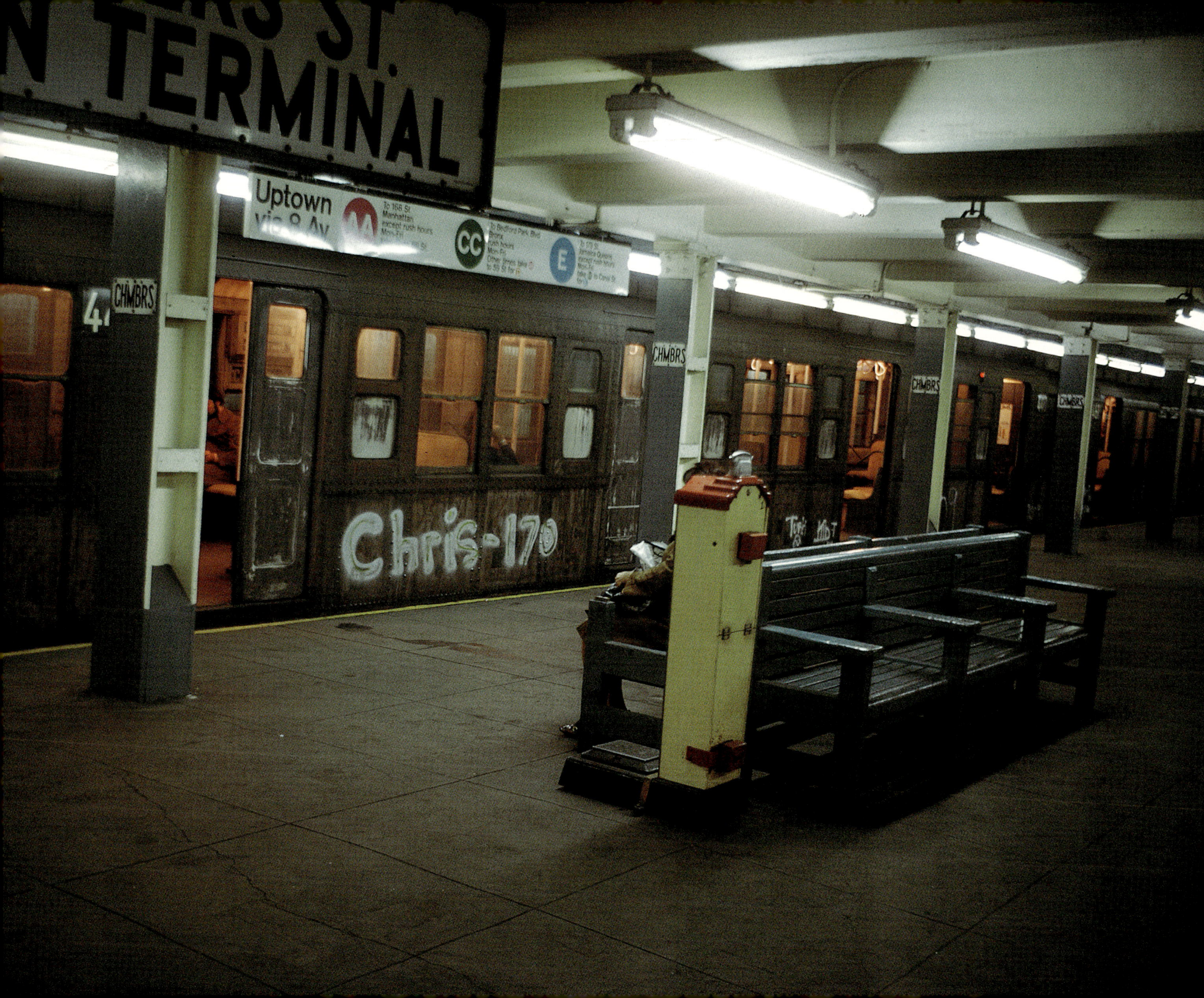

R-4, CC line, Chambers St.–Hudson Terminal, Manhattan, 1971

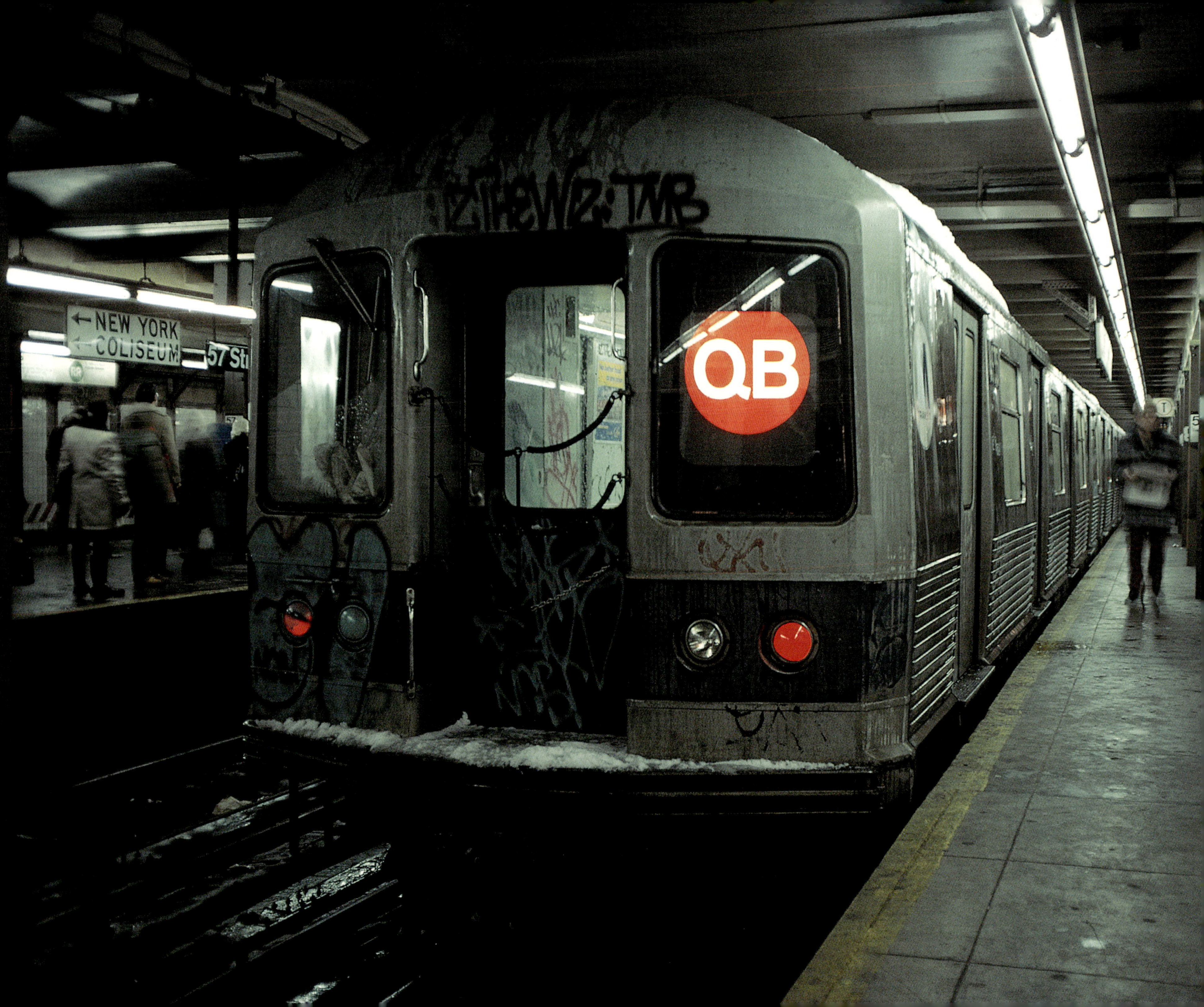

R-42s, QB line, 57th St.–7th Ave., Manhattan, 1978

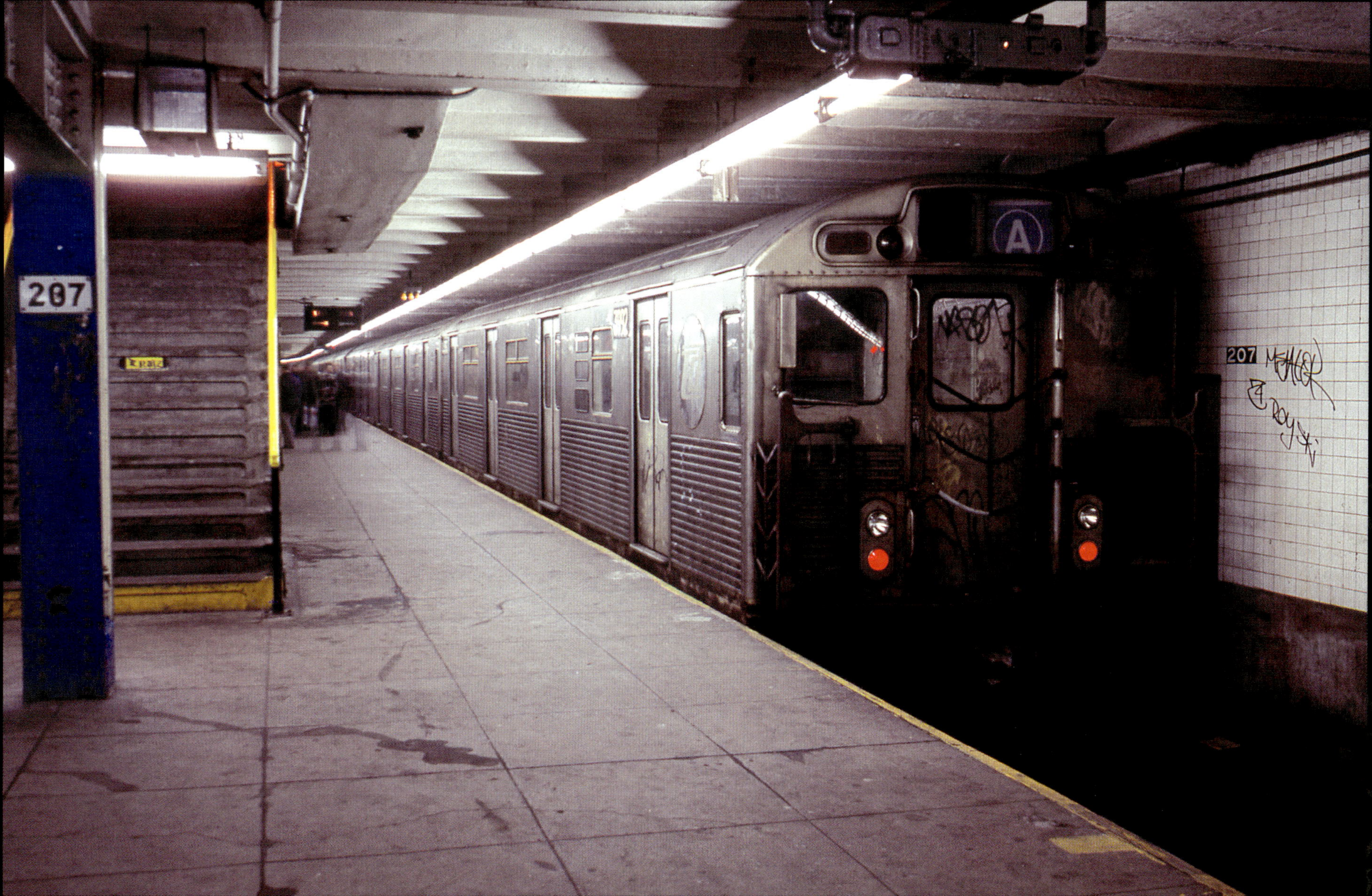

e, 207th St., Manhattan, 1980

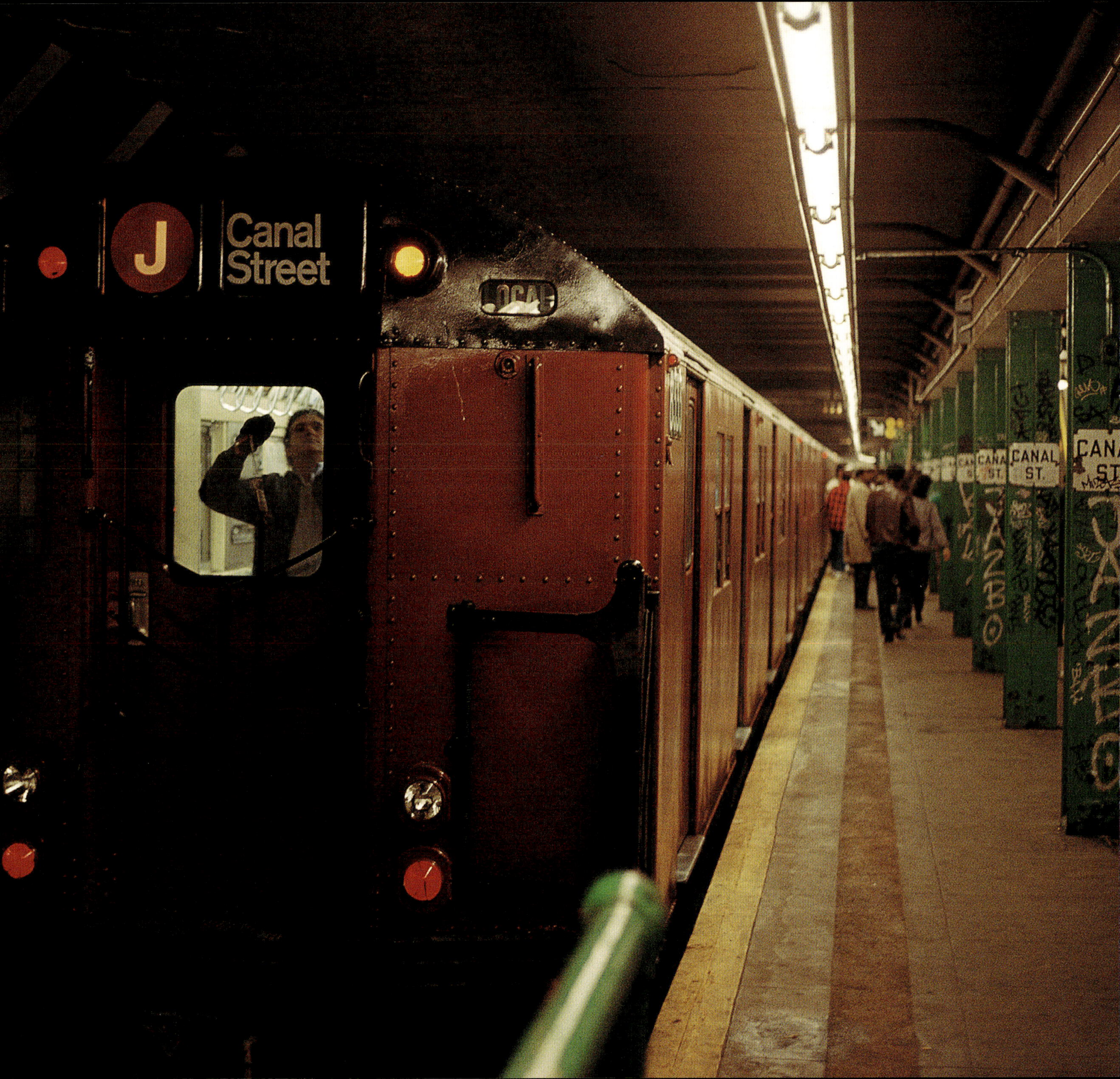
J
Canal
Street
LOCAL
CANAL
ST.

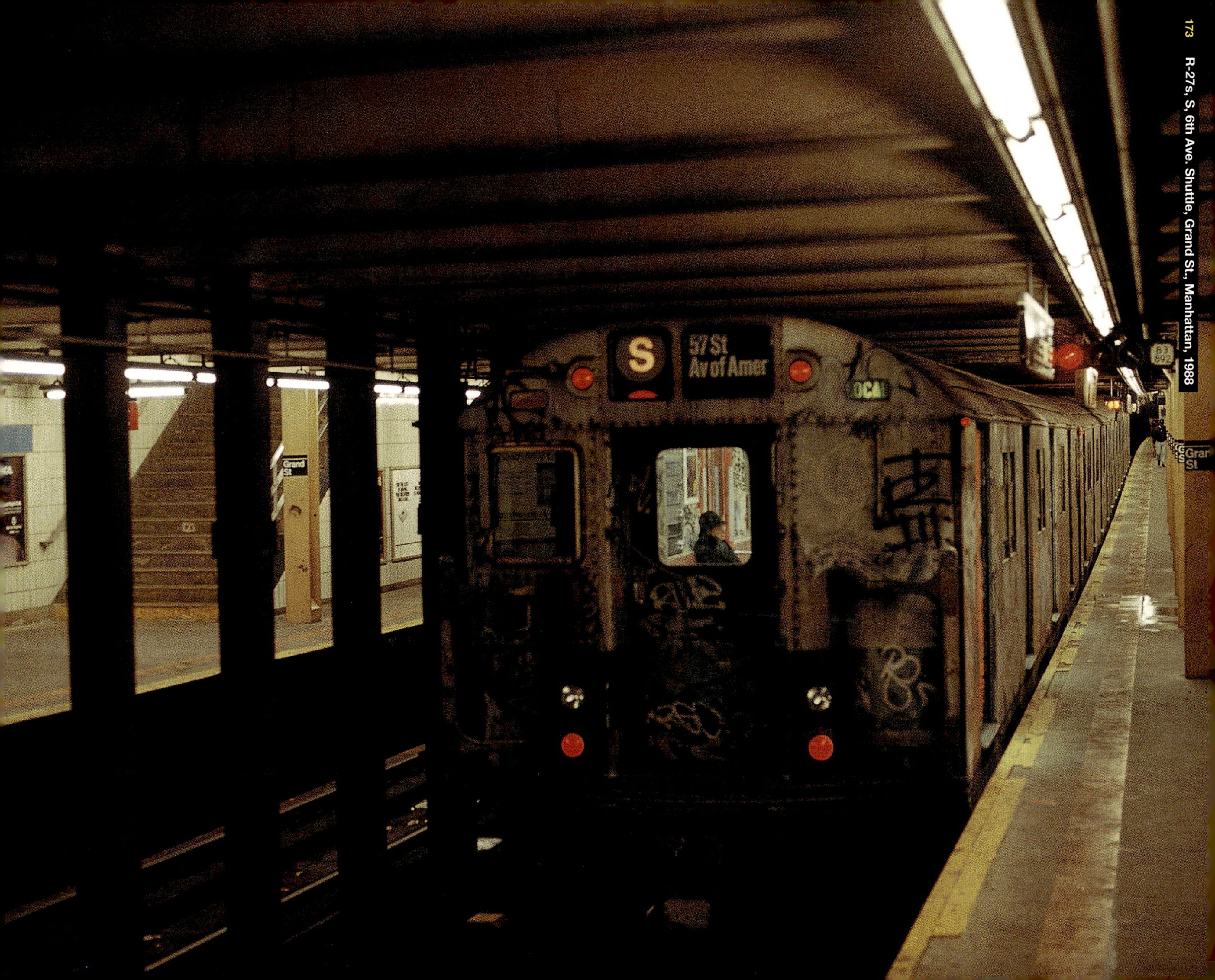

R-27s, S, 6th Ave. Shuttle, Grand St., Manhattan, 1988

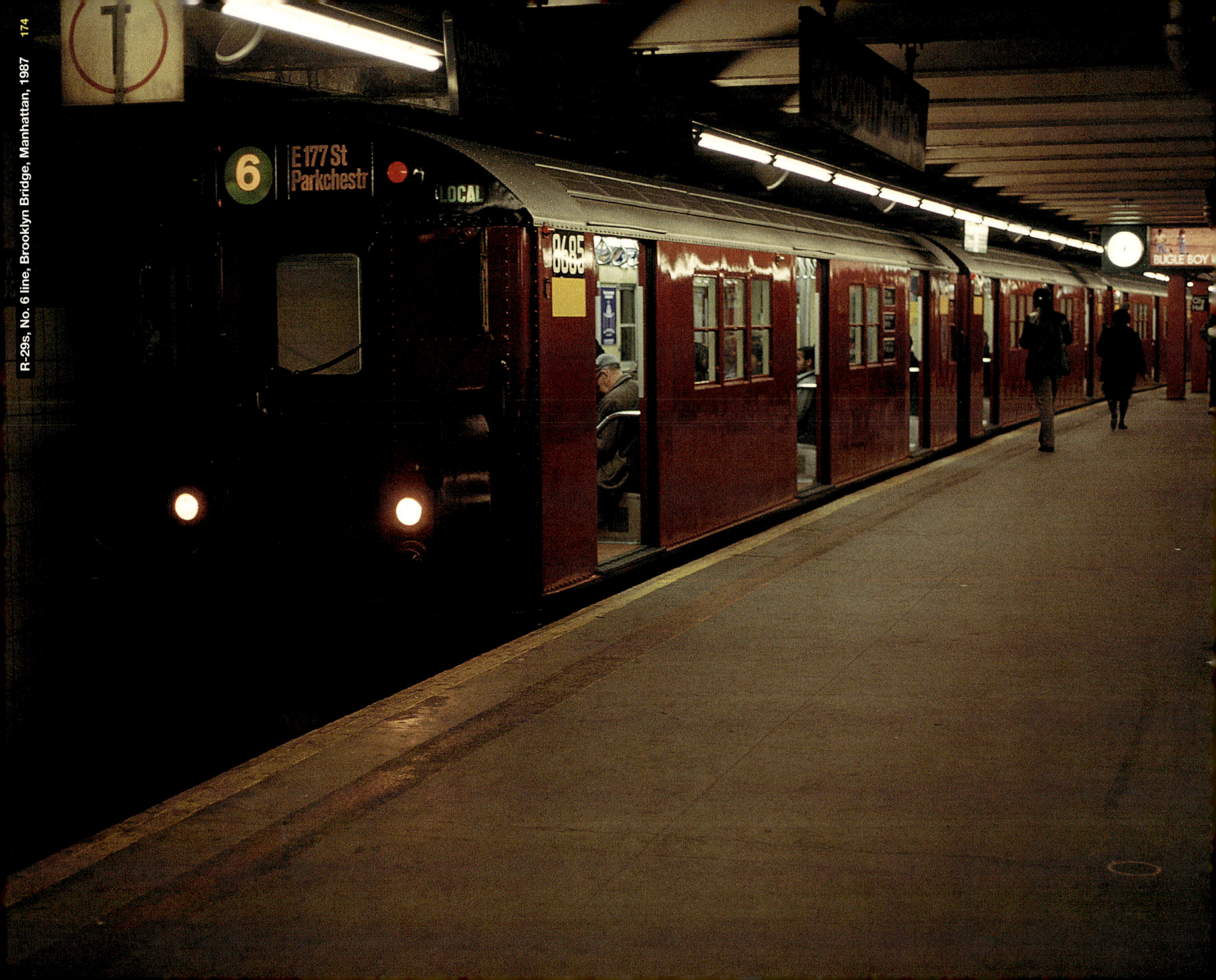

R-29s, No. 6 line, Brooklyn Bridge, Manhattan, 1987

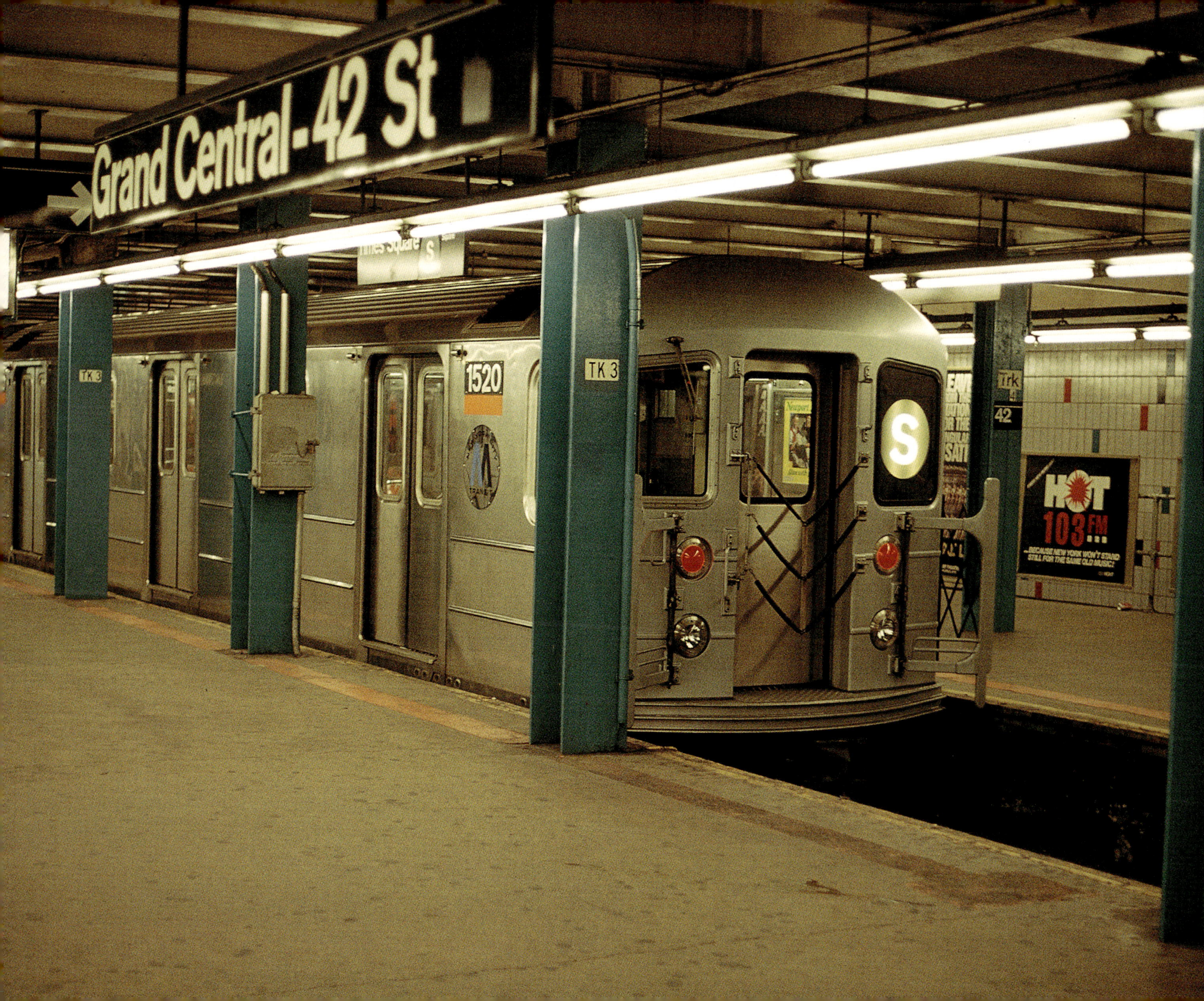

R-62, S, 42nd St. Shuttle, Grand Central-42nd St., Manhattan, 1987

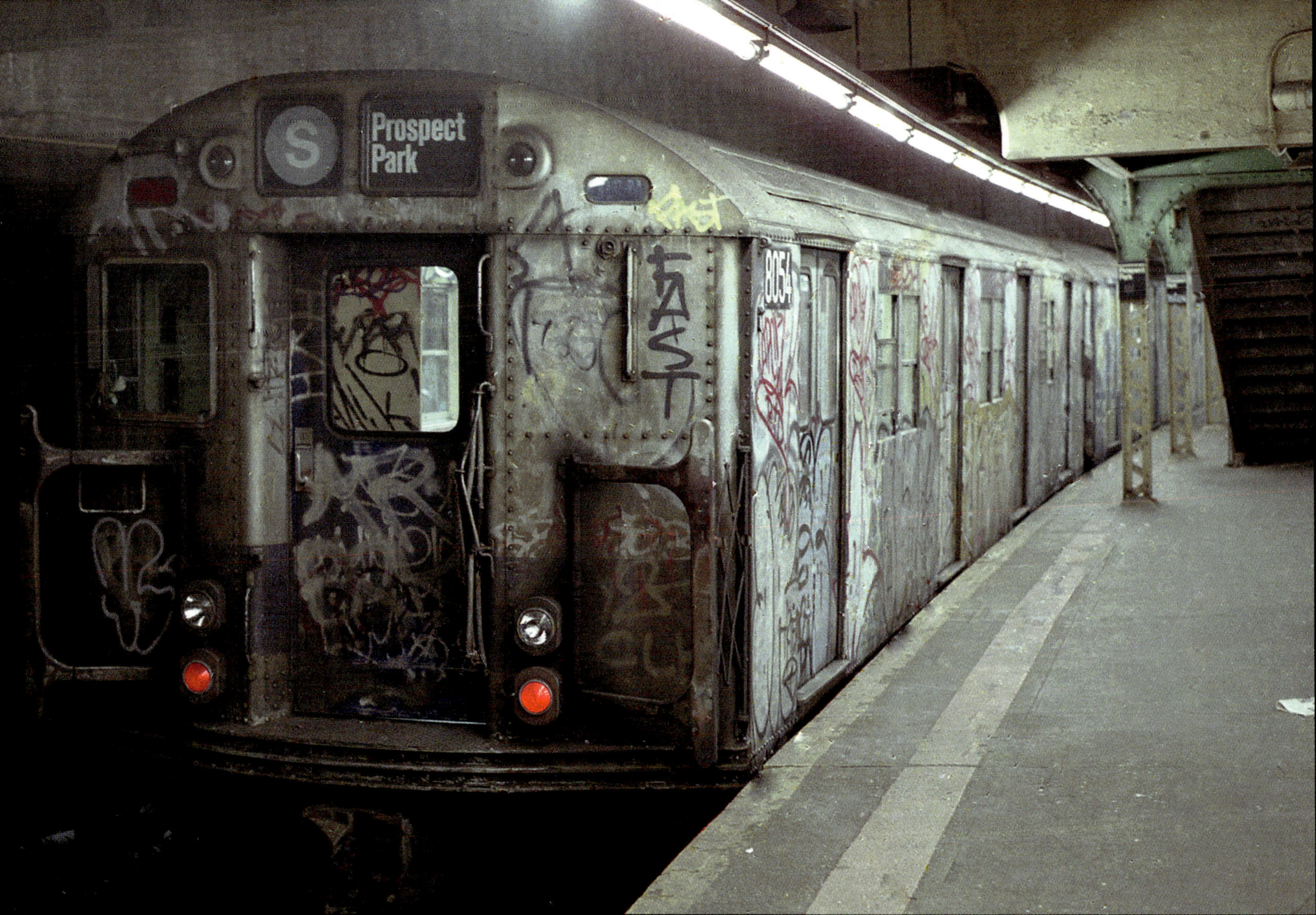
S
Prospect Park
8054

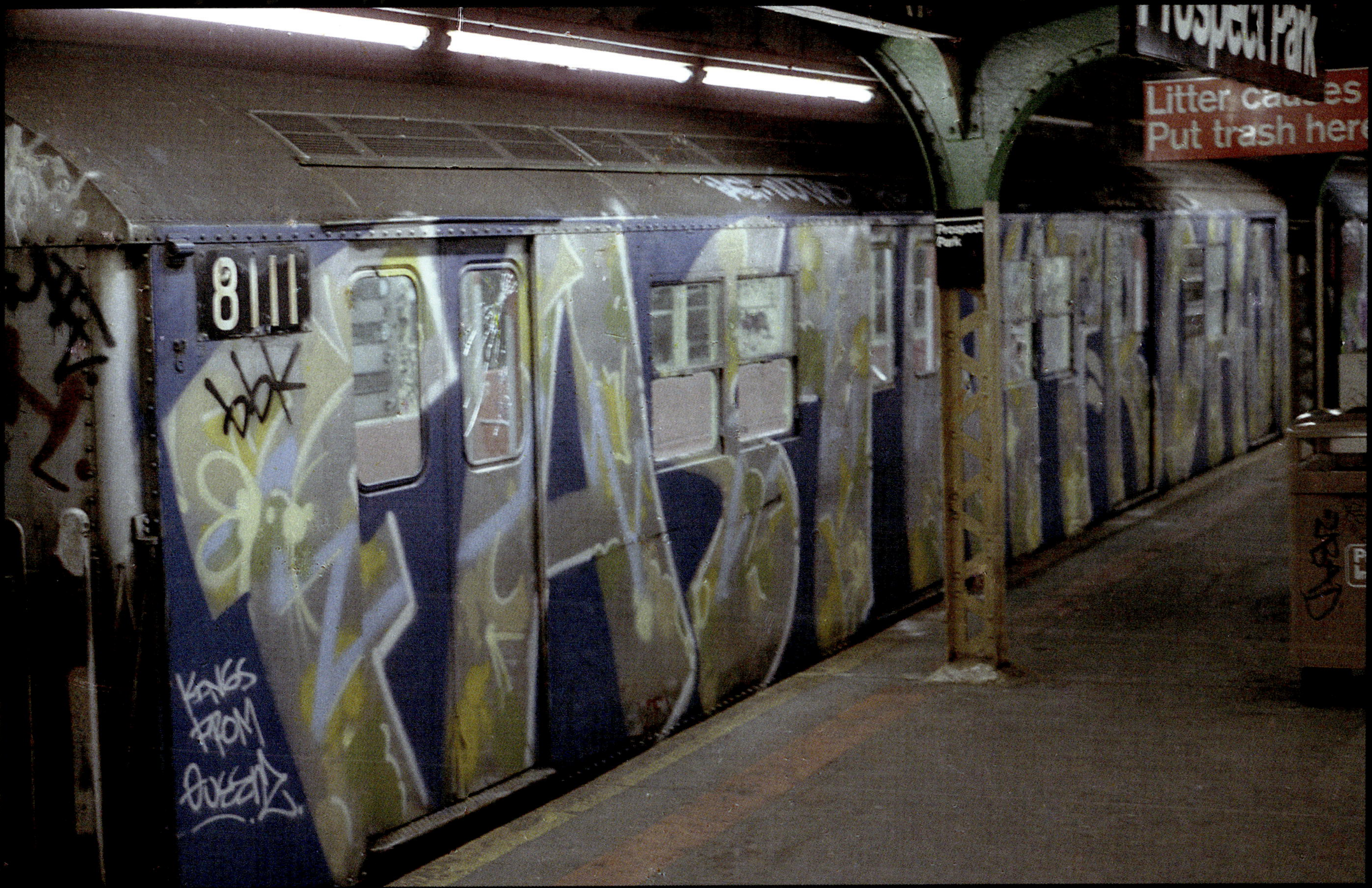

R-27, S, Franklin Ave. Shuttle, Prospect Park, Brooklyn, 1988

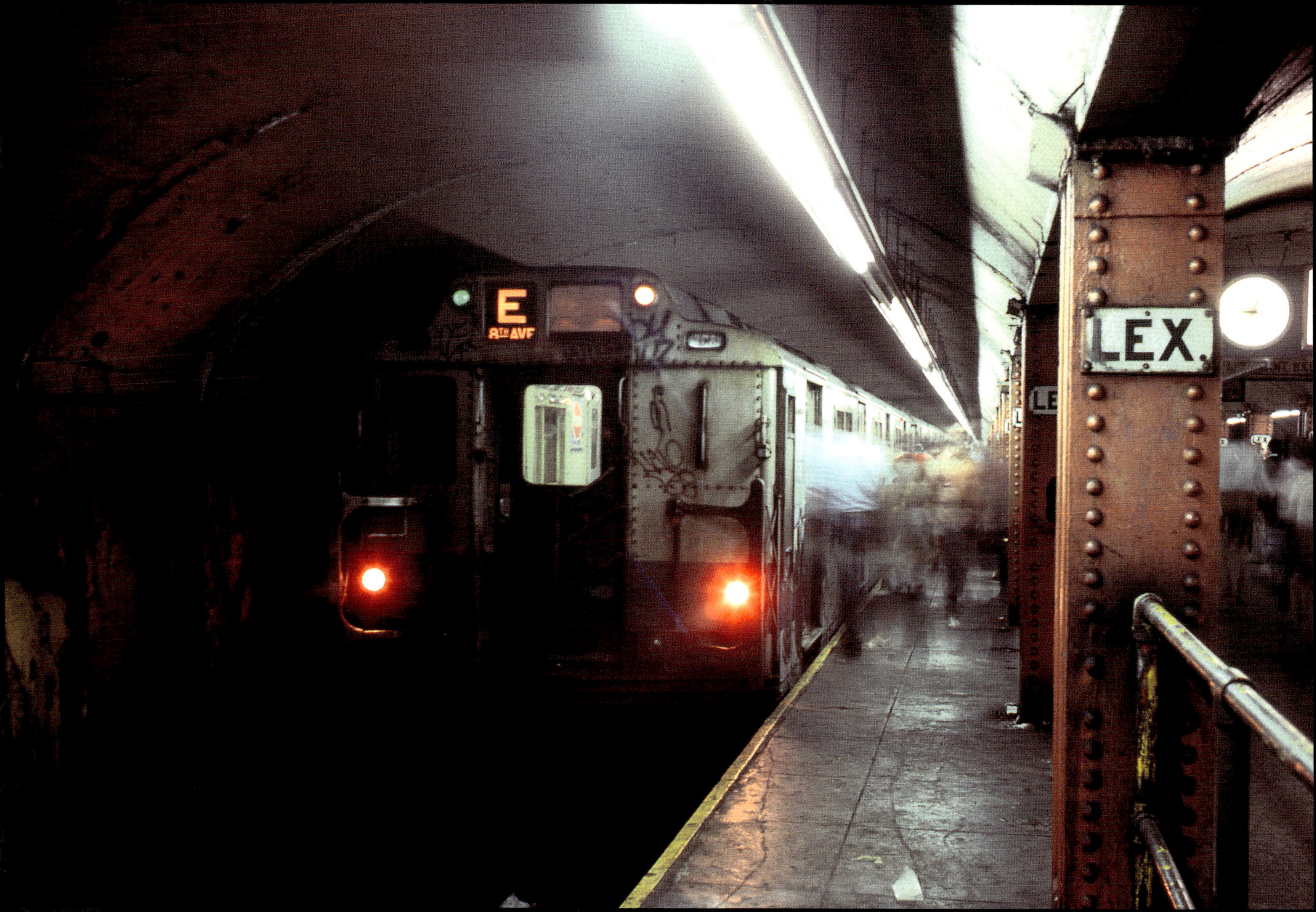

R-10, E, 8th Ave. line, Lexington Ave., Manhattan, 1980

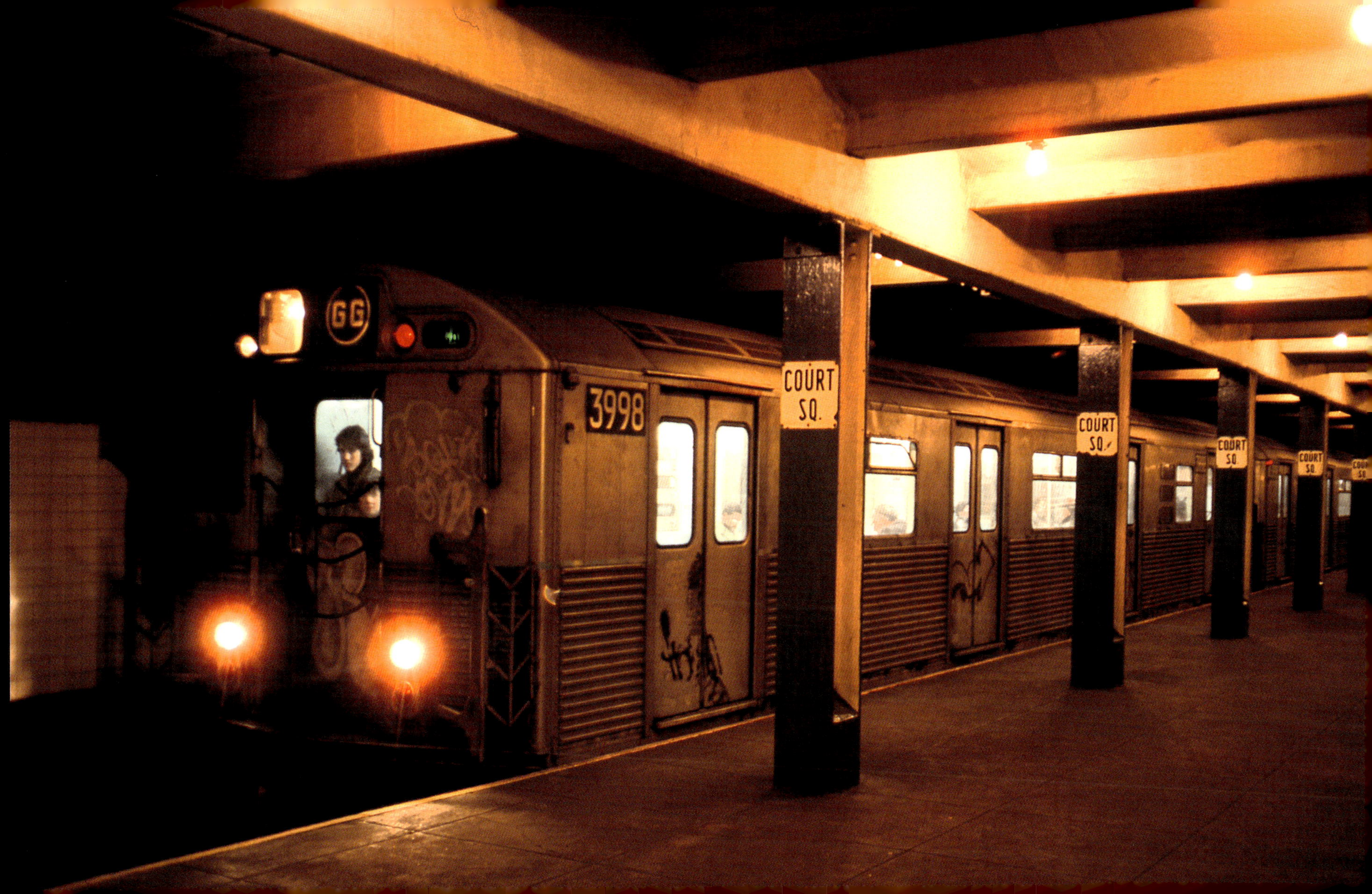
GG
3998
COURT SQ.
COURT SQ.
COURT SQ.
COURT SQ.

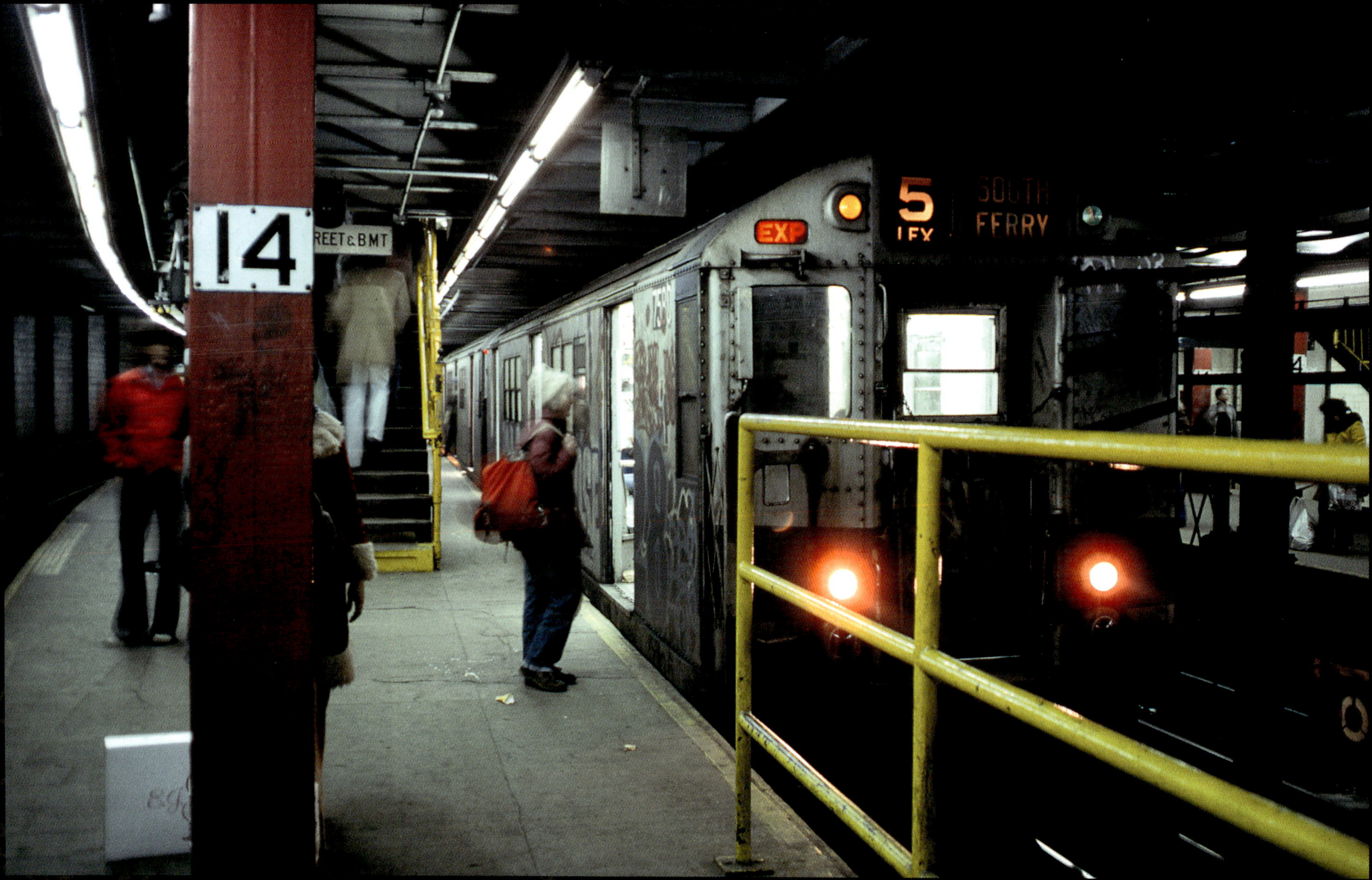

R-22, No. 5 line, 14th St., Manhattan, 1977

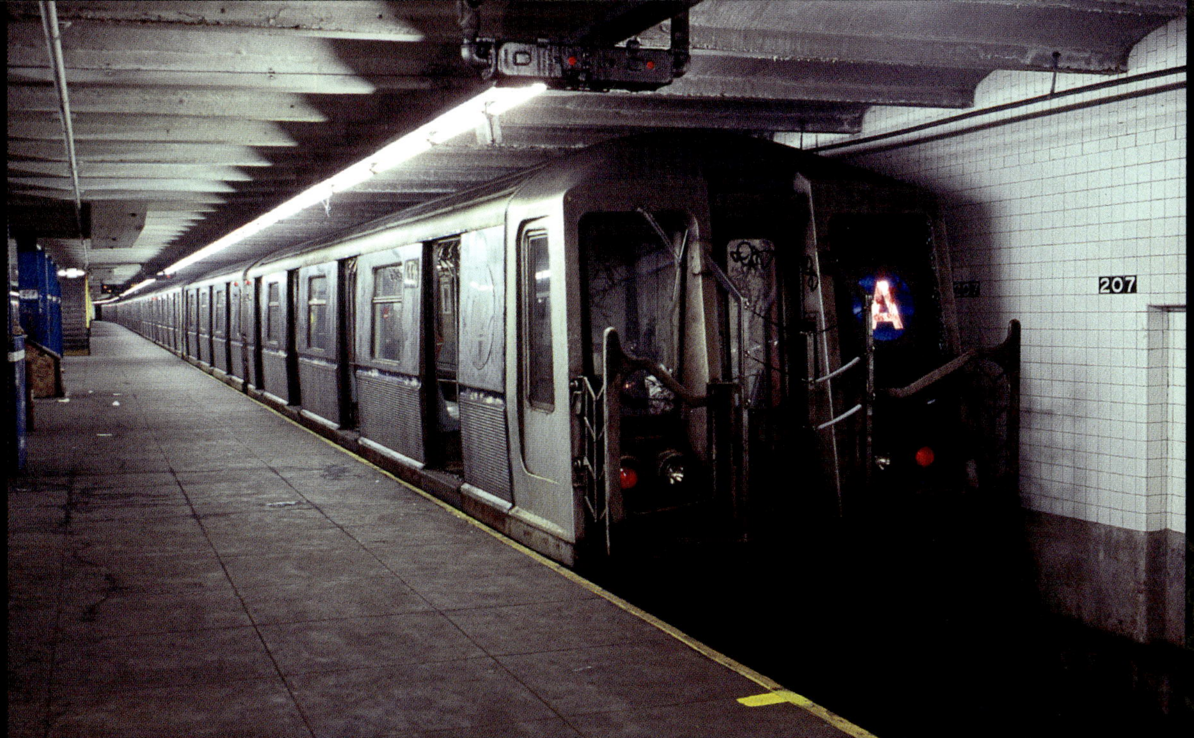
207
A

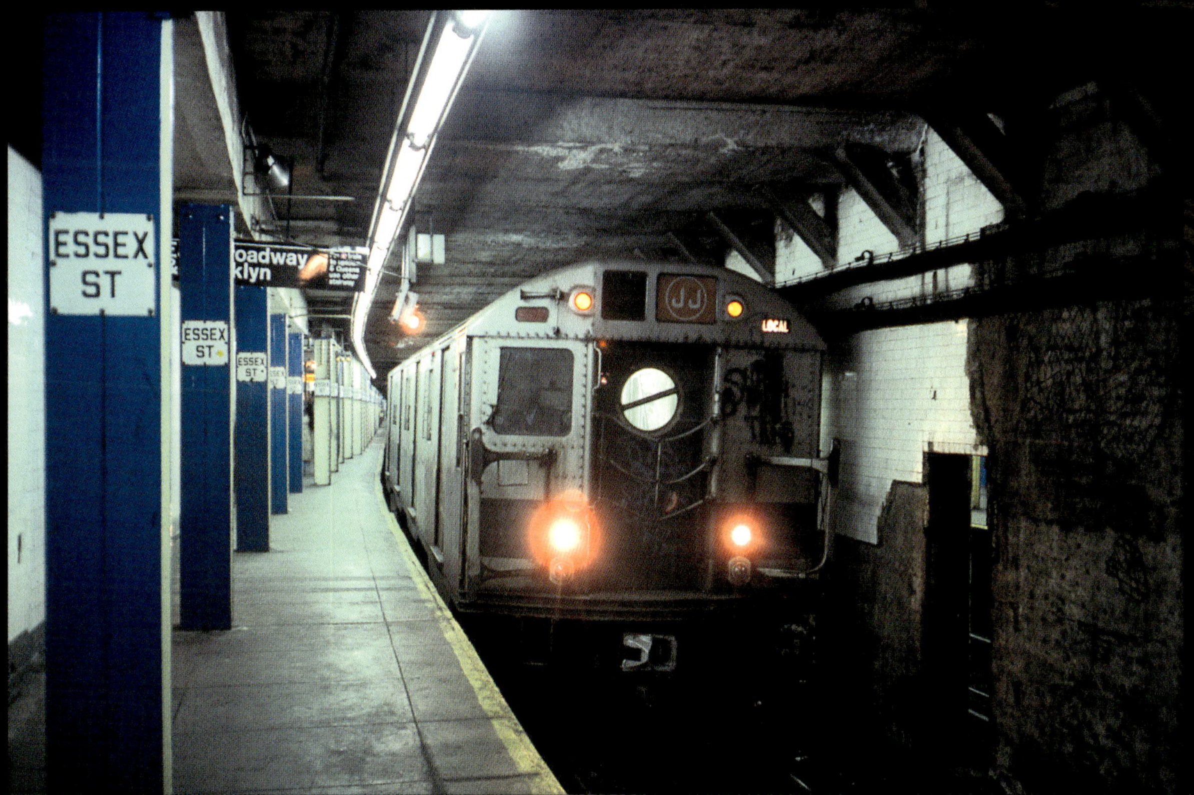
ESSEX
ST
ESSEX
ST
oadway
klyn
JJ
LOCAL

The Graffiti Cars

New York
Subways & Stations
1970–1990

CHAPTER 5

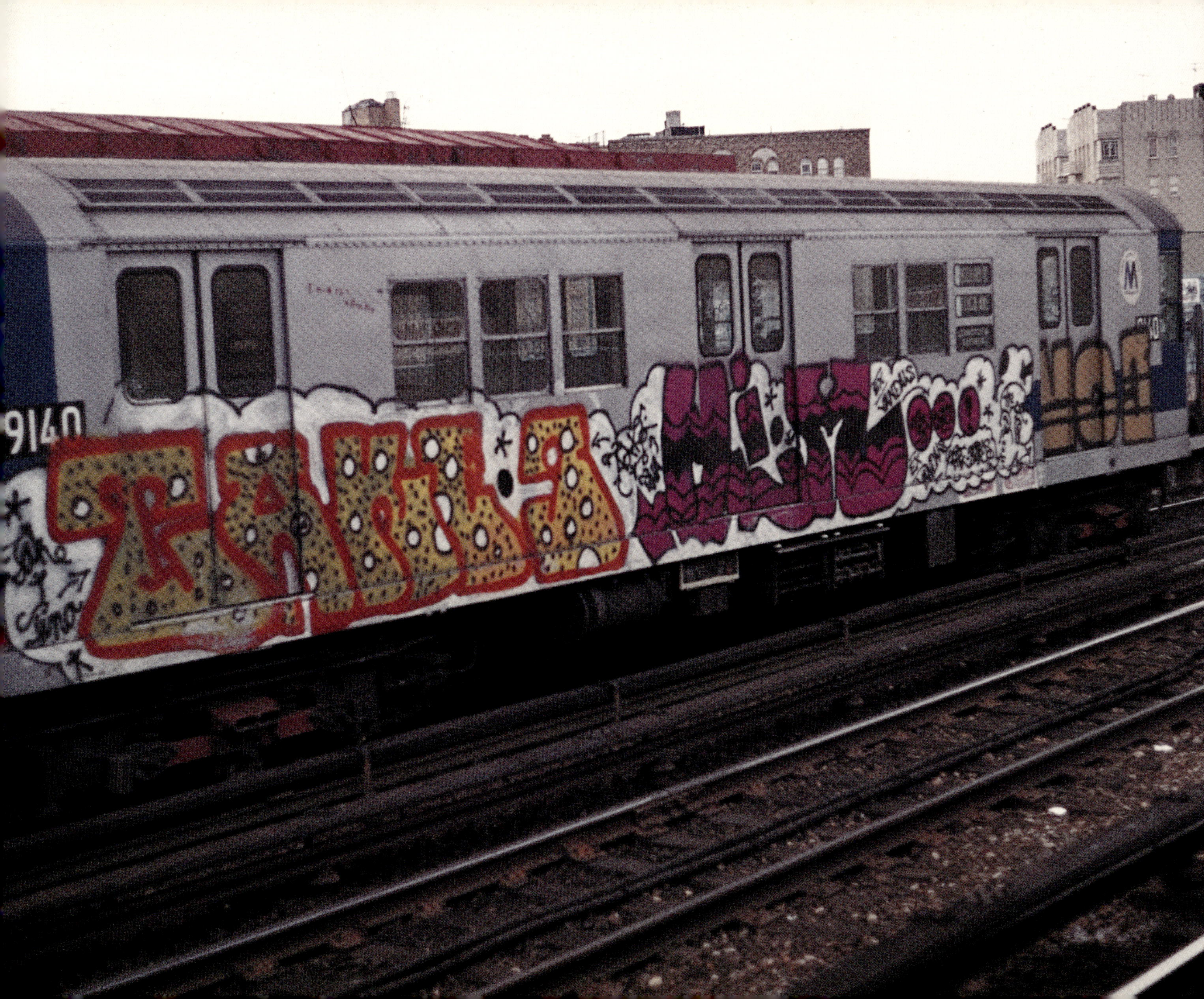

R-33, No. 4 line, Lexington Ave.–Jerome Ave. Exp., Bedford Park Blvd., Bronx, 1973

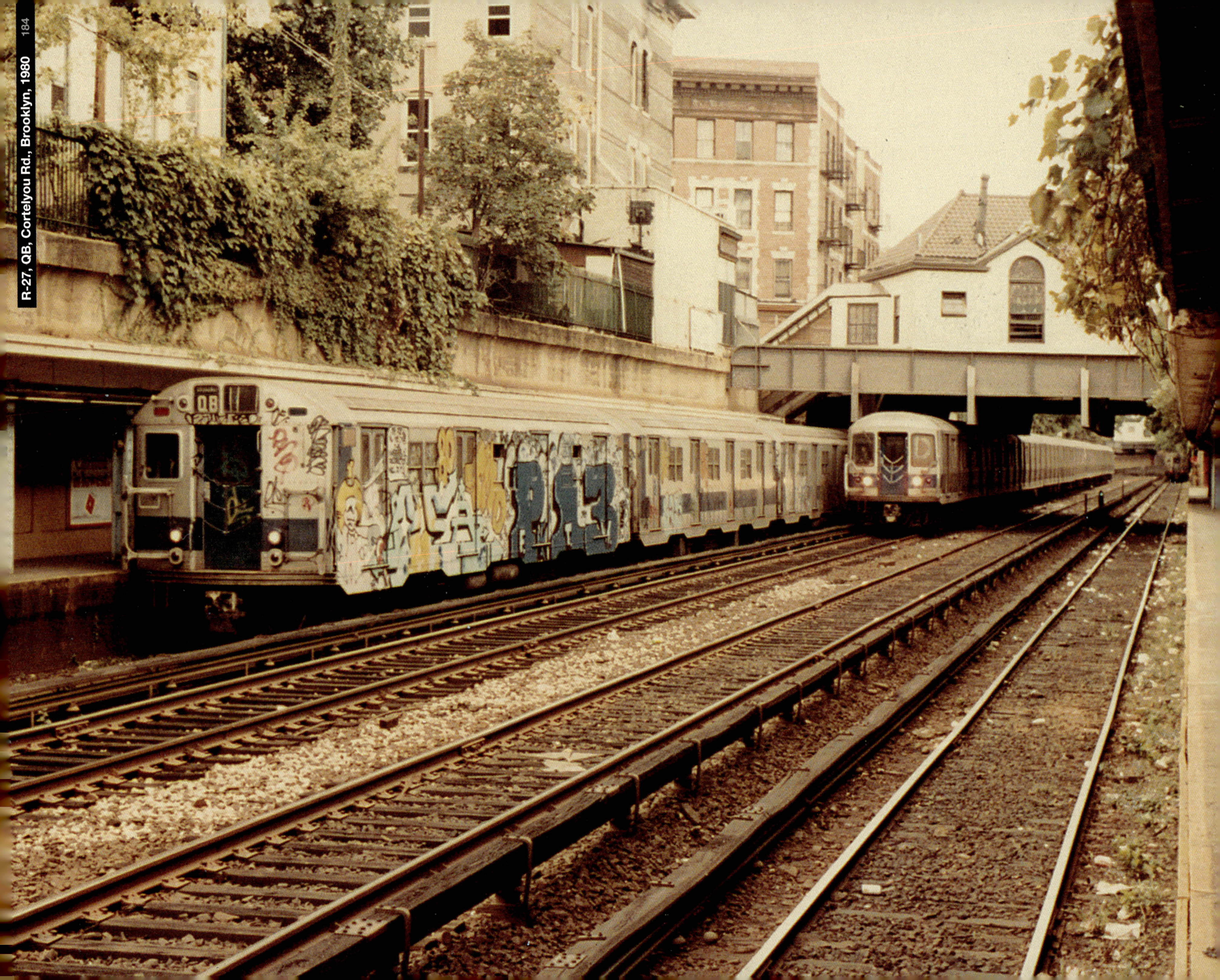

R-27, QB, Cortelyou Rd., Brooklyn, 1980

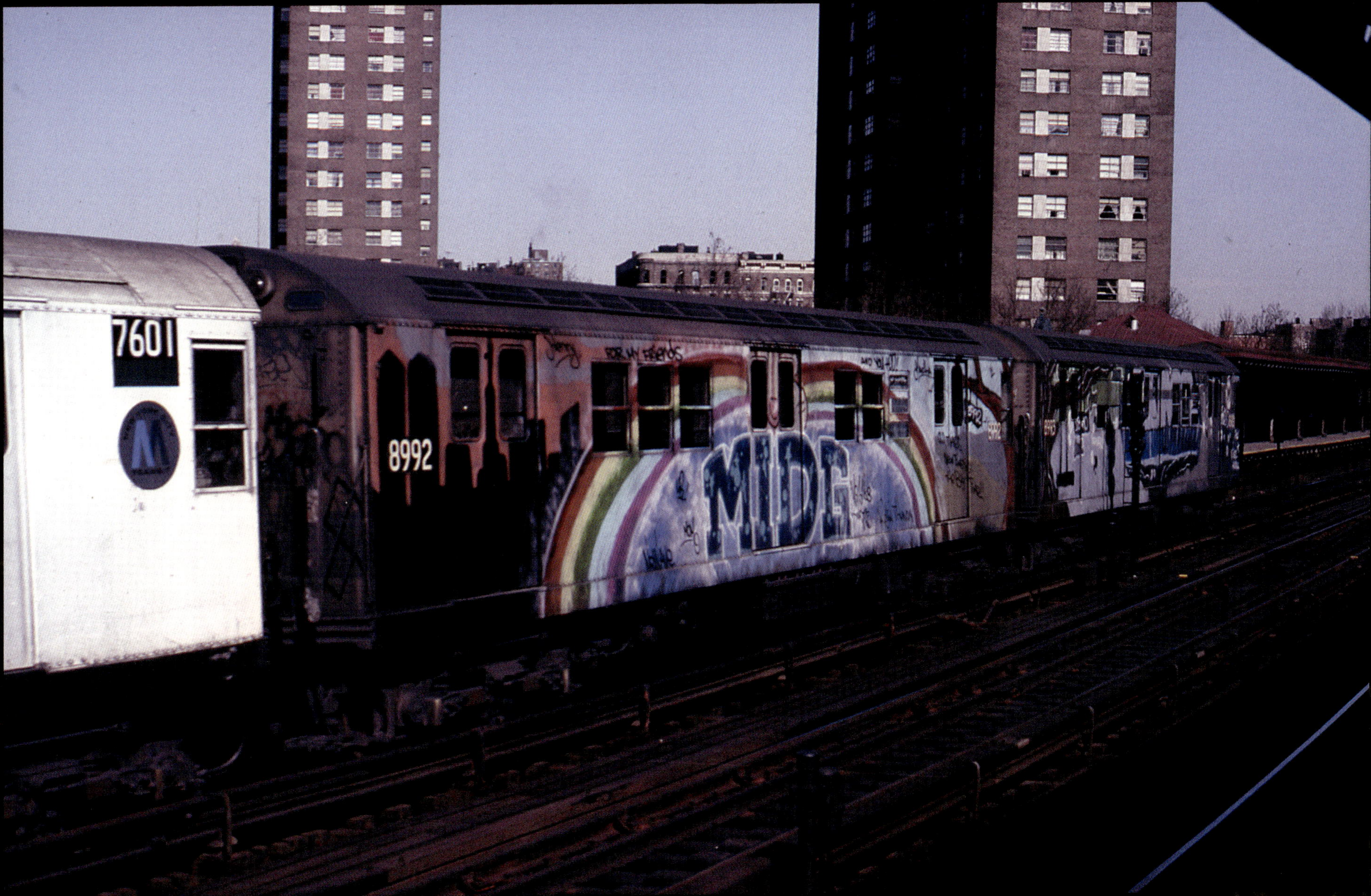

R-33, No. 5 line, Jackson Ave., Bronx, 1983

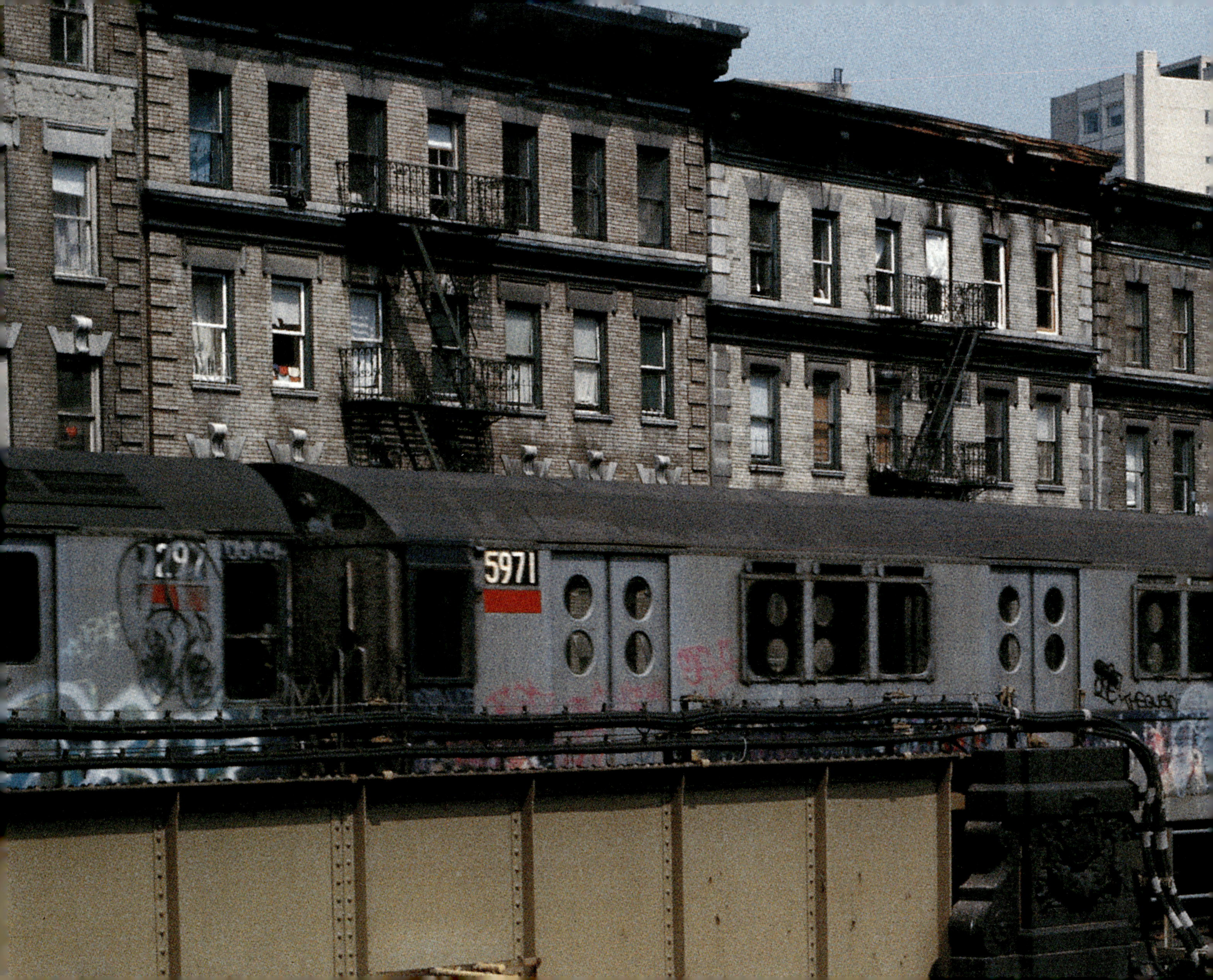
5971

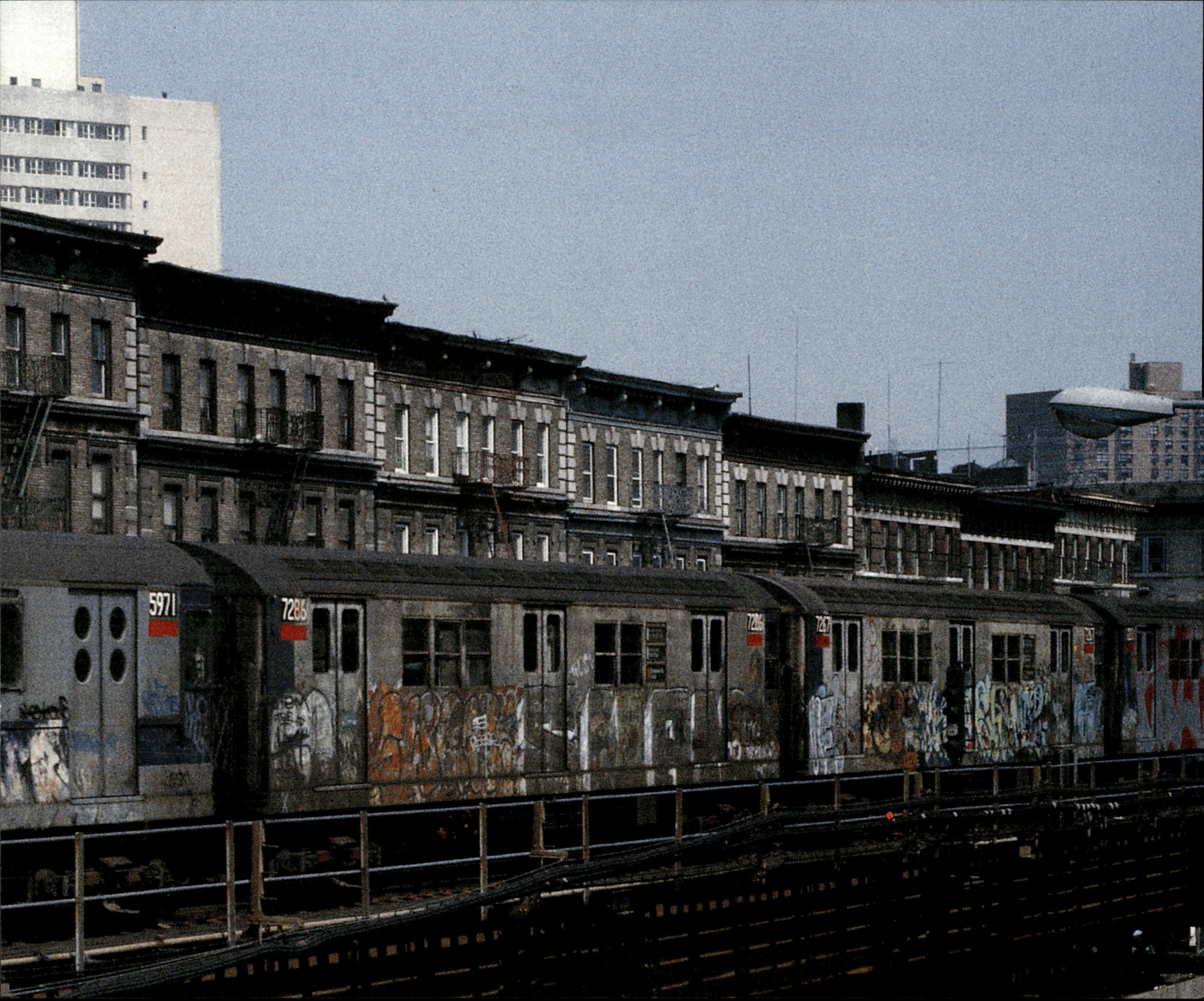

No. 1 Broadway Line, near 125th St., Manhattan, 1984

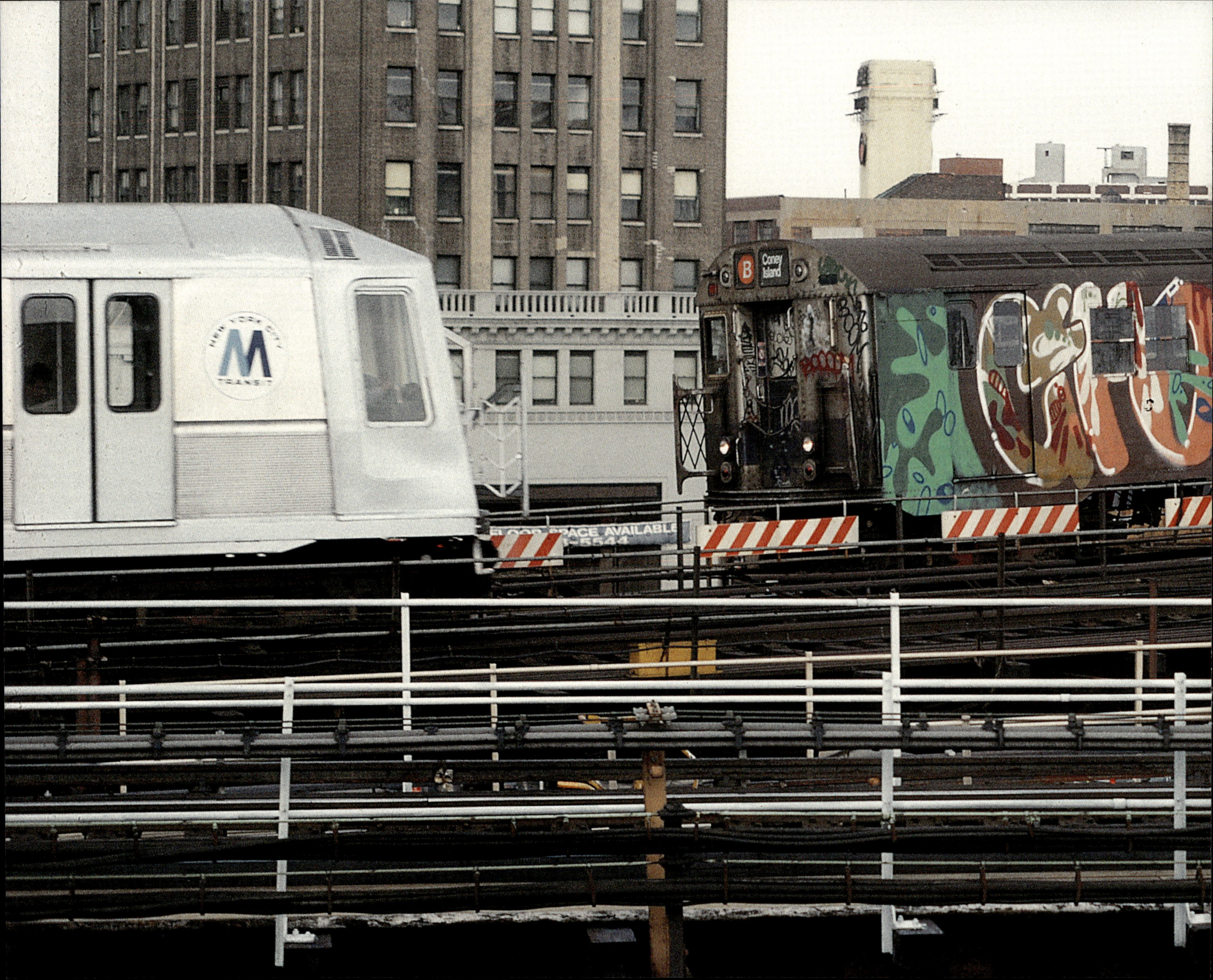
NEW YORK CITY
M
TRANSIT
B
Coney Island

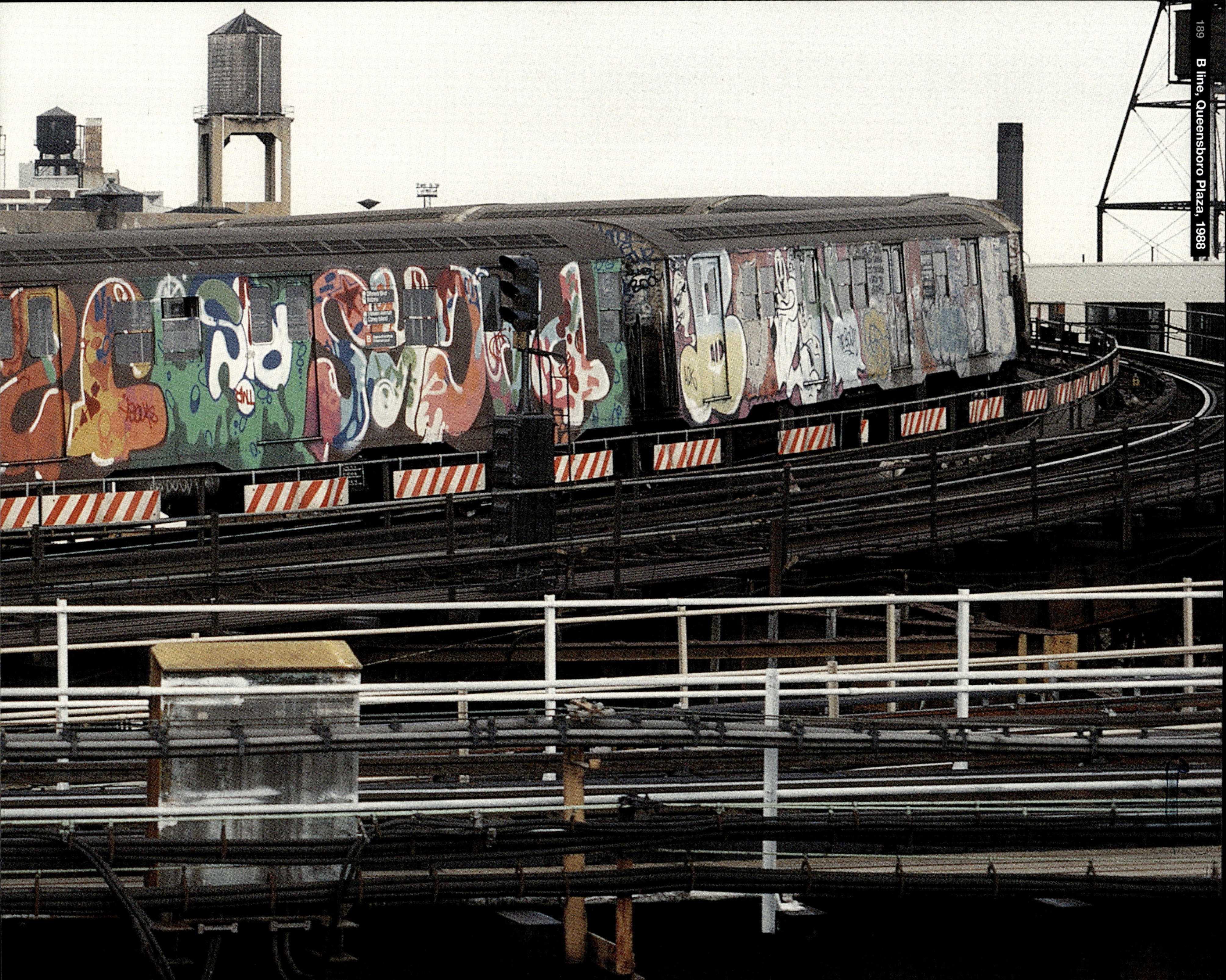

B line, Queensboro Plaza, 1988

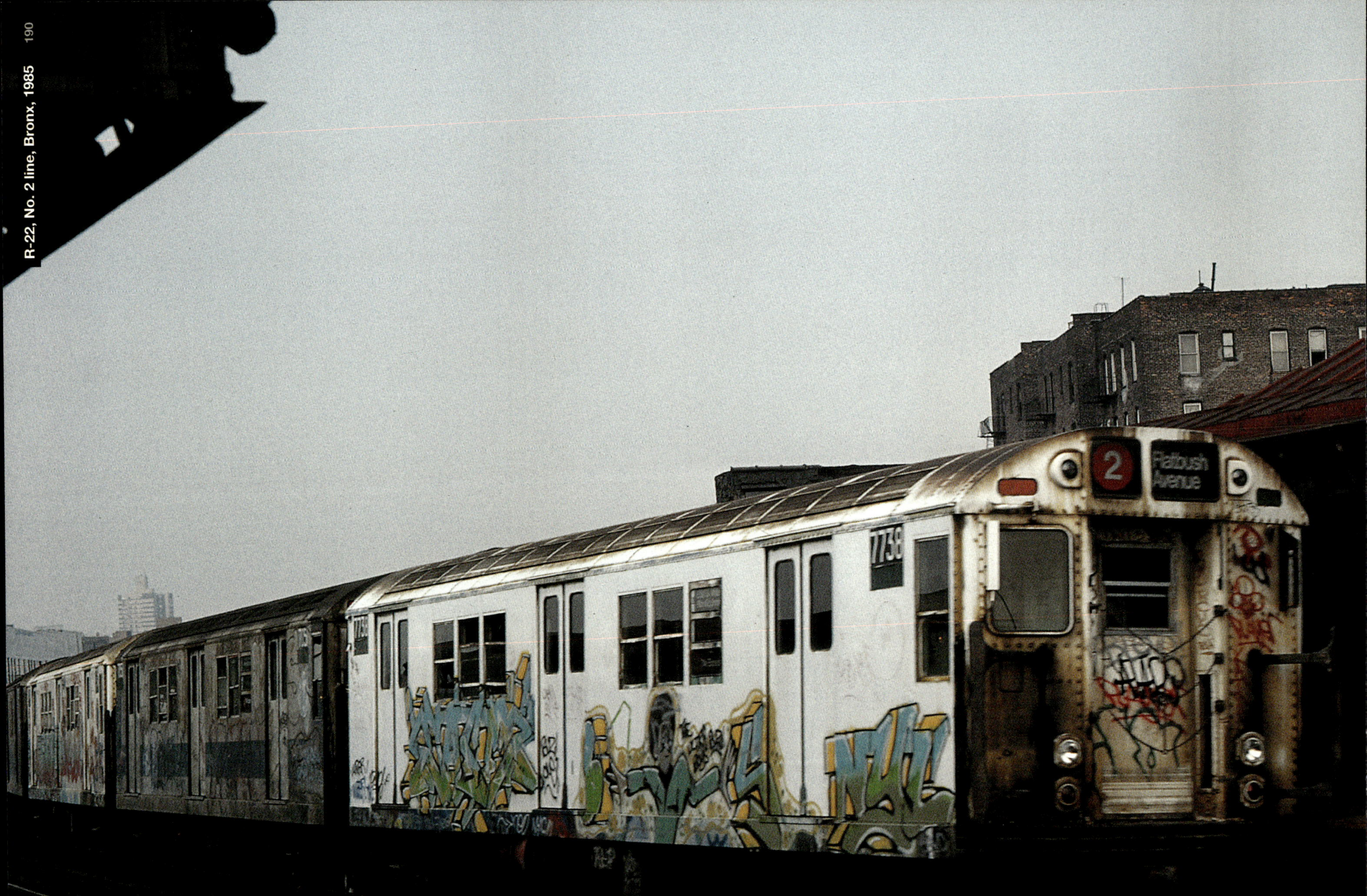

R-22, No. 2 line, Bronx, 1985

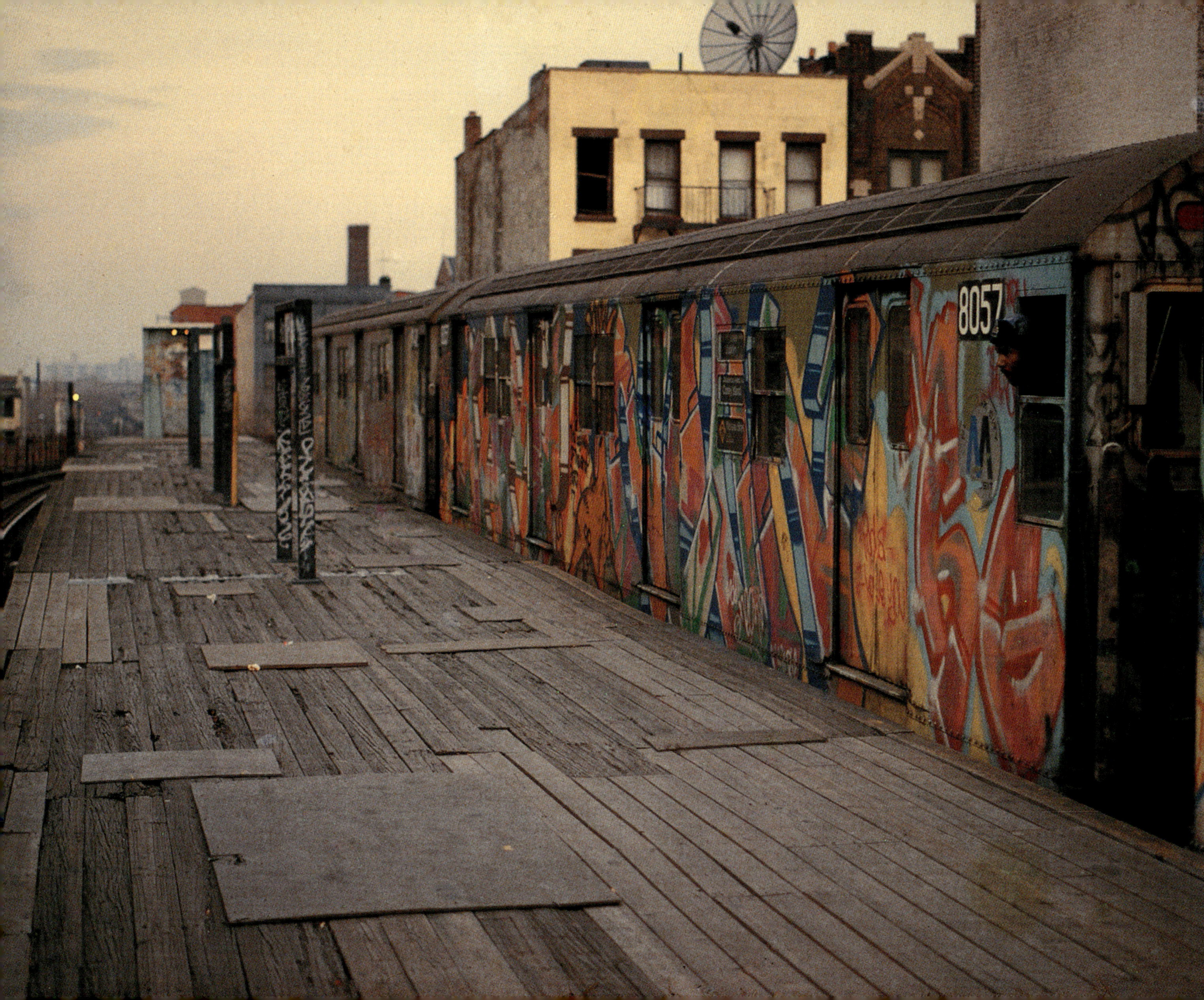

R-27, Franklin Ave. Shuttle, Park Place, Brooklyn, 1988

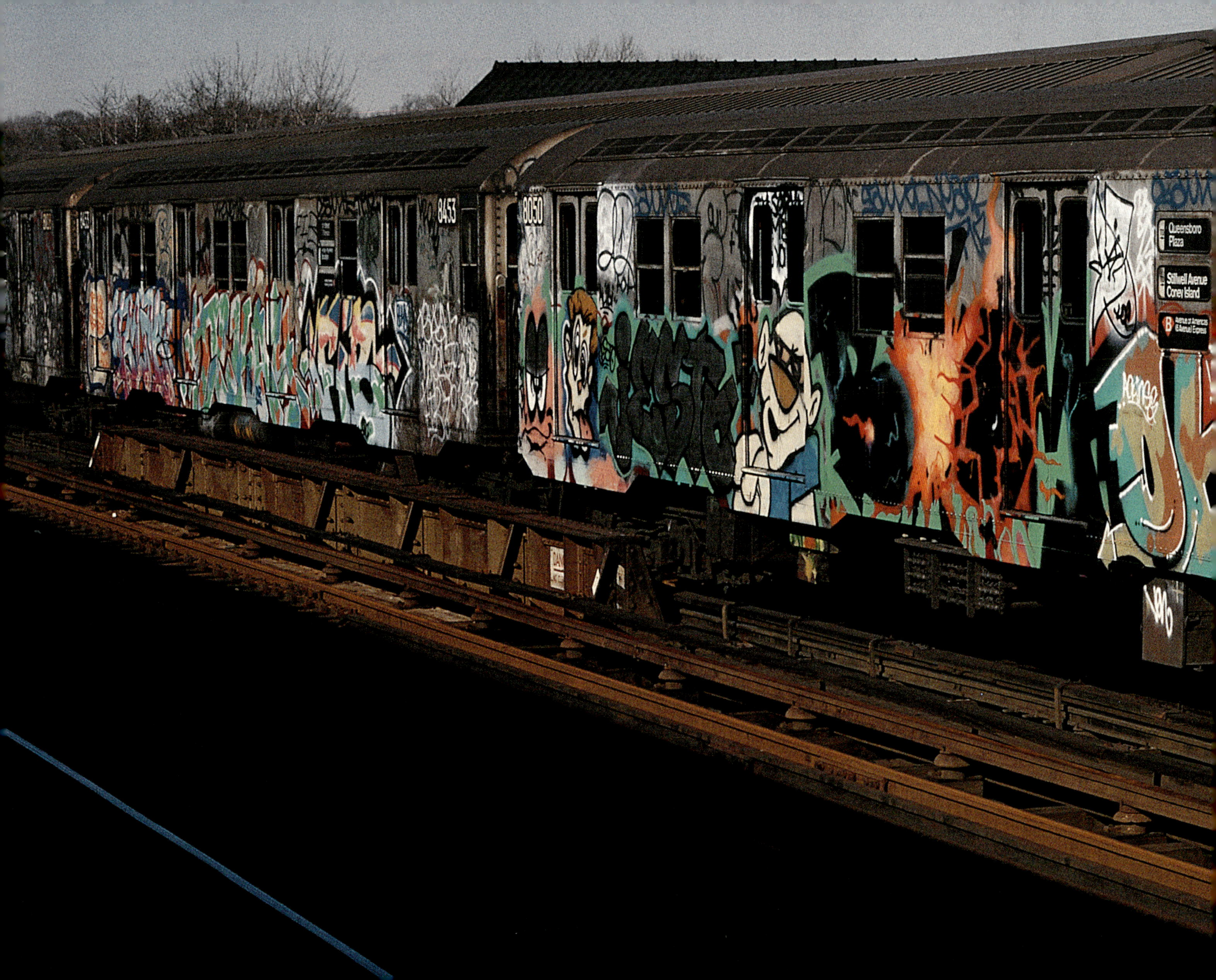

8453
8050
Queensboro Plaza
Stillwell Avenue Coney Island
B

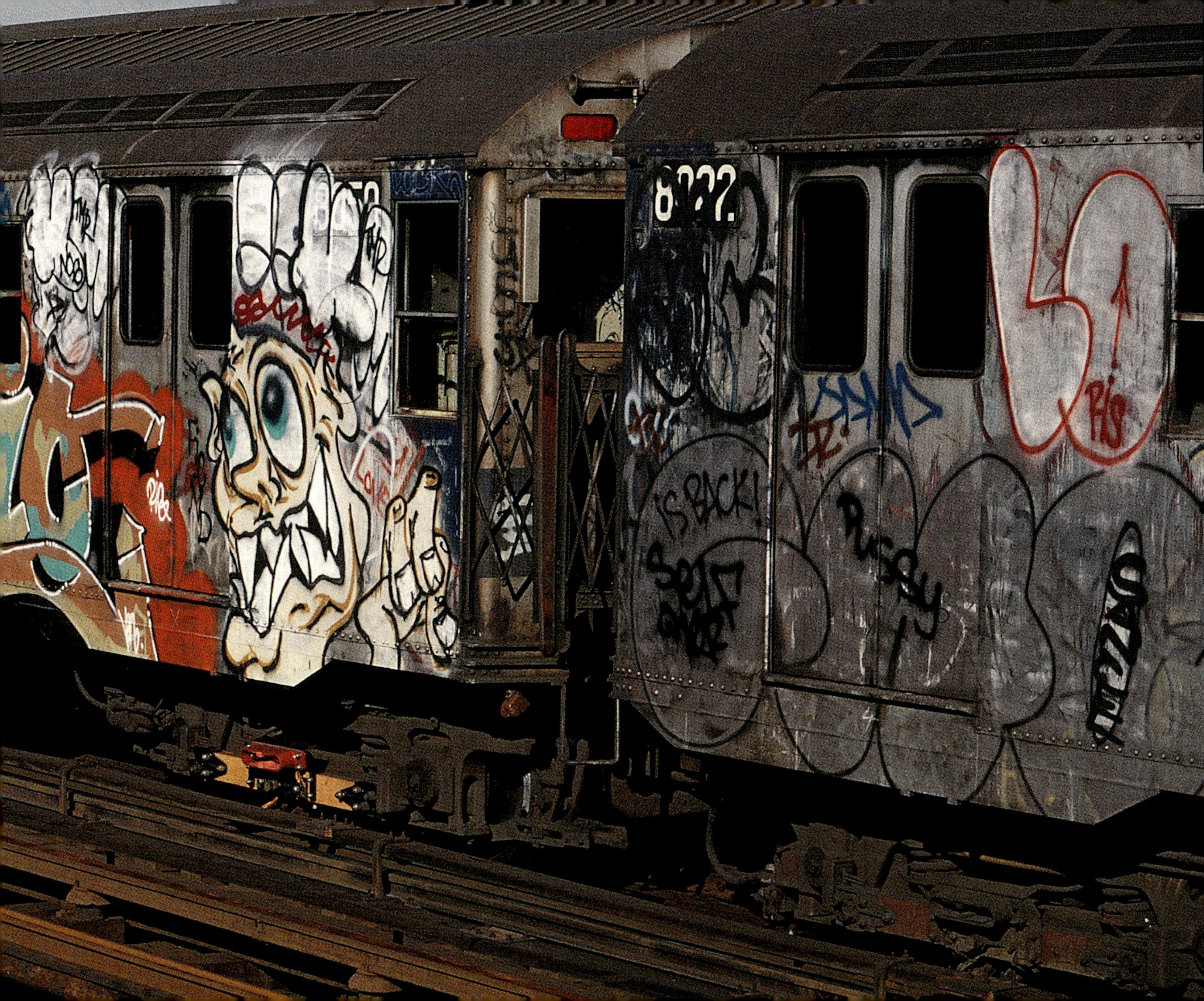

R-27, B line, 1988

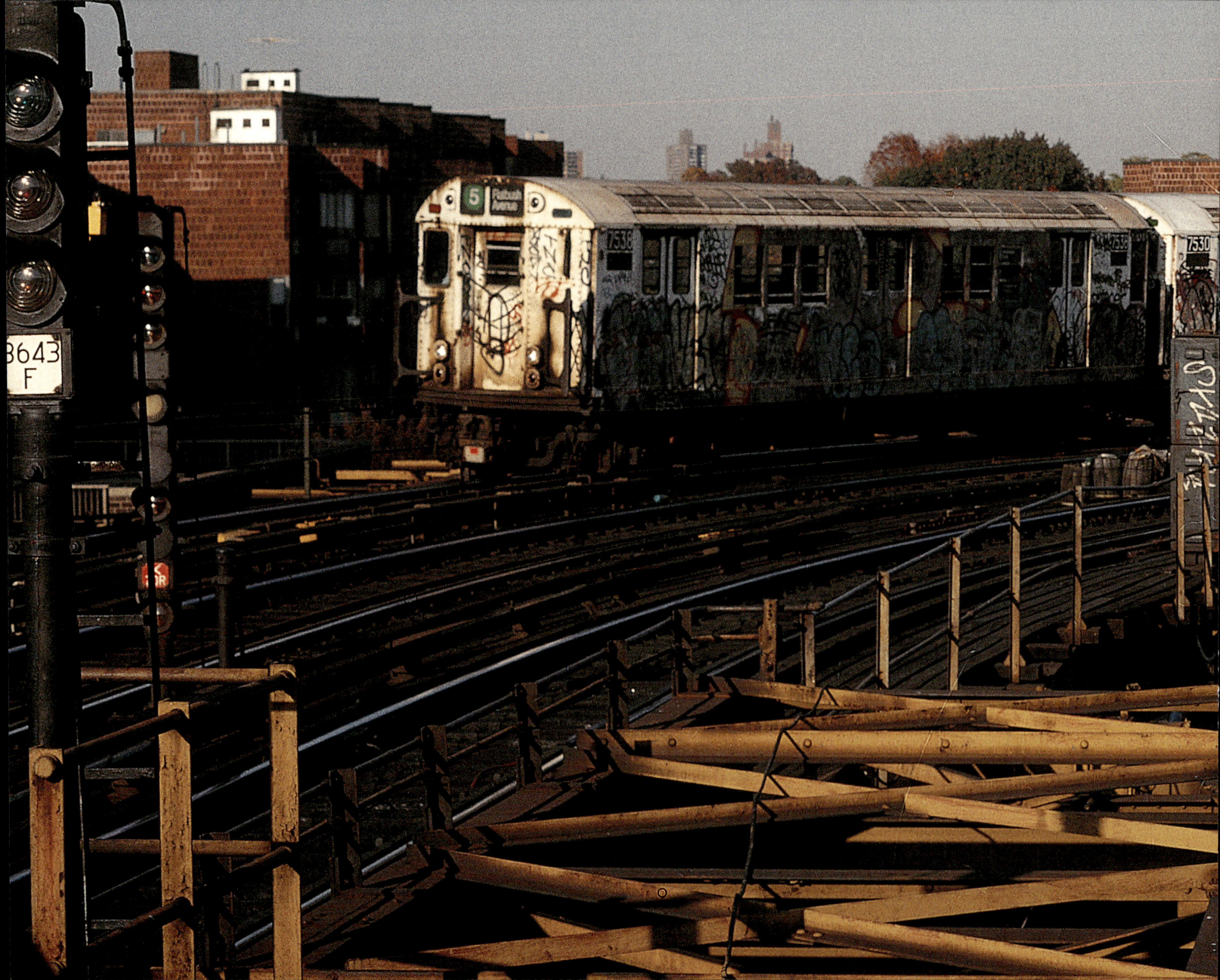
5
3643
F
7538
7530

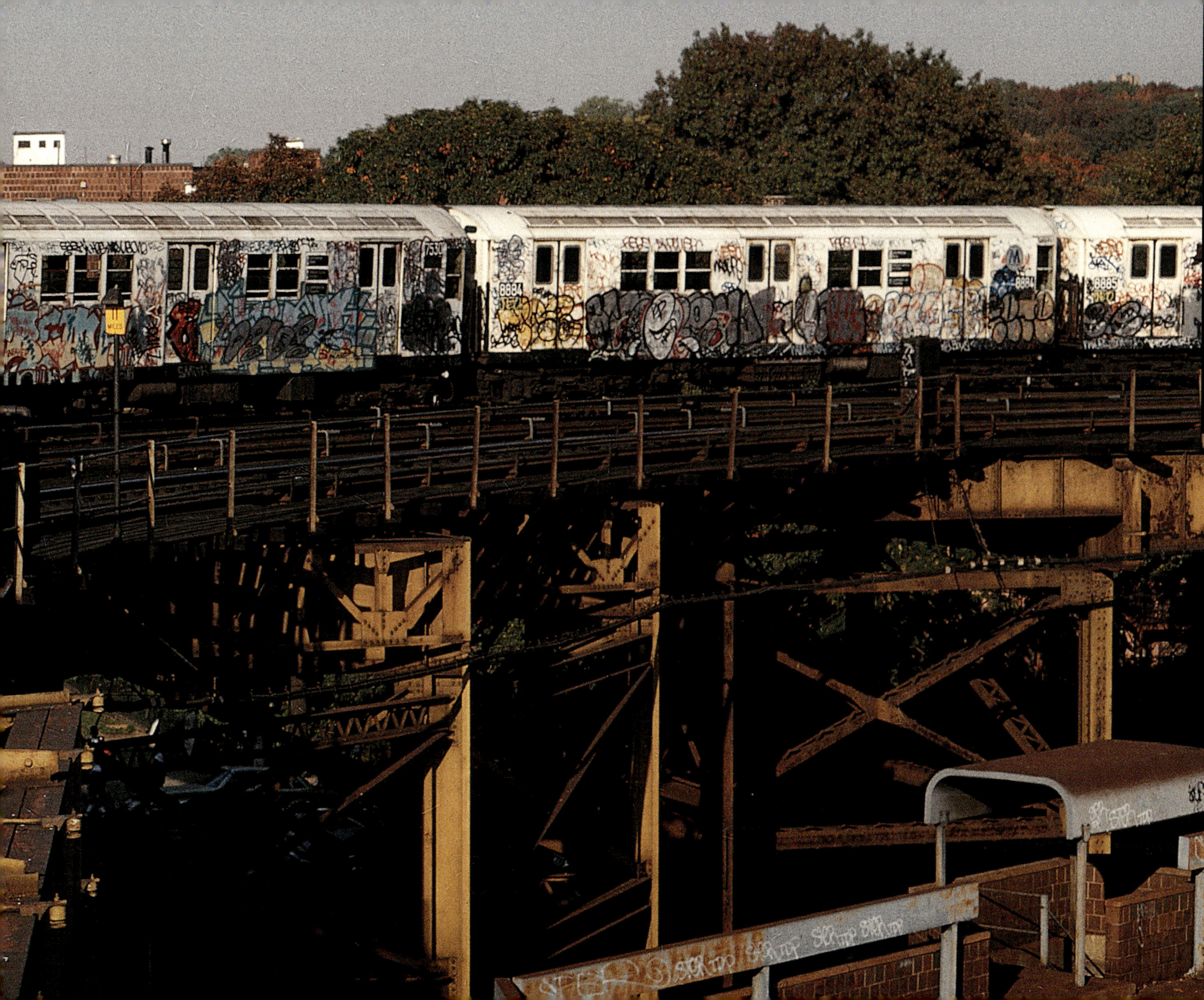

No. 5 line, East Tremont Ave.–West Farms Sq., Bronx, 1987

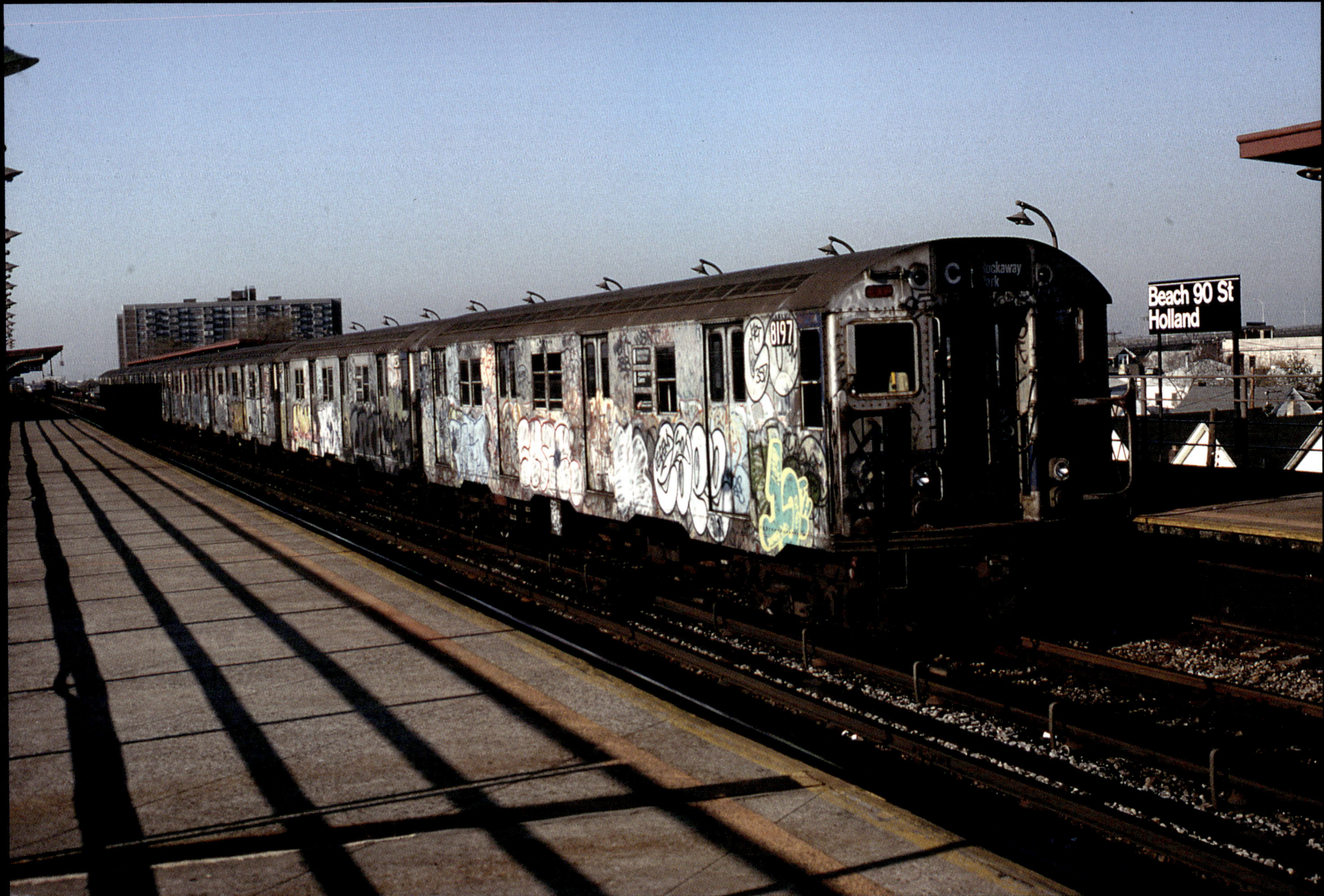

R-27, C, Rockaway Park line, Beach 90th St.–Holland, Queens, 1988

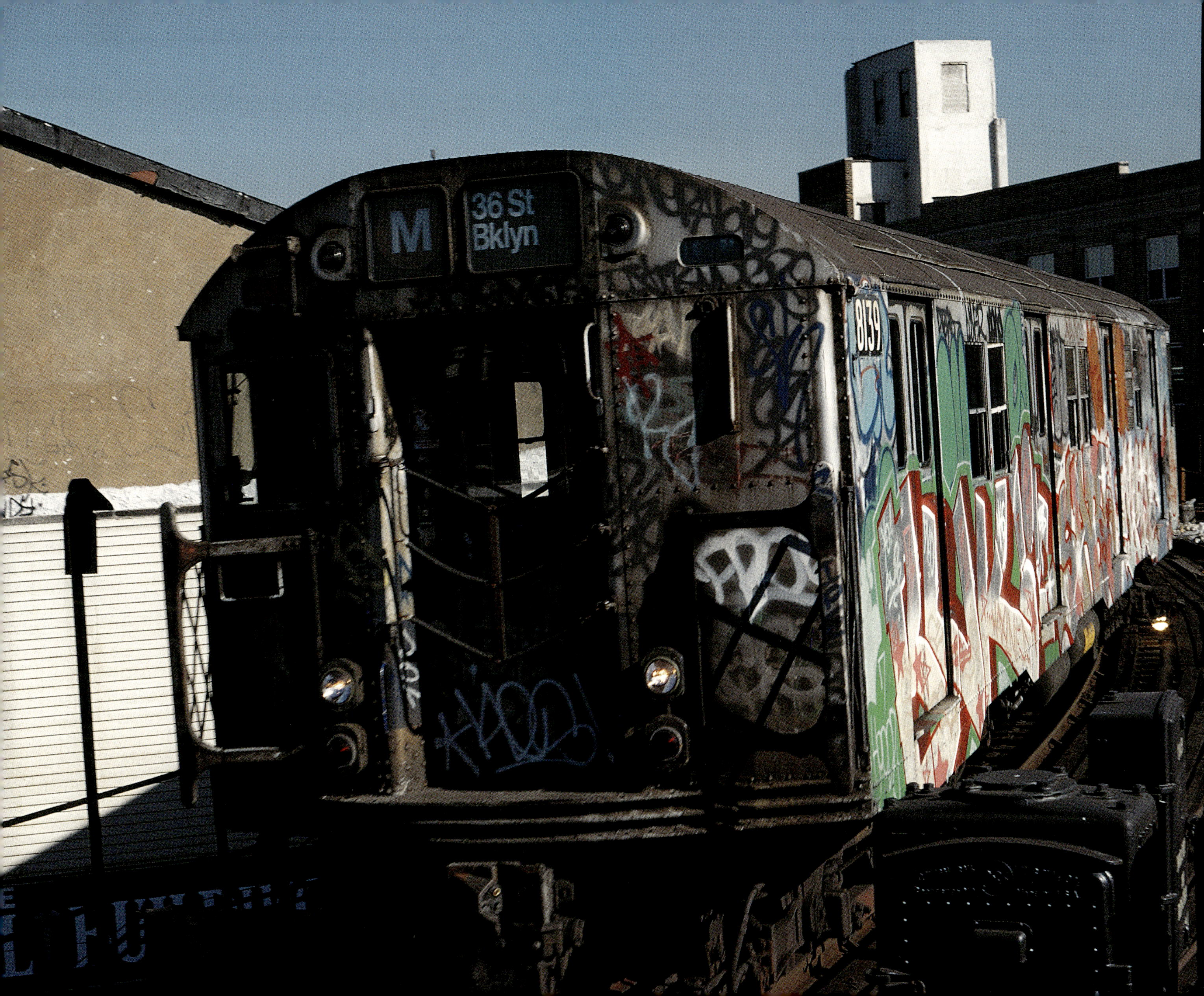

R-27, Myrtle Ave. line, Wyckoff Ave., Brooklyn, 1988

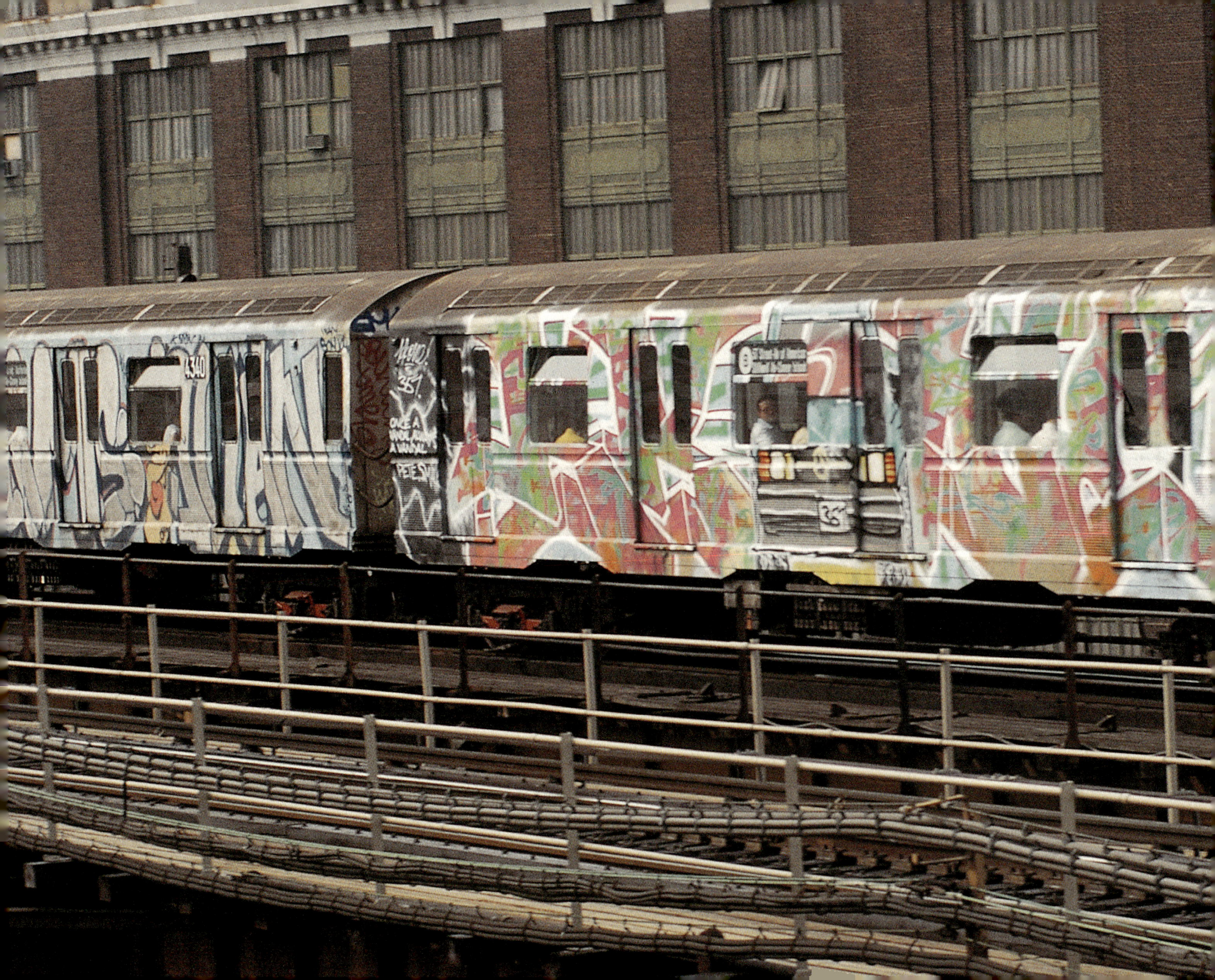
4340

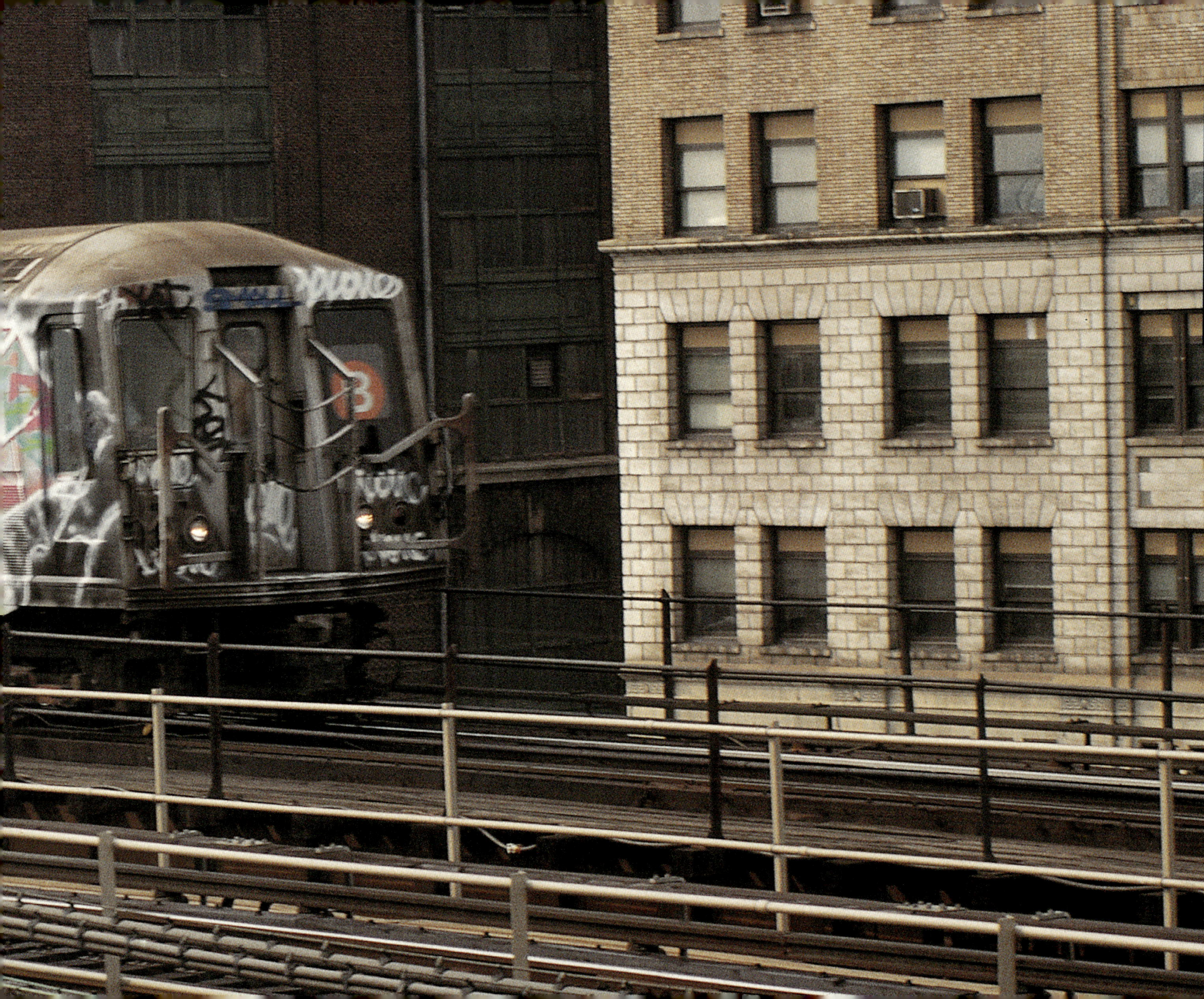

R-40, B line, east of Queensboro Plaza, 1988

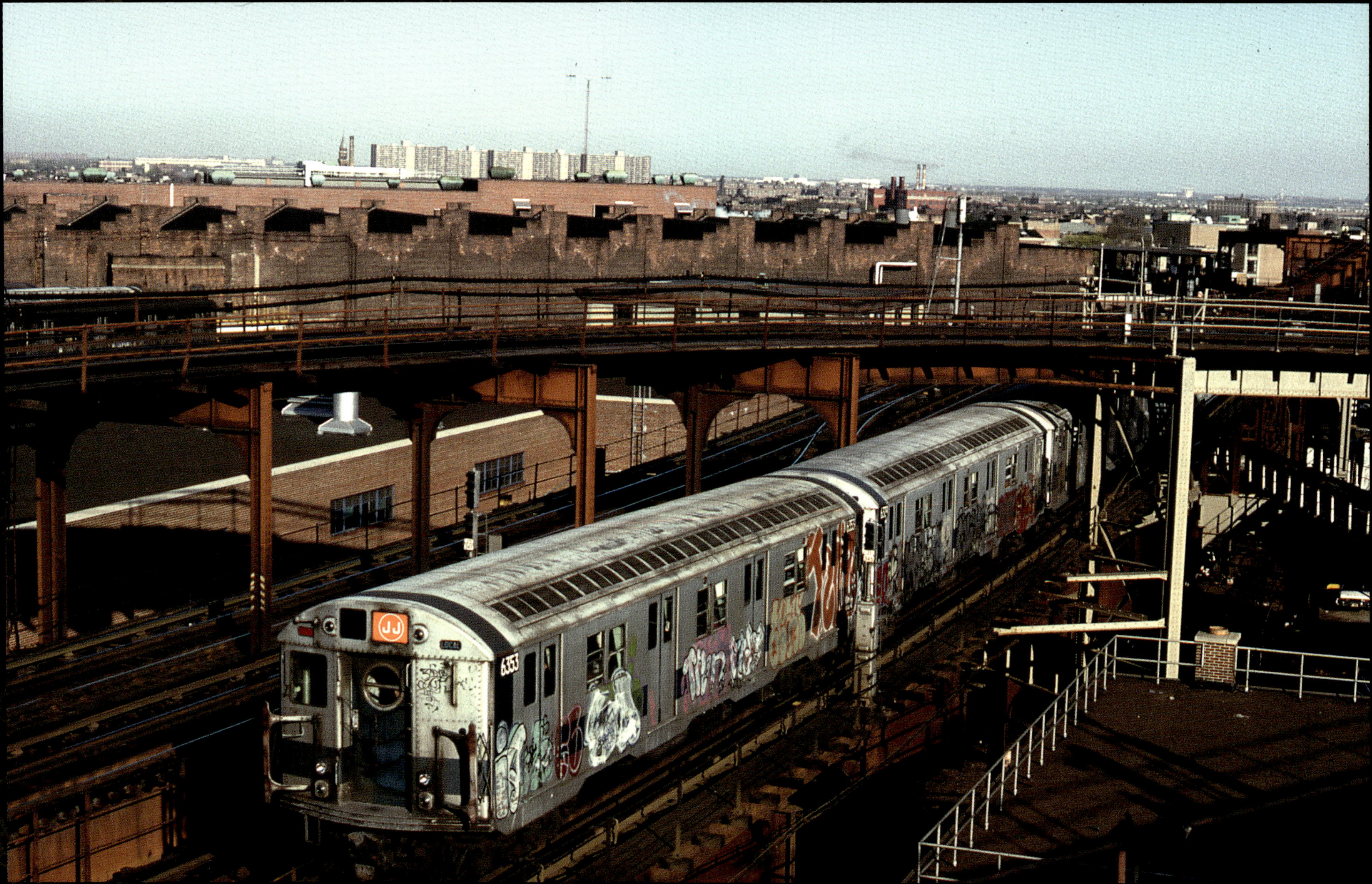

R-16s, J line, between Eastern Parkway & Broadway junction, Brooklyn, 1976

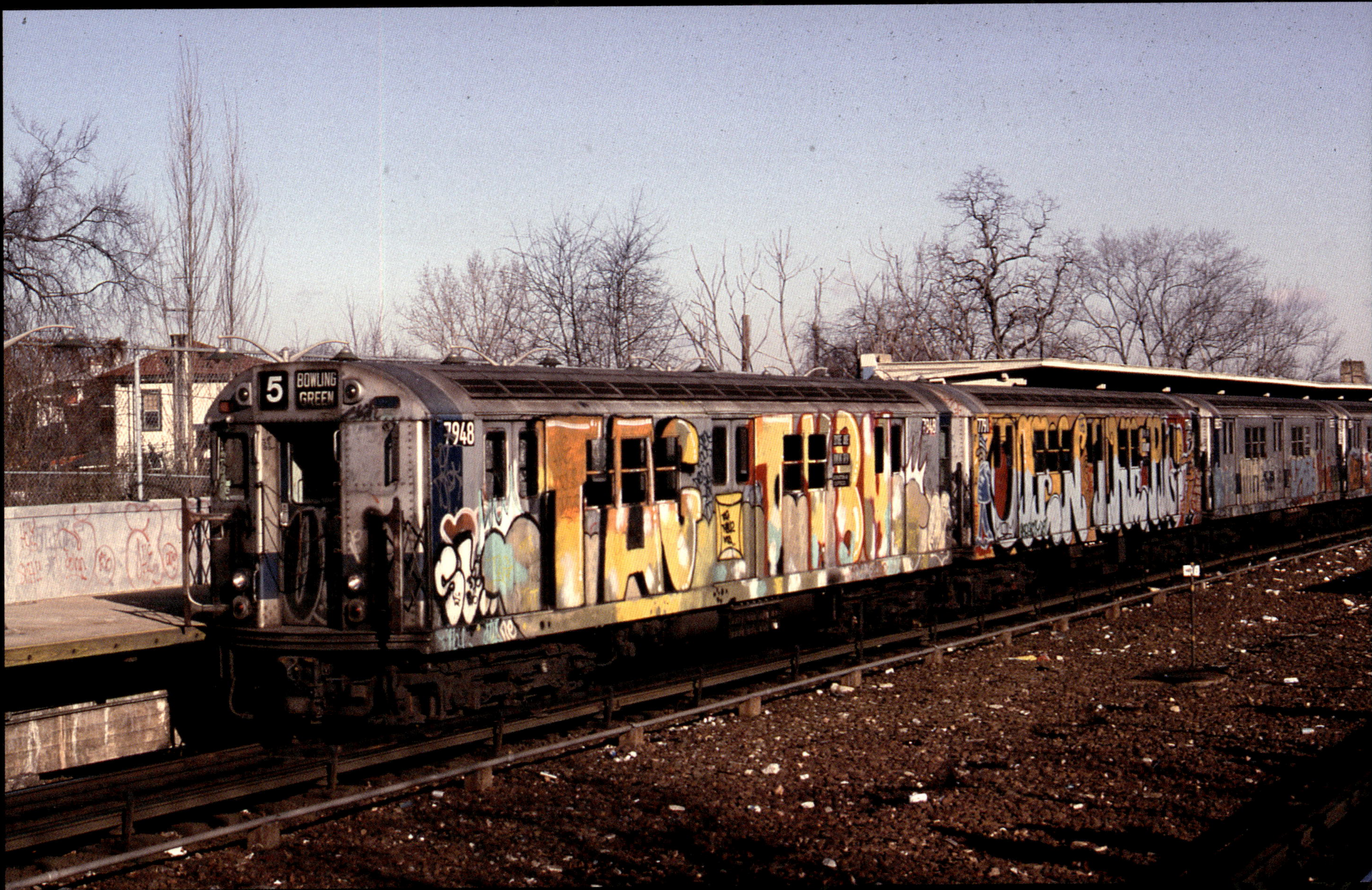

R-28, No. 5 line, Baychester Ave., Bronx, 1977

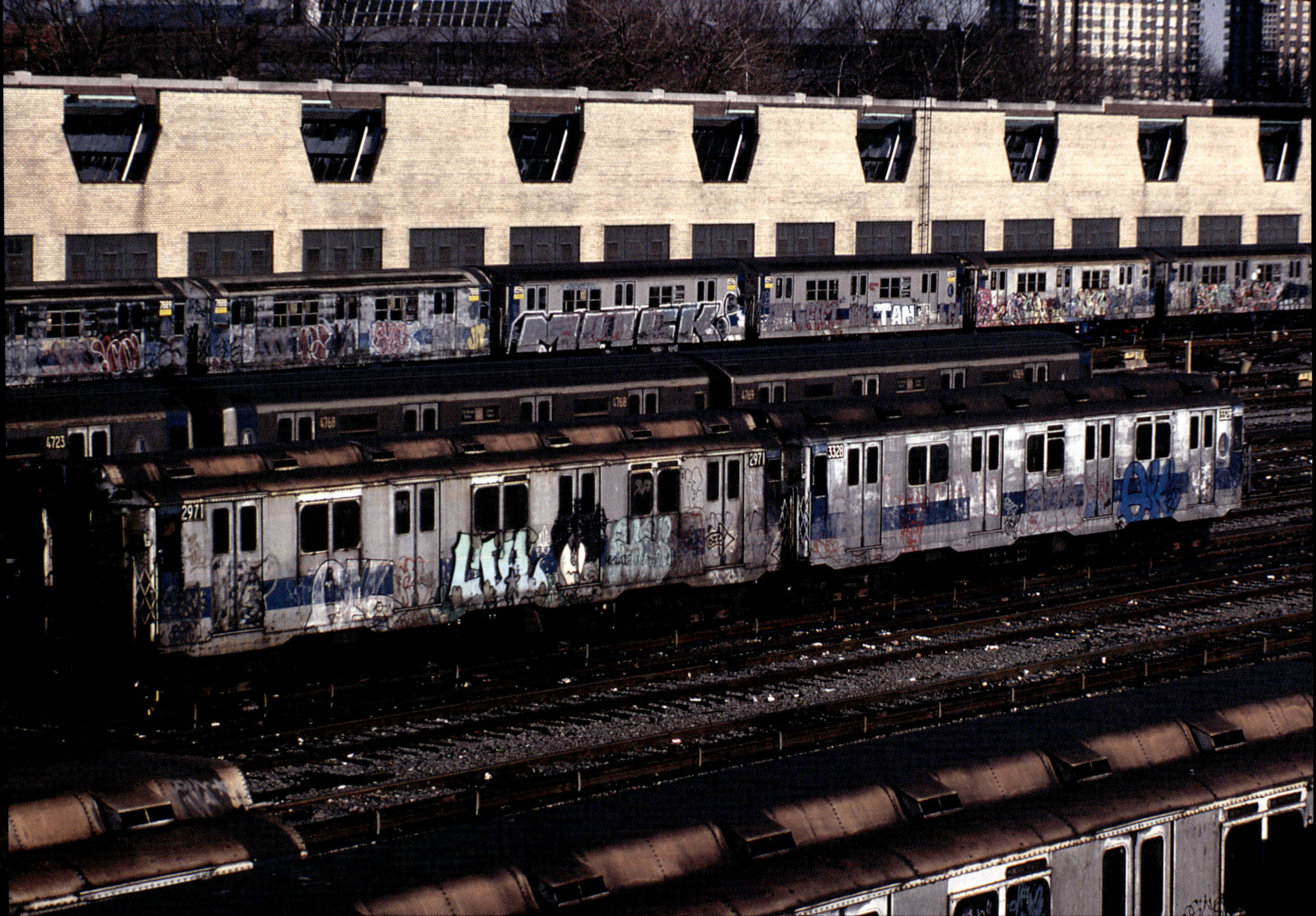

Concourse Yard, Bronx

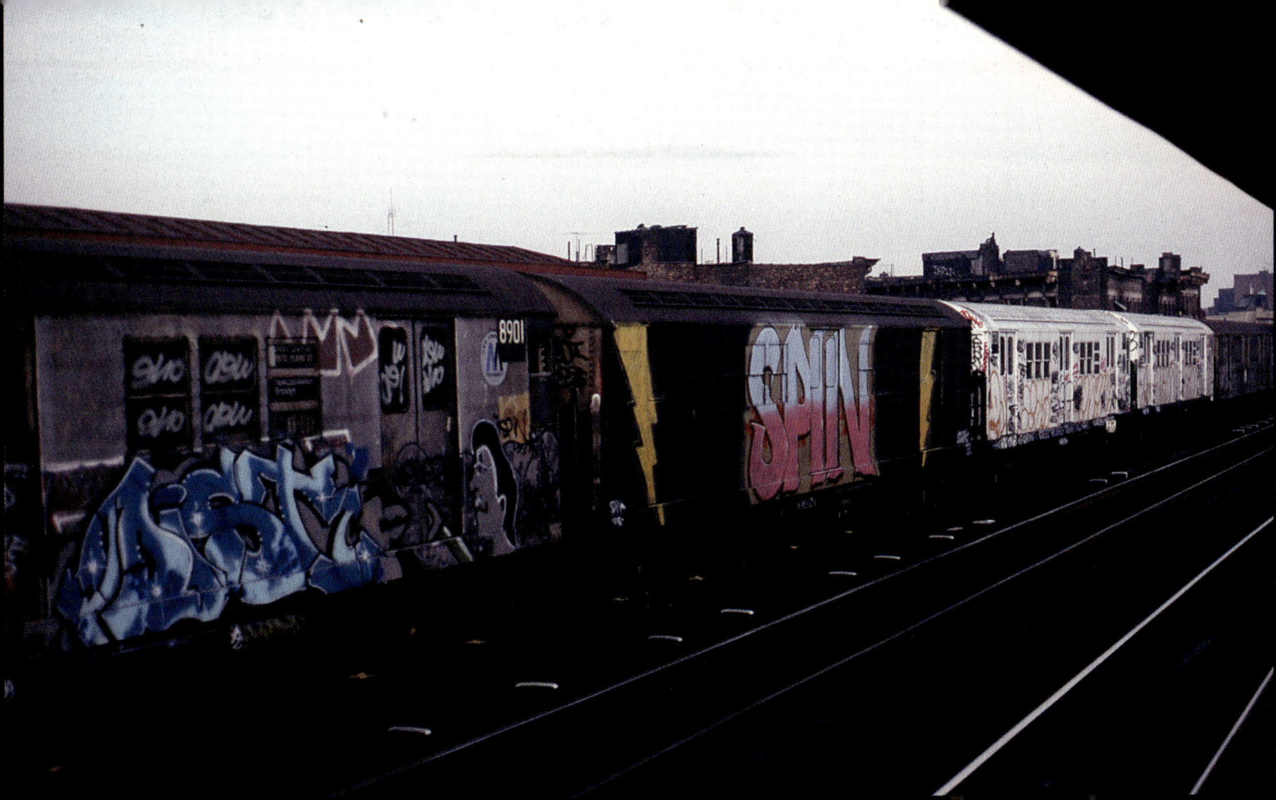

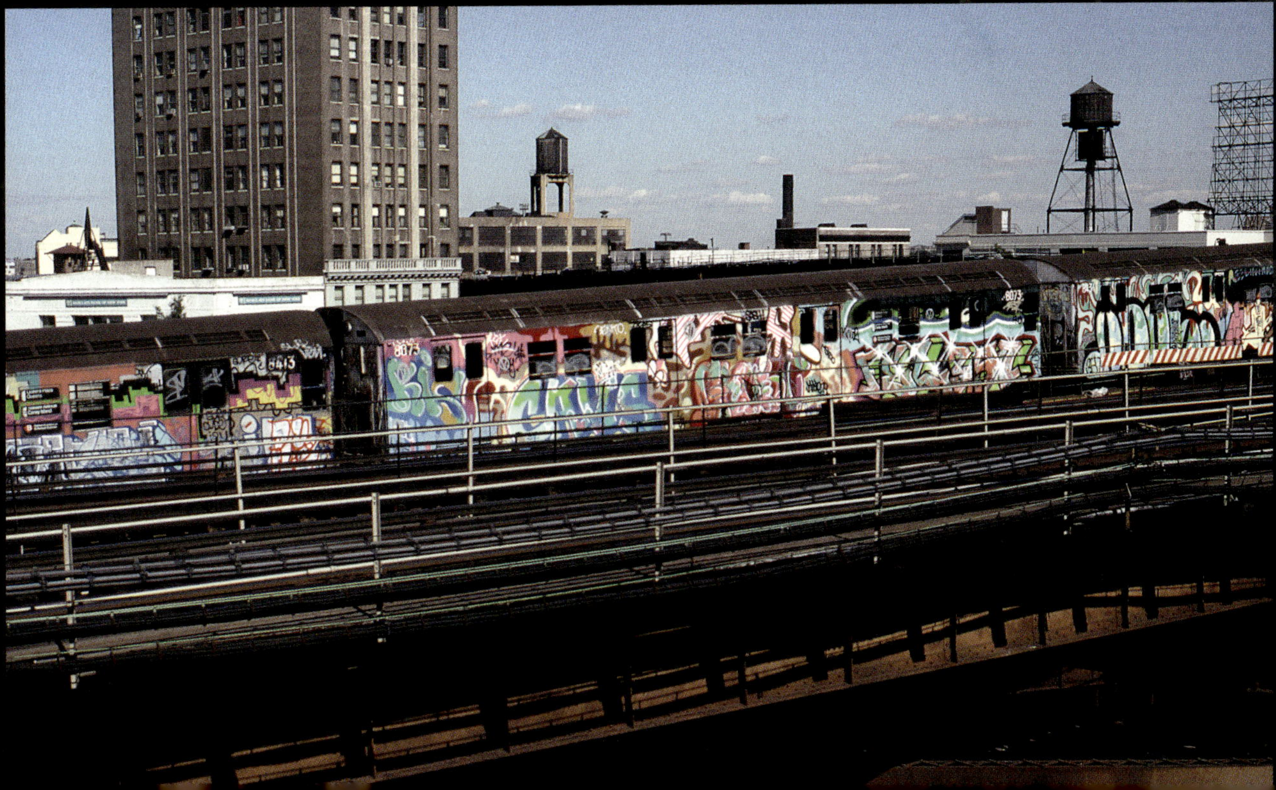

R-33, No. 2 line, Intervale Ave.–163rd St., Bronx, 1982 | R-30/R-27, B line, east of Queensboro Plaza, 1988

Work Equipment

New York Subways & Stations 1970–1990

CHAPTER 6

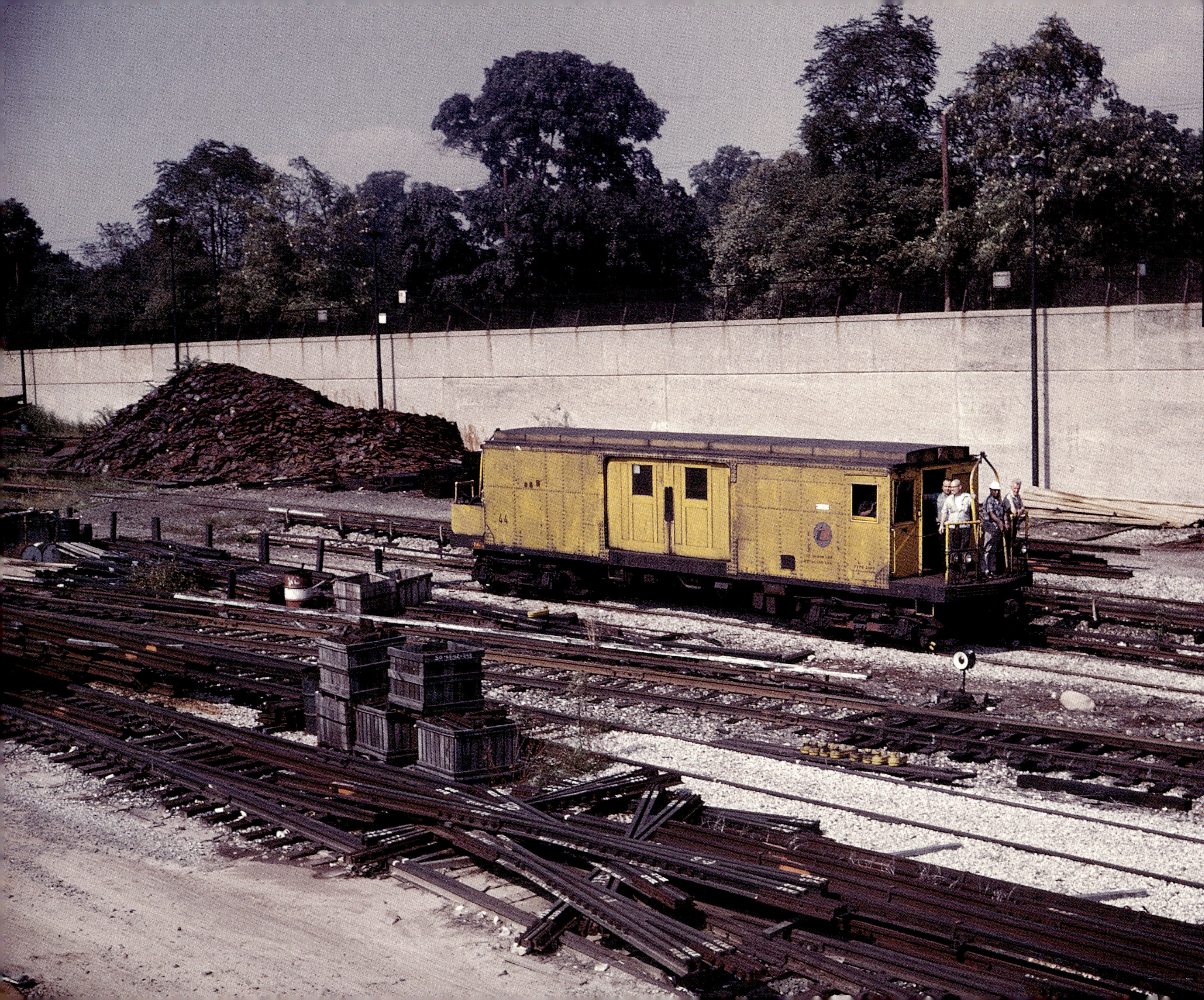

Locomotive, 36th St. Yard, Brooklyn, 1970

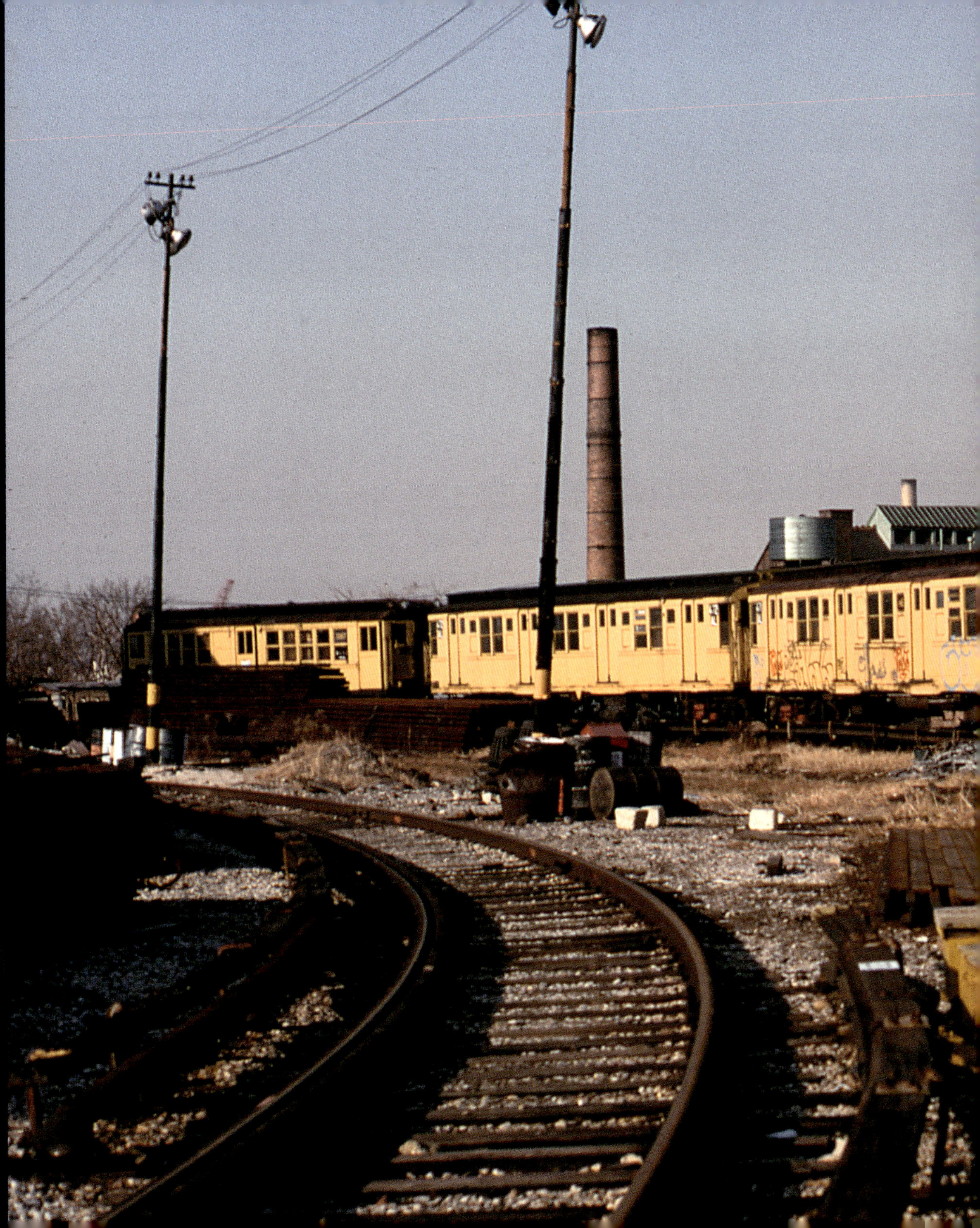

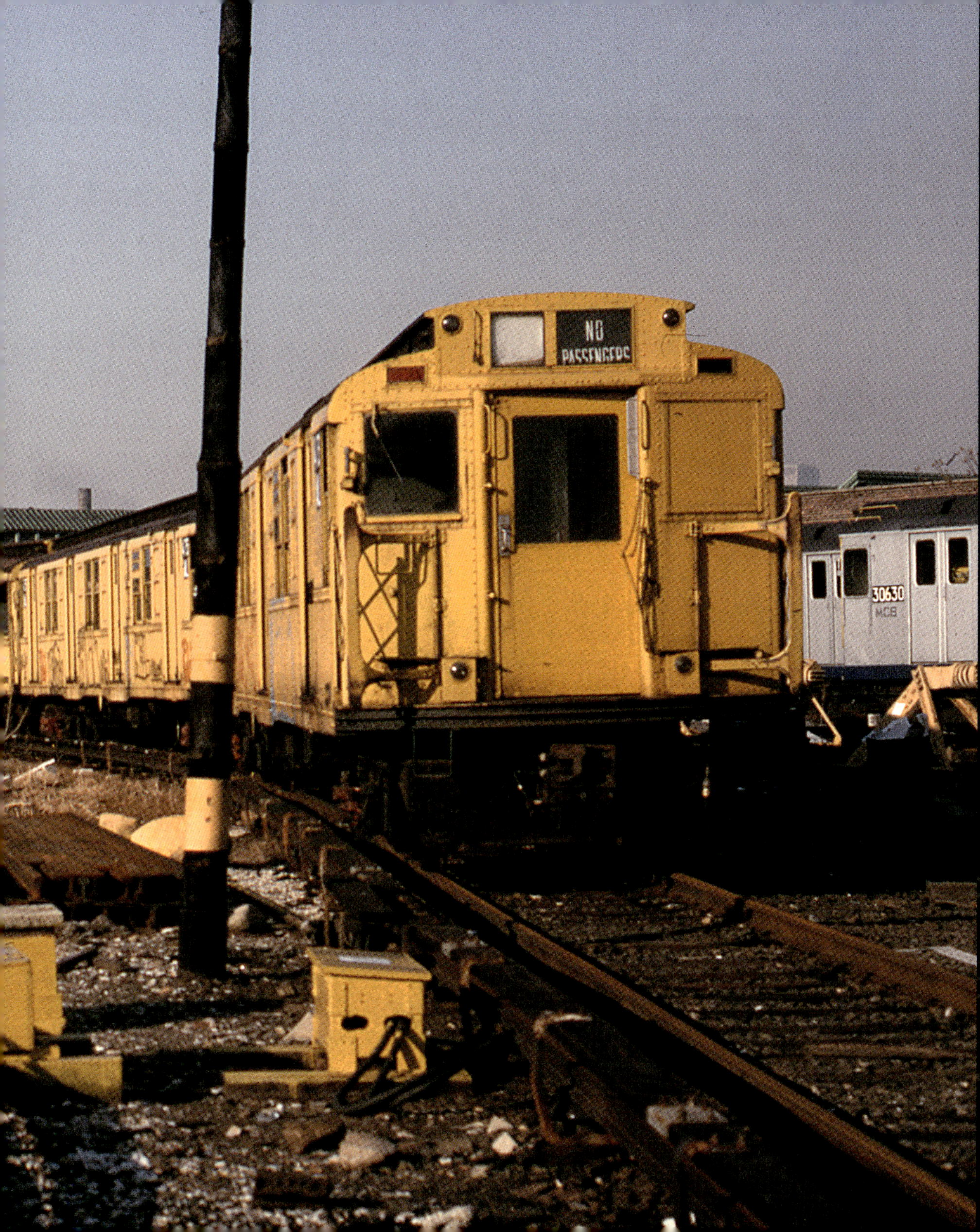

IND Snow Equipment, 36th St. Yard, Brooklyn, 1975

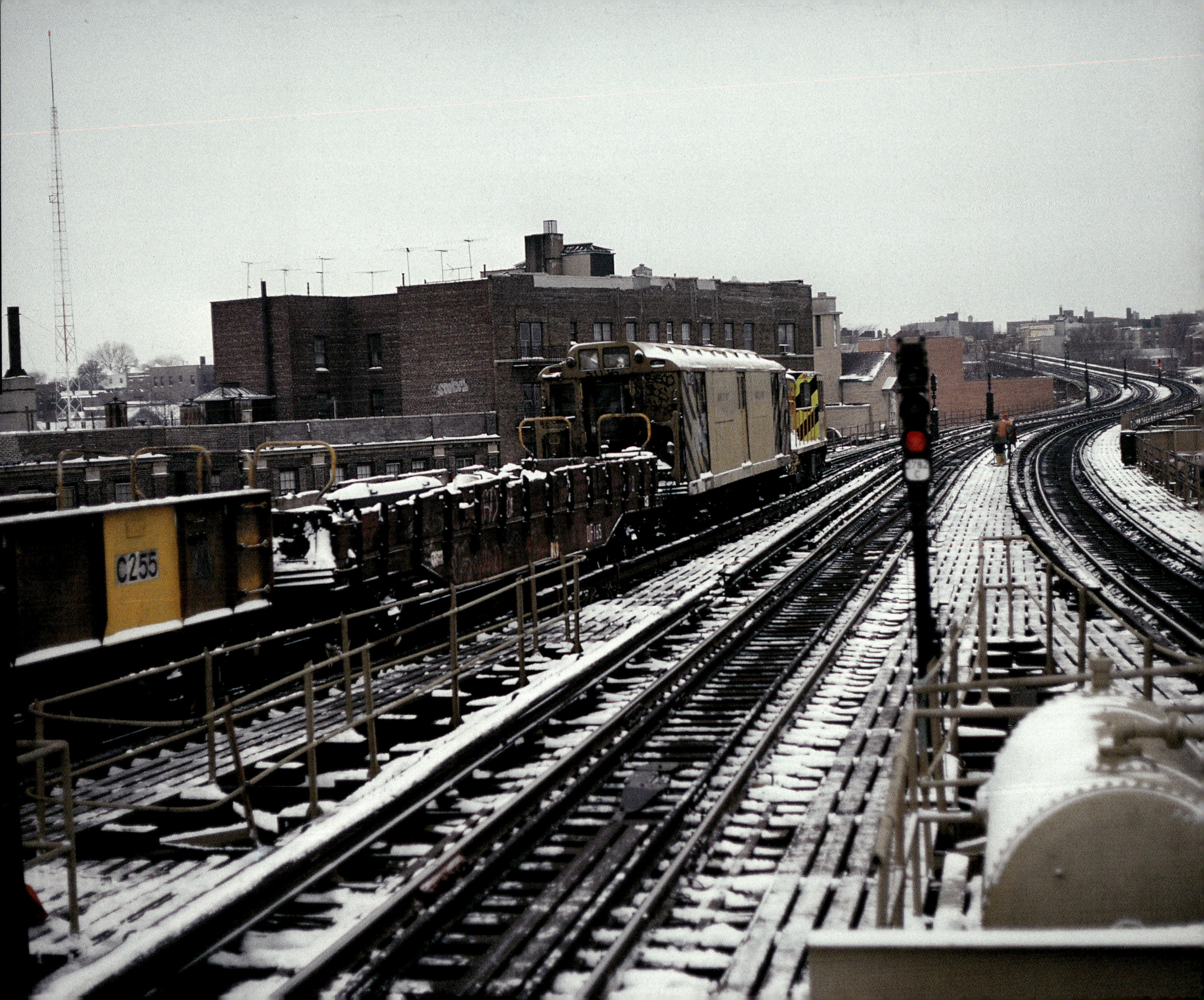

No. 7 Flushing line, 61st St.–Woodside, Queens, 1985

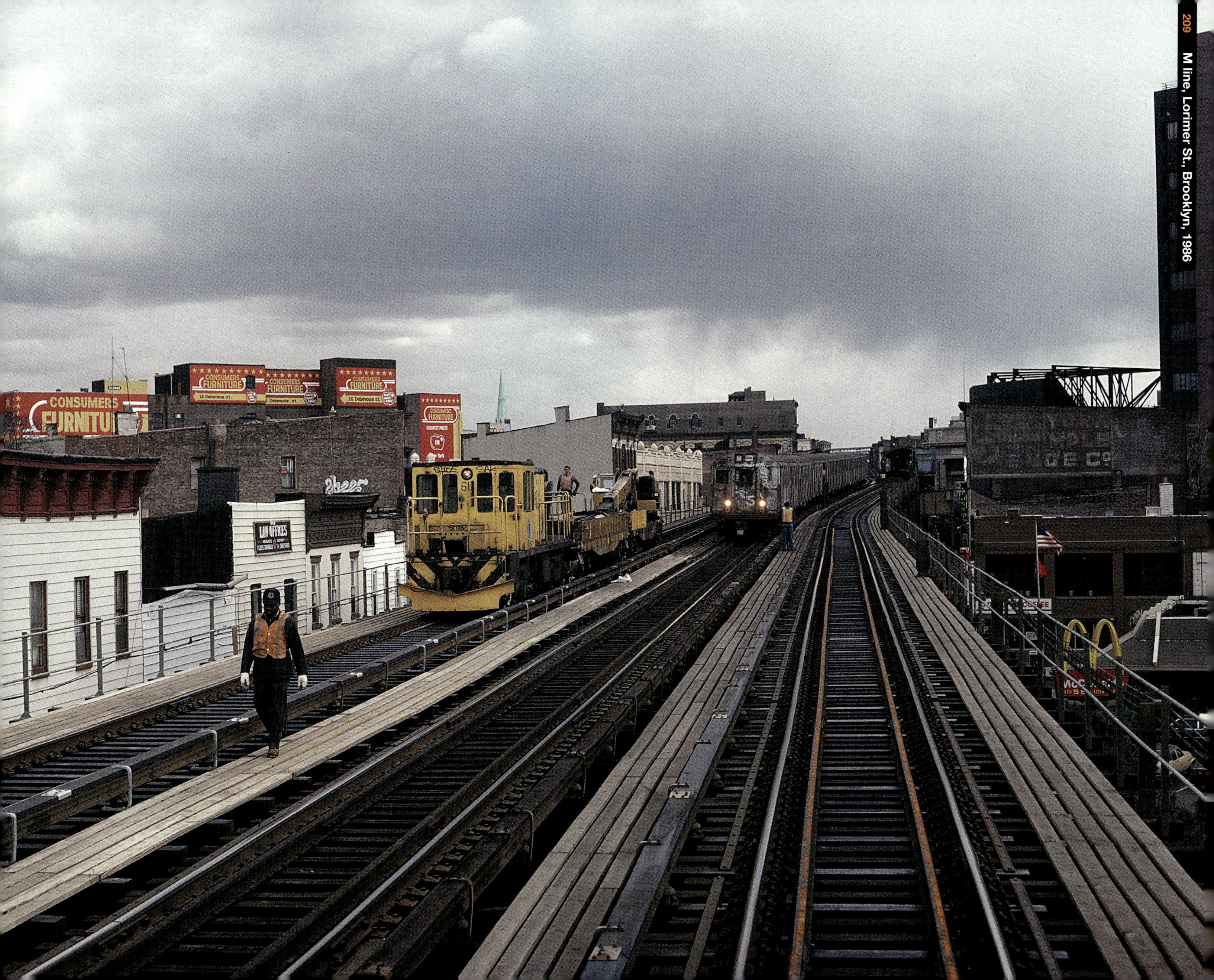

M line, Lorimer St., Brooklyn, 1986

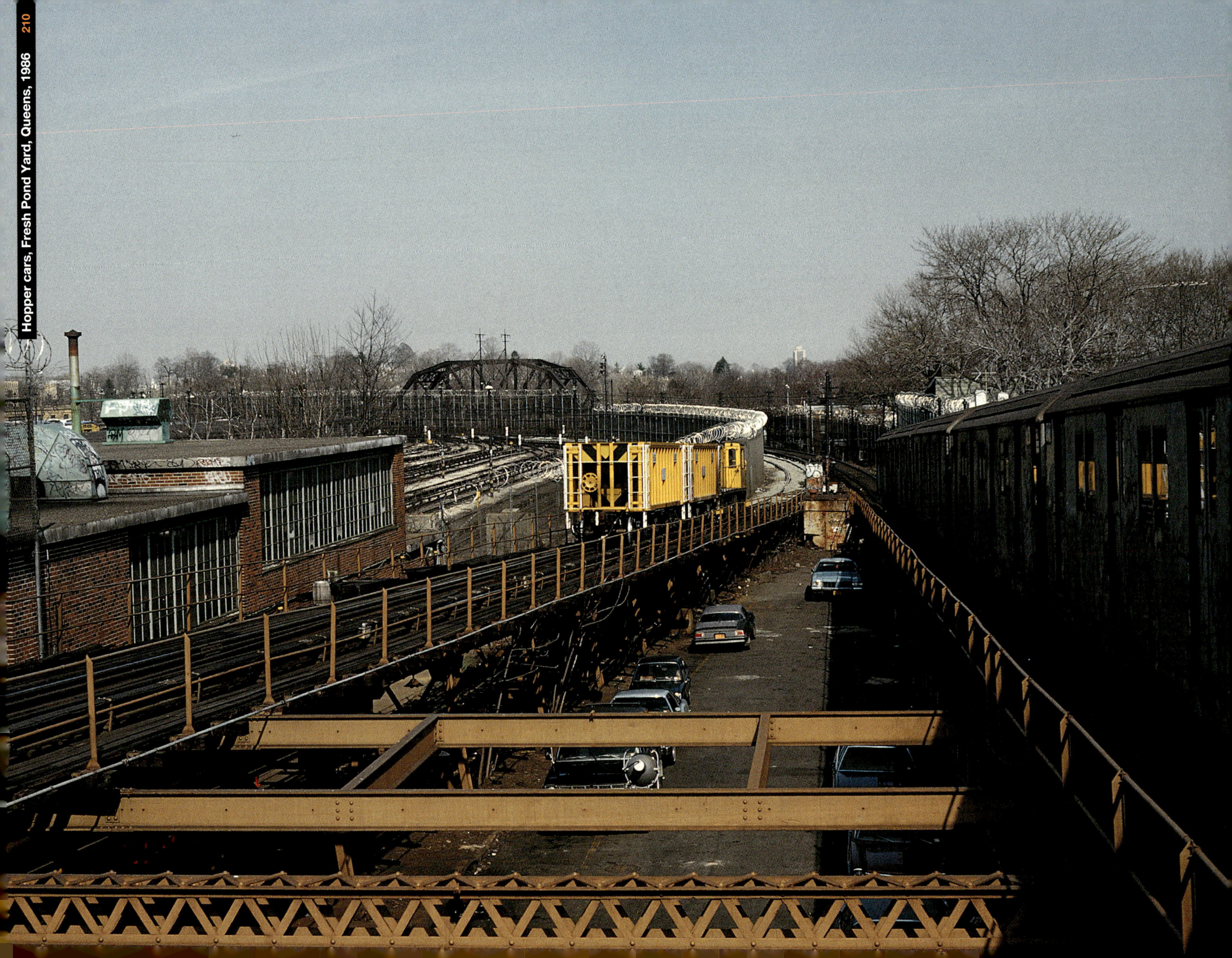

Hopper cars, Fresh Pond Yard, Queens, 1986

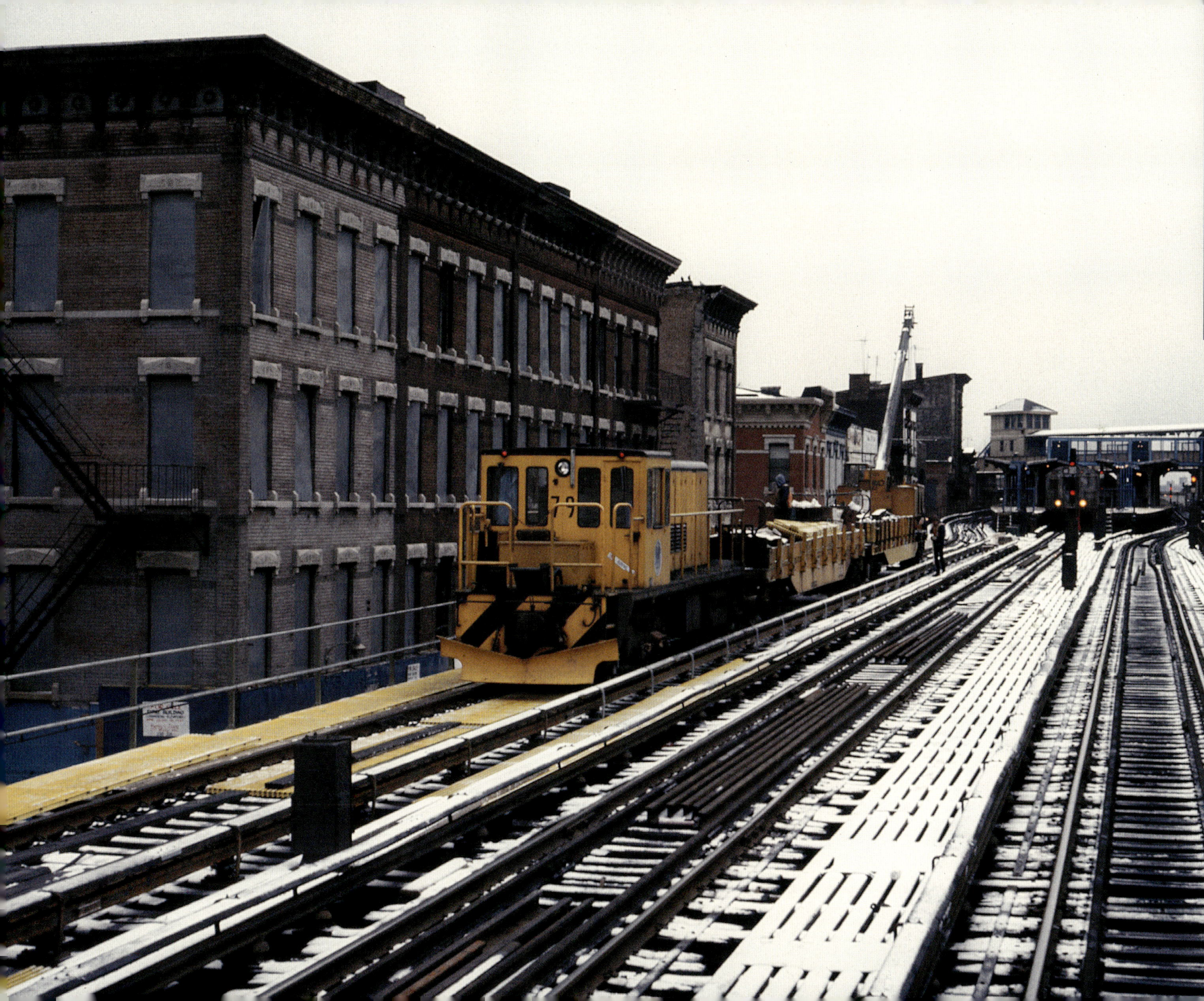

West of Myrtle Ave. Station, Brooklyn, 1986

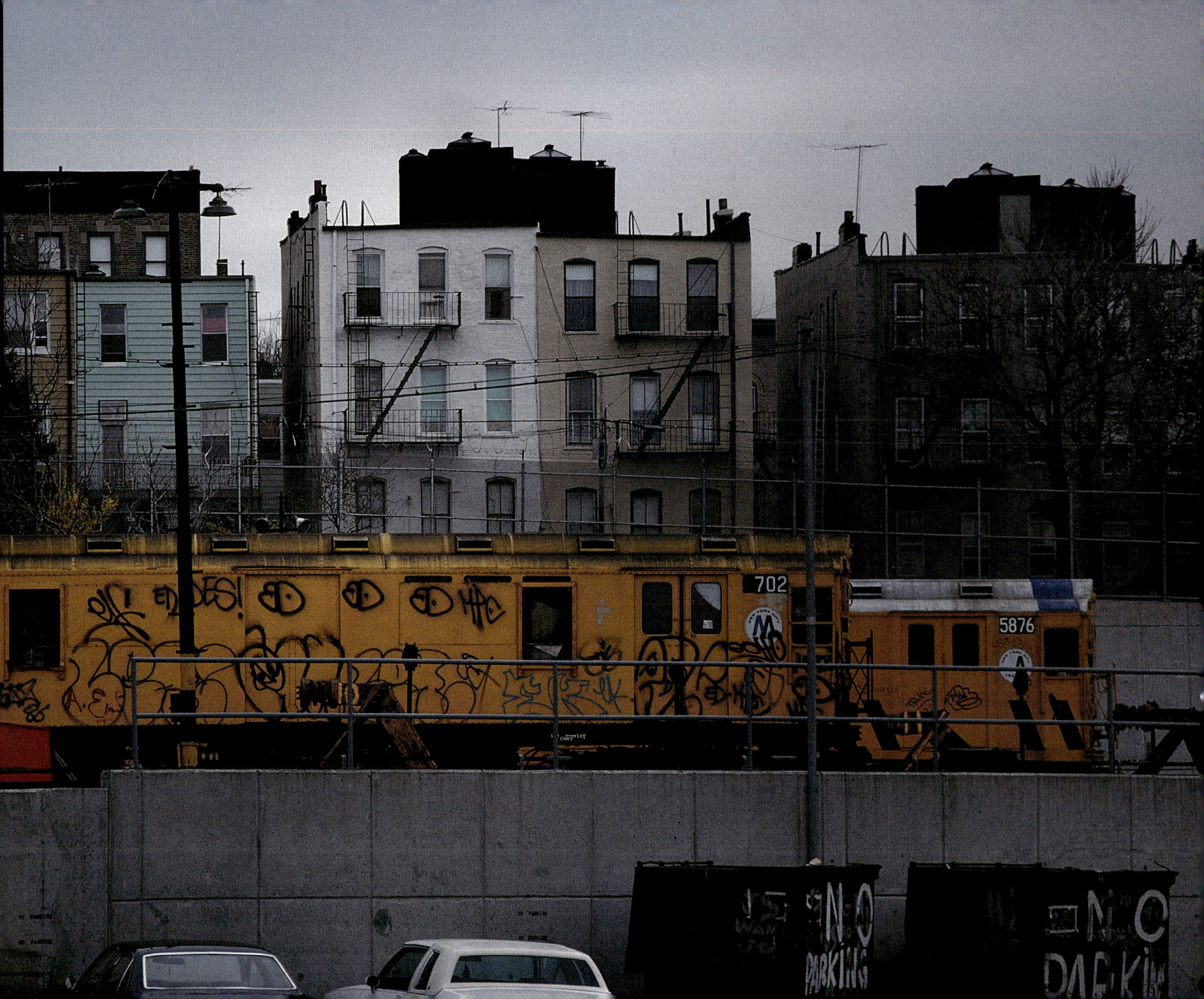

R-12, revenue collector car, 36th St. Yard, Brooklyn, 1987

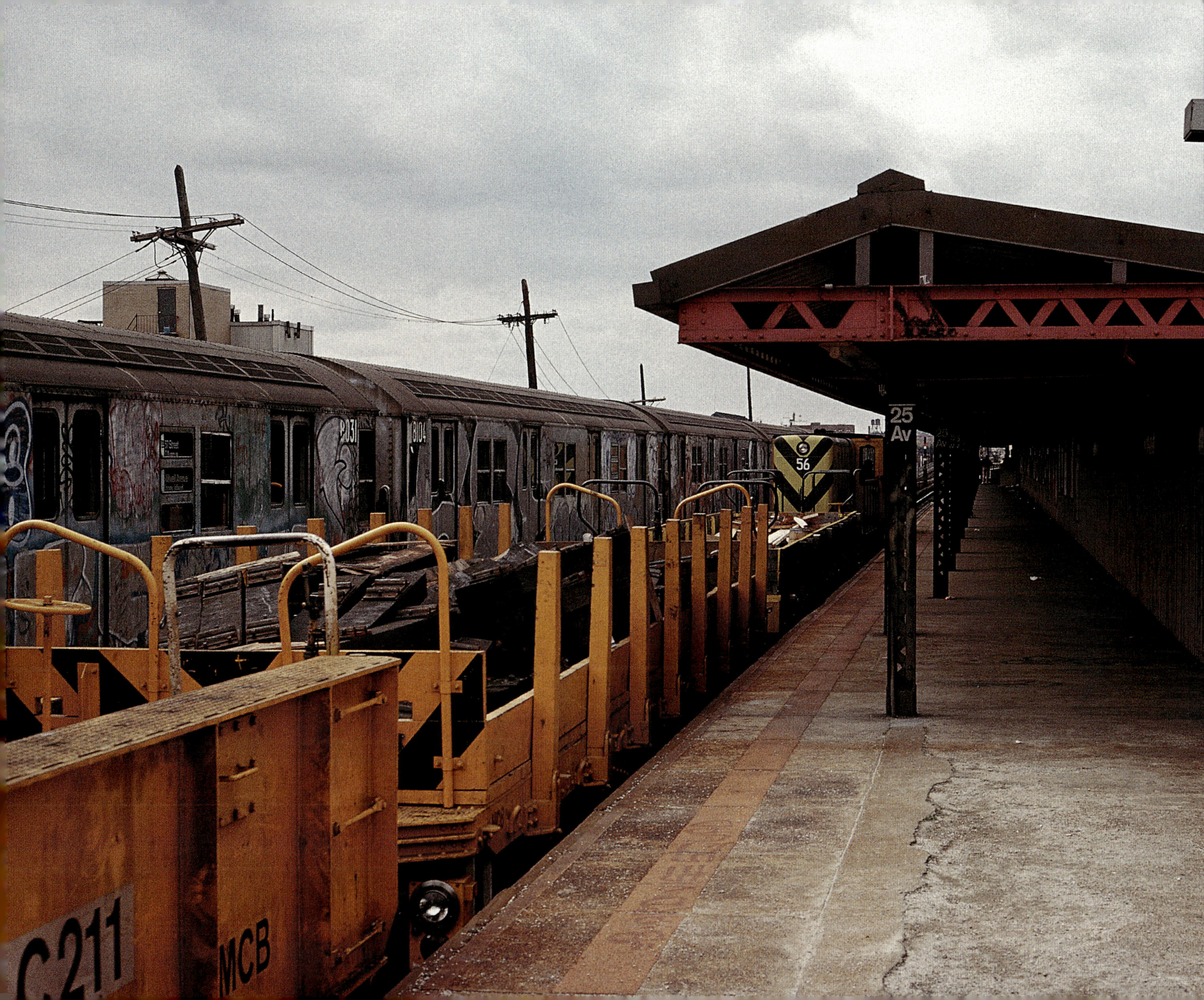

Work train, R-27s, West End line, 25th Ave., Brooklyn, 1988

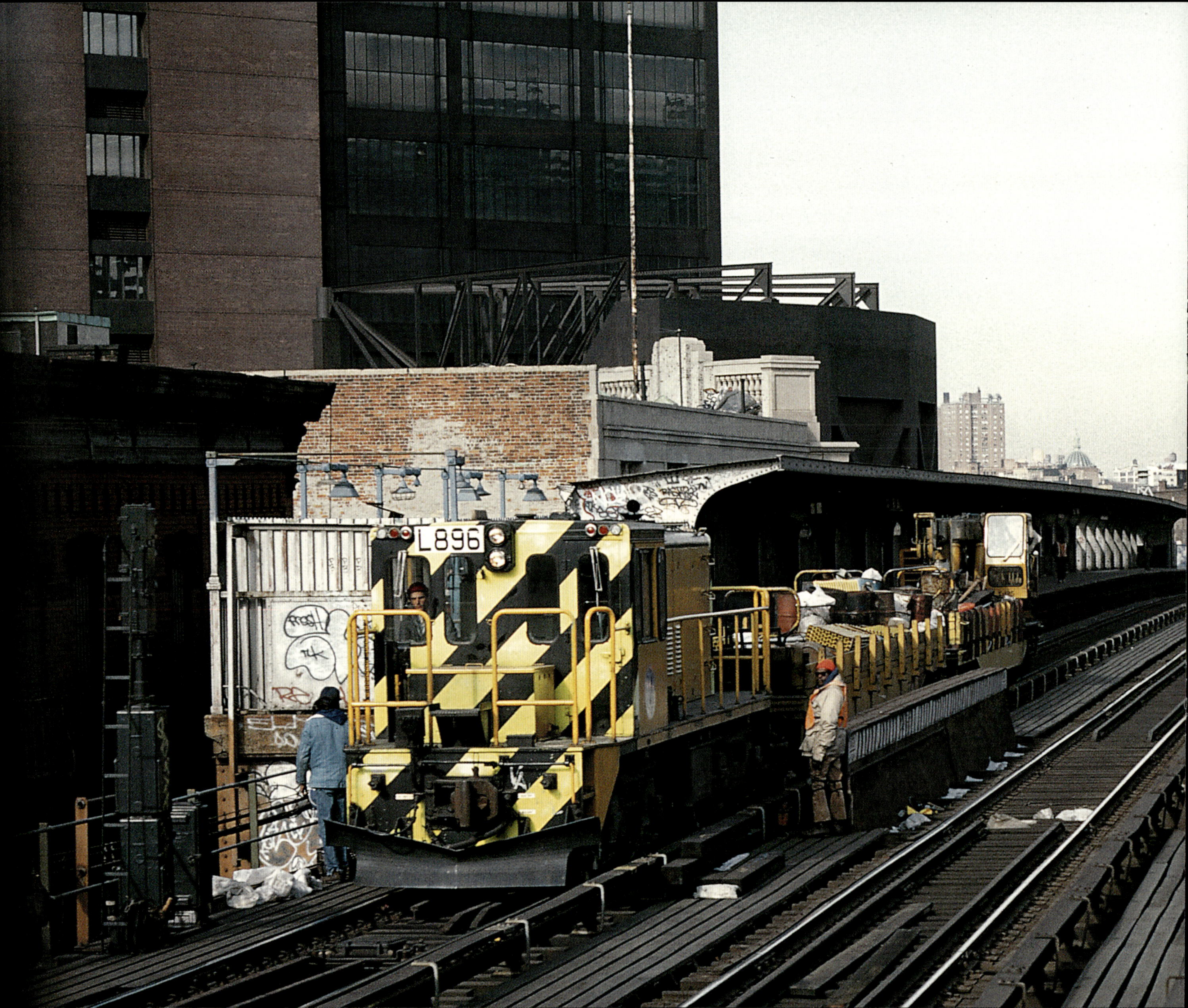
L896

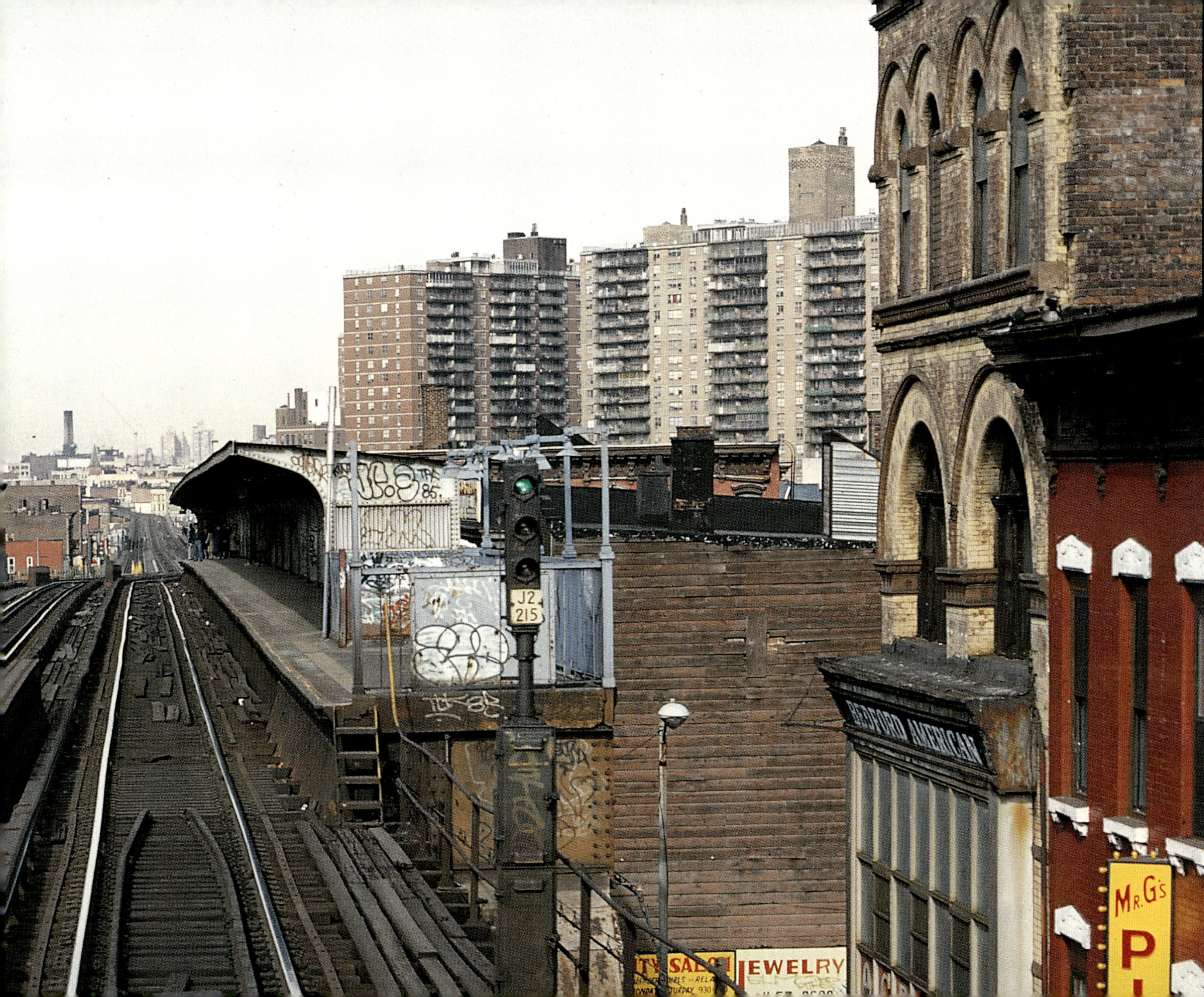

215

Flushing Ave. Station, Brooklyn, 1987

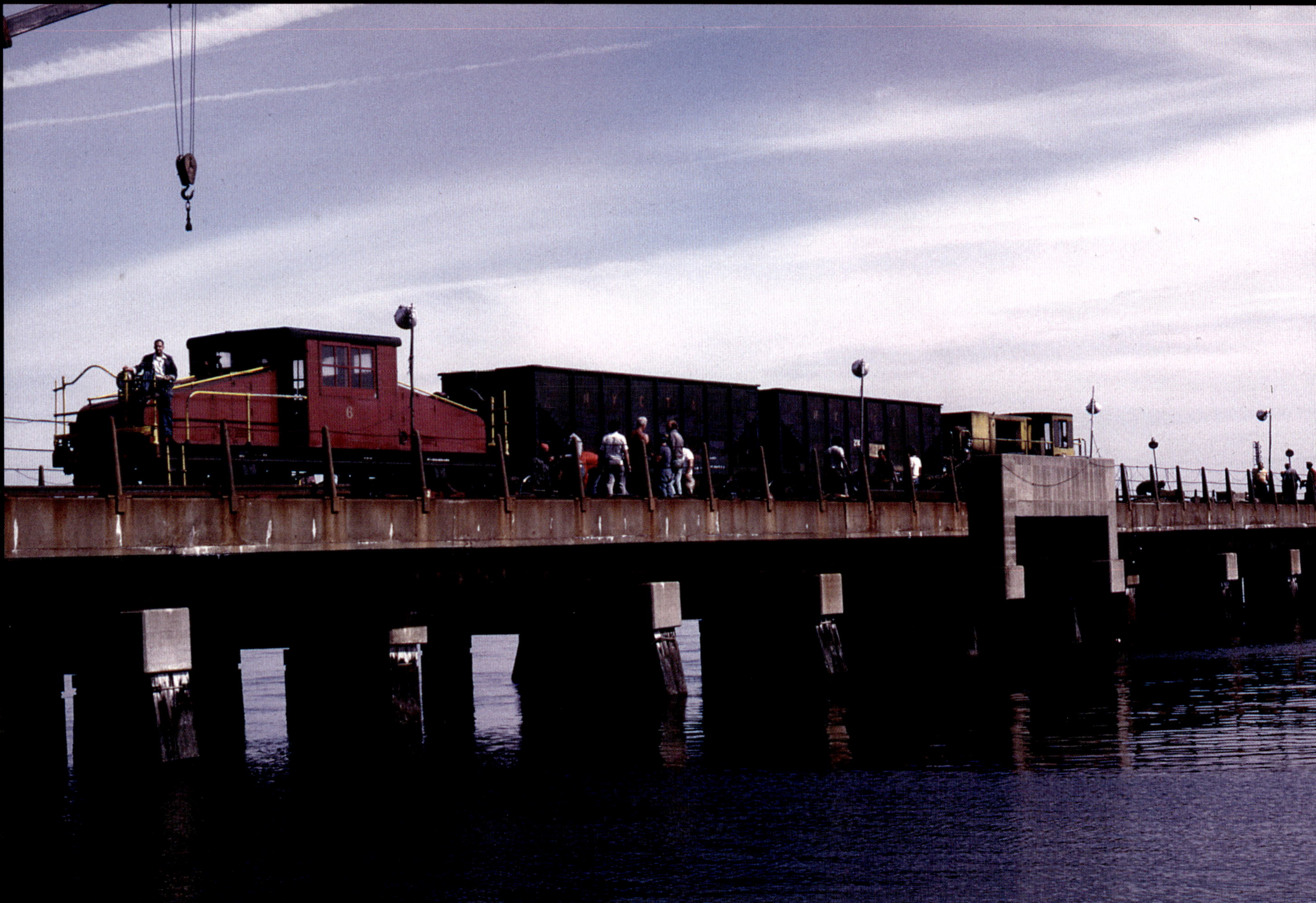

Locomotive #6, Rockaway line, near Broad Channel, Queens, 1973

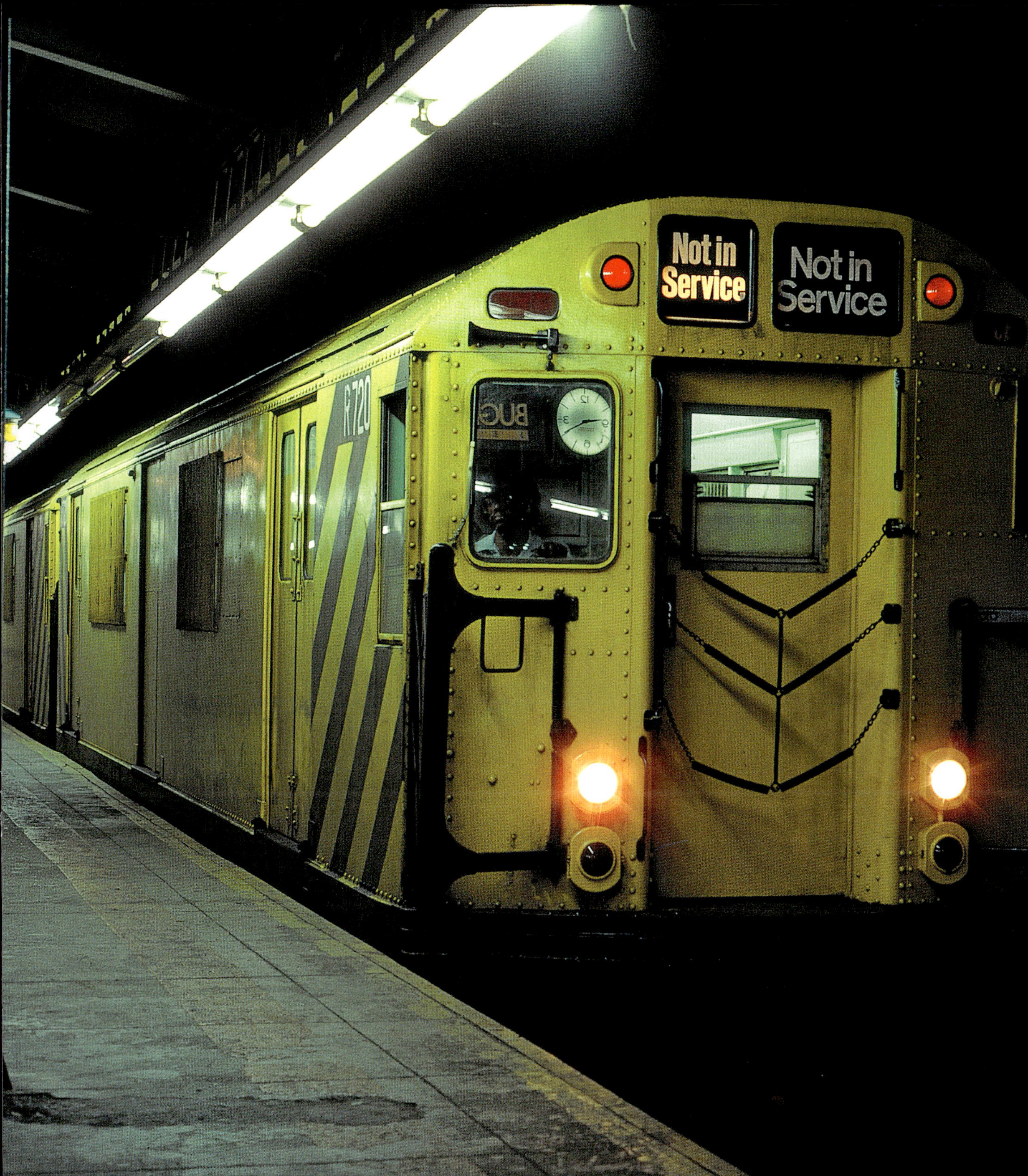

Not in Service
Not in Service
R720

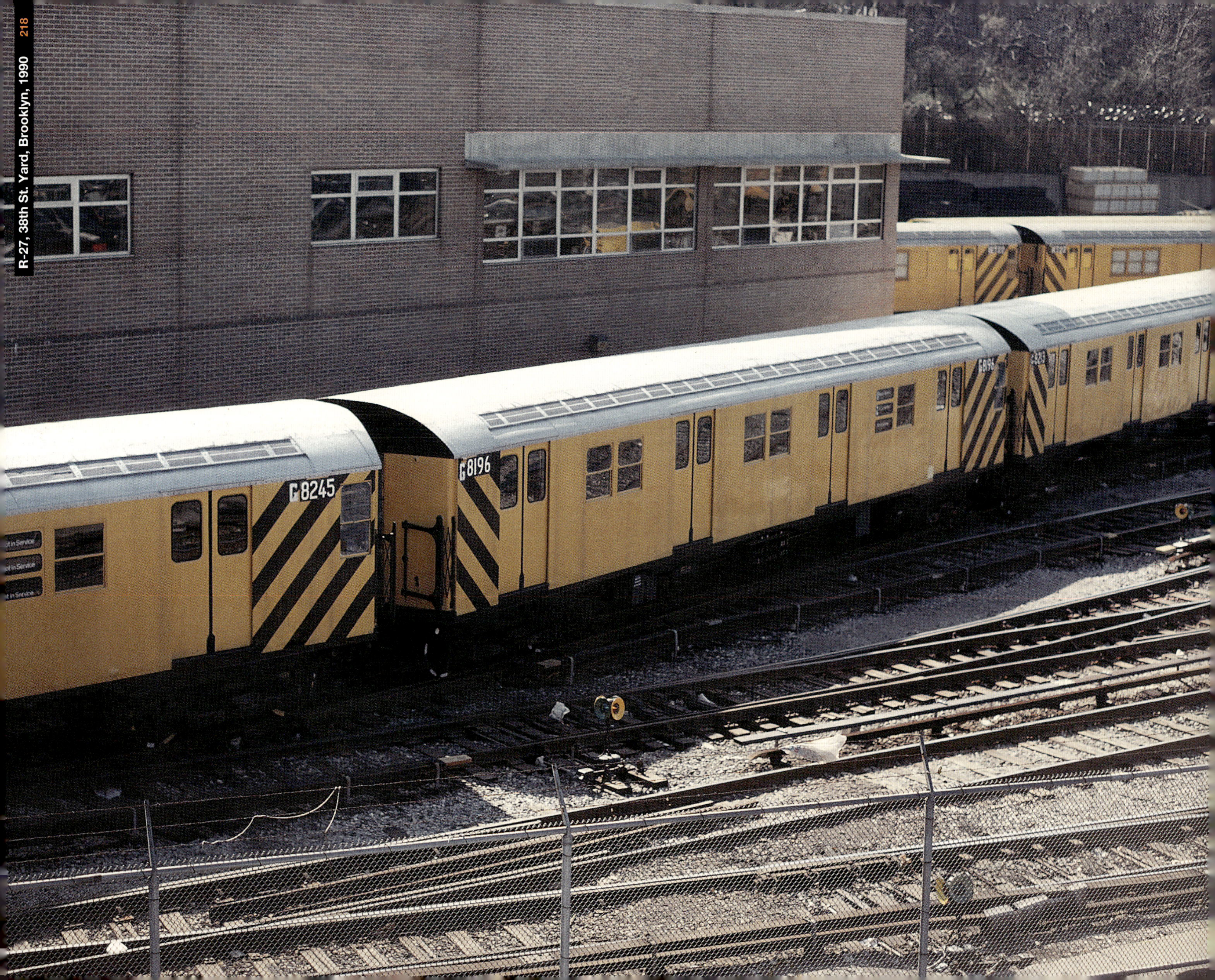

R-27, 38th St. Yard, Brooklyn, 1990

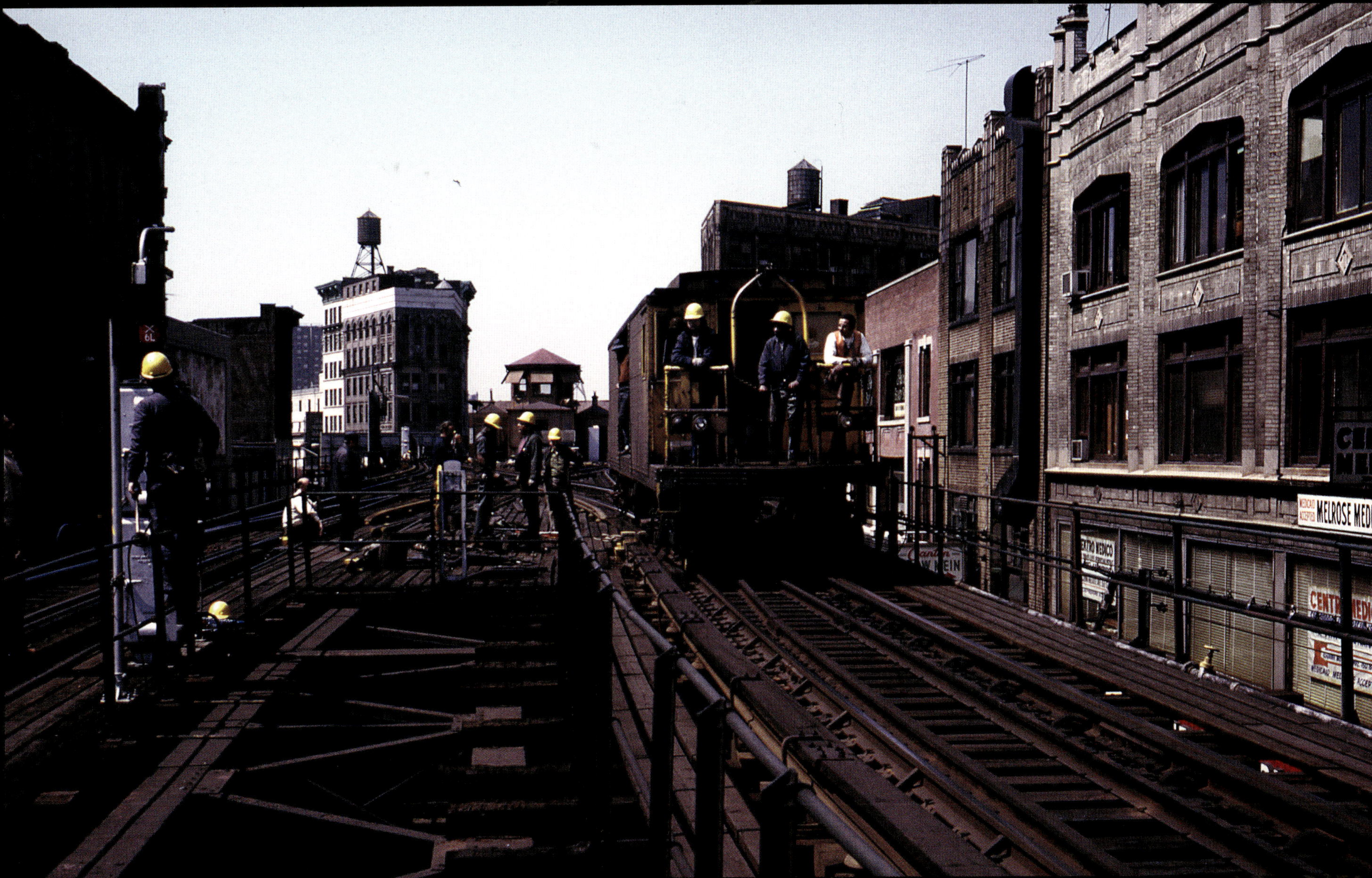

Signal dolly, 3rd Ave. El, 149th St., Bronx, 1973

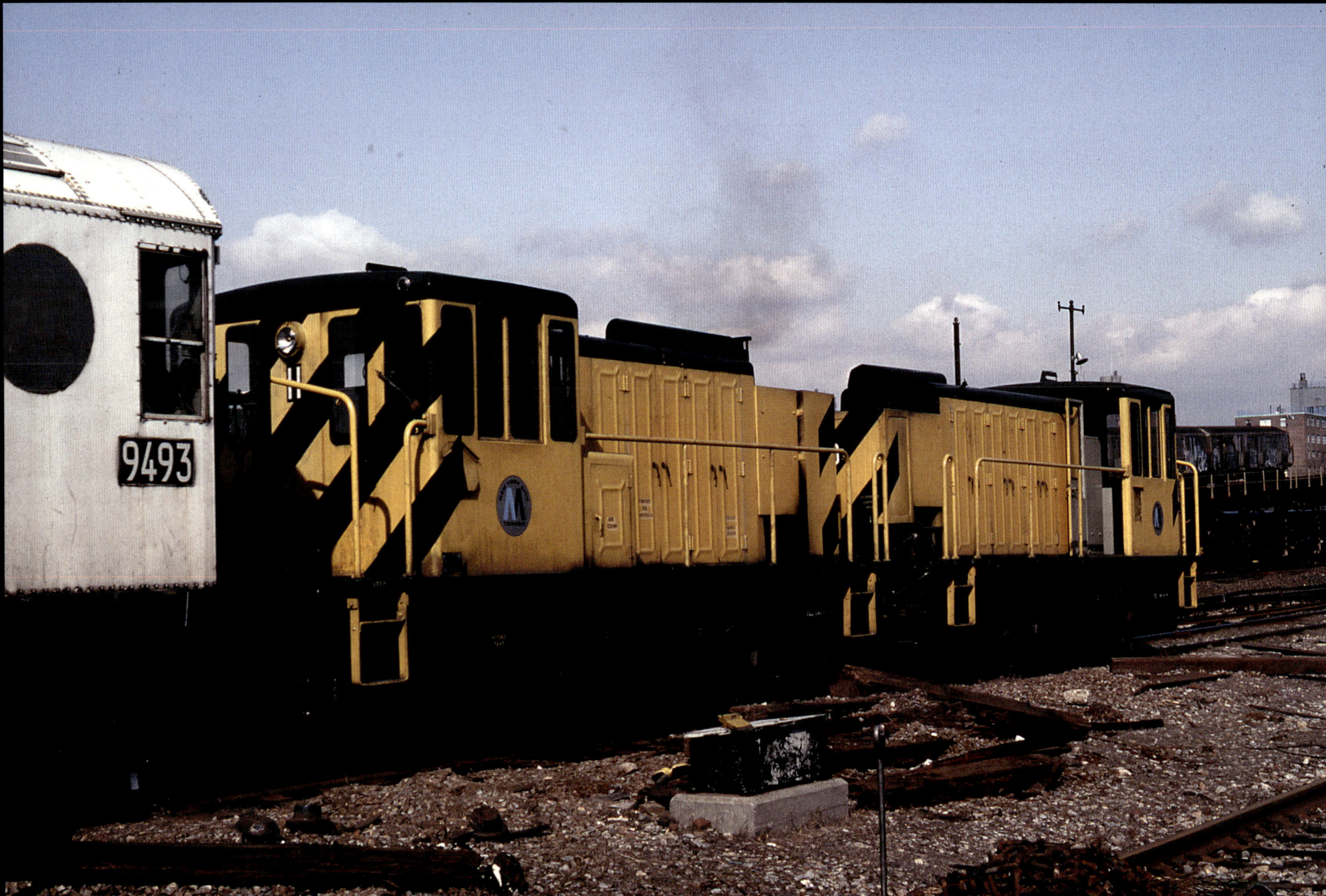

Diesel locomotives, Coney Island Yard, Brooklyn, 1984

Scrap Trains

New York
Subways & Stations
1970–1990

CHAPTER 7

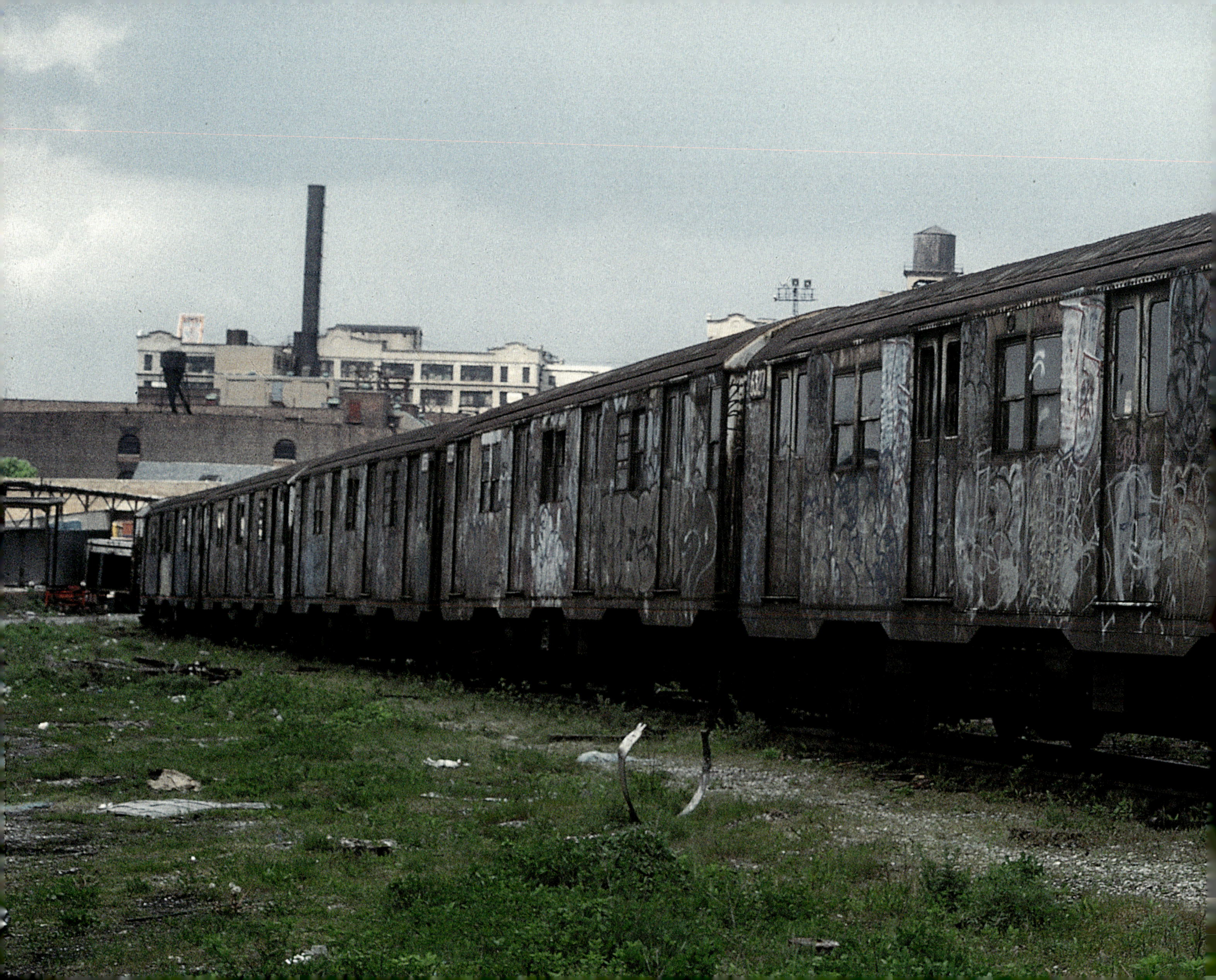

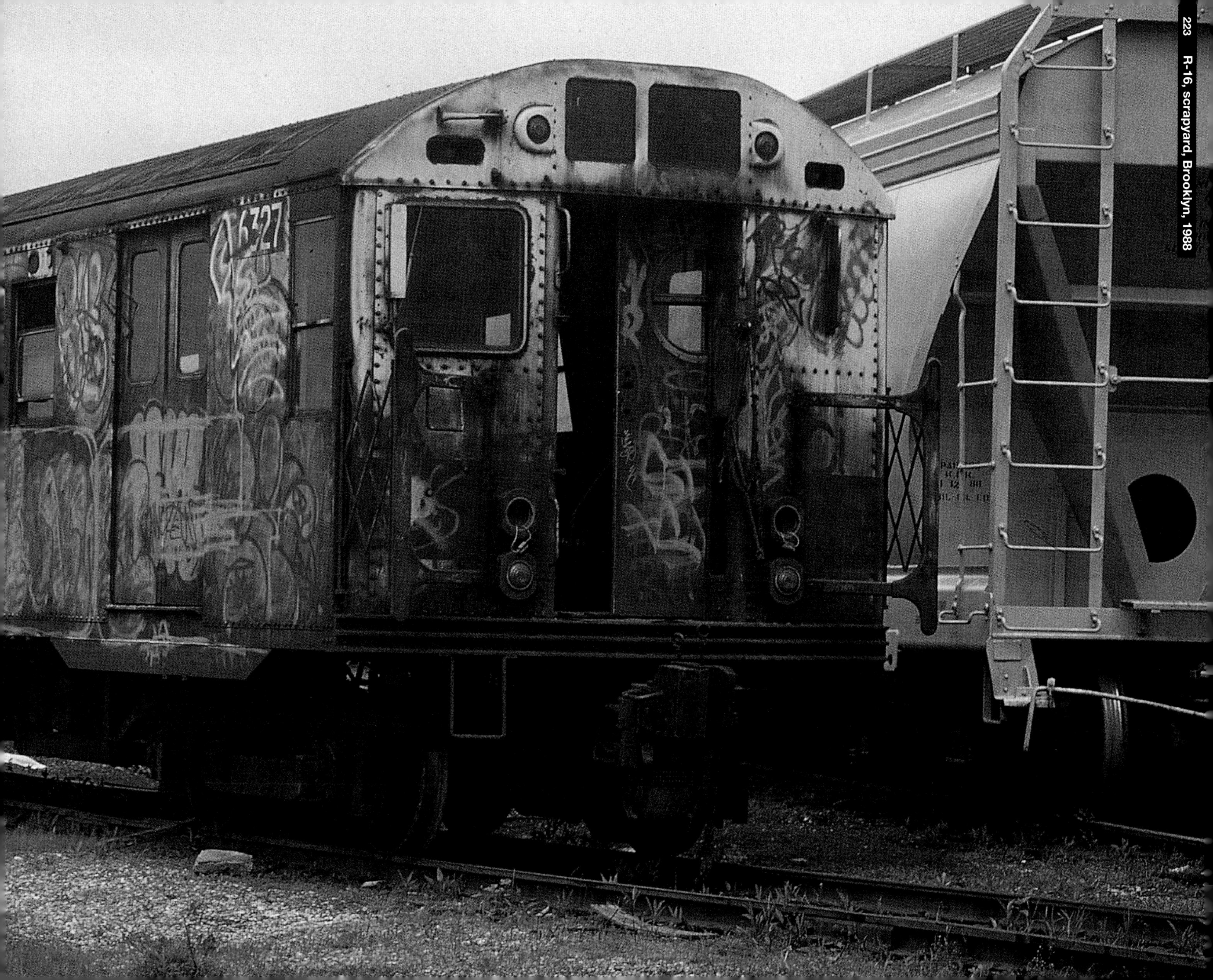

R-16, scrapyard, Brooklyn, 1988

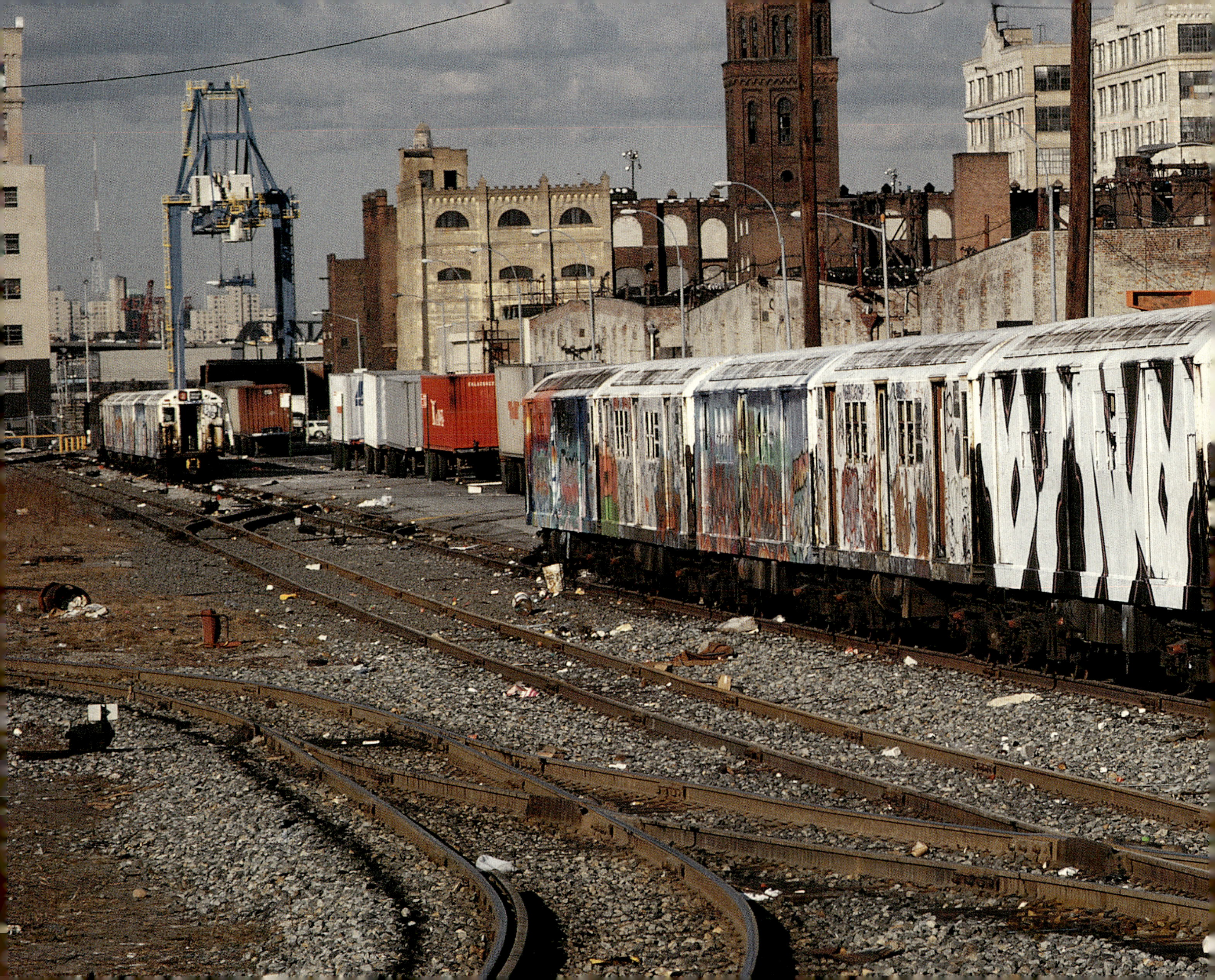

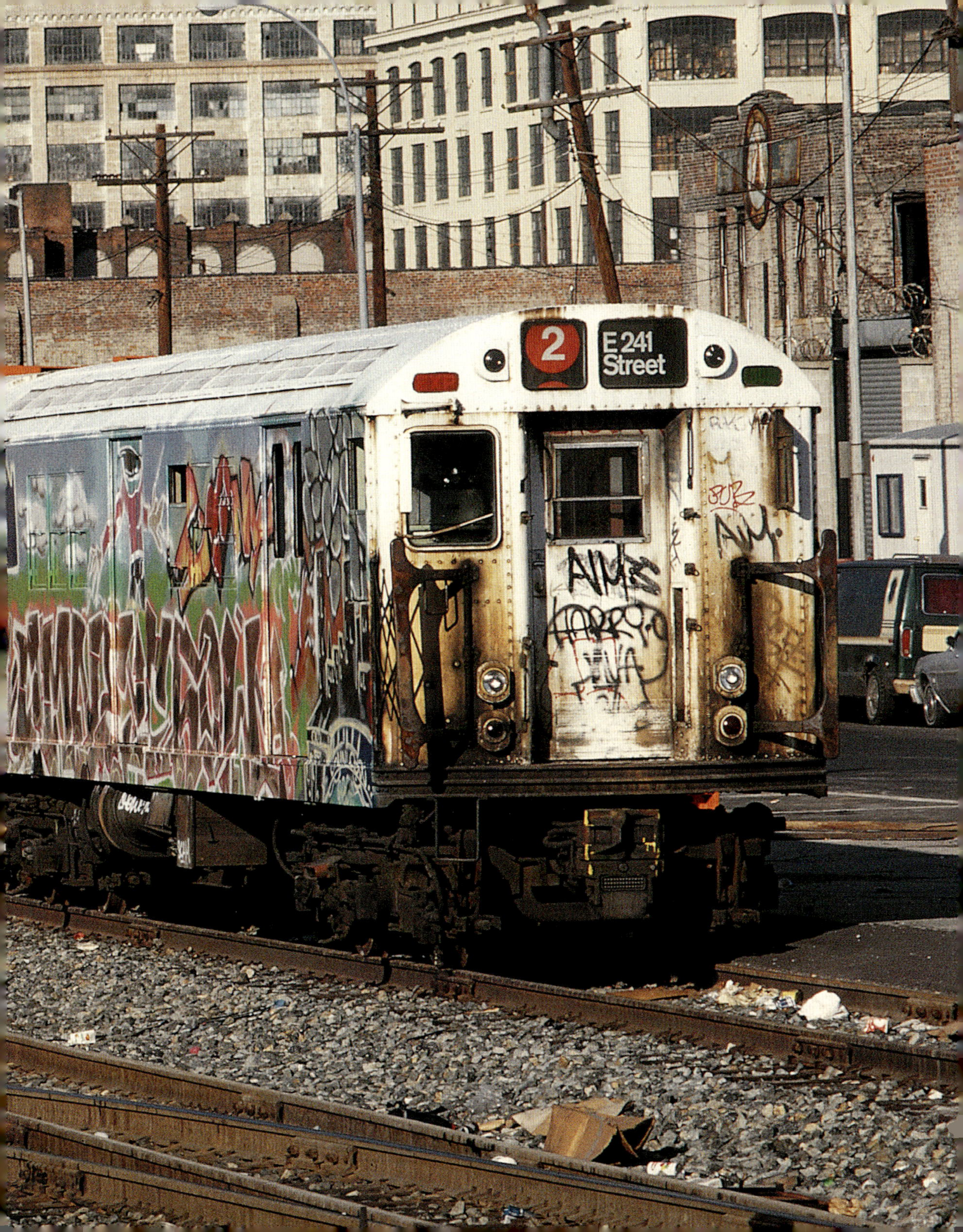
2
E 241
Street

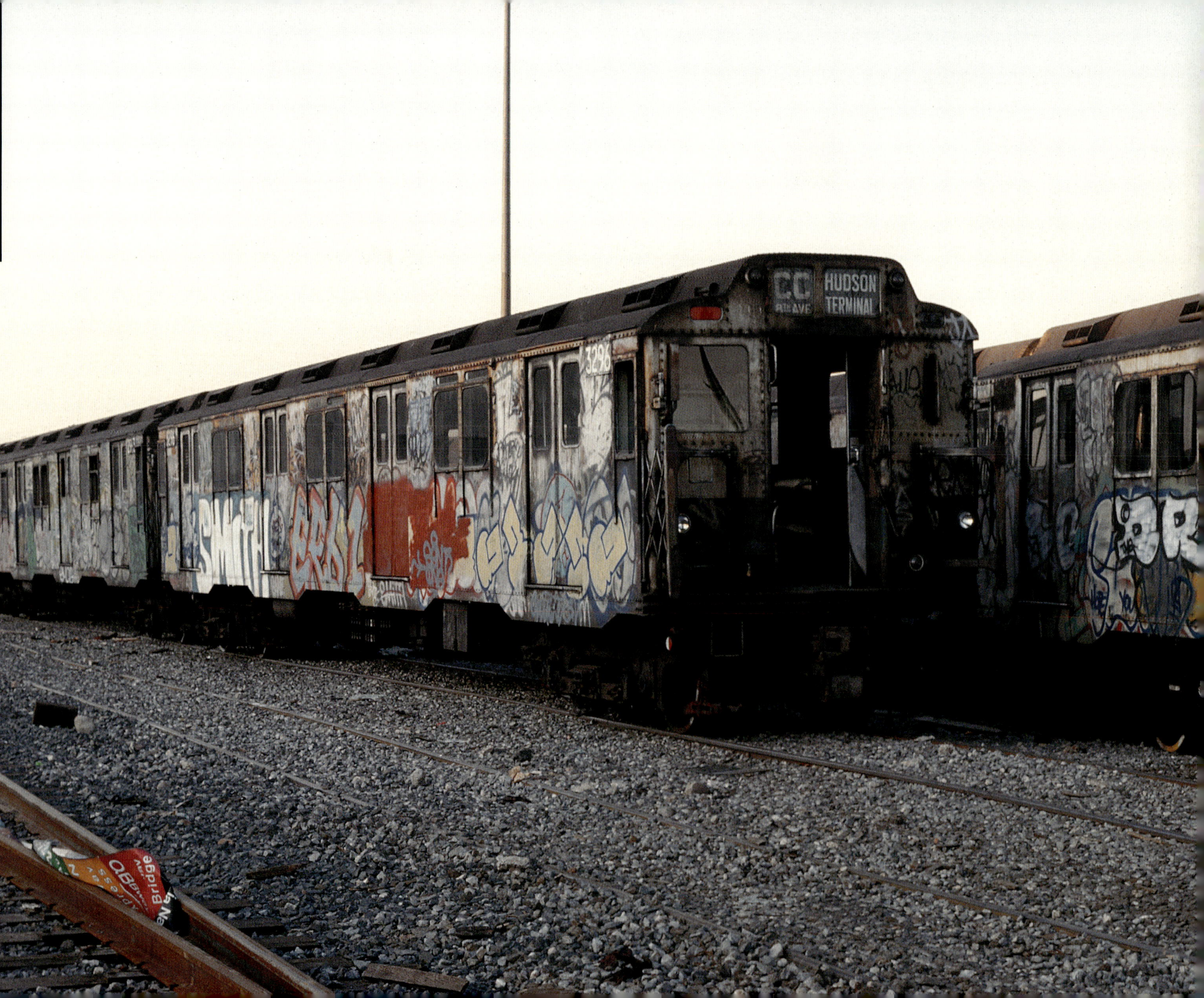

R-10, scrapyard, Brooklyn, 1988

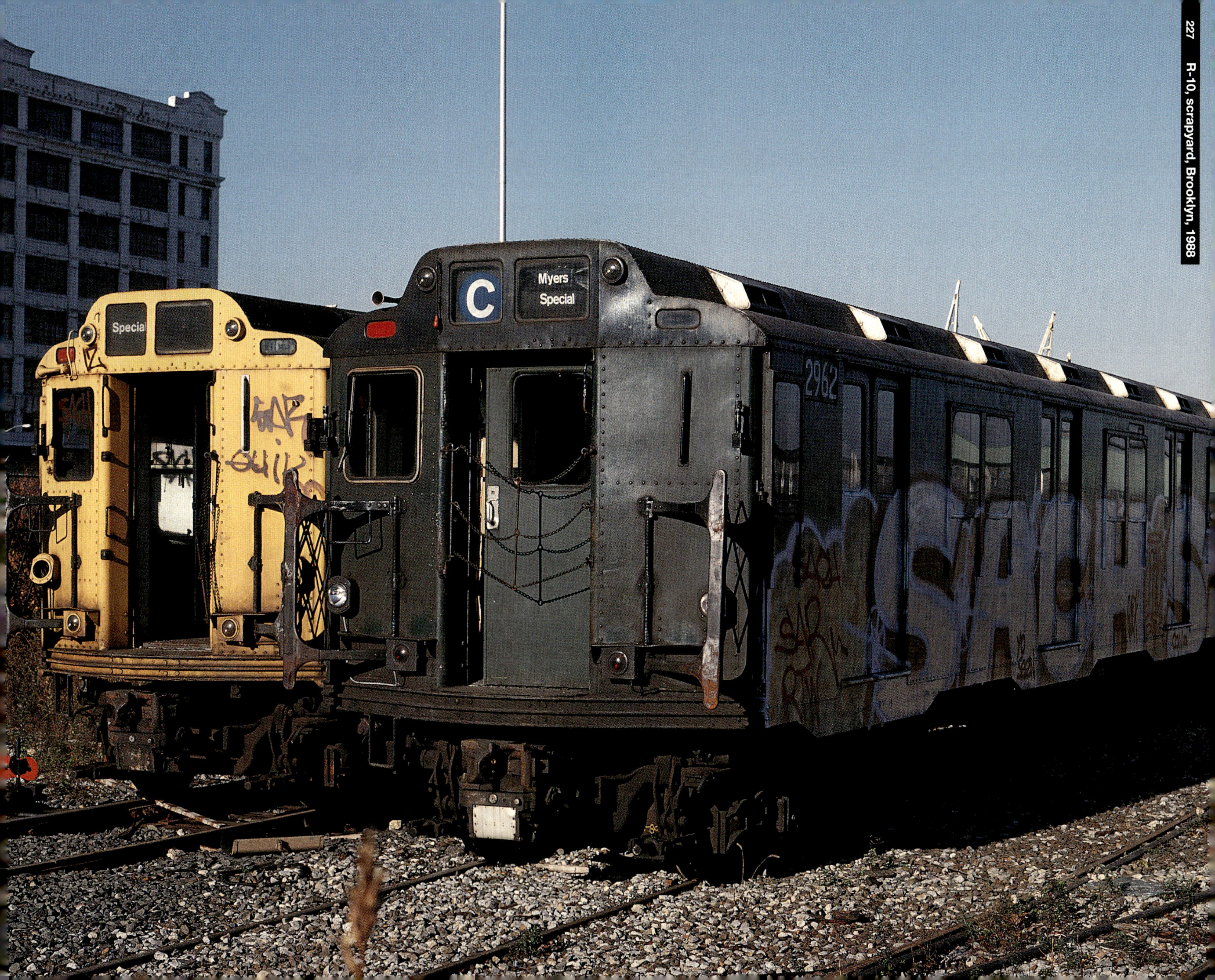

R-10, scrapyard, Brooklyn, 1988

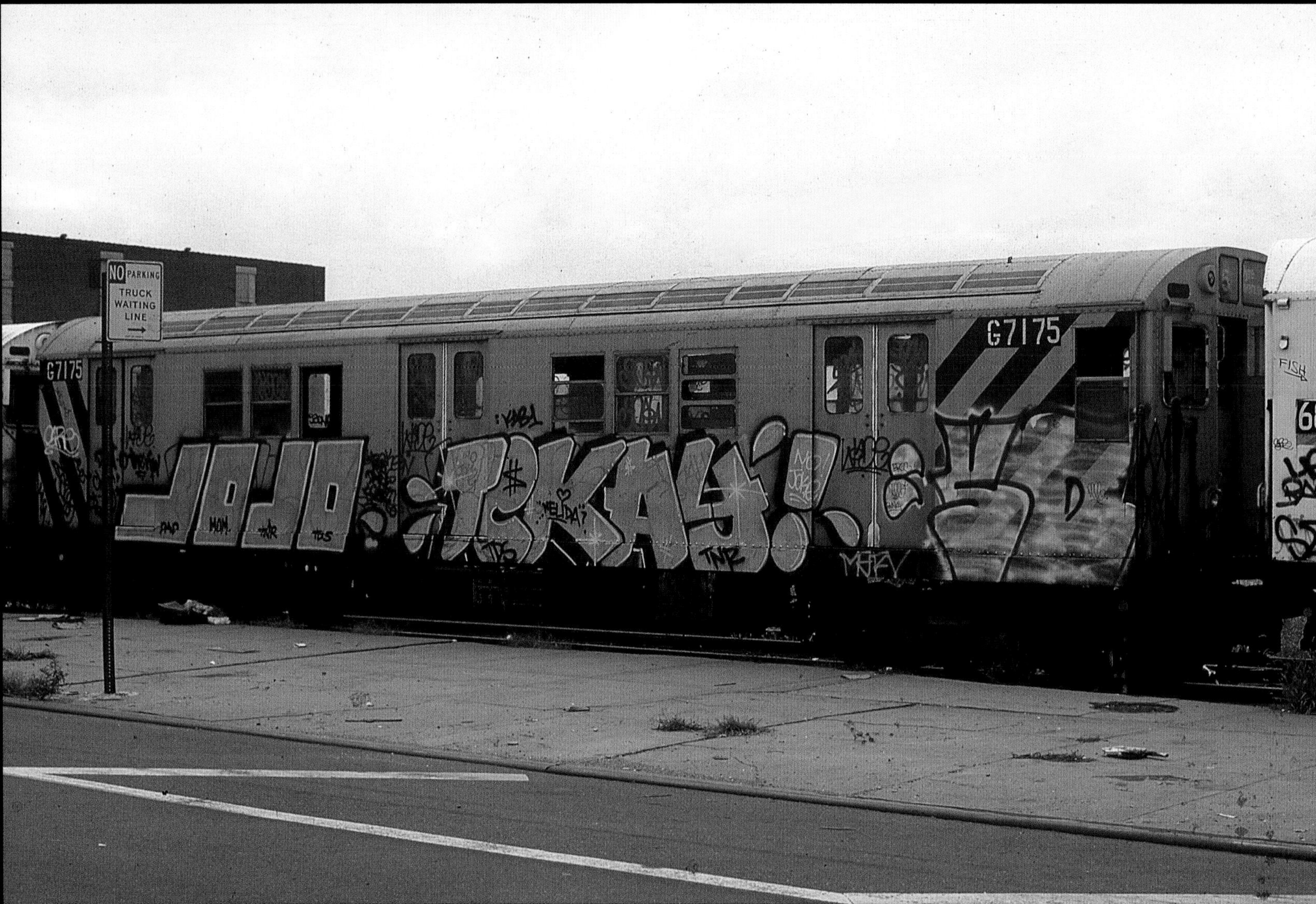
NO PARKING
TRUCK
WAITING
LINE
G7175
G7175

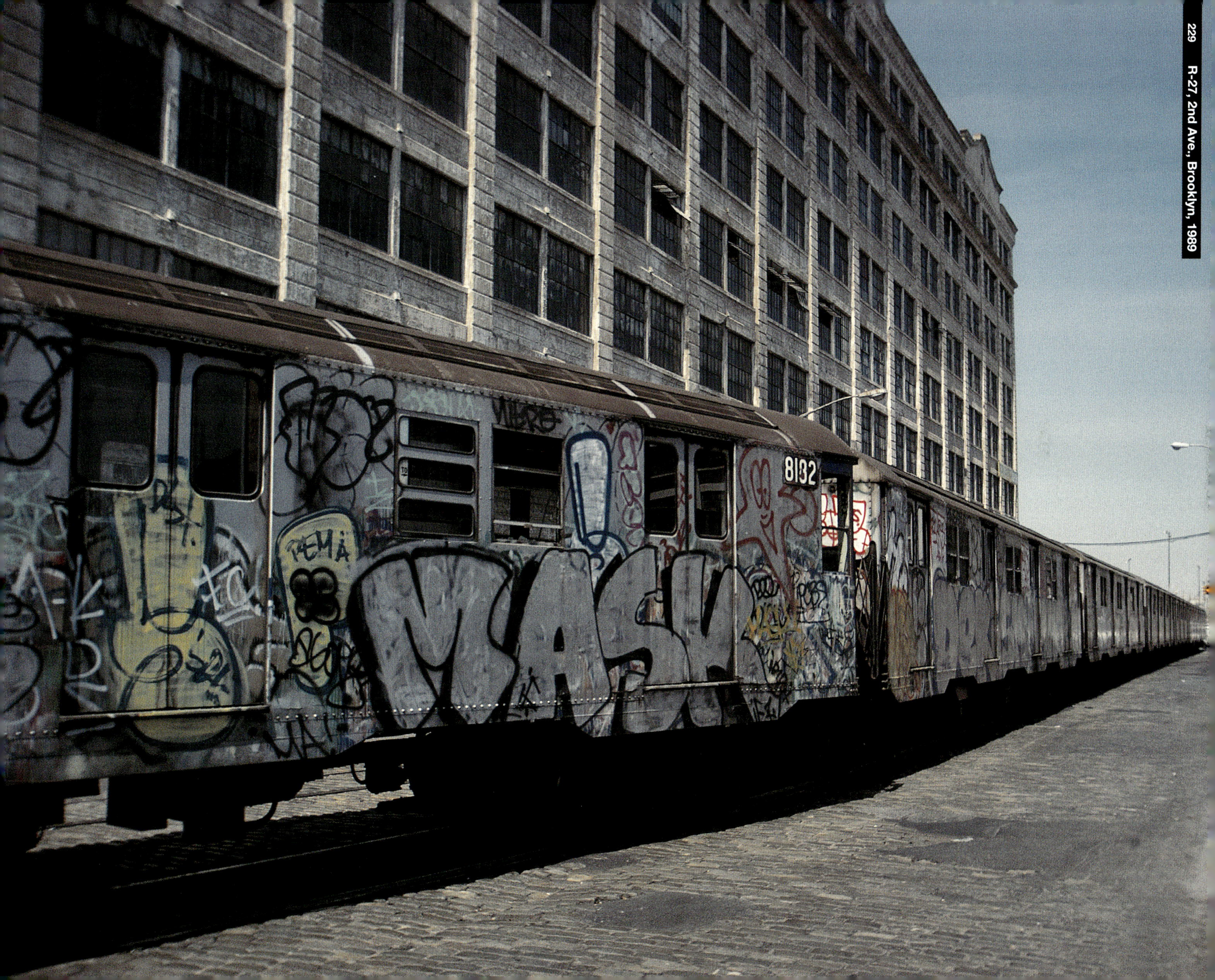

R-27, 2nd Ave., Brooklyn, 1989

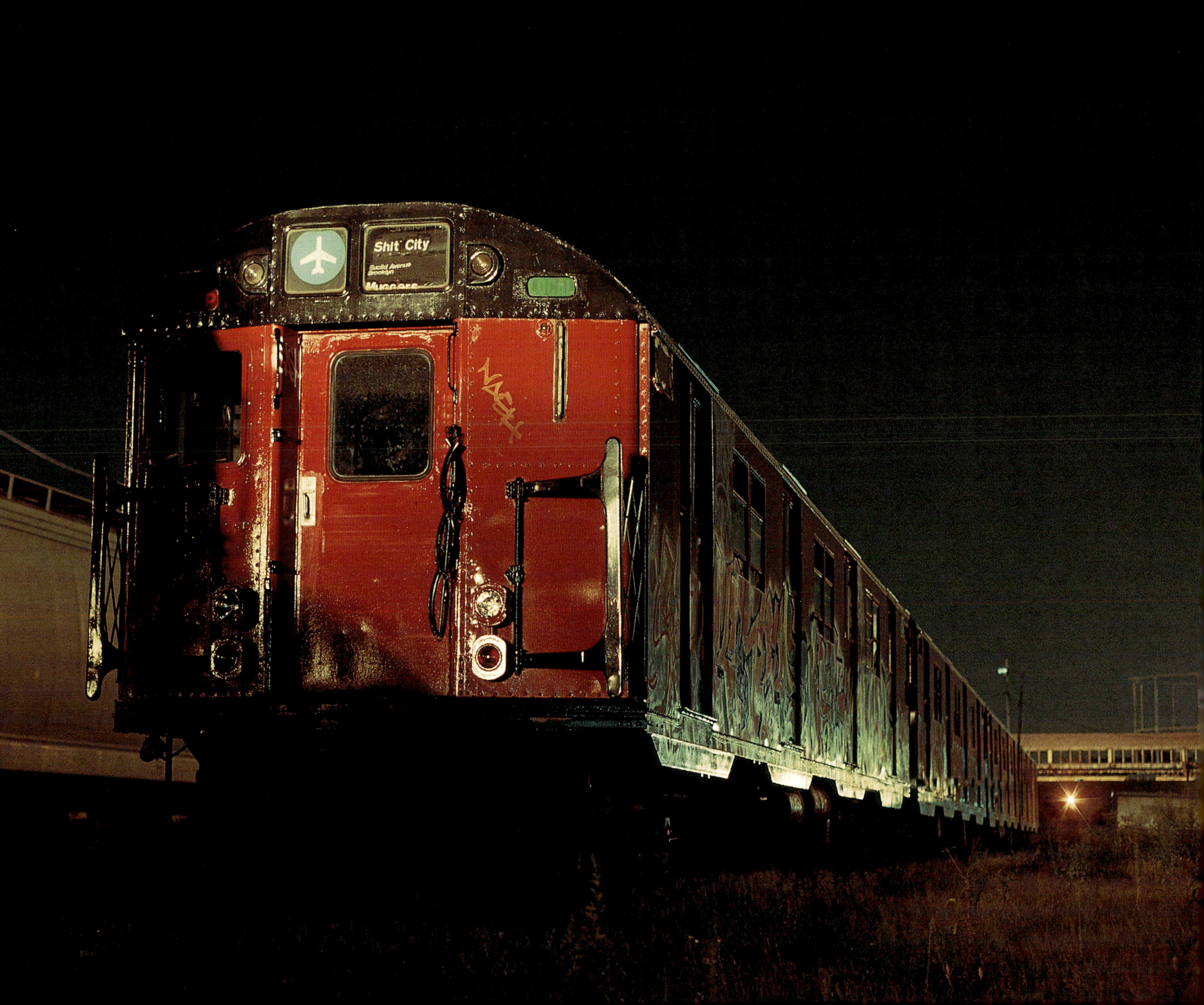

R-27/30, scrapyard, Brooklyn, 1989

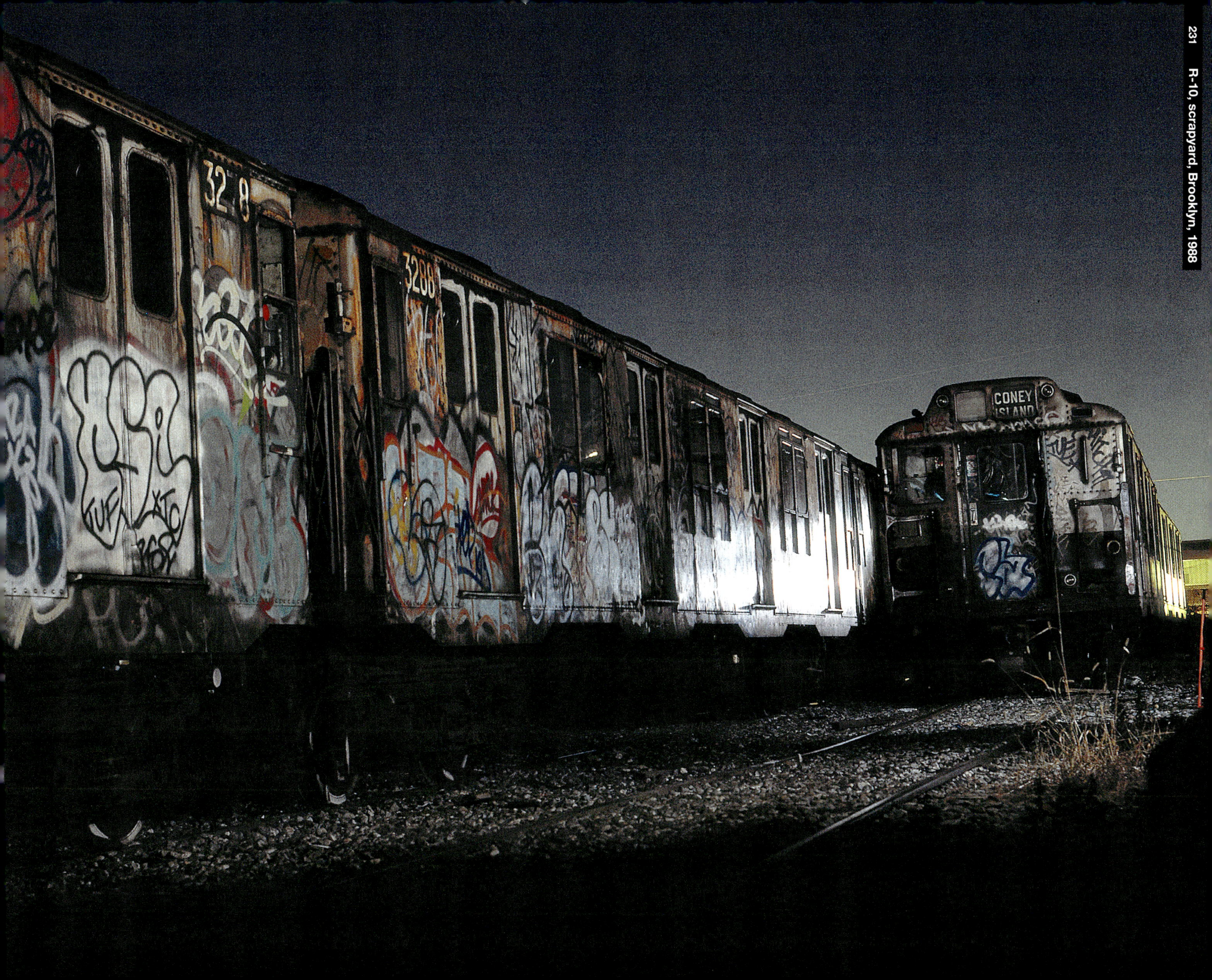

R-10, scrapyard, Brooklyn, 1988

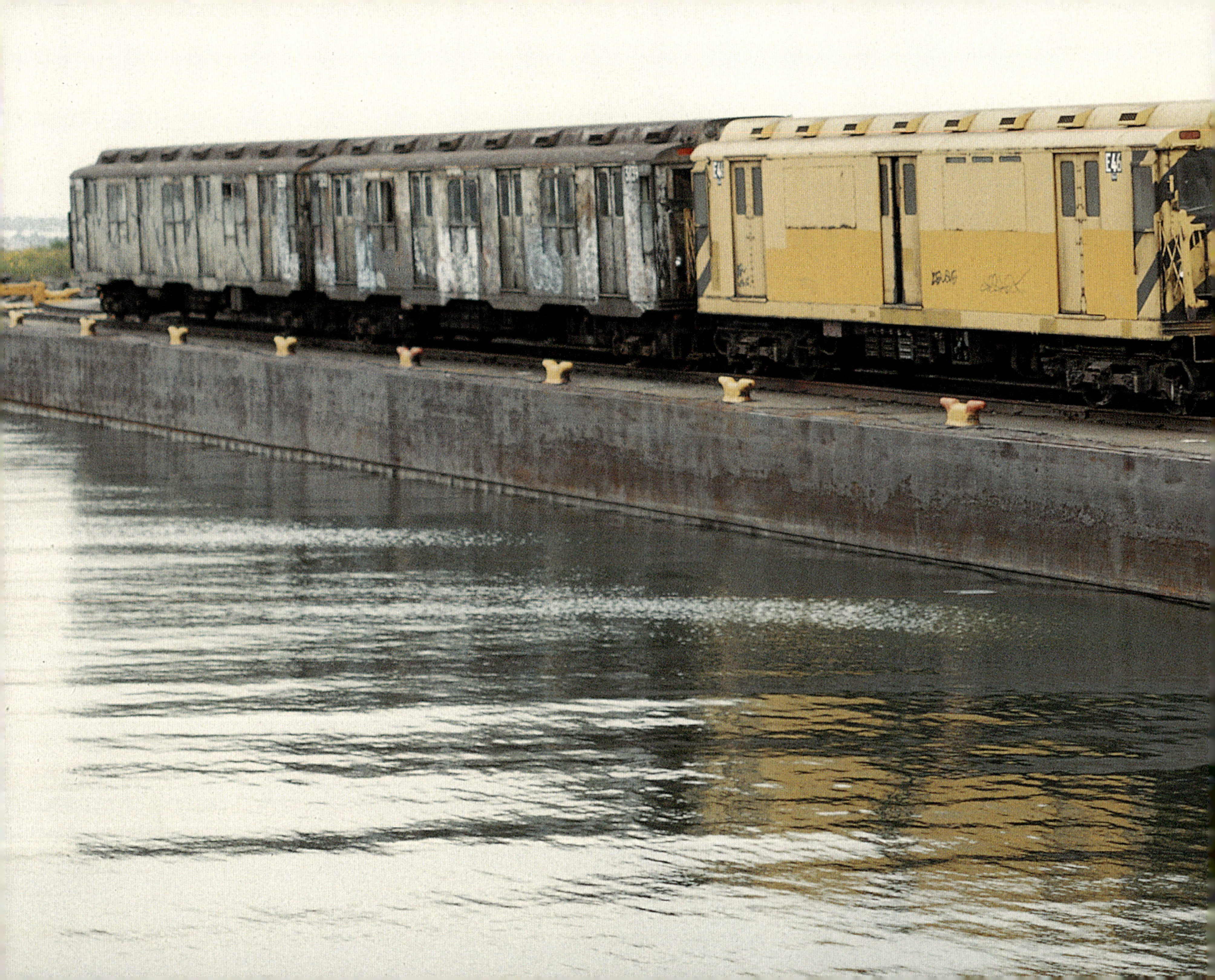

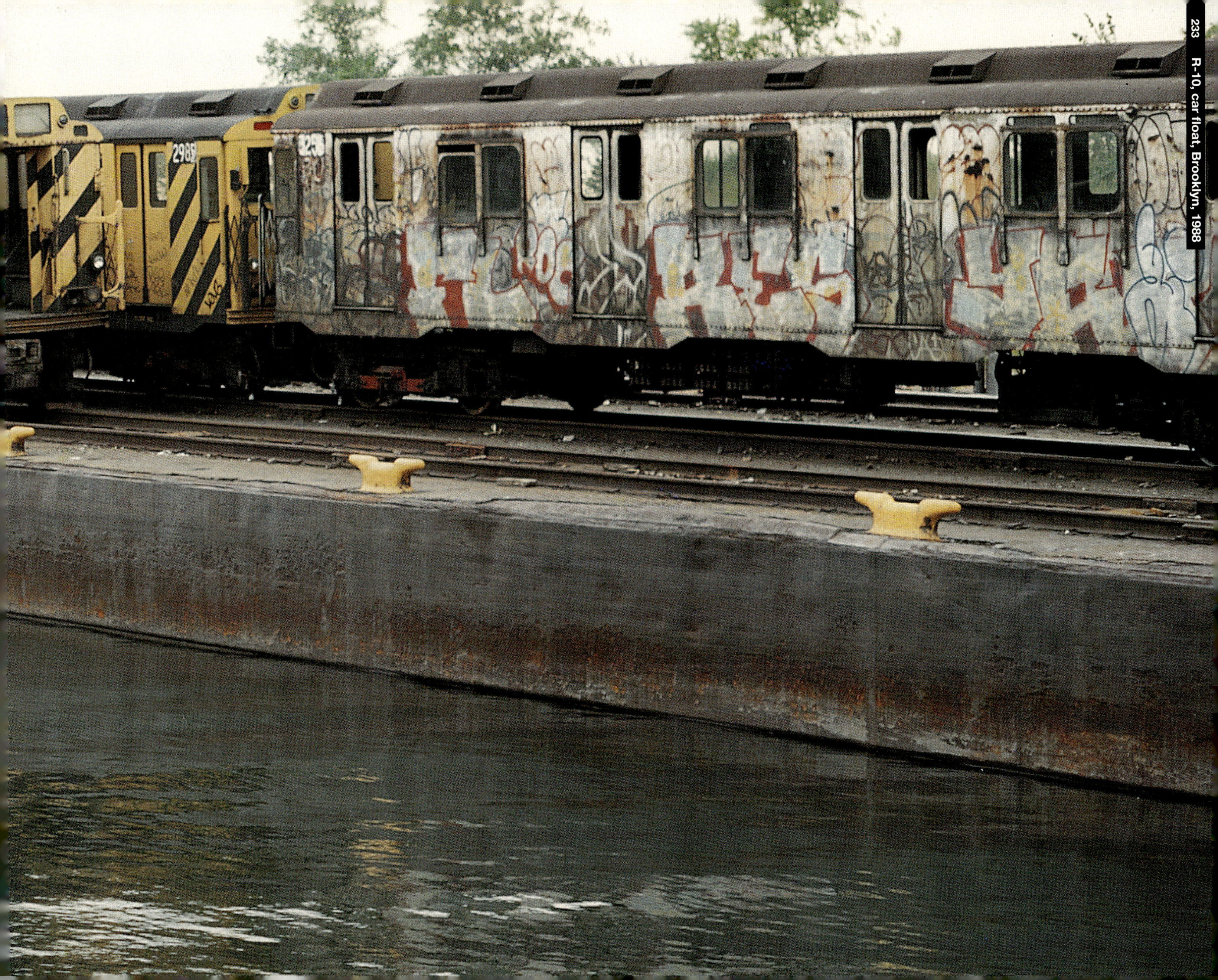

R-10, car float, Brooklyn, 1988

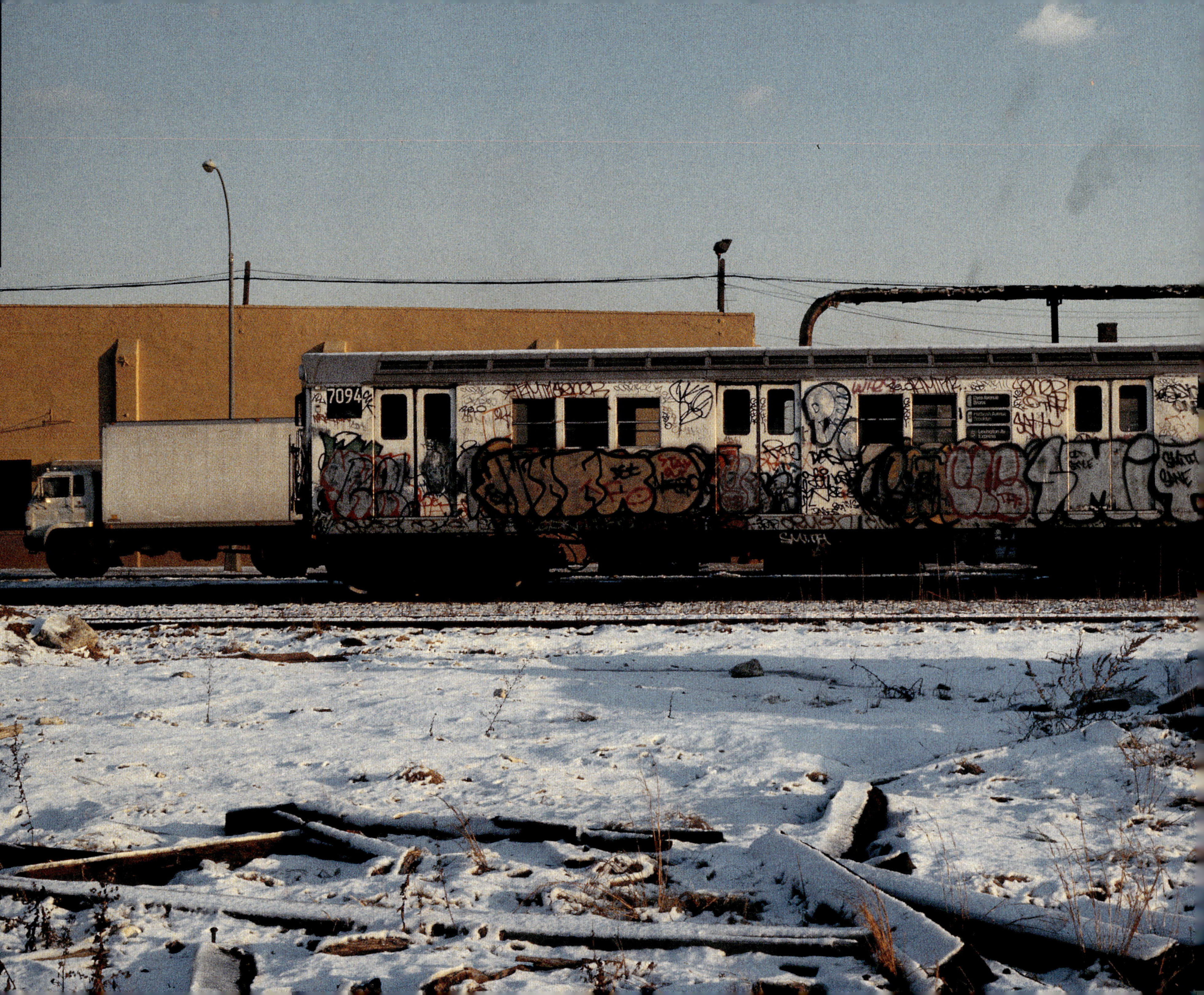

R-21, scrapyard, Brooklyn, 1988

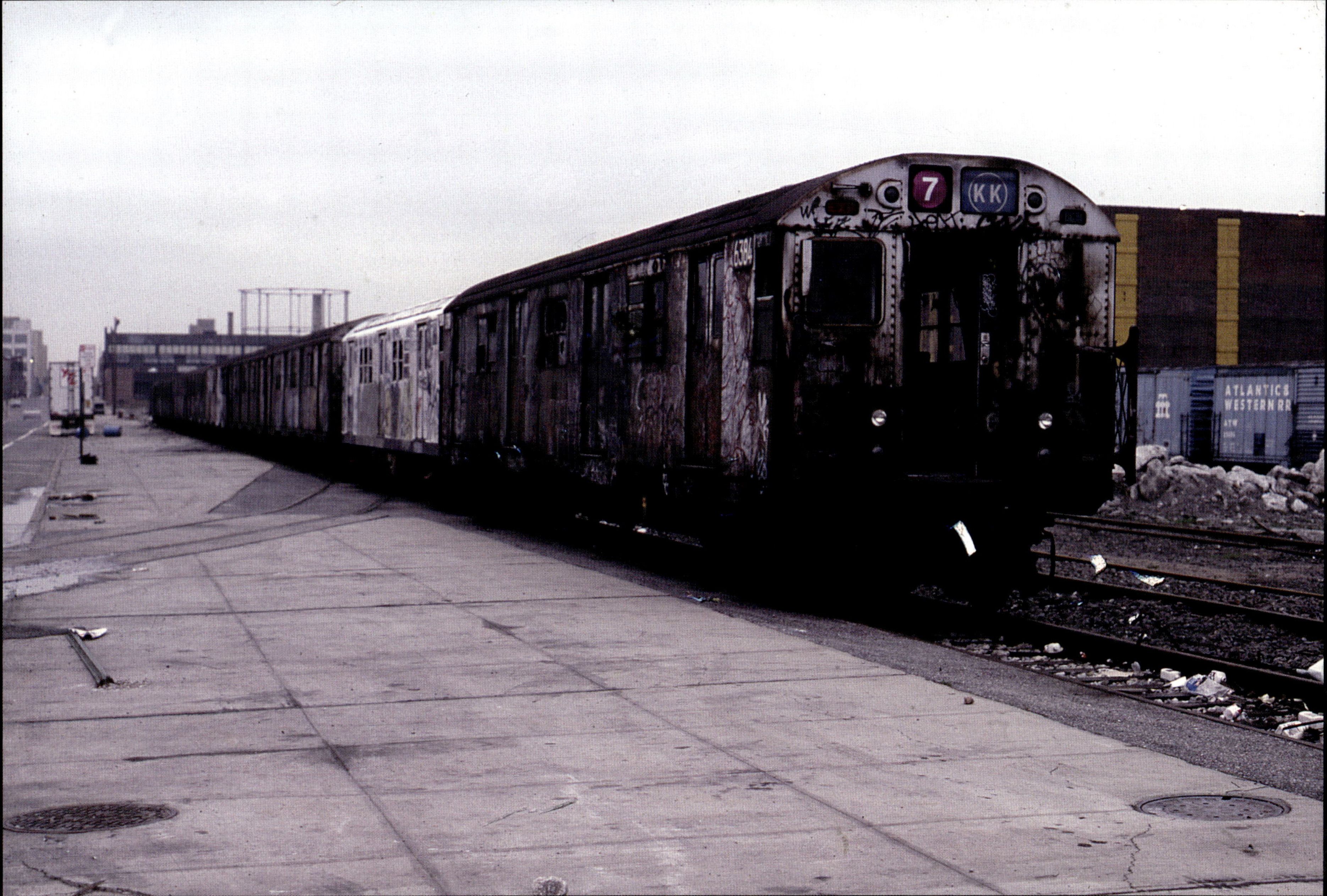

rapyard, Brooklyn, 1987

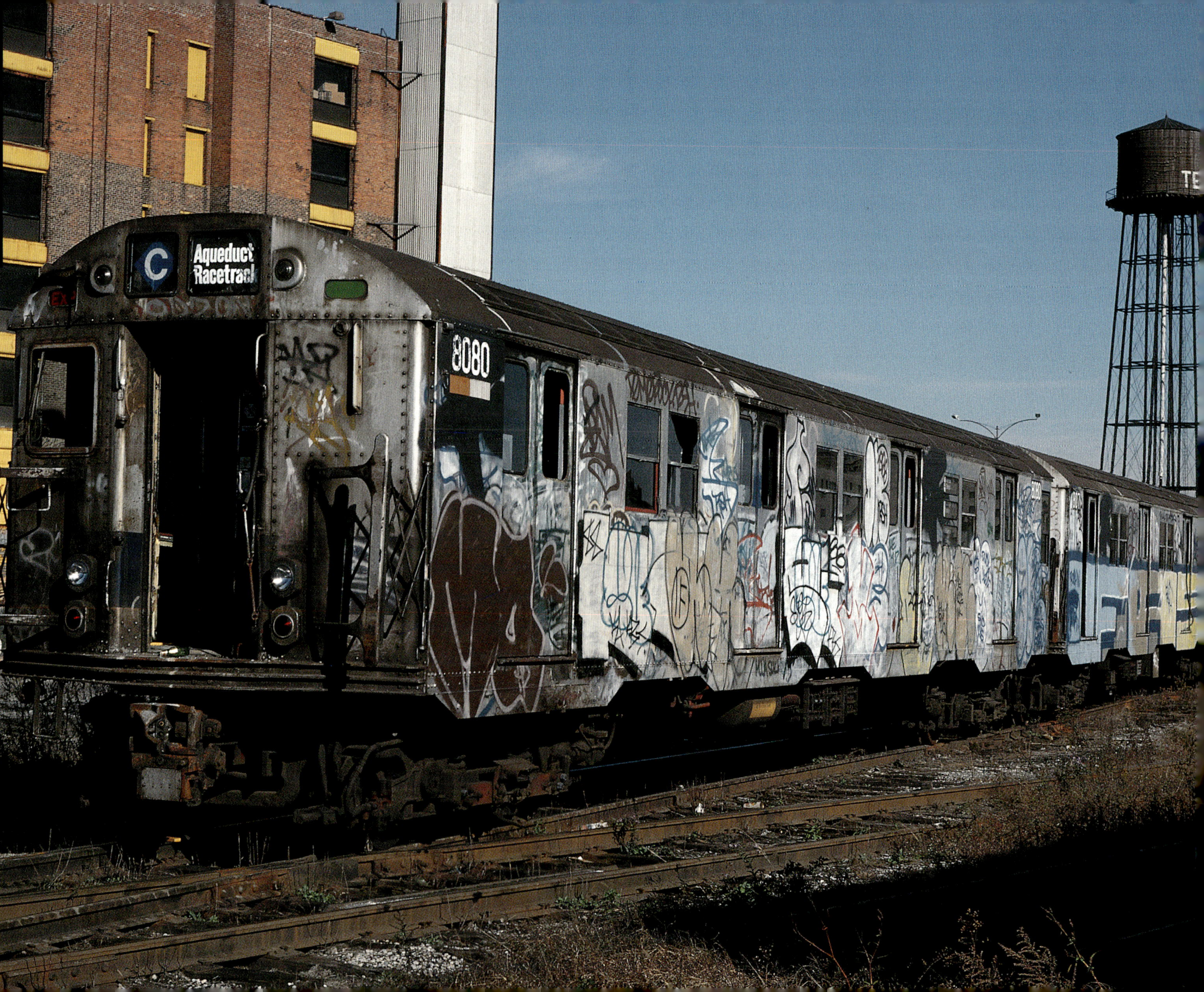

R-27, scrapyard, Brooklyn, 1989

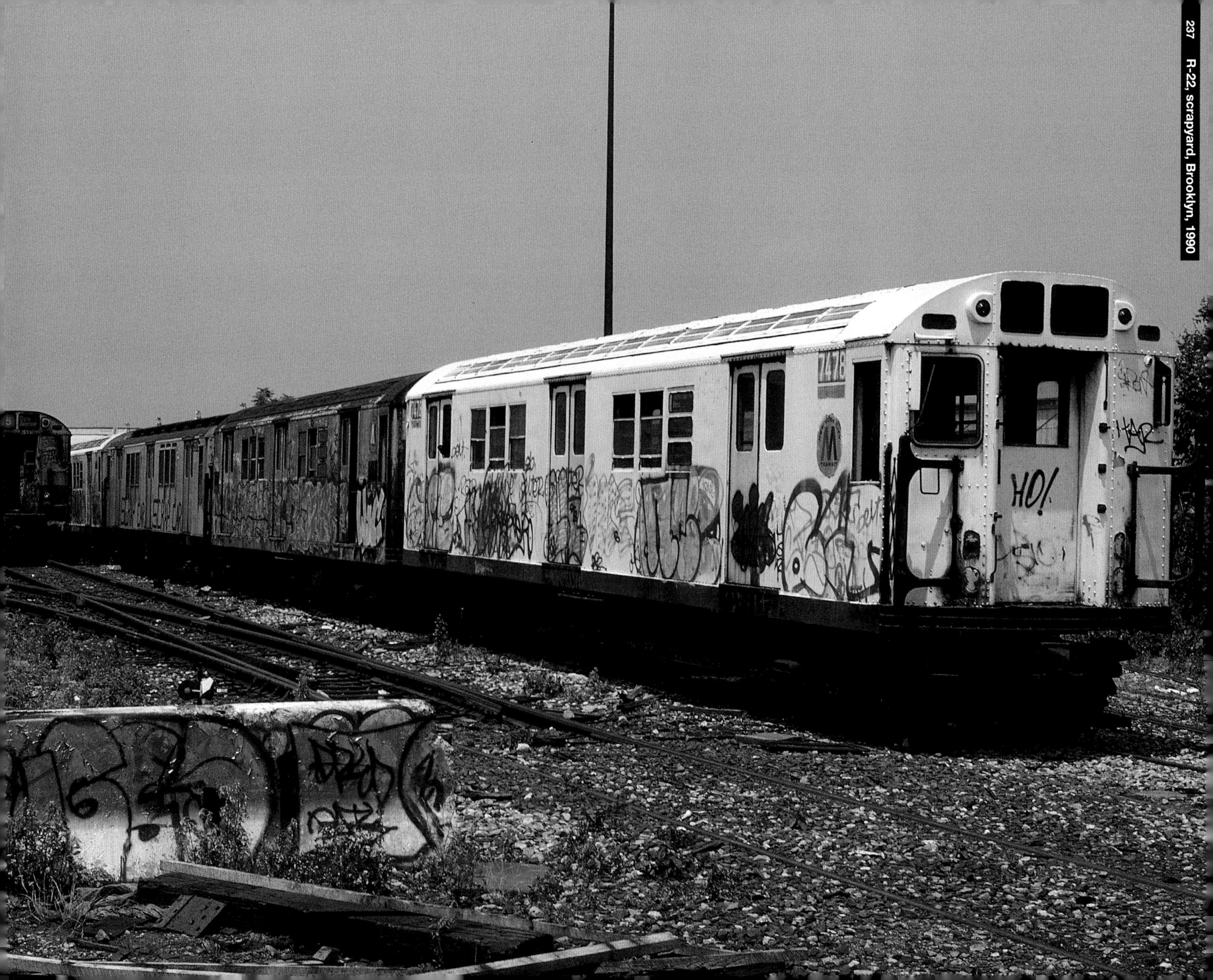

R-22, scrapyard, Brooklyn, 1990

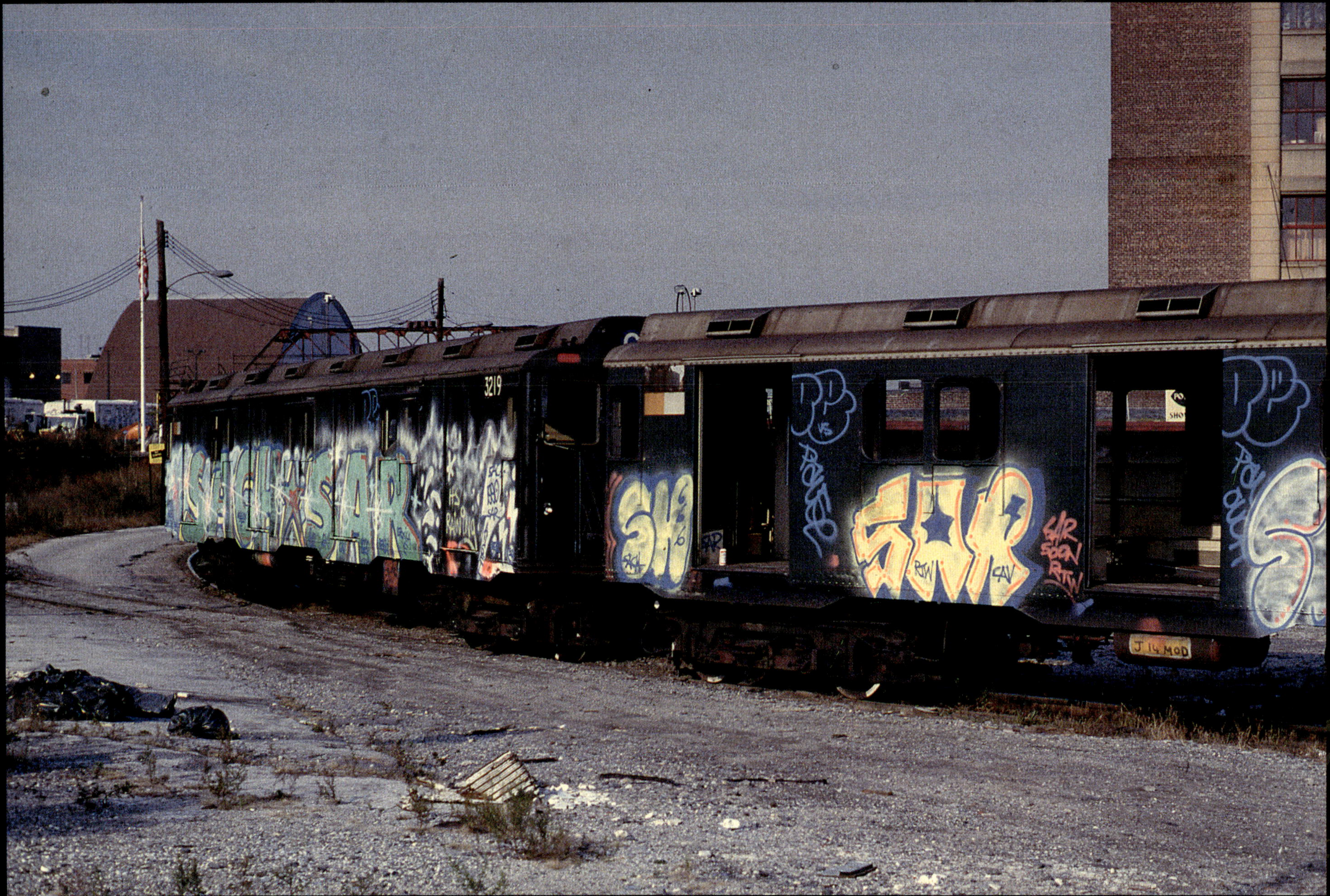

R10s, scrapyard, Brookly

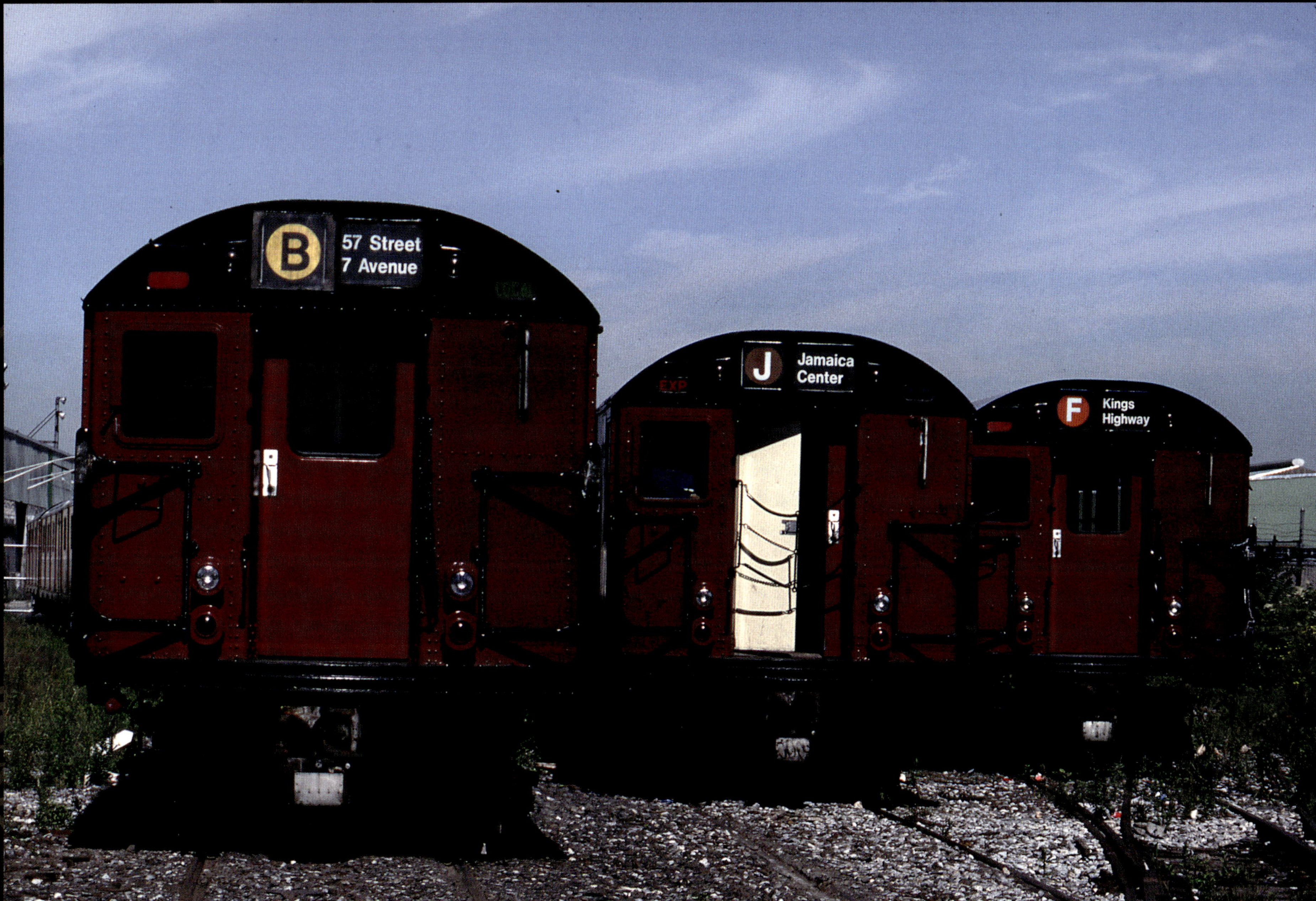

7s, scrapyard, Brooklyn, 1989

Subway Car Interiors

New York Subways & Stations 1970–1990

CHAPTER 8

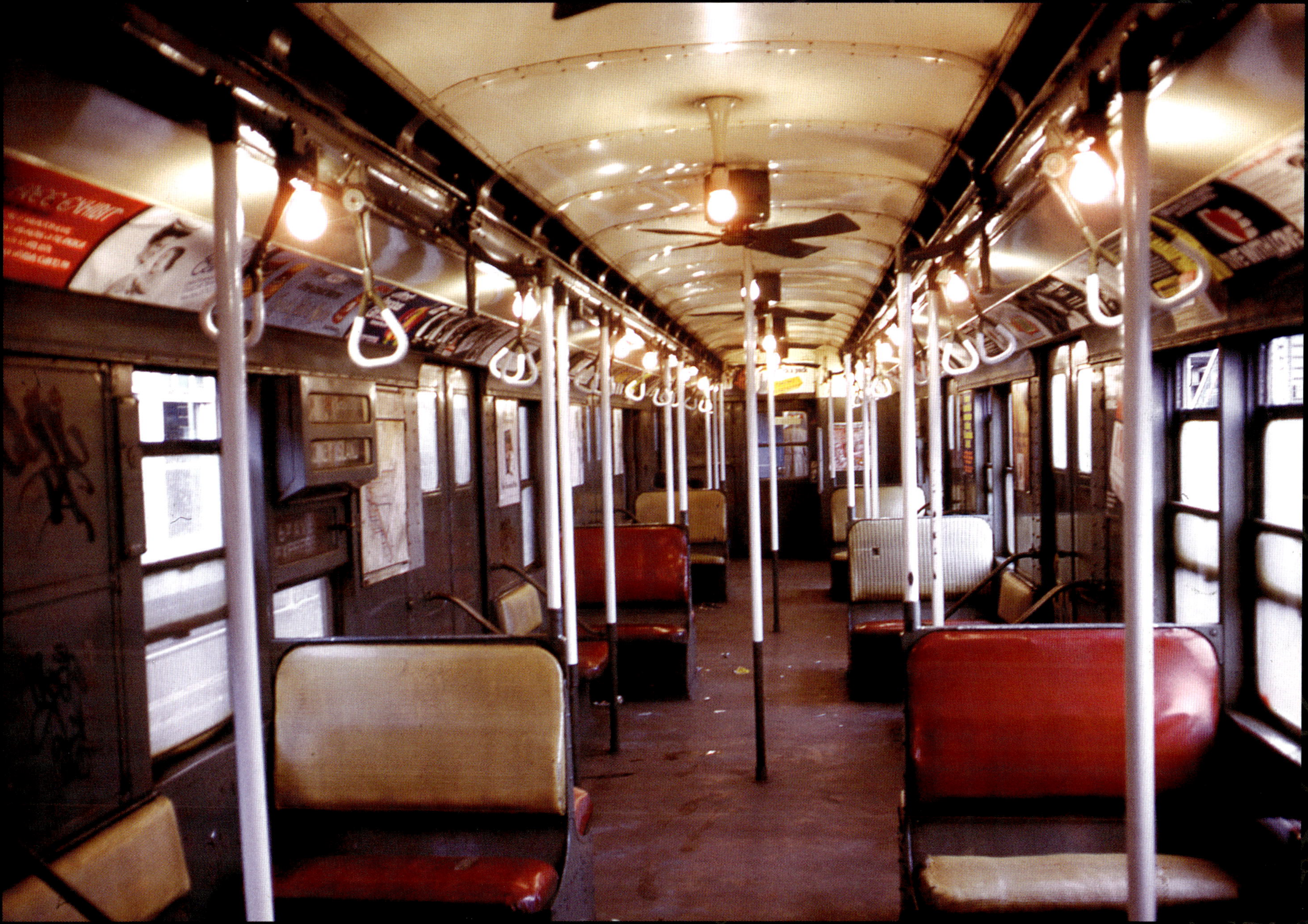

IND, R-6, #1058, F line, 1975

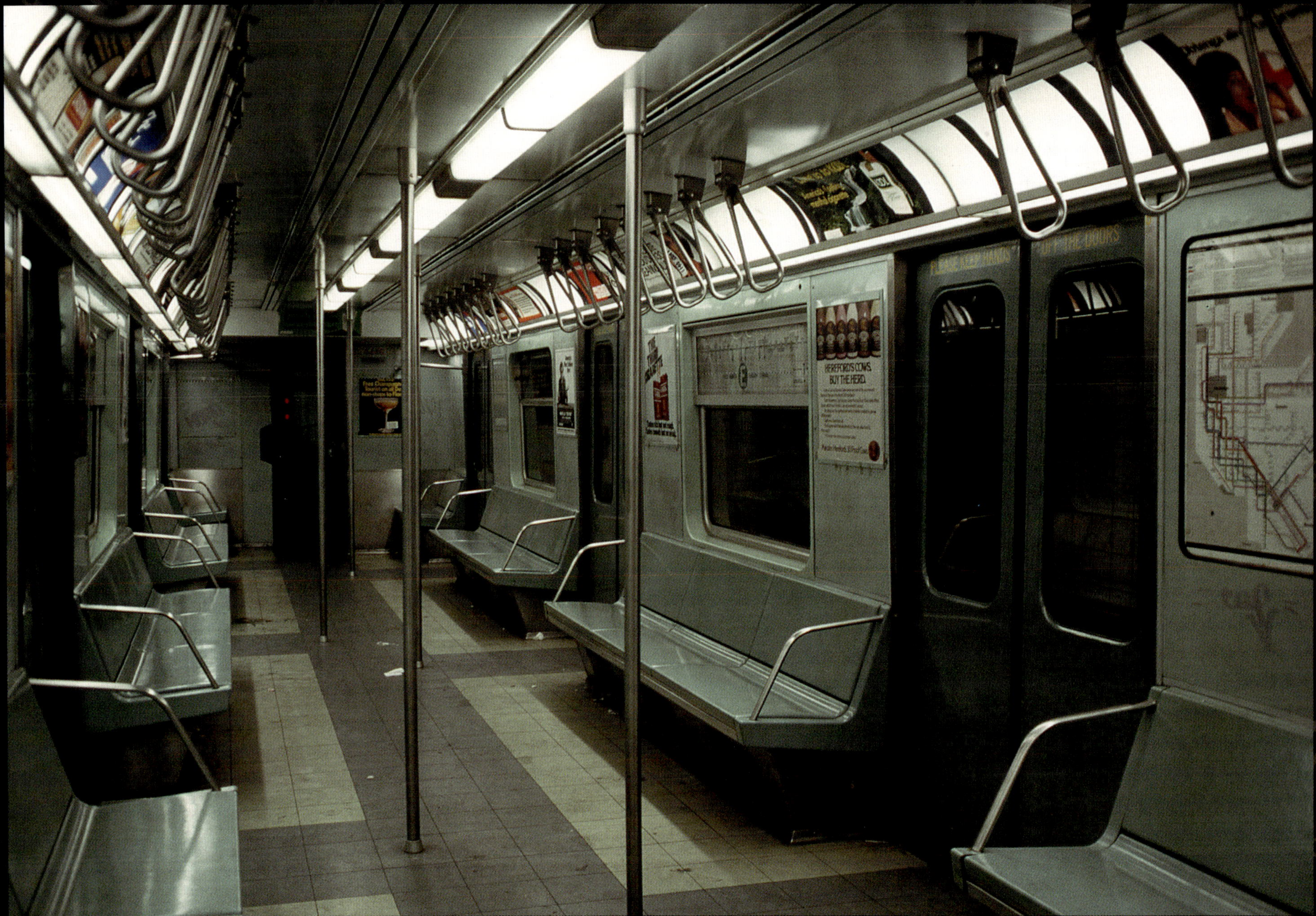

IND, R-40, #4436, E line, 19

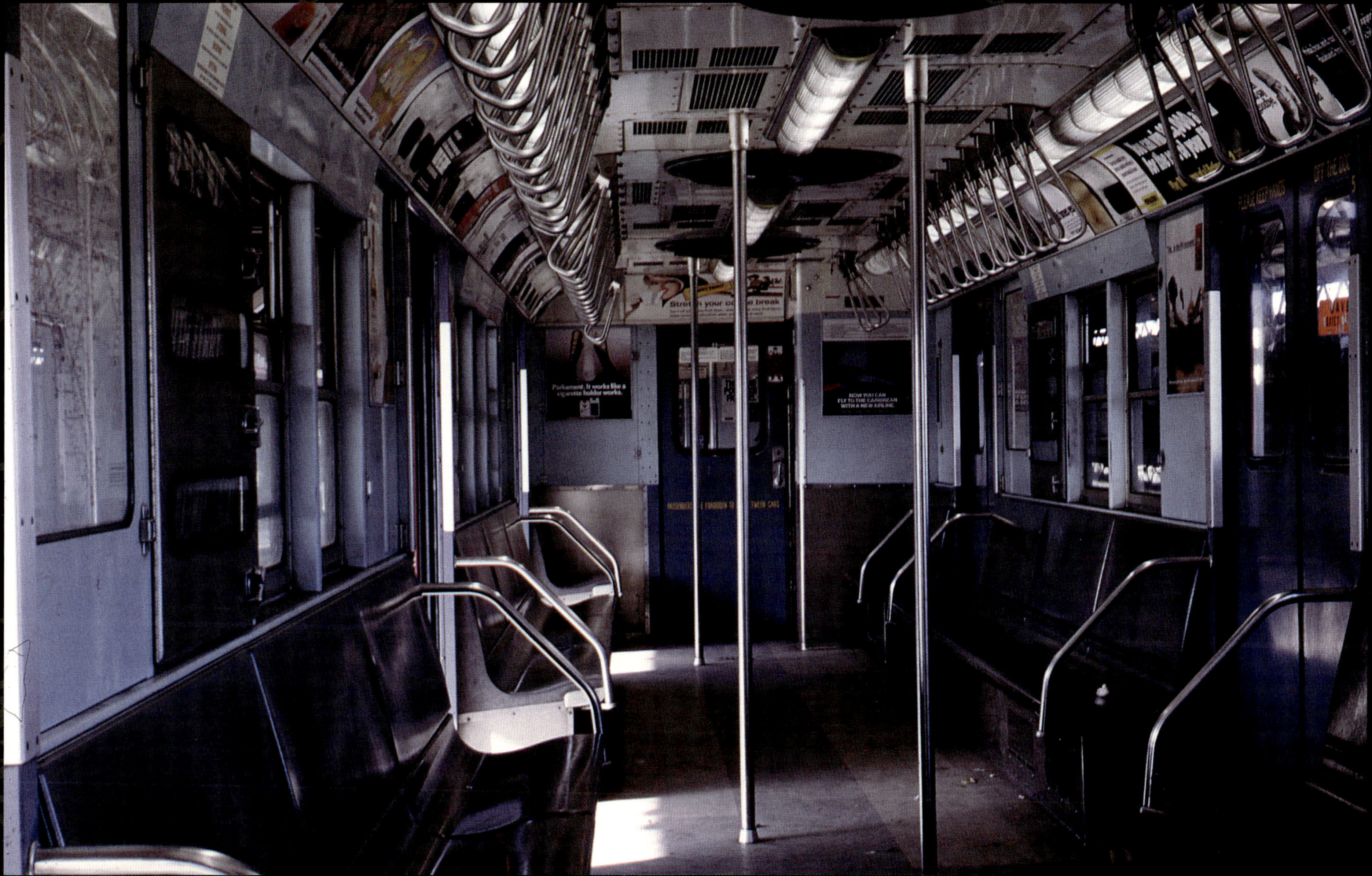

IRT, R-29, #8635, No. 1 line, 1971

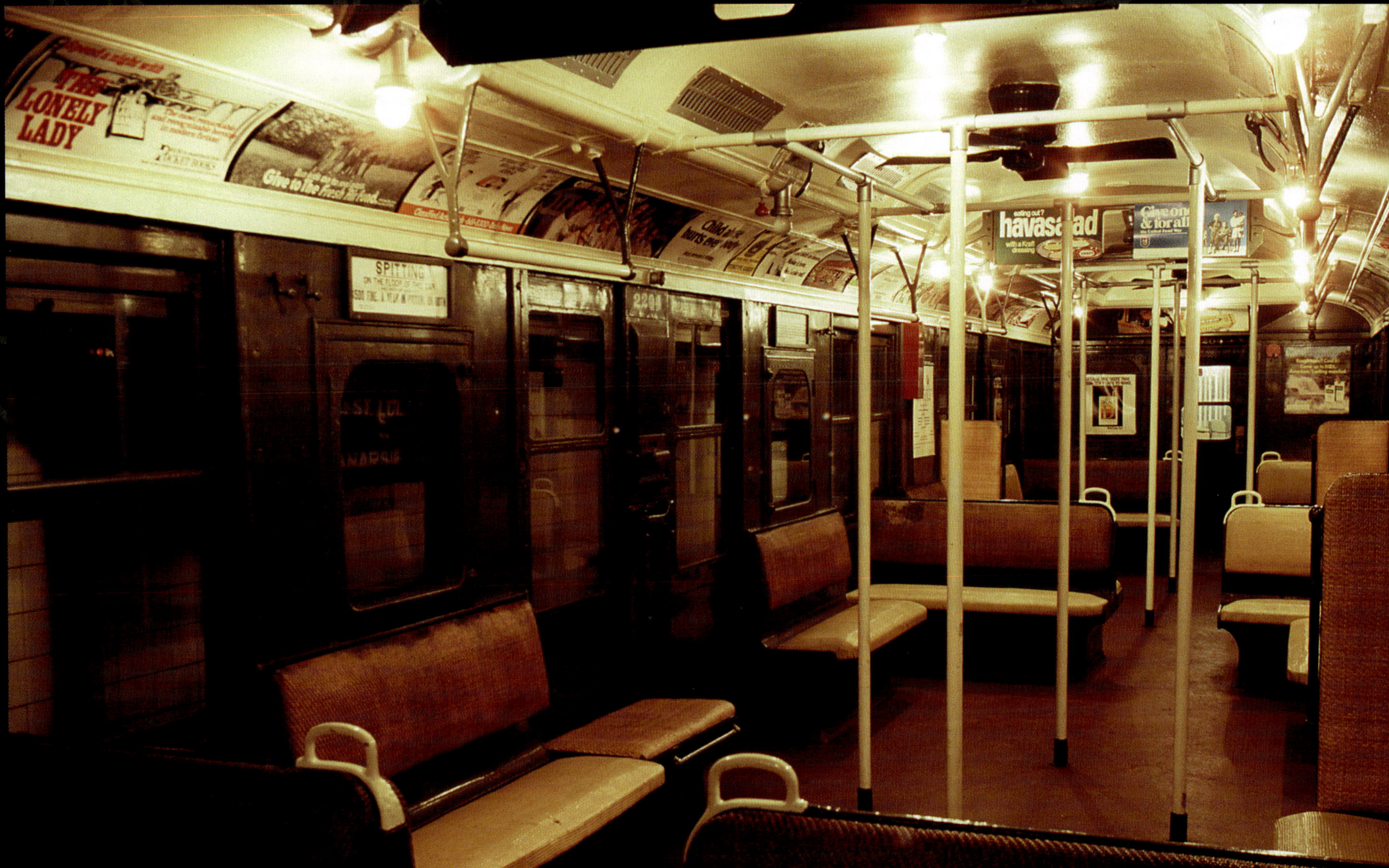

BMT Standard, #2204, museum car, 1979

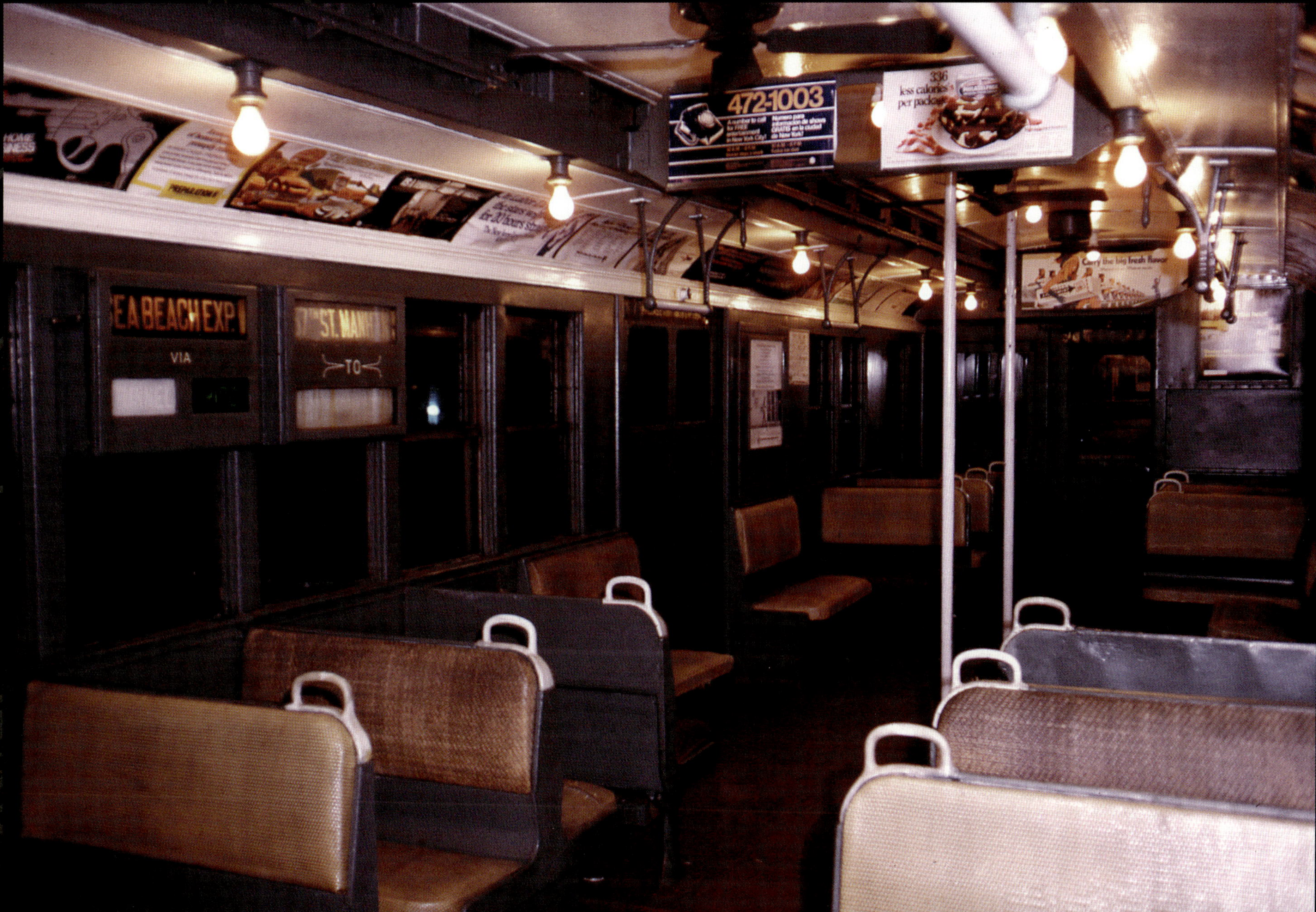
472-1003
SEA BEACH EXP
VIA
TO

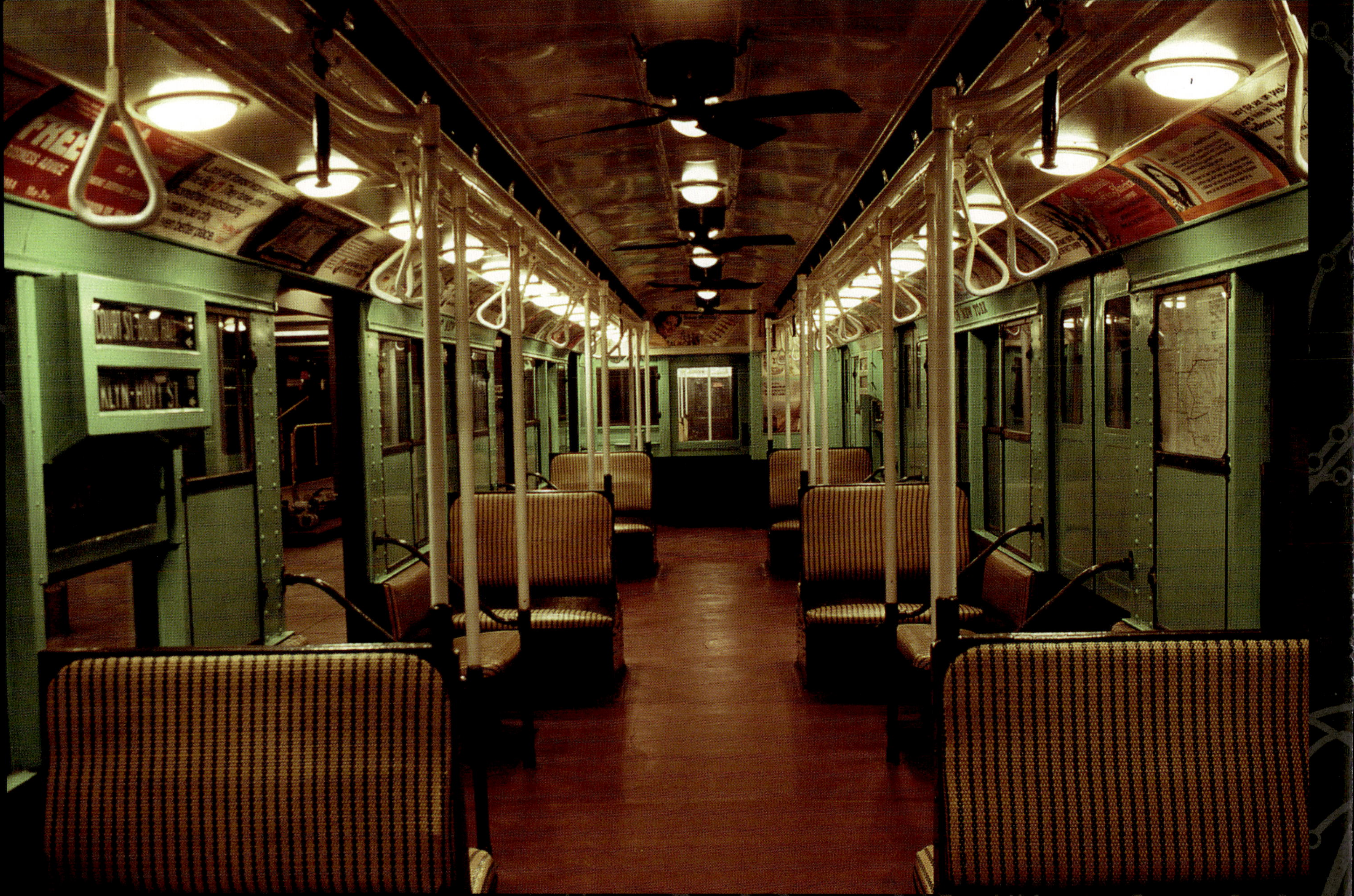

IND R-4, #484, museum

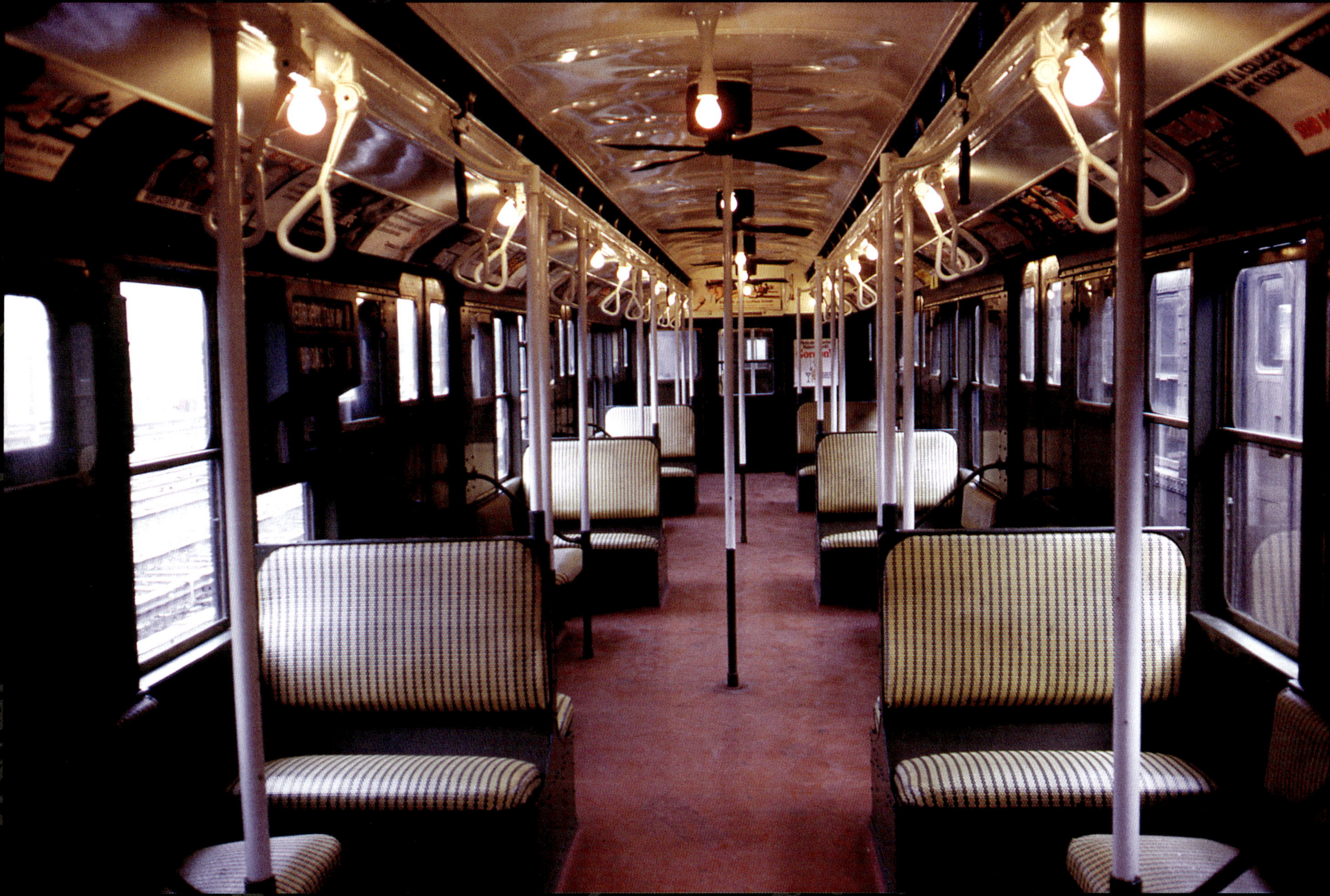

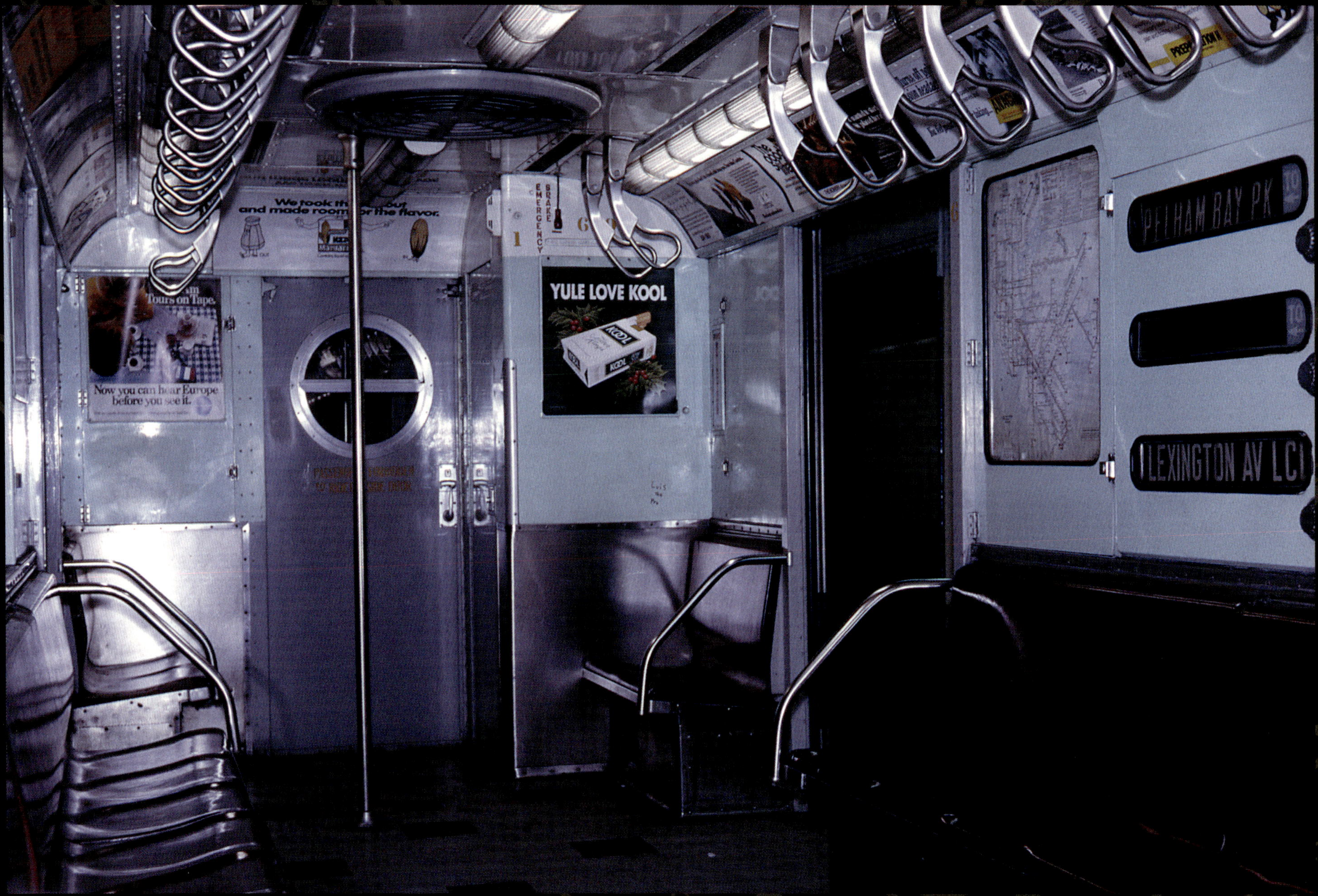

IRT, R-17, #6809, No. 6 line, 1970

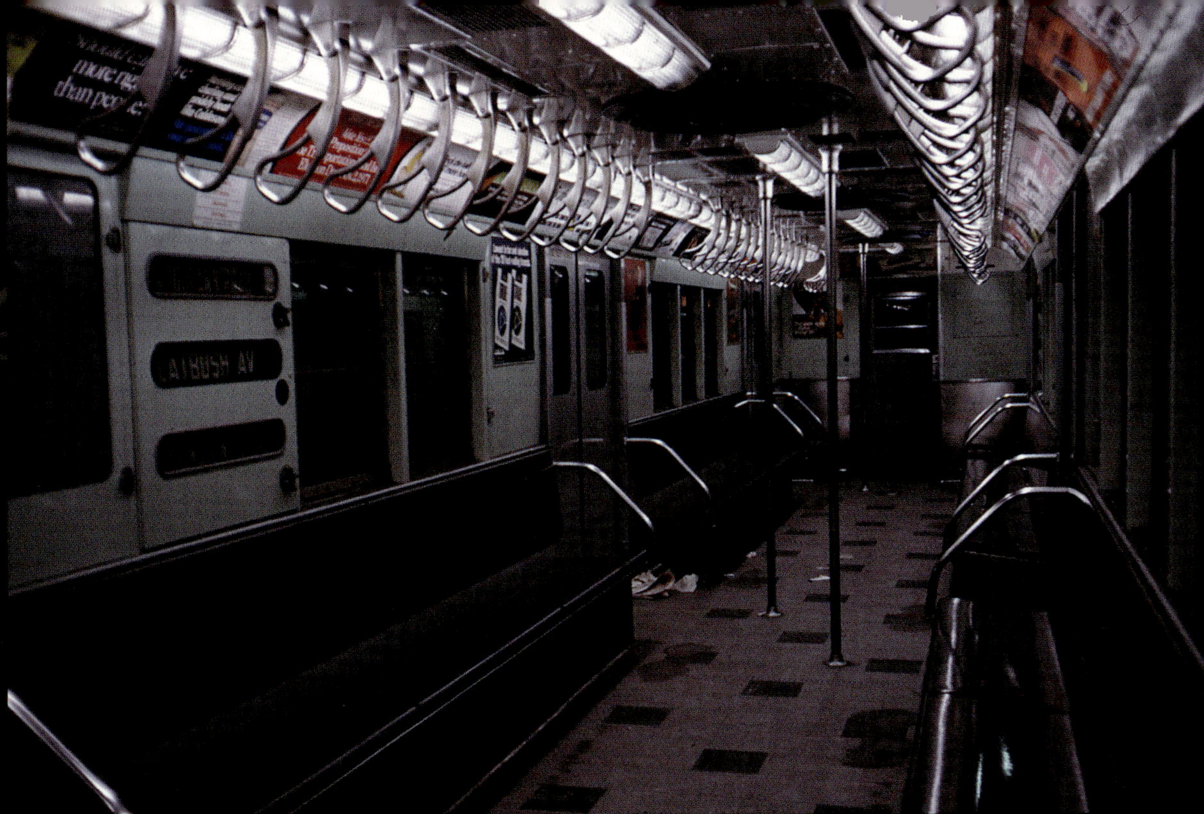

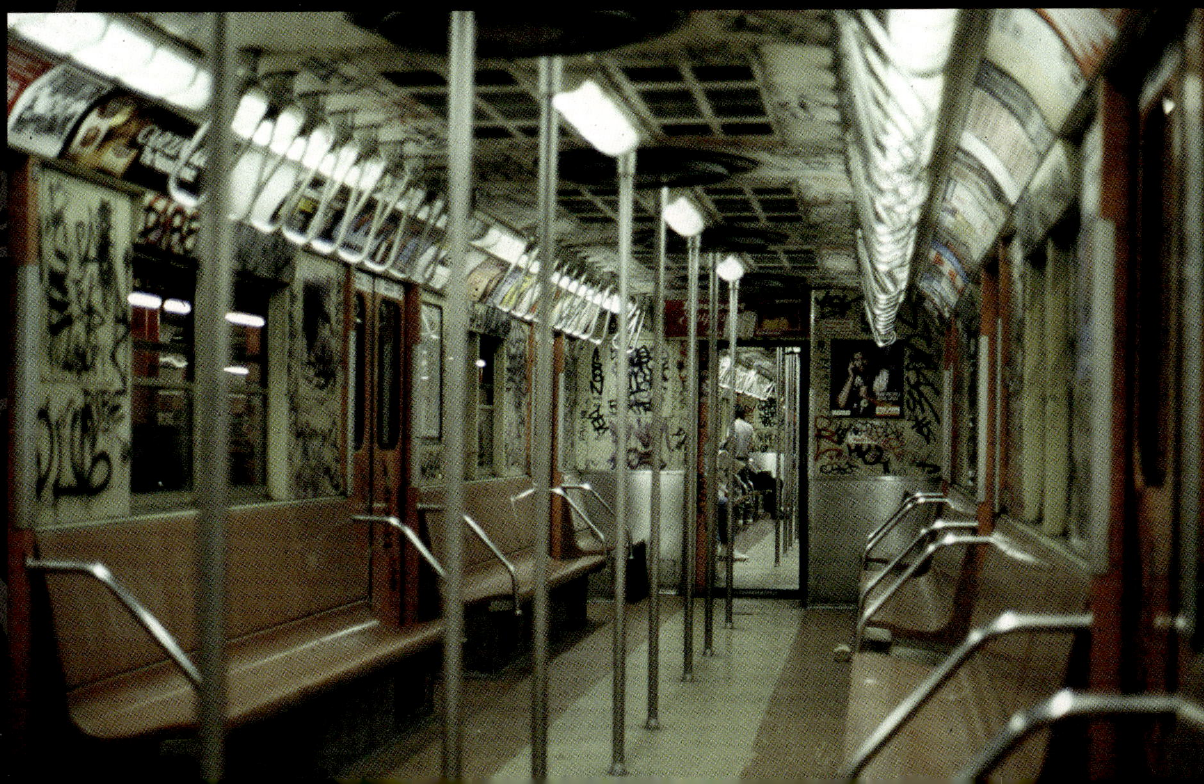

IRT, R-21, #7130, No. 4 line, 1971 | BMT, R-30, 1960s

True New York Subway Legends

New York Subways & Stations 1970–1990

CHAPTER 9

They say New York has many hidden treasures. One of the best treasures I found was a gentleman named Bill Myers—a classic New York photographer with a passion for transit and a generous person whose photos grace this book and many others. He also shared some of his gems in *New York Subway Graffiti*. He's one of the most versed photographers I've ever seen. His photos are alive and filled with a history of decades gone by—powerful, thought-provoking images! He captured transit from Brooklyn to the Bronx, uptown/downtown, and everywhere in between. A prolific New York photographer who truly earned the title! Here is a little about him.

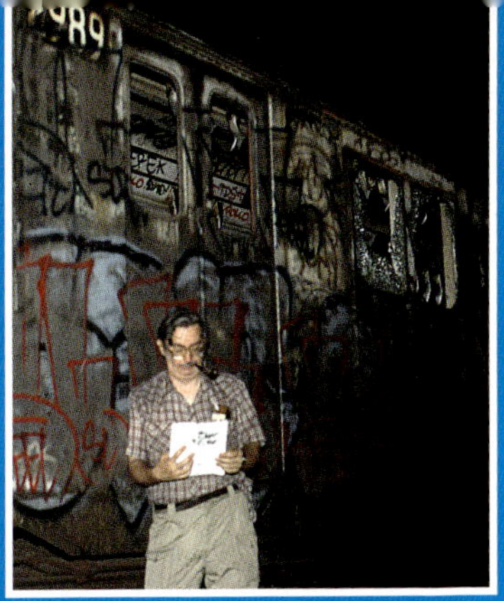

Brooklyn 1988

Bill Myers

1944–2025, Rest in Peace

I was born in Manhattan in 1944. We lived in Pennsylvania for a while. That's where I saw and liked steam locomotives. My uncle Frank worked at the Enola Yards. He took me into the roundhouse in the 1950s. It was amazing back then! We moved back to New York and lived near the Flushing line. That is where I would watch the El trains. I remember going to New York Hospital with my mother. I would be hanging out the window as we went by the Sunnyside Yard in Queens. As a kid I saw my first orange Queensboro Bridge trolley. My mother said I got very excited when I saw it. I did not even know what it was at that time. As I got older, I discovered a subway map. It had all sorts of El trains and shuttles on it. It cost fifteen cents back then. I would play hooky and ride the Els all day long. I got a camera for grade school graduation, and thus was born a lifelong interest in photography. I took black and white at first. That's what most railfans did. I went to Aviation High School. From my English-class window, I was able to take pictures of the 7 line. I tried to take slides with my 127 camera; some actually came out. Some of my first slides were on the #7 Flushing line. I still have the slides. I got a 35 mm camera in 1963. At that time there was so much to shoot. You never had enough film. I joined the Electric Railroaders Association (ERA) in 1963 and have been on many fan trips. I'm still a member. I moved to Long Island City in the 1970s and stayed ever since. I worked in the camera industry until I got a job with the transit authority in the 1980s. I put in twenty years and retired. I still enjoy trolleys and steam locomotives and El trains. I don't get around like I used to. I keep busy with the computer and video games, when I can't get out. I find the subway system very boring now. The really exciting time was in the 1970s and 1980s. With all the different paint schemes and cars! I'm glad I took slides back then. I'm very pleased to share them with you.

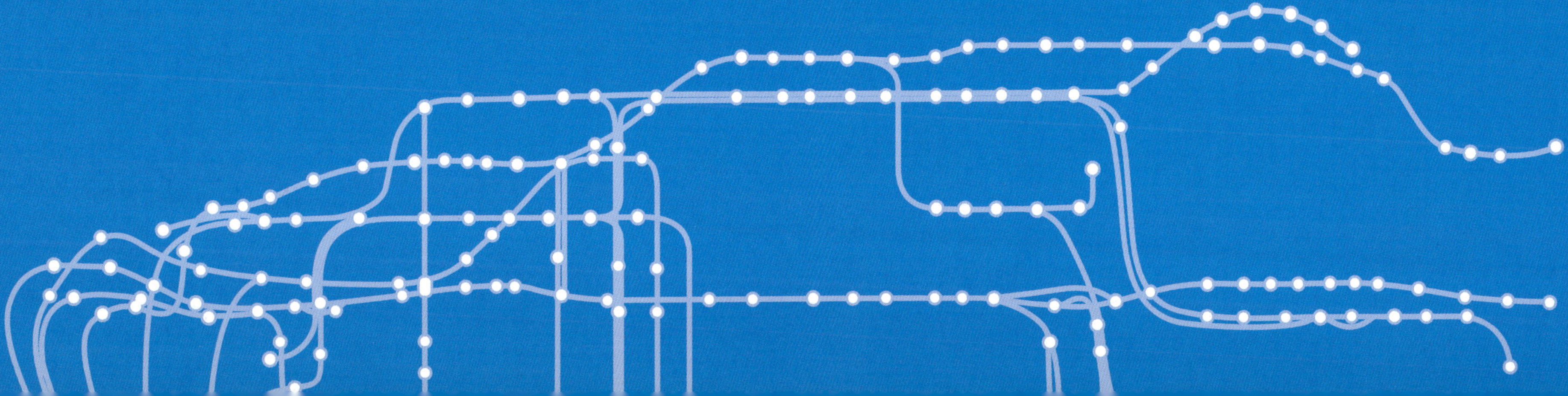

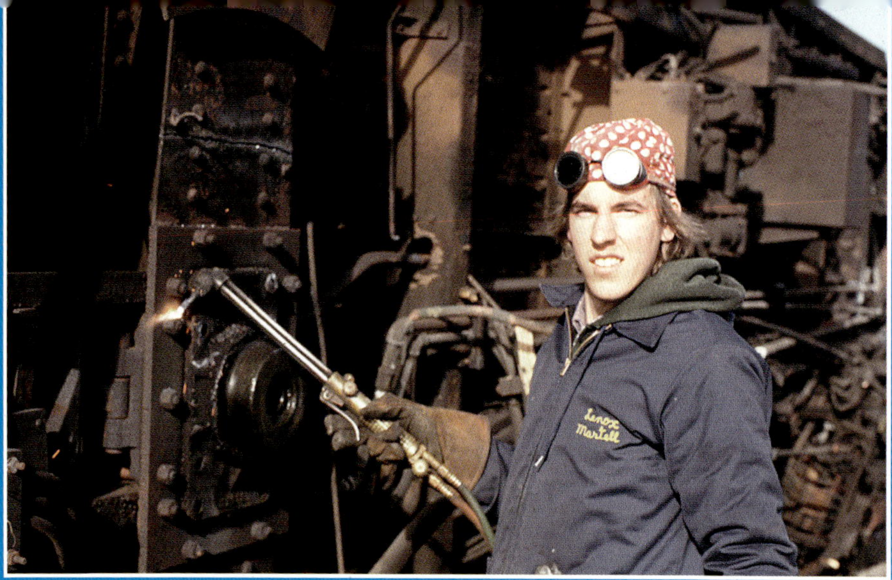

Cutting MBTA 0539's underbody, 1986

Bill Pollman

Railroad enthusiast William A. Pollman was born on November 22, 1965, in Everett, Massachusetts, 5 miles north of Boston. Bill's fascination with trains began at the tender age of five, when his parents bought him his first train set. Bill remembers the many rides on the Charlestown El with his parents and grandmother en route to downtown Boston.

His father was very much into photography and photographed the Charlestown El, Boston's Orange Line that closed in 1975. Bill was close at hand with his father while he photographed the El. As Bill grew older, he carried on the tradition of taking photographs of trains and began photographing in New York City in the early 1980s. The number 7 line / Main St. Flushing–Times Square is his all-time favorite numbered line. His favorite lettered line is the M, J, Z from Essex St. over the Williamsburg Bridge to Metropolitan Ave. on the Myrtle Line and out to 168th St. on the Jamaica Line, which closed in 1977. Bill went on many fan trips, which consisted of running old cars that the NYCTA Transit Museum hosted.

Through this endeavor of taking slides using Kodachrome 64 film, Bill became acquainted with several other railroad friends, both in Boston and New York City. This circle of friends introduced him to the Seashore Trolley Museum, located in Kennebunkport, Maine. The Seashore Trolley Museum is a nonprofit, educational, and historical society consisting of mostly volunteers. Bill frequents the museum mostly on the weekends and has been for the past twenty-eight years. This museum houses the largest collection of electric railway equipment, which consists of trolleys, interurbans, and subway cars.

Bill's photography led to his quest to preserve and transport subway cars from Boston, New York City, Philadelphia, and Chicago. In 1988, two NYCTA R-9s became available for purchase or they would have been scrapped. Bill seized the opportunity to outbid the junkman and successfully transported the R-9s from Coney Island shops to the museum in Maine in 1989. This process entailed several trips to New York to prepare the cars, find a truck route, and photograph the remaining old cars in service at that time; these images served as a curatorial guide to correctly restoring the cars Bill purchased.

Another endeavor started in 2001, when the NYCTA was reefing the redbirds. Upon seeing the pictures and reading the article in the *New York Times*, Bill was inspired to save a pair of them. In 2004, when the last redbirds were taken out of service, Bill obtained a pair and moved them to the museum in Maine in 2005.

Bill currently works for the MBTA Commuter Rail as a locomotive technician. He has invested twenty-one years (and counting) of service. Bill not only fixes real trains and volunteers his time at the museum but also enjoys his hobby of model trains. Bill's father once said that Bill was the only person he knows who turned his hobby into a career.

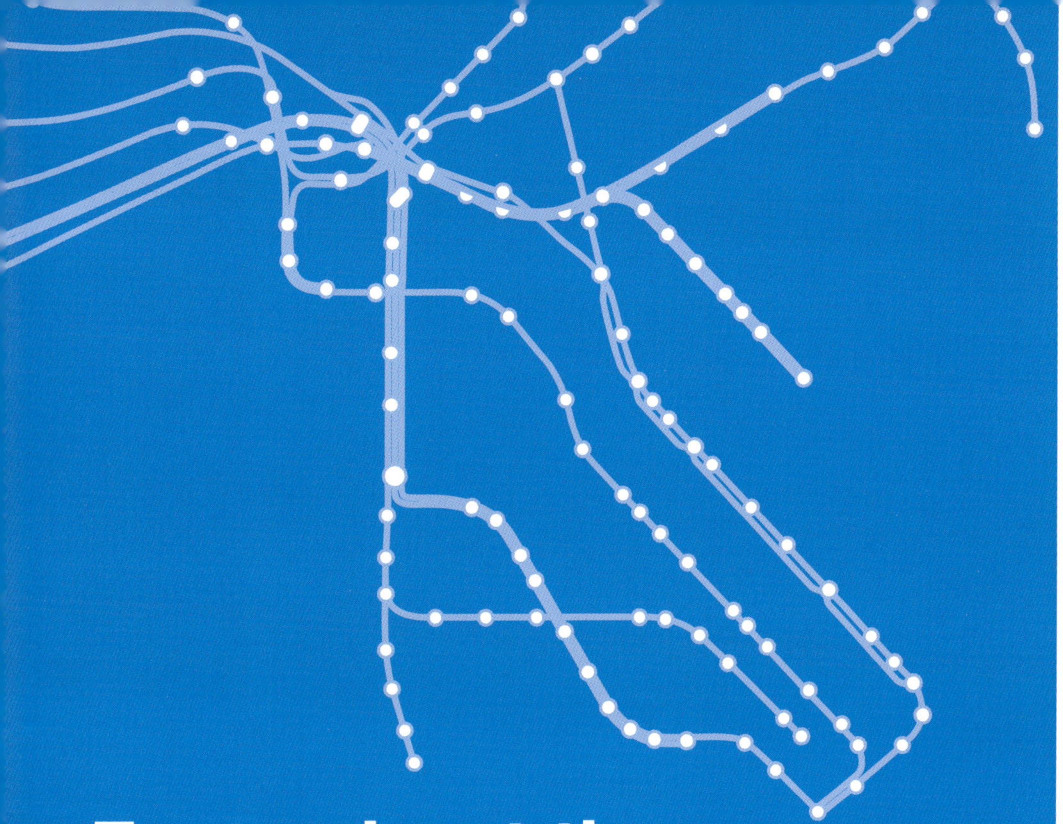

Facts about the Four New York Cars:

Car 800 (R-4) was built in 1932 and **Car 1440 (R-7)** was built in 1936. Both were in service until March 31, 1977. They were used in the Nostalgia Special from 1976 to 1983. These two cars appeared in the movie *Night Hawks*, starring Sylvester Stallone, in 1981. They moved to the Seashore Trolley Museum in 1989.

Car 7371 (R-22), built in 1957, ran in service until December 31, 1987, and was used as a work car until 2004. This car was one of twelve cars used in the 1974 movie *The Taking of Pelham 123*, starring Walter Matthau and Robert Shaw. It was moved to the Seashore Trolley Museum in 2005.

Car 9327 (R-33s) was built in 1963 for the 1964 World's Fair. It is the only subway series 2000 car left and ran until 2004. It was moved to the Seashore Trolley Museum in 2005.

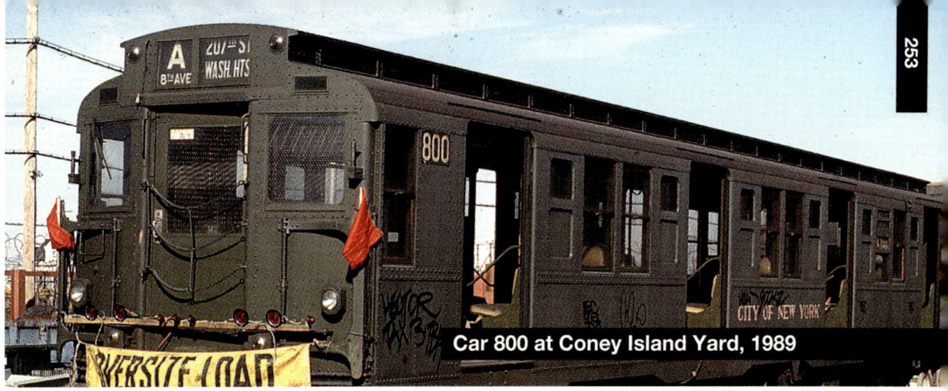

Car 800 at Coney Island Yard, 1989

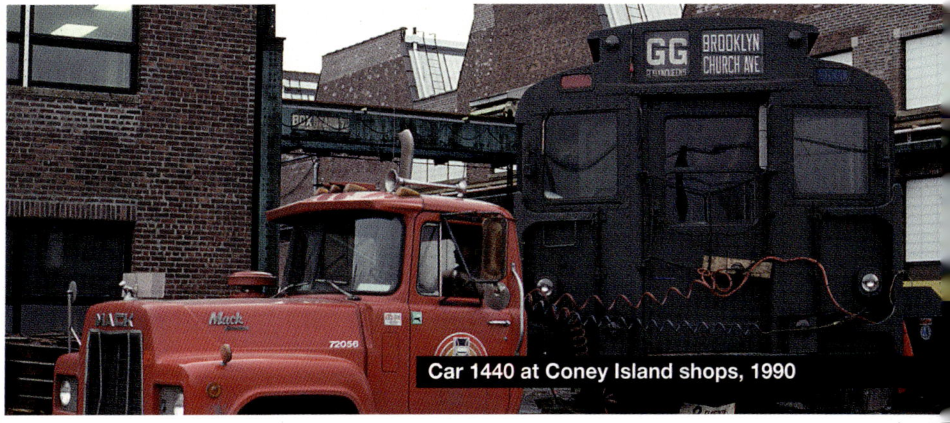

Car 1440 at Coney Island shops, 1990

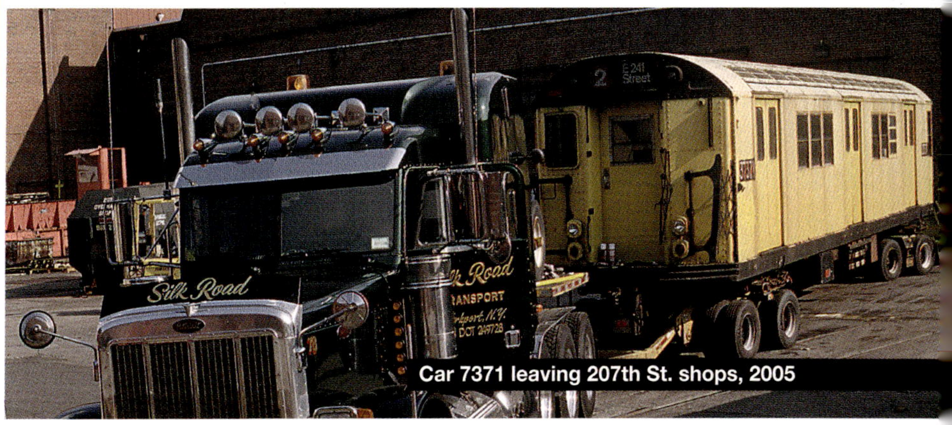

Car 7371 leaving 207th St. shops, 2005

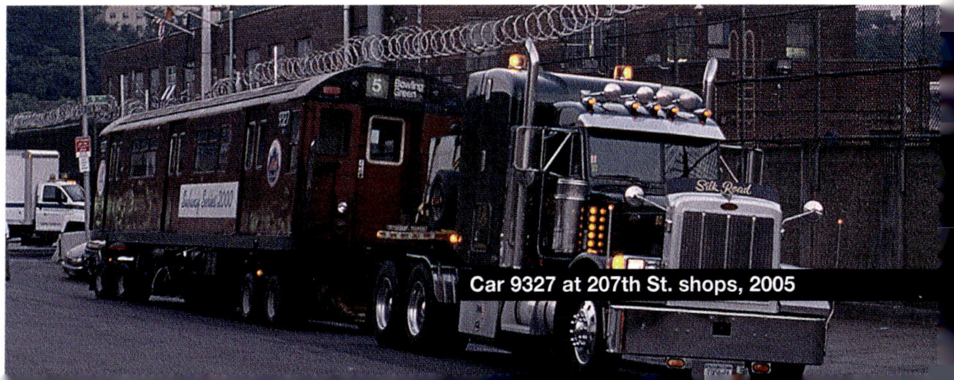

Car 9327 at 207th St. shops, 2005

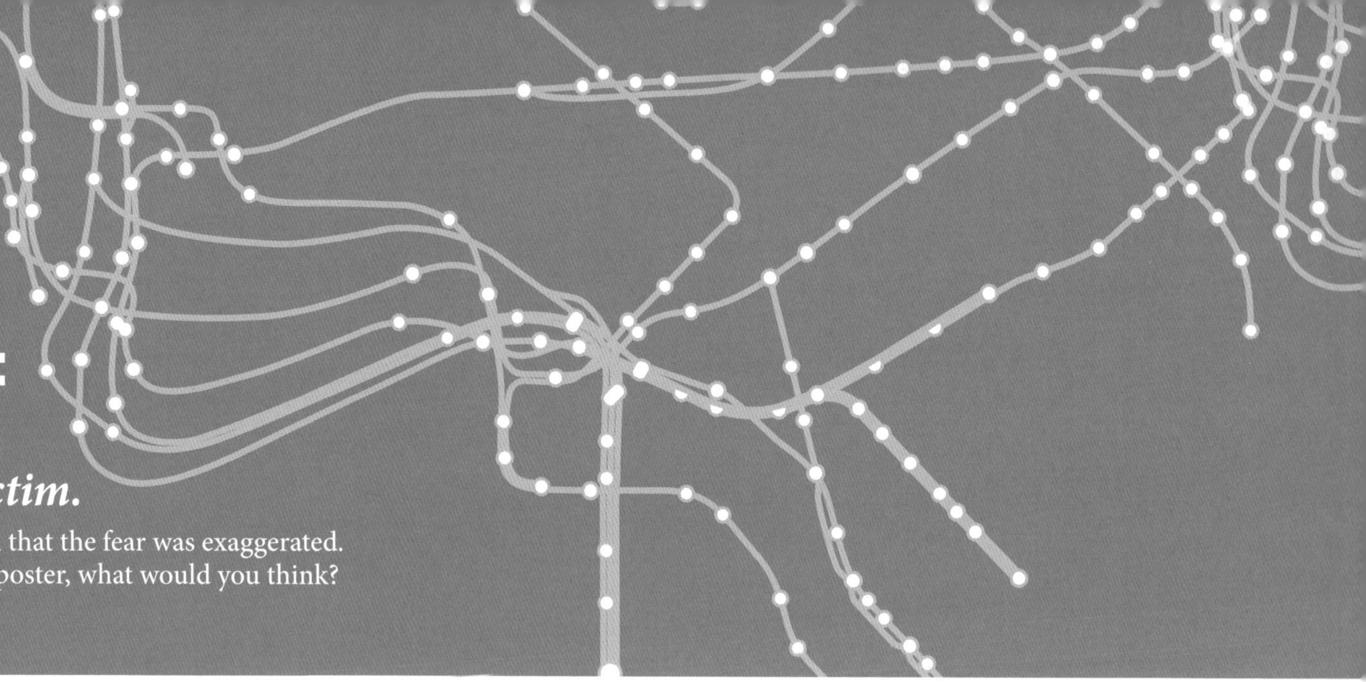

The impression of the subway back then was this:

If you ride the subway …
you are guaranteed to be a victim.

Perception became reality after a while. Some feel that the fear was exaggerated. But if you walked into a subway car and saw this poster, what would you think?

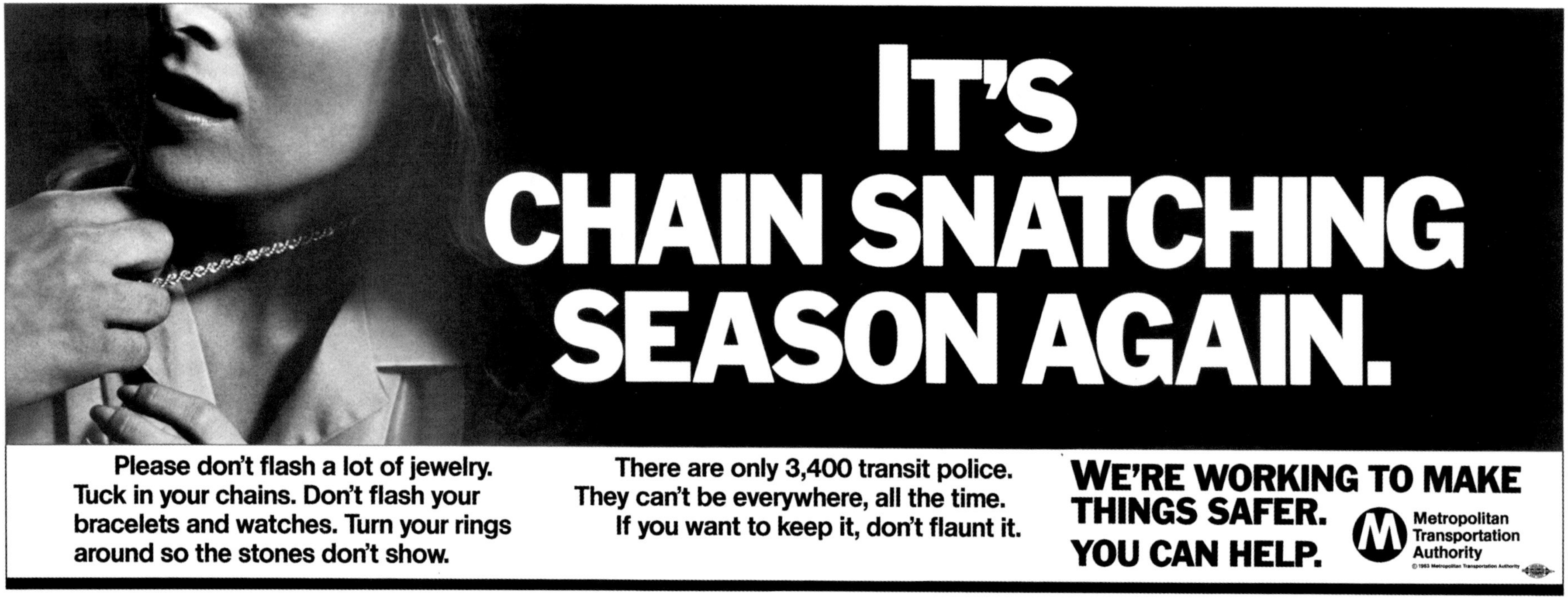

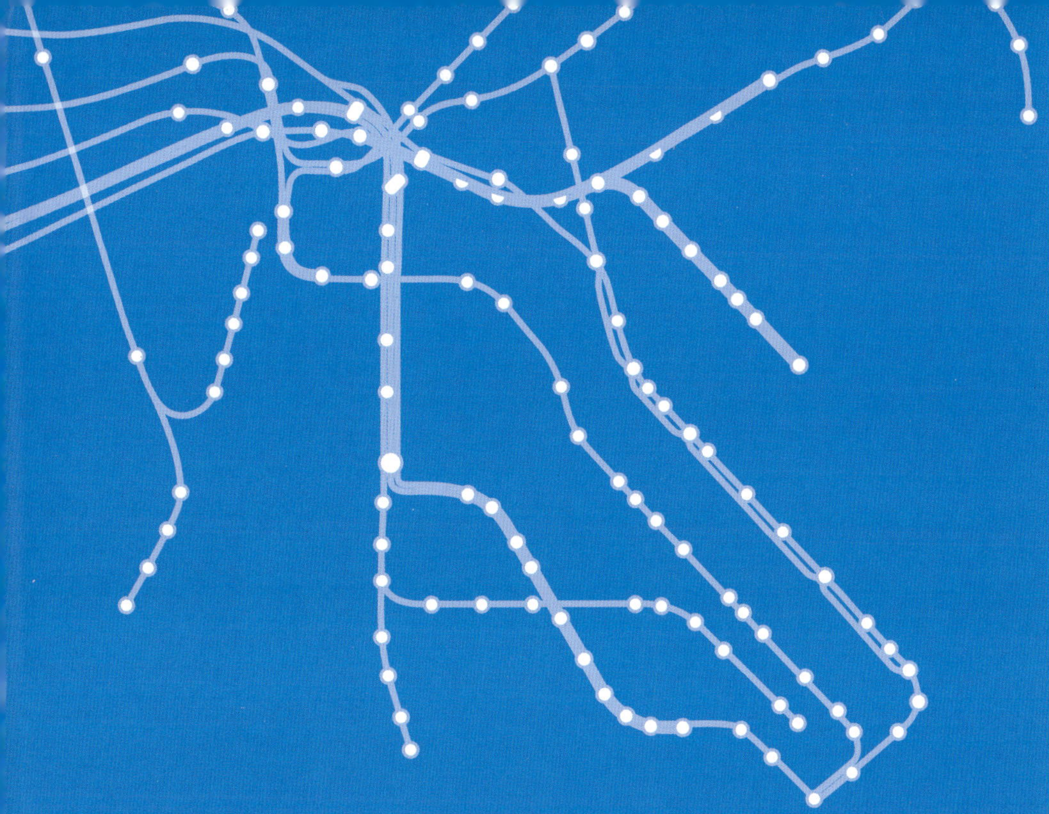

More Schiffer books from the author:

New York Subway Graffiti | 978-0-7643-3339-2
Truck Art | 978-0-7643-3493-1
Born to Run | 978-0-7643-5642-1
Vintage New York City Subway Signs | 978-0-7643-6920-9

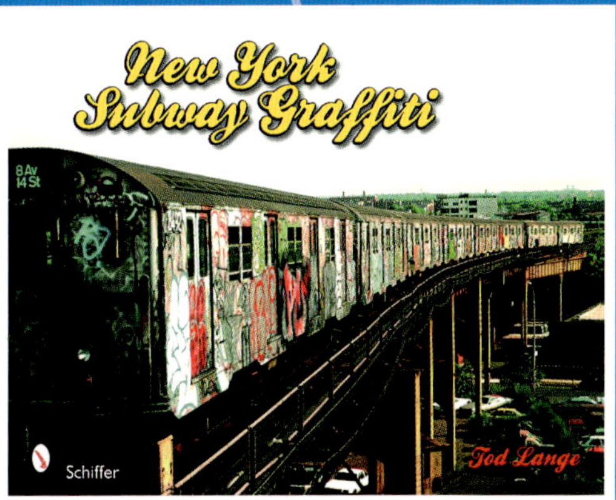

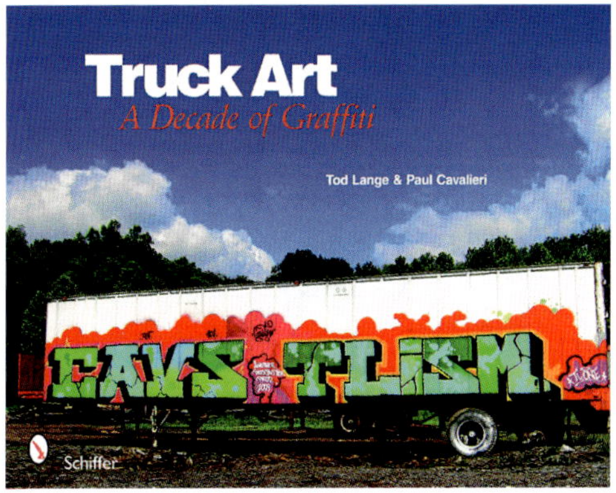

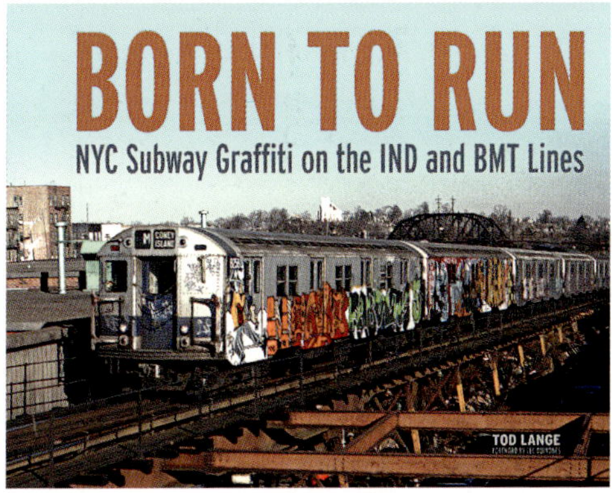

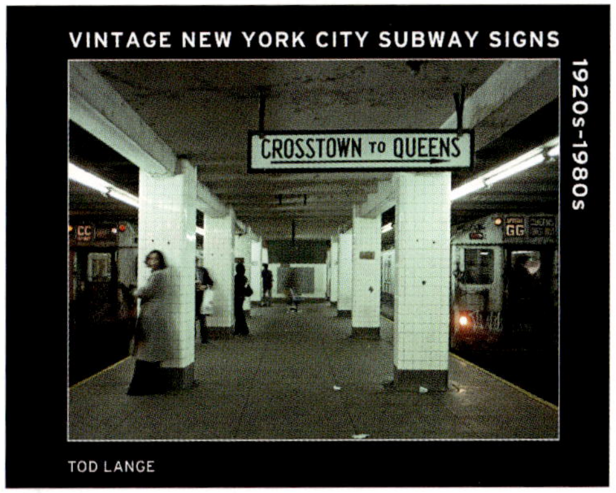

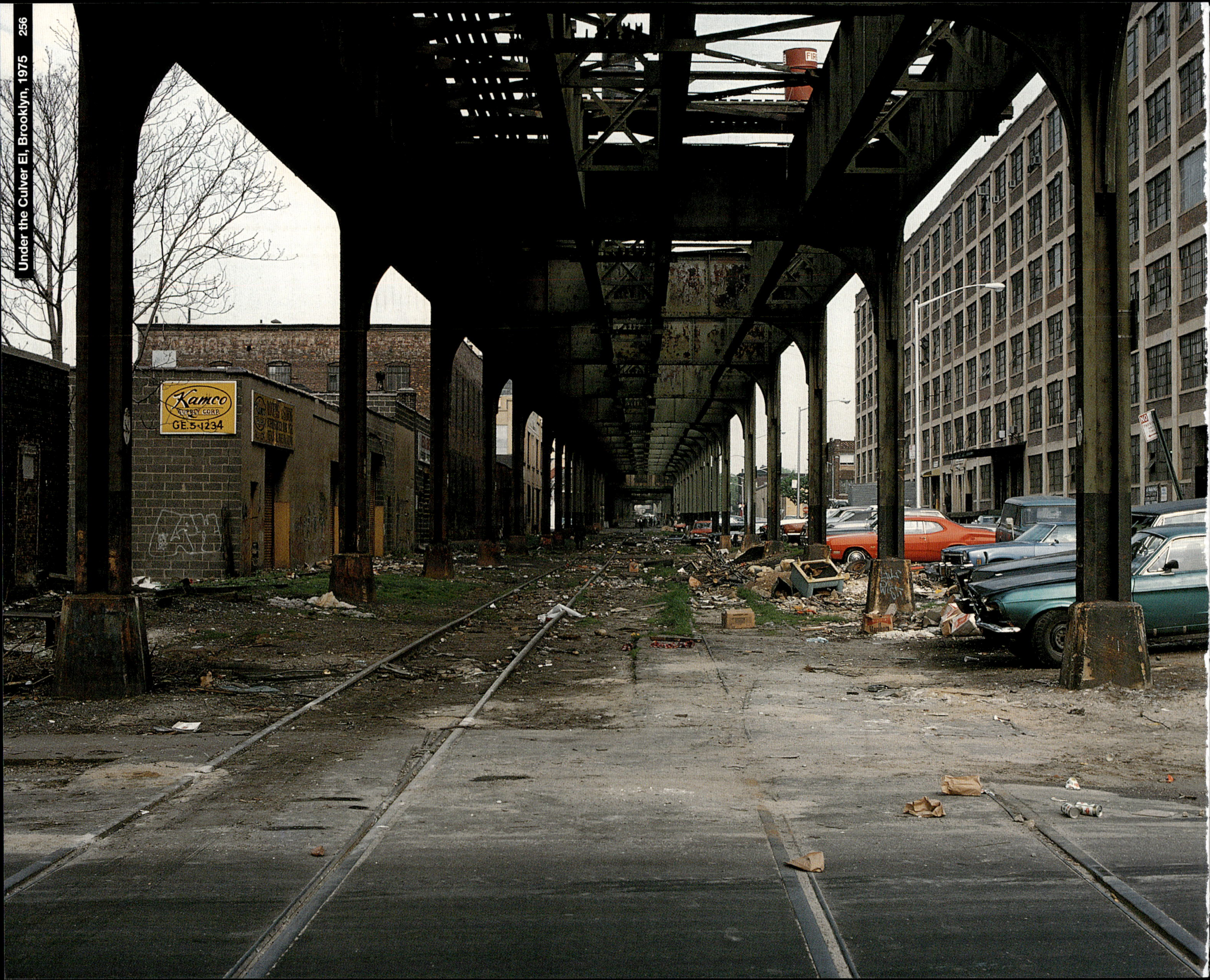

Under the Culver El, Brooklyn, 1975

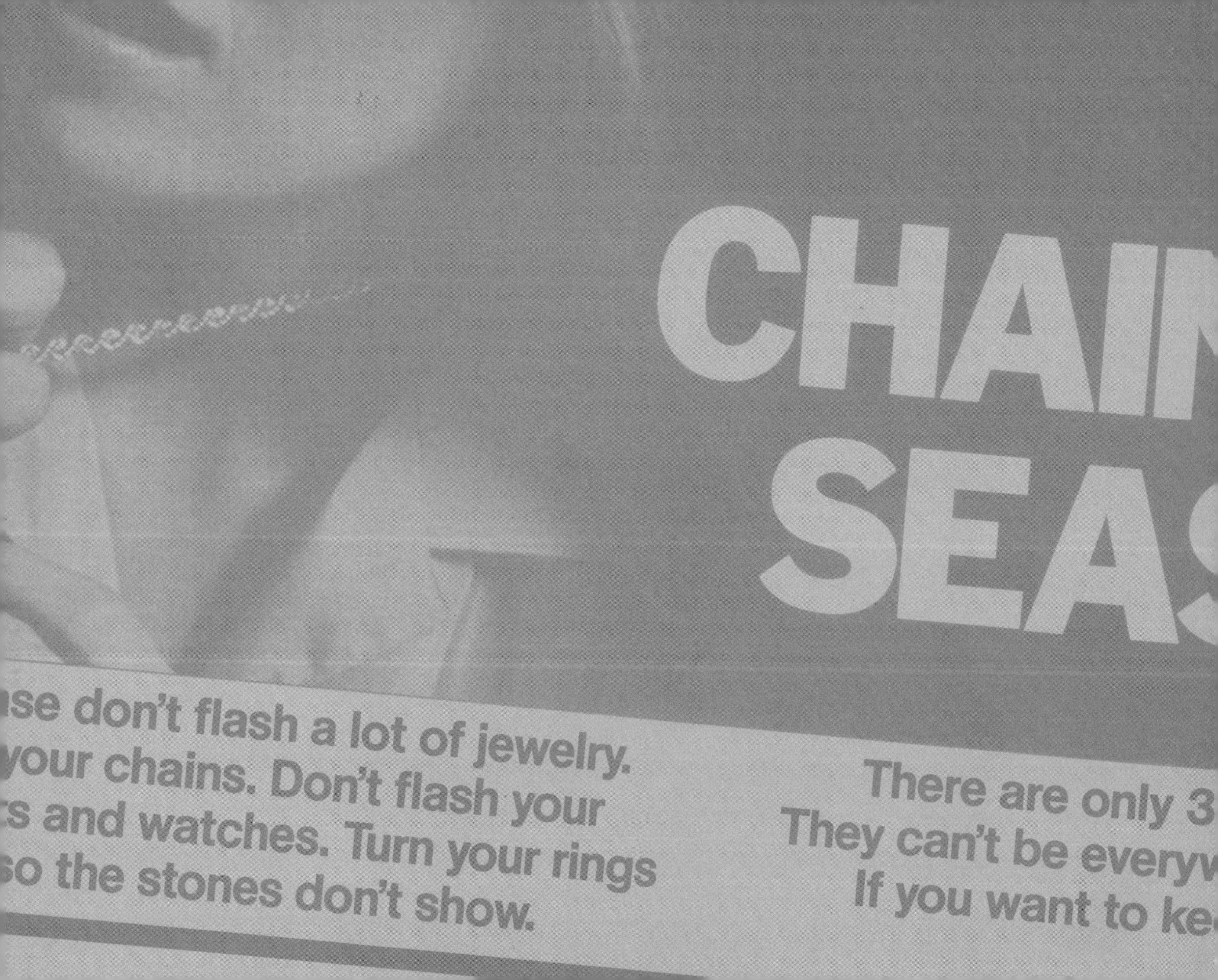
CHAI
SEAS
se don't flash a lot of jewelry.
your chains. Don't flash your
s and watches. Turn your rings
so the stones don't show.
There are only
They can't be every
If you want to